# making worlds

# making worlds

## GENDER, METAPHOR, MATERIALITY

EDITORS

SUSAN HARDY AIKEN
ANN BRIGHAM
SALLIE A. MARSTON
PENNY WATERSTONE

THE UNIVERSITY OF ARIZONA PRESS
TUCSON

The University of Arizona Press
© 1998 Arizona Board of Regents
All rights reserved

02  01  00  99  98  97    6  5  4  3  2  1

Library of Congress Cataloging-in-Publication Data
Making worlds : gender, metaphor, materiality / editors, Susan Hardy
Aiken ... [et al.].
p.   cm.
ISBN 0-8165-1779-7 (cloth : acid-free paper). —
ISBN 0-8165-1780-0 (pbk. : acid-free paper)
1. Feminist theory.   2. Women—Social conditions.   3. Space
perception.   4. Geographical perception.   5. Spatial behavior.
6. Place (Philosophy)   I. Aiken, Susan Hardy, 1943–
HQ1190.M33   1998   97-21106
305.42'01—dc21   CIP

British Library Cataloguing-in-Publication Data
A catalogue record for this book is available from the British Library.

Acknowledgments of previously printed material appear on page 309.

Cover illustration: Detail from the installation *Poem No. 423 "The Months
have ends—the Years—a knot—,"* by Barbara Penn, title from *The Complete
Poems of Emily Dickinson,* edited by Thomas H. Johnson. Photograph by
Keith Schreiber.

# contents

# acknowledgments

This book was made possible in part by funding from the Rockefeller Foundation as part of a five-year Humanist-in-Residence grant to the Southwest Institute for Research on Women (SIROW) at the University of Arizona. We owe special thanks also to Patricia Bowman for her donation in support of this book in memory of her daughter, Barbara Fairfax Bowman Durning.

We want to thank Janice Monk, Executive Director of SIROW, who co-organized the conference from which this book evolved. We're also grateful for the contributions of those conference participants whose work is not represented here: Barbara Babcock, Fran Leeper Buss, Barbara Hooper, Nancy Rose Hunt, Katie King, Gwen Raaberg, Kerstin W. Shands, Diane Waldman, and Iris Marion Young. Thanks to Janet Jakobsen for her generosity in sharing her office and library during the completion of this project, and to Mary Contreras, Jo Ann Troutman, and Marisa Walker for invaluable assistance in various stages of its production.

Finally, and preeminently, we are indebted to Esther Gale, who typed the entire manuscript. Without her this book could not have been completed.

# making worlds

SUSAN HARDY AIKEN

ANN BRIGHAM

SALLIE A. MARSTON

PENNY WATERSTONE

# introduction

This book grew out of a series of questions that resonate with increasing urgency in our current global environment: How is space imagined, represented, arranged, and distributed? What are the lived consequences of these configurations? And how are these questions inflected by conditions of gender, articulated with other socially constructed forms of "difference"—race, ethnicity, sexual orientation, class, nationality? How, in sum, are the symbolic formations of "place" and "space" marked by cultural ideologies that carry across into the places and spaces we inhabit, the institutions we establish and maintain? It was with these questions in mind that we organized a symposium at the University of Arizona, inviting distinguished feminist activists, artists, and scholars from many fields to consider the constructions of gender, place, and space in contemporary feminist theories and practices. *Making Worlds* is the product of conversations begun at that gathering.

In juxtaposing the terms *metaphor* and *materiality* in the context of world making, we gesture toward the problematic polarities that have too often divided discussions of space and place. Although the construction of spatialities has in recent years become a subject of intensive analysis in many academic fields and in debates beyond the academy, few of these inquiries have crossed the boundaries of individual disciplines or contested the inside/outside dichotomy that has traditionally opposed the academy to "the world."[1]

These divisions are registered in the diverse discourses of spatiality currently produced across a wide variety of semantic contexts. As any reader of contemporary cultural studies will recognize, the textual landscape (to invoke one of the terms in question) has long been crowded with references to borders, ground, terrains, margins, sites, zones, displacements, and placelessness, while critical activity is represented repeatedly through metaphors of mapping, traversing, locating, revisiting, and unpacking.[2] Such rhetoric produces a decidedly geographical inscription of "reality"—an explicitly spatialized narrative that figures criticism variously as a form of travel, exploration (often with unintended imperialist overtones), surveying, cartography, or tourism. Obviously, the meanings of these terms shift markedly among disciplines, as well as within them, and from one linguistic context to another.[3] "Mapping," for example, signifies something quite different in the nomenclatures of a cartographer, a geographer, or a historian concerned with the permutations of national boundaries, than in the vocabulary of a literary critic proposing to explore the symbolic structures of a text, or of a scholar of Native American cultures for whom European cartographic expeditions register the territorial expansions of colonialism.

Such differences, though based in lexical distinctions, are not simply semantic. As Michel Foucault, for one, has demonstrated, in the dynamics played out through the production and legitimization of knowledge, power accrues to those who set the standards of signification. It is hardly surprising, then, that some materially based feminist activists might accuse academics of dealing in metaphoric abstractions that evade the pressures of raw, lived experience or that empiricist scholars may react ambivalently when semioticians deploy spatial terms in what seems a purely figurative fashion.[4] On the other hand, students of poststructuralist theory would rejoin that even the most empirical articulations of spatiality are already symbolic constructs and that such constructs perform quite "real" cultural and political work.[5]

In order to open numerous approaches to these vexed and vexing issues, we sought to include in the Arizona symposium academic discourses from many disciplinary perspectives as well as practices ordinarily construed as distinct from the academic: personal essays, activist political rhetoric, poetry, iconography, theatrical spectacle. We hoped that a diverse assemblage of scholars, artists, and activists from different locations around the country might address issues of gender, metaphor, and materiality in new ways, engaging in a collaborative conversation that might amplify our understanding of spatial dialectics beyond what any of those groups alone could accomplish.

As a result, the symposium itself was a heady brew of voices and perspectives. Not surprisingly, its very diversity made it the occasion for some sharp debate and generated additional questions that, whether spoken or unspoken, formed an undercurrent to our discussions and echo in the essays of *Making*

*Worlds*: What counts as theory? What counts as praxis? And in the world beyond the academy, what theories, what practices, really count? In allowing all these problematics to come into play, the symposium became a space of encounter and contestation, a focused site and synecdoche for some of the current crises in criticism.

The conceptual issues of place and placement found material counterparts in the sites of the conference itself. Aware that the setting of our conversations would, in several senses, frame the dialogues, we sought a location dissociated from the conventional spatial typology of academic conferences. Rather than meeting at the university, we held our discussions at Tohono Chul ("Desert Corner"), a forty-eight-acre nature preserve near the edge of Tucson, where urban landscape meets the Sonoran Desert. Like all parks, Tohono Chul is a categorical hybrid, a paradoxical nexus of apparent opposites, where nature and culture, wildness and cultivation, randomness and structure intermingle in a lovely but uneasy conjunction. A desert garden that for all its natural vegetation is nevertheless a kind of well-(in)tended simulacrum—wilderness preserved, miniaturized, and contained—the place in its peculiar doubleness seemed an appropriate symbol of some of the subjects our discussions would enact and explicate.

Ironically, however informal or marginal our meeting place, its internal configurations reconstituted a familiar scene: meeting rooms with panelists at one end, behind tables or podiums, facing the audience in the classic agonistic confrontation. So obviously overdetermined were these arrangements that one panel ("The Place of the Letter") made them the focus of its inaugural deconstructive move, a gesture of radical decentering. Rather than gathering in a unified linear space behind a conference table, the panelists situated themselves randomly throughout the room, so that their discussion shuttled, weblike, from point to point, involving the audience in its weavings with an immediacy impossible in traditional panel settings.

In different but comparable ways, Judith Roof called attention to the politics of space through a send-up of the temporal constraints of academic conference presentations. In an ironically self-reflexive performance, she held before her a large cardboard clock face with movable hands and literally pushed time forward with increasing speed as her talk proceeded, explicitly staging the chronological dimensions of space. Such a one-time, one-woman show, like the gendered "stunts" Mary Russo discusses in this volume, defies replication. While we reproduce Roof's paper here, its status as performative event is, like a play, literally untranslatable into the space of page and print.

The politics of the space/time continuum that Roof so cleverly dramatized found an unexpectedly ironic reiteration in an event that occurred later in the conference. Because the park management relentlessly closed down the meeting hall at 5 P.M. every day whether discussions had ceased or not, Rina Swentzell's presentation, on the forced marginalization of Native American discourses on space, was itself literally forced outside the space of the conference room into the natural world Swentzell invokes—or at least into the imitation wilderness of Tohono Chul. There, in a stone amphitheater overlooking desert and mountain range (but echoing with the roar of traffic from the thoroughfare just out of sight), Swentzell delivered an eloquent commentary on natural spaces sacred to her people and on their embattled relationship to colonial constructions.

Finally, in another kind of space whose very name recalls the origins of drama as a form of sacred ritual—the Temple of Music and Art—the women's acting troupe Bloodhut delivered a multilayered performance on woman's place and women's places in contemporary Western culture. Their presentation—represented in this volume by Lori Scheer's "Dancing for Dollars"—powerfully embodied the etymological link between theater and theory and thus merged almost seamlessly with Mary Poovey's keynote address at the same site, spotlighting the degree to which academic presentation is itself a performative spectacle. Wearing a bright red miniskirt and red stiletto heels, Poovey simultaneously displayed and playfully dismantled both the theater of the academy and the theatrics of gender.

Thus our gathering made and remade itself as it unfolded. Like the conceptions of space we considered and the material spaces we occupied, our positions—conceptual as well as corporeal—shifted as the symposium progressed. This mobility of place and positionality anticipated the subjects and structures of *Making Worlds*. Obviously, the sectional sequences we have chosen represent only one of many possible arrangements. Some of the groupings replicate the conference structure; some have evolved subsequently, in the process of compilation and revision. Most essays could have been situated otherwise, producing thereby an alternative set of configurations and dialogues.

The first section, "Locating the Issues," brings together social activists and scholars from geography, history, cultural studies, and Latin American studies to consider the politics of location and mobility. Beginning with Geraldine Pratt's inquiry into the movements of spatial vocabularies among academic disciplines, the section continues with a series of essays that both respond to Pratt's analysis and elaborate alternative positions. Speaking as a Native American, Holly

Youngbear-Tibbetts develops a critique of the spatial discourses of privileged Anglo-American feminists, which, she argues, tend to emphasize autonomy over affinity, alienation over community. Tessie Liu, Melanie Kaye/Kantrowitz, and María Lugones examine both the unstable vocabularies of spatiality and the material implications of their deployment, especially with reference to ethnic positionalities and social justice. Finally, Caren Kaplan argues that we must historicize whatever metaphors we use in our theoretical accounts of "the social relations that produce material conditions."

The issues of gendered theory and praxis these authors raise recur in different registers in the second section, "Bodies Politic." Following Mary Poovey's analysis of the construction of "abstract space" in industrial capitalist societies, scholars from history, political science, African American studies, and literary/ cultural studies scrutinize diverse signifying practices through which space is articulated and organized and consider how these constructions function at the intersections between social and individual bodies in varying historical conditions. By tracing the representations and uses of specific political geographies from the eighteenth century to the present, Mary Pat Brady, Joan Dayan, Joan Landes, and Susan Geiger elucidate the complex local manifestations of large-scale structural forces such as capitalism and imperialism.

The third section, "The Place of the Letter," marks a radical departure from the discursive mode of earlier exchanges. In order to elicit more experimental and intimate discussions than ordinarily occur in academic venues, we asked four conference participants—from geography, literature, critical theory, and cultural studies—to engage in an extended correspondence for several months prior to the symposium. In the remarkable epistolary colloquy that ensued, Elizabeth Meese, Angelika Bammer, Minrose Gwin, and Cindi Katz simultaneously question and perform metaphoric and material constructions of subjectivity, exploring what it means to "position" oneself in the spaces of discourse. At once public and private, theoretical and quotidian, personal and professional, serious and playful, their exchanges engender a different kind of writing that dislocates traditional structures of academic rhetoric and self-representation.

Like the multifaceted conversation that emerges from this chain letter, the essays in "A Different Script" also challenge received discursive distinctions, reflecting on the connections of the "real" and the "figurative" in the construction of moral geographies. The writers—who work, variously, in religious studies and queer theory (Jakobsen), Native American studies and architecture (Swentzell), anthropology and women's studies (Mascia-Lees and Sharpe), literature (Mairs), African studies and history (White)—here ponder the role of boundaries in ethical claim making by examining the politics of inclusion and exclusion inherent in the fashioning of value-laden worlds.

Issues of inclusivity and exclusivity also inform the final section, "Sites and Spectacles," which engages the placement of women's labor in many senses of the term. And like the authors in "Locating the Issues" or "The Place of the Letter," the scholars and artists here—Ofelia Zepeda, Helena Michie, Raquel Rubio-Goldsmith, Lori Scheer, Mary Russo, and Judith Roof—consider the cultural work performed by such concepts as "public" and "private" as well as the various performative modes through which women resist or transgress the traditionally designated boundaries such categories assume. By analyzing diverse material sites—obstetrical wards, Mexican American gardens, strip joints, southwestern landscapes, the plazas of Dar es Salaam, an academic conference room—the authors expose the ideological complexity of naturalized or seemingly mundane, unproblematic spaces.

As this summary suggests, although the essays now stand categorized in what appear to be neatly fixed positions, they also speak to each other across the artificial boundaries of their published placement. Thus, *Making Worlds* might best be read not as a closed structure but rather as a contingent, mobile series of engagements. In the spirit of dis-location that has persistently characterized the project, we offer it as a fluid work in progress, one stage (in both senses) of an evolving conversation about the relations of gender, metaphor, and materiality in feminist theory and practice.

## NOTES

1. A notable exception is *Sexuality and Space,* ed. Beatriz Colamina (New York: Princeton Architectural Press, 1992), but it focuses rather exclusively on architectural spaces. Instances of the growing analytical interest in space are too numerous to list, but see, for example, Henri Lefebvre, *The Production of Space,* trans. Donald Nicholson-Smith (Oxford: Basil Blackwell, 1991); Edward Soja, *Postmodern Geographies: The Reassertion of Space in Critical Social Theory* (London and New York: Verso, 1989); Rosalyn Diprose and Robyn Ferrell, eds., *Cartographies: Poststructuralisms and the Mapping of Bodies and Spaces* (North Sydney, NSW, Australia: Allen & Unwin, 1991); Trevor J. Barnes and James S. Duncan, eds., *Writing Worlds: Discourse, Text, and Metaphor in the Representation of Landscape* (London and New York: Routledge, 1992); Jon Bird et al., eds., *Mapping the Futures: Local Cultures, Global Change* (New York: Routledge, 1993); Roger Friedland and Deirdre Boden, eds., *Now Here: Space, Time and Modernity* (Berkeley: University of California Press, 1994); Margaret R. Higgonet and Joan Templeton, eds., *Reconfigured Spheres: Feminist Explorations of Literary Space* (Amherst: University of Massachusetts Press, 1994); Elizabeth

Grosz, *Space, Time and Perversion: Essays on the Politics of Bodies* (New York: Routledge, 1995); and David Sibley, *Geographies of Exclusion* (New York: Routledge, 1995).

2. For more extensive analysis of this point, see Kathleen M. Kirby, "Thinking through the Boundary: The Politics of Location," *Boundary* 2, no. 20 (Summer 1993): 2–a journal whose title exemplifies the phenomenon to which we refer; and Janet Wolff, "On the Road Again: Metaphors of Travel in Cultural Criticism," *Cultural Studies* 7 (1993): 224–39.

3. For further discussion of this issue, see Kathleen Kirby, *Indifferent Boundaries: Spatial Concepts of Human Subjectivity* (New York: Guilford Press, 1996); Neil Smith and Cindi Katz, "Grounding Metaphor: Towards a Spatialized Politics," in *Place and the Politics of Identity*, ed. Michael Keith and Steve Pile (London and New York: Routledge, 1993), 67–83; and Doreen Massey, *Space, Place, and Gender* (Minneapolis: University of Minnesota Press, 1994).

4. For an example of one empirical geographer's reaction to poststructuralist configurations of spatiality, see Pauline Rosenau's characterization of the use of space and spatial referents in postmodernist discourses as an intentional blurring of the distinction between metaphor and materiality, a conscious construction of location as something that cannot be definitely determined: "These skeptics question every aspect of geographical space as normally conceived by turning it inside out and reformulating it as a mentally constructed set of relationships. Post-modern hyperspace is dramatically at odds with the philosophical material world of conventional science, where concrete objects, located in an objective geographical space, are charted in terms of latitude and longitude, where one inch on the map equals linear miles on earth. Conventional geography assumes that, once located, things stay put or, if they move around, they do so in predictable patterns." *Postmodernism and the Social Sciences: Insights, Inroads, and Intrusions* (Princeton: Princeton University Press, 1992), 69. See also Sallie Marston and Andrew Kirby, "Living in a Material World: The Political Problems of Everywhere and Nowhere," paper delivered at conference on "Metaphor and Materiality in the Social Construction of Space and Nature," Rutgers University, 1992.

5. For extensive discussions of these issues and debates, see Linda Hutcheon, *The Politics of Postmodernism* (London and New York: Routledge, 1989); and Linda J. Nicholson, ed. *Feminism/Postmodernism* (New York and London: Routledge, 1990). The relationship between poststructuralisms and materially based postcolonial theories is an explicit concern of Gayatri Spivak and Trinh T. Minh-ha, among others. See Spivak, *In Other Worlds: Essays in Cultural Politics* (New York and London: Methuen, 1987) and *The Post-Colonial Critic: Interviews, Strategies, Dialogues,* ed. Sarah Harasym (New York and London: Routledge, 1990); Trinh, *Woman, Native, Other: Writing Postcoloniality and Feminism* (Bloomington: University of Indiana Press, 1989) and *When the Moon Waxes Red: Representation, Gender, and Cultural Politics* (New York and London: Routledge, 1991); and Alison Blunt and Gillian Rose, eds., *Writing Women and Space: Colonial and Postcolonial Geographies* (New York: Guilford Press, 1994). As an instance of the metaphorization of a material space in activist discourse, consider Gloria Anzaldúa's *Borderlands/La Frontera: The New*

*Mestiza* (San Francisco: Aunt Lute Books, 1987). For diverse (and by no means exhaustive) examples of recent attempts to bring poststructuralist perspectives to bear on geography, see Barnes and Duncan, *Writing Worlds;* Derek Gregory, *Geographical Imaginations* (Cambridge, Mass.: Blackwell, 1994); Soja, *Postmodern Geographies;* and David Harvey, *The Condition of Postmodernity: An Enquiry into the Origins of Cultural Change* (Oxford and New York: Blackwell, 1989).

# PART I

## locating the issues

Beginning with Geraldine Pratt's inquiry into the movement of spatial vocabularies among disciplines, this inaugural section brings together social activists and scholars from geography, history, cultural studies, and Latin American studies to explore issues of location and mobility in theory and practice. Claiming that "metaphors are only representational strategies" that help "articulate certain ways of being," Pratt examines the areas of closure that certain spatial metaphors impart when used as static representational devices. Arguing that we must attend to what such closures elide, Pratt advocates a fuller examination of the relations between places and subject formations. In response, Holly Youngbear-Tibbetts asserts the transcultural persistence of certain fundamental metaphors, the most potent of which is landscape. Speaking as a Native American, Youngbear-Tibbetts argues that privileged Anglo-American feminists who have "abdicated their responsibilities to place" tend to favor spatial metaphors that reflect "socioscapes" or "mentascapes" rather than landscapes. In so doing, she contends, their discourses reflect the ethos of institutions or systems of organization, emphasizing autonomy over affinity, alienation over communality.

Other contributors—Tessie Liu, María Lugones, Melanie Kaye/Kantrowitz, and Caren Kaplan—advance the discussion by interrogating such ubiquitous oppositions as *global* and *local, home* and *away, margin* and *center,* or *rootedness* and *diaspora,* noting their intersections and internal instabilities. Liu cautions us not to equate material situations, even though we might use the same metaphors to represent them. Thus, in her reflexive meditations on her disciplinary "marginalization" as an academic feminist, she is careful to distinguish her marginality from that of the late nineteenth-century women she studies. María Lugones's elaboration of "doing theory" takes these kinds of reflections still further in an explicitly activist application of the questions raised by the earlier analyses. Melanie Kaye/Kantrowitz addresses the problematic nature of constructing accurate maps of social relations and discourses by examining the neighborhood interactions between African American and Jewish communities in New York City and Los Angeles.

The concluding essay by Caren Kaplan provides a useful vantage point from which to re-view the major concerns of the preceding essays. Echoing several of the other authors, Kaplan argues that we must historicize whatever metaphors we use in our theoretical accounts of the "social relations that produce material conditions." Finally, then, the essays in this section point to the importance of understanding, in Kaplan's words, both the continuities and the discontinuities among metaphors, practices, and subject positions.

GERALDINE PRATT

1

# geographic metaphors
# in feminist theory

As a geographer, I look upon the prolifera-
tion of spatial metaphors within feminist theory with a good deal of
interest and excitement.[1] Dislocation, exile, nomadism, marginalization, borderland, sandbar are some of the metaphors that feminist
theorists have used to represent their sense of self and self-location.
Metaphors are only that: representational strategies that help us to
think and articulate certain ways of being; in Elspeth Probyn's words,
"they [organize] the field of the thinkable."[2] In so organizing, they
open up some avenues of thought and necessarily close down others.

I am struck by areas of closure that some metaphors of geography impart. As metaphor, geography is often used as a static representational device and seems to freeze even the material, particular
historical geographies filtered through it. As Neil Smith and Cindi
Katz have argued, this is precisely why geographical referents can be
effective as metaphor.[3] As the presumed concrete, static, familiar
meaning system, they donate meaning to a more elusive domain. In
the case of feminist theory, the more elusive domain is that of subjectivity and feminist politics. From a geographer's perspective, this setup
is somewhat problematic because geography, space, and places are
not static and self-evidently familiar. The very static aspect of geographic metaphors, which under some circumstances have rendered
them politically effective, can also lead to both misreadings of and failures in feminist attempts to express decolonized feminist consciousness and politics.

## CENTERS, MARGINS, AND SHUTTLING BETWEEN

Metaphors of centers and margins are pervasive in contemporary feminist writing. Metaphors of marginality have been used to insist upon differences between women and a distance from hegemonic cultures. For bell hooks, for example, marginality is a site of resistance, a position from which to resist colonization by the dominant (white) culture, one that allows a space to imagine alternative ways of existing and the opportunity to create counter-hegemonic cultures.[4] The margin is not an easy location or a safe place or a "mythic" abstraction. hooks grounds it in her lived experience, particularly in her experiences growing up in a small Kentucky town where the railroad tracks divided the residences of African Americans—shacks and unpaved roads—from the town of whites. African Americans would cross those tracks, as service workers, and she argues that it is the recognition of this intimate connection between margin and center—the knowledge and experiences of both separation and connection—that engenders oppositional consciousness.

hooks struggles to maintain her marginality because it is a location that nourishes her capacity to resist. Her insistence on choosing the margins is an intervention against the position of marginality imposed by oppressive structures and by oppressors who say, "Tell me your story. Only do not speak in a voice of resistance. Only speak from that space in the margin that is a sign of deprivation, a wound, an unfulfilled longing. Only speak your pain."[5] hooks chooses the margins as a place of strength and as a site from which to imagine alternative ways of living.

Other feminists represent marginality, less as a way of centering a type of identity politics, and more as a means to decentering feminist consciousness. Teresa de Lauretis lists "marginality as location" as one of the key characteristics of postcolonial feminism.[6] We also see the valorization of outsider status in the concluding sections of Minnie Bruce Pratt's narrative of travel and self-discovery in her now classic essay, "Identity: Skin Blood Heart."[7] At the end of the narrative, Pratt is living as a solitary white lesbian woman in an African American neighborhood in Washington, D.C.—very much an outsider—choosing this location in part as a vehicle for continuously destabilizing her sense of identity. Liz Stanley and Sue Wise take up Pratt's residential choice as a feminist model: "Pratt is located in an immediate social context in which the original and oppressed 'other' becomes in a sense the norm . . . her account is a suggestive one."[8]

The metaphors of exile and marginality, and the idea of a continuous shuttle between center and margins, have been used to articulate a type of consciousness, what Kathy Ferguson calls (metaphorically) "mobile subjectivities."[9] This is a subjectivity that is in process, unstable and interpellated by diverse and sometimes contradictory subject positions. Trinh T. Minh-ha describes this consciousness through the image of "a permanent sojourner walking bare-footed on multiply de/re-territorialized land." Drawing in part on Zen teachings, she writes, "*If you see the Buddha, kill the Buddha!* Rooted and rootless . . . walking on masterless and ownerless land is living always anew the exile's condition."[10] For Trinh, movement and exile are metaphors that articulate an attempt to displace continuously boundaries between center and margin, thereby displacing controlling reference points. Gillian Rose has labeled this space, which "simultaneously grounds and denies identity," as paradoxical space. "This geography describes . . . subjectivity as that of both prisoner and exile; it allows the subject of feminism to occupy both the centre and the margin, the inside and the outside." Building from the work of others, Rose argues that recognizing our doubled positions (both inside and outside) can be politically productive because it both allows us to exhaust the meanings of margin and centrality and sharpens our critical capacity. By understanding that we as individuals move between/across margins and centers, we can destabilize unexamined dualisms and boundaries as we begin to see the inherent connections between inside/outside, center/margins, same/other.[11]

I support this vision of feminist consciousness and politics, what Spivak has termed a "feminis[m]-in-decolonization . . . the sign of a(n) (l)earned perspective"; but I do not think that the metaphors of margins and center, and notions of shuttling between the two, help us to articulate this vision.[12]

I am struck, for example, by the contradictory readings of bell hooks's writings, interpretations that situate her politics alternatively within identity politics and poststructuralist readings of decentered consciousness. I think that the multiplicity of readings is tied not only to the different political aims of the readers (which are not necessarily those of hooks) but also to the inadequacy of the metaphors of margins and center, both to the ways that hooks uses them and to the varying preconceptions that readers bring to their readings of her use of these metaphors. On the one hand, Sara Suleri argues that whereas

> hooks claims to speak beyond binarism, her discourse keeps returning to the banality of easy dichotomies: "Dare I speak to oppressed and oppressor in the same voice? Dare I speak to you in a language that will take us away from the boundaries of domination, a language

that will not fence you in, bind you, or hold you? Language is also a place of struggle." The acute embarrassment generated by such an idiom could possibly be regarded as a radical rhetorical strategy designed to induce racial discomfort in its audience, but it more frequently registers as black feminism's failure to move beyond the proprietary rights that can be claimed by any oppressed discourse.[13]

On the other hand, Gillian Rose writes that

> hooks describes a politics which fragments the territorial logic of white masculinity by describing a place both within and outside the dominant culture.... hooks's essay, then, is not placed on a territorial imagined geography, where center and margin are permanently marked and mutually exclusive. Instead, she positions herself in a fluid and multidimensional topography, doubled between two poles but finding that tension productive in the imagining of an elsewhere.[14]

Other geographers, such as Soja and Hooper, also read hooks in this way, attributing to hooks the creation of "a 'third space' of political choice, containing more than simple combinations of the original dualities."[15]

Suleri's less than generous reading of hooks is facilitated by hooks's use of the metaphor of center and margins and the way that hooks grounds it in her anecdotes of lived experience. Even if boundaries are conceived as socially constructed, metaphors of inside/outside, center/margins at least temporarily homogenize experience on either side of the boundary. It is arguable, as Suleri recognizes, that as a strategic intervention it is important for white women to experience this act of reductive homogenization, which they have no doubt practiced upon others. But it is a representational strategy that rigidifies differences among women. The metaphors of exile and margin help us to see difference, but they encourage us to lose sight of commonalities.

Further, there is an interesting way in which the presumed givenness of real geographies is used by hooks to harden the dichotomies already inherent in the metaphor of margin and center. Consider the simplified social geography that she presents in her mapping of her childhood town in Kentucky: black and white divided by a line, a railroad track. The social geography of the town may have been this simple; I do not know, but I doubt it. Mapped through the lenses of class, ethnicity, and religion, the solid spaces of blackness and whiteness would likely look more complex. For example, white women were probably also employed as low-paid service workers. Jews may have been excluded from "white" social institutions. hooks has mapped race onto class (and other social categories) in an extremely simplified way, and a more nuanced landscape would emerge if the contradictions and points of intersection were represented. For strategic reasons, hooks may wish to suppress this complexity, but my point is that the seeming self-evident facticity of actual places, which are always only representations, has been layered onto spatial metaphors of margins and centers in such a way as to reinforce the exclusions of dichotomous thought.

Rose's sympathetic reading of hooks's work rests on her willingness to accept a temporary (and possibly strategic) homogenization around the racial categories of "black" and "white" as a means to achieving a new political geography "structured by the dynamic tensions between such poles." Rose also foregrounds individual mobility across boundaries, as in hooks's description of the shuttle between white and black worlds by African Americans who crossed into white geographical and social spaces as service workers, returning daily to strictly segregated black residential space. Following hooks, Rose interprets this "doubling between poles" as productive of a critical consciousness, by giving "insight into the contradictions between the ideology and the practice of the dominant group."[16]

Although I appreciate Rose's reading of hooks and her vision of a decentered feminist consciousness, her own rendering of paradoxical spaces and feminist consciousness is difficult to imagine because of her use of the sociospatial metaphors of center/margins, inside/outside, and prisoner/exile. Rose attempts to deconstruct binary oppositions by tracing the shuttle between, by asserting that centers and margins are in contradiction but not in opposition, and by invoking Fuss's metaphor that "every outside is also an alongside." She wants to describe a subjectivity that is multidimensional (e.g., gender, sexual orientation, race, class) and doubled: "Any [subject] position is imagined not only as being located in multiple social spaces, but also as at both poles of each dimension. It is this tension which can articulate a sense of elsewhere beyond the territory of the master subject."[17]

Abstract assertions aside, in her concrete examples of this feminist consciousness, Rose works through one dimension at a time: white lesbians and gays who act straight gain the vantage of inside as an outsider; African American domestic workers who have a doubled perspective enforced by the necessity of working in white households. I do not think that the fact that Rose works through one identity at a time is sheer accident; it is very difficult to hold an image of center and margin—a duality—in relation to a multiplicity of subject positions. The metaphor seems to impede our shared revisioning of feminist subjectivity. If the task of the metaphor is to allow us to make sense of the unthinkable, this is a serious failing.[18] We need a different language to speak this complexity.

As an attempt to speak the "unthinkable" without relying on the metaphor of center and margin, we can consider Kathy Ferguson's use of the metaphor of mobile subjectivities; this metaphor accentuates movement without defining what it is that subjects move between, to, or from. Ferguson presents the metaphor as a strategy to disrupt dualistic thinking and essentializing around any social categories: "I have chosen the term *mobile* rather than *multiple* to avoid the implication of movement from one to another stable resting place, and instead to problematize the contours of the resting one does." "Class, like race, gender, erotic identity, 'etc.', can be a crucial but still temporary and shifting resting place for subjects always in motion and in relation."[19]

It is difficult to assess Ferguson's claims for mobile subjectivities because it is unclear what status she is staking for them: "The attraction of mobile subjectivities is at heart ethical and political, not simply epistemological." If we take seriously her epistemological claims, we must question both whether Ferguson overextends the metaphor of mobility and the adequacy of a perspective that undertheorizes the "resting places" of subjectivity. Against Ferguson's focus on the discursive construction of categories and her observation that "women of color and white women become unstable categories, shaky representations, regulatory impositions concealing enormous turbulence,"[20] we must place hooks's recognition that the residential segregation of African Americans in her childhood town was defined by a material border enforced by law: "There were laws to ensure our return [at the end of the work day]. To not return was to risk being punished."[21] While Ferguson recognizes that mobile subjectivities are "material as well as semiotic actors," she gives little attention to the boundaries that anchor identities.[22] Janet Wolff notes that one of the dangers of travel metaphors is that they lull us into forgetting that centers still exist.[23] There are many forms of domination, many borders, operating at different scales, and we continue to be situated within and by them. It seems important to thematize the construction of these boundaries and to understand the complexity of this boundary construction in ways that take us beyond the dualities of center and margin.

## FREE-FLOATING BODIES

Without following through on the recommendation, Ferguson recognizes that understanding how subjectivities get anchored and disrupted requires careful attention to the specifics of geography and particular locales.[24] The value that is placed on both marginality and mobility in many recent feminist accounts of subjectivity-in-decolonization tends, I think, to work against this recommendation.

Critiquing the use of the metaphor of exile in cultural theory, Jenny Bourne Taylor notes how the metaphor of exile, and the narratives that are structured around it, rest on some notion of bedrock experience, a simplified and relatively static notion of home, that "home is always the place you come back to, and always from a place of greater complexity."[25] So, too, in many feminist narratives of self-discovery, it is only through leaving home places that an understanding of the complexity of social location is attained.[26] Within much feminist theory in which the metaphors of dislocation, exile, and marginality are employed, the place of greater complexity is usually a social location that is unconnected to place, and actual places tend to be treated as relatively simple and static entities. Writers such as hooks and Anzaldúa, who try to articulate a new vision of home, speak about subjective location conceived apart from specific places. Home, hooks writes, "is no longer just one place. It is locations. Home is that place which enables and promotes varied and ever-changing perspectives, a place where one discovers new ways of seeing reality, frontiers of difference."[27] Anzaldúa's vision of home is a new culture—*una cultura mestiza*—a culture beyond dualisms in which there is tolerance of ambiguity and contradiction.[28]

Against this optimism about revisioning home is a more general skepticism toward home and home places. Kathy Ferguson equates a desire for a stable subjectivity with home and claims that "such homes always end up requiring much policing to monitor the fringes and basements."[29] Gayatri Spivak expresses reservation about subjective location in home places: "As far as I can tell," she says, "one is always on the run, and it seems I haven't really had a home base—and this may have been good for me. I think it's important for people not to feel rooted in one place. So wherever I am, I feel I'm on the run in some way."[30] In her discussion of feminist consciousness, Gillian Rose lays the metaphor of prisoner/exile onto the metaphor of inside/outside: there is no identification with the inside of paradoxical space.[31]

The idea that a decolonized feminist consciousness is attained partially through detachment from place requires closer examination. First, in a naive way, I wonder who is going to care about real places, like old-growth forests and neighborhoods vulnerable to gentrification and profit-driven densification, if we all attain the ideal of being "on the run" or if we all experience the inside only as prisoner. There seem serious reasons for reexamining the positive ethics of dwelling in place and for holding these in close tension with the rhetoric and romance of margins and mobility.

This is poignantly illustrated by Jamie Daniel in her discussion of Adorno's unhappy decade of exile in the United States and his return to Germany in 1949. She argues that Adorno's most "resistant gesture" was his refusal to concede his claim to Germany as a home. It is because he claimed Germany as a home that he returned to reconstruct it as a home, "to expose and dismantle its false foundations—the false sense of a reconciled and homogeneous community and nation," in other words, a false sense of home. If we have no sense of placement, we have no stake in places—both locally and globally (this is not a plea for parochialism)—and we have no reason to either preserve or change them.[32]

Another problem flowing from the ideal of detachment is that it may help us to forget that we are always situated in particular places and have effects on those as well as other places. As a way of understanding this point, consider Minnie Bruce Pratt's location at the end of her narrative of self-discovery. As a white woman living within an African American neighborhood in Washington, D.C., Pratt displays extreme sensitivity to her multiple social locations and the effects that these have on her various encounters with different people on the street at various times of day. At the same time she seems oblivious of the impact her presence might have on the neighborhood—as potential first-wave gentrifier. As an outsider she is nevertheless situated in place. Although she is attempting to dismantle her consciousness of privilege, Pratt is nevertheless marked by that privilege, and her body situated in specific places can change those places because of this marking. Given contemporary constructions of "whiteness" in the United States, the presence of her white body in particular places can change those places, in ways that she neither wishes nor intends. Pratt no doubt has unintended and unacknowledged effects on other places as well, in ways that I cannot presume to describe.[33]

What I am advocating is a fuller examination of the relations between places and subject formations, to move feminist thinking about geography and subjectivity away from the extremes of dualistic metaphors of margin/center on the one hand and metaphors of mobility on the other. This entails taking Ferguson's recommendation seriously and giving close attention to the specifics of geography and particular locales. I should say that I am by no means the first to argue or demonstrate this; there is a rich tradition of feminist geography, of which Rose's book is an important example, and many feminists blend multiple readings of geography—metaphorical and material—in compelling ways.[34] Anzaldúa's use of the metaphor of borderland in relation to the specific border between Mexico and the United States is one such example.[35] In the two empirical vignettes that follow, I focus on boundary construction and try to show how place-based and social boundaries are intertwined and mutually constitutive but exceed the dualisms of center/margins. The shift to case studies is not meant to signal a prioritizing of "real" geographies over metaphorical geographical referents; I hope it is clear that metaphors and cultural representations structure material relations (and vice versa). Nor does the material evidence stand on its own. My reading of this evidence is heavily indebted to the theoretical discussions that I criticize. In what follows I am attempting to push at the limits of this theorizing by using material evidence to trace out the complexity of boundaries and the interface between subjectivity and geography. My strongest claim is that when geography is treated *only* as a metaphor, it is deadened in a way that obscures the mutual constitution of place and identities.

## BOUNDARIES/SUBJECTIVITIES
### Crossing Boundaries and Reproducing Differences

The first spatial story is about the difficulty of crossing boundaries and the reinscription of differences through symbolic geographies that mark the crossings. I draw upon an ethnography by Williams of one block in a racially integrated, rapidly gentrifying inner-city neighborhood in Washington, D.C.[36] Most of the whites living on the block were relatively recent arrivals. In occupation terms, they were classified as political activist lawyers, environmental activists, university professors, newspaper reporters, and the like. These people bought into the area in part because they were attracted by its varied racial composition. Despite the attractions of racial heterogeneity, the realities of labor market segmentation were translated starkly into the housing market, and strict racial segregation persisted: all of the white households owned row houses on the one side of the street, while long-term African American residents lived in rental apartments facing them. Members of neither group entered the homes of the other.

Williams's analysis of the television-viewing habits of these residents is particularly interesting to me because mass television can be taken as an index of the nationalization and indeed globalization of culture and as a vehicle for crossing boundaries. In fact, residents on one side of the street rarely watched the same programs as those on the other. Instead, they watched each other through programs that seriously distorted each other's lives and perpetuated stereotypes of race and urban living. African American women living in the apartments, who did most of the television viewing in their households, watched programs like *Dallas* and *Dynasty,* dramas of wealthy, troubled white families living in large houses. The white homeowners watched what Williams terms gentrified television, programs like *Hill Street Blues* and *St. Elsewhere.* Although these latter programs have been represented as self-conscious attempts to undermine racial and gender stereotypes and to portray urban life in realistic ways, Williams argues that they simply reproduce these stereotypes and a vision of city life as chaotic, violent, and unpredictable, in which liberal, well-intentioned people are vulnerable to attacks from gangs and drug addicts, and in which lower-income people live uniformly sordid and violent lives. She sees these programs as "extraordinary urban vehicles for cross-class communication" that guided assumptions the white homeowners made about everyday life. These programs led the homeowners "to interpret and frame ambiguous scenes with more unease, fear, and distrust [than they might have otherwise]. These programs thus [spoke] powerfully to the uncertainties of [the] new owners, although a direct connection between watching them and growing more hostile [to their neighbors across the street] might be difficult to prove."[37] The liberal whites were attempting to live in a place of cultural variety, but the cultural representations they watched on television portrayed a dichotomous cultural urban space that partially structured, through fear and hostility, their relations in their neighborhood, reproducing dichotomized urban places.

The television preferences of the African Americans can be interpreted as a sign of their contradictory status: they were drawn to the ethics of home ownership but unable to gain entrance to these property relations. Their in-between and contradictory status was apparent in their relations with the Latino families in their building. In recent years about a half-dozen extended Latino families, refugees from El Salvador, had moved into the apartment building inhabited by African Americans. One result was a fair amount of conflict between African American and Latino residents, centering around (or at least articulated through) their different ideas of how the building should be used. The categories of race and difference were worked through the material use of the building. Many African Americans attributed declining conditions within the building to the presence of Latino families. They were critical of what they perceived to be overcrowding on the part of Latinos as well as the tendency of Latinos to domesticate semipublic spaces, such as the laundry room and hallways. As one African American woman put it, "Spanish people use the hall like a porch." In appealing to the management company, African American residents distinguished themselves from Latino families and employed the rhetoric of home ownership, citing their personal morality, concern about the building, and residential stability. Williams writes that "black women tenants argue that by settling in and taking an active moral interest in a building you can act like a homeowner. This ethos then frames the rhetoric through which they demand particular privileges and services."[38] By tying African Americans so closely to the ideals of home ownership, Williams positions them within the same ideological space as the homeowners across the street.

The boundaries on this one street were multiple and drawn in different places in different ideological spaces. Material boundaries (homeowner/renter; different traditions of drawing lines between public and private spaces) underlined racial categories. Cultural representations of race reproduced material divisions. I am struck not only by the multitude of boundaries but by the loss of political agency that flowed from them. As the deterioration of living conditions, likely due to disinvestment on the part of the landlord, was interpreted as the consequence of racial difference among tenants, the potential for effective tenant organizing was undermined. As the whites, whose gentrifying impulse was prompted by the ideals of cultural and racial diversity (bracketing the material consequences of this impulse for their neighbors across the street and the responsibility that they may bear for the disinvestment on the part of the landlord), burrowed into the security of their private homes, their vision of an urban experience that sought out diversity was lost. Sorting through the boundaries and overlapping ideological spaces—seeing the boundaries and points of intersection—is a very preliminary step toward building alliances that might work against the homogenizing forces of gentrification.

This ethnography also raises questions about the naming of marginality. Who is marginalized in this spatial story? Whites have been constructed as dominant, as property owners having the material capacity to withdraw and to draw a line between their houses and their inner-city neighbors. In one sense this is true, but other interpretations see widespread home ownership among the middle and working classes as a co-optive strategy on the part of the state and capitalists that fundamentally divides and weakens working-class opposition both within residential communities and within workplaces.[39] One can question a simple reading of homeowner as "dupe," but certainly this reading places a different interpretation on the white homeowners in this gentrifying block in Washington, D.C.; it shifts them from a position of dominance to acquiescence. Moving through different socio-spatial scales and different social dimensions, lines of marginality shift in and out of focus. Can something politically productive come out of this refocusing exercise, something that feels different from claims to dualistic social spaces and, alternatively, mobile subject positions?

*Crossing Boundaries and Discovering Differences Within*

A second vignette comes from research I have done with Susan Hanson in Worcester, Massachusetts.[40] In this case I am interested in exploring how existing boundaries and spatial separations might work to open up differences within *individual* women rather than differences between different women. In this sense this example builds more optimistically toward a contemporary notion of decentered subjectivity. Once again my focus is on boundaries and spatial separations.

Many women live out the fragmentation of their identities in space. That is, there is a spatialization to the fragmentation of many women's identities that is less typical for men in our society.[41] For the sake of simplicity I will outline the argument only in relation to middle-class heterosexual women living in dual-headed households. The argument builds from the recognition that sex-based occupational segregation persists in our societies and that most women still find work in traditionally female-dominated occupations that tend to have relatively low status, poor benefits, and low remuneration. This means that many women living in middle-class households (defined in terms of their partners' jobs) in relatively affluent neighborhoods work in working-class occupations.[42] As an index of this, using 1980 census data from Worcester and looking only at households in which women and men are employed, in one-quarter of the households in which the male's job is classified as managerial and professional, the woman is employed in a so-called nonskilled white-collar job. This would be a job like telephone operator, cashier, waitress, or retail clerk. One could argue that these women literally move through class locations during the day. At their jobs they are working class; at home they are middle class. For most men in our societies, residential location reinforces work class location; for many women there is a radical disjuncture between these two class experiences. Rather than interpreting this as a movement between center (middle-class residence) and margins (working-class job)—as a type of doubled perspective described by Rose—the working-class status of middle-class wives can be read in part as an extension of their subordinated position in the family.[43] At the very least we are compelled to find a richer vocabulary (than "center" and "margin") to express the layers of power relations and of privilege and oppression that these women experience in their daily lives.

There is something very interesting about the fact that many women live out the fragmentation of this part of their identity both temporally and spatially. The implications of this for spawning the type of consciousness described within contemporary feminism have scarcely been explored, and one would clearly have to draw on more than census data to understand how the spatial-ization of subjectivity works. I can only speculate. It may be that contradictions thrown up by multiple class locations are managed by compartmentalizing dif-ferent parts of one's life and identity, and that the spatial separation of home and workplace encourages this. Rosemary Pringle, for example, notes that the relations of home and work are lived differently for middle-class (to some ex-tent in terms of their own jobs and through their husbands' class standing as managers) and working-class secretaries (who tend to be employed in lower secretarial jobs and to be married to men in the trades). The former tend to compartmentalize the two parts of their lives more completely: "As far as they were concerned, their home life was not relevant to what they did at work: they assumed a separation." Pringle observes that middle-class women are re-luctant to bring their private lives to work ("their 'middle-classness' required that they be able to resist intrusions on their 'private' lives"), while working-class secretaries speak openly and predominantly about their families and so-cial activities.[44] This difference may be tied to attempts on the part of middle-class secretaries to manage their experiences of class disjuncture.

Alternatively, different class locations may disrupt each other. On the one hand, the multiplicity of class locations inhabited by women in the same occu-pations may impede workplace organization. This is precisely what Cho con-cludes from her participant observation study of women working at Microtek in Silicon Valley. Most of the unskilled assembly jobs at Microtek were filled by women, but taking into consideration the rest of their lives and identities, these women were situated in diverse class circumstances: "One Korean woman worker's husband was a medical doctor, while one American woman's boy-friend was a fabrication operator at a firm in Silicon Valley. . . . In general, a sig-nificant number of the married women's husbands had high-income jobs, such as chemical engineering. There were also quite a few single women who had two jobs to meet their living expenses." Cho argues that the diverse cultural and class backgrounds discouraged women from discovering and pursuing their common interests as assembly workers. She reports that many of the married women "never read [their] pay checks with care" and it was a single mother who discovered that the company was violating its own regulations by failing to pay overtime.[45]

On the other hand, and in a different place, the fact that many women ex-perience different class locations may have transformative effects. Working women may bring back to their middle-class residential communities a knowl-edge of a greater range of experiences and needs. This may partially explain the gender gap in electoral politics and women's greater support for social services, which have been noticed in the United States at least since 1980.[46] We get clues of how these gender differences might translate into the transformation of places from a large survey conducted in the Greater Vancouver region in 1990. Women were much more likely than men to support such statements as "Housing developments should contain a variety of income groups"; "The single family house is not essential for a 'true' family life"; and "I like the variety and stimulation one finds in the city" and less likely to agree with a statement like "Attempting to mix lifestyles in any one part of the city leads to friction."[47] (Unfortunately, differences among women were not pursued.)

My causal scenario for why many women are seemingly more accepting than are men of cultural and architectural diversity is extremely speculative, but given the potential significance of these patterns for the places in which we live, they are well worth speculating about. I am tracing an argument about how class-based residential segregation and the journey of many middle-class women across different class positions during the course of their days may transform our cities by encouraging the creation of more diversity in place. Decentered consciousness may find concrete, material expression in our built environments.

## CONCLUSION

I hope that my comments are not interpreted as being a statement against geographical metaphors. This would be an absurd position, given that Lakoff and Johnson claim that "most of our fundamental concepts are organized in terms of one or more spatialization metaphors."[48] I do think that some geographical metaphors are more useful than others for framing contemporary feminist ideas about consciousness. Elsewhere I have argued that the metaphor of borderland is especially provocative because it conveys a sense of political contestation and invites consideration of particular historical geographies.[49]

I recognize that a discussion of "the most useful" metaphor may be meaningless in the abstract. The utility of a metaphor to some extent depends on the specific circumstances in which it is used, and there are no doubt times when a static, simplifying metaphor may be useful precisely because it obscures detail and other viewpoints for the sake of a specific political (and polemical) aim. Nevertheless, we must continually remind ourselves of what we are closing off through these strategic closures; the aim of this paper is to encourage this process of remembering.

Quite beyond championing the "best" or most useful geographical metaphor, my point is that feminist theorizing about subjectivity has much to gain from an expanded treatment of geography and place and from giving closer attention to the ways that geographical metaphors and material relations are intertwined with constructions of identities. Each of us is situated in many worlds, and we continue to be situated by those geographies in ways that metaphors of mobility and marginality scarcely begin to suggest. If we want to change these worlds, we have to understand how they have constructed us and claim them as our own.

## NOTES

1. I thank the SFU/UBC/Emily Carr Feminist History and Representation Reading Group for a vigorous critique of a draft of this paper. Thanks also to Trevor Barnes, Lynne Bell, Robyn Dowling, Derek Gregory, Susan Hanson, Jennifer Hyndman, and Rose Marie San Juan for detailed comments on the draft. I also learned much through the process of presenting this paper at the "Making Worlds" conference but have resisted incorporating all of what I learned, thereby anticipating the papers and comments that follow in this volume.

2. Elspeth Probyn, "The Body Which Is Not One: Speaking an Embodied Self," *Hypatia* 6 (1991): 116.

3. Neil Smith and Cindi Katz, "Grounding Metaphor: Towards a Spatialized Politics," in *Place and the Politics of Identity,* ed. Michael Keith and Steve Pile (London and New York: Routledge, 1993), 67–83.

4. bell hooks, *Yearning: Race, Gender, and Cultural Politics* (Toronto: Between the Lines, 1990).

5. Ibid., 152.

6. Teresa de Lauretis, "Eccentric Subjects: Feminist Theory and Historical Consciousness," *Feminist Studies* 16 (1990): 115–50.

7. Minnie Bruce Pratt, "Identity: Skin Blood Heart," in *Yours in Struggle: Three Feminist Perspectives on Anti-Semitism and Racism,* ed. Elly Burkin, Minnie Bruce Pratt, and Barbara Smith (New York: Long Haul Press, 1984), 10–63.

8. Liz Stanley and Sue Wise, "Method, Methodology and Epistemology in Feminist Research," in *Feminist Praxis: Research, Theory, and Epistemology in Feminist Sociology,* ed. Liz Stanley (London: Routledge, 1990), 33.

9. Kathy Ferguson, *The Man Question: Visions of Subjectivity in Feminist Theory* (Berkeley: University of California Press, 1993).

10. Trinh T. Minh-ha, "Cotton and Iron," in *Out There: Marginalization and Contemporary Culture,* ed. R. Ferguson et al. (New York and Cambridge, Mass.: New Museum of Contemporary Art and MIT Press, 1990), 334–35.

11. Gillian Rose, *Feminism and Geography: The Limits of Geographical Knowledge* (Cambridge, Mass.: Polity, 1993), 155.

12. Gayatri C. Spivak, "Acting Bits/Identity Talk," *Critical Inquiry* 18 (1992): 771.

13. Sara Suleri, "Women Skin Deep: Feminism and the Postcolonial Condition," *Critical Inquiry* 18 (1992): 764.

14. Rose is referring to "Choosing the Margins as a Space of Radical Openness," in hooks, *Yearning*.

15. Ed Soja and Barbara Hooper, "The Spaces That Difference Makes: Some Notes on the Geographical Margins of the New Cultural Politics," in *Place and the Politics of Identity*, ed. Michael Keith and Steve Pile (London and New York: Routledge, 1993), 192.

16. Rose, *Feminism and Geography*, 155, 152.

17. Ibid., 151.

18. Donald Davidson, "What Metaphors Mean," *Critical Inquiry* 5 (1978): 31–47. I thank Trevor Barnes for calling my attention to this phrase. There are other questions to ask about Rose's theoretical account. For example, is it really the case that all subjects are placed at both poles of a dimension? Within this generalization, are there some important differences? Caren Kaplan has asked, for example, that we think carefully about the specificity of material positions of first-world and third-world feminists who claim the status of exile: "[We] have to pay attention to whether or not it is possible for me to *choose* deterritorialization or whether deterritorialization has been chosen for me." Caren Kaplan, "Deterritorializations: The Rewriting of Home and Exile in Western Feminist Discourse," *Cultural Critique* 6 (1987): 191.

19. Ferguson, *The Man Question*, 158, 177.

20. Ibid., 154, 160.

21. bell hooks, *Feminist Theory: From Margin to Center* (Boston: South End Press, 1984), iii.

22. Ferguson, *The Man Question*, 162.

23. Janet Wolff, "On the Road Again: Metaphors of Travel in Cultural Criticism," *Cultural Studies* 7 (1993): 224–39.

24. Ferguson, *The Man Question*, 162.

25. Jenny Bourne Taylor, "Re: Locations—From Bradford to Brighton," *New Formations* 17 (1992): 92–93.

26. Through successive departures many feminists have narrated a process of losing a naive relation to their various cultures so as to not uncover and create multiple layers of social identity. Through traveling to Cuba from the United States, for example, Johnetta Cole recalls how she began to understand herself in gendered and not just racialized terms: "There I was," she says, "seeing for the first time the possibility that the race thing was not forever and ever; and then the other -ism [sexism] was right up there saying, what about me?" (Cole is one of several women whose biography is told by Mary C. Bateson, *Composing a Life* [New York: Plume, 1990], 45). Teresa de Lauretis tells of the importance of immigrating to the United States for her awareness of ethnic difference: "[My] first (geographical) displacement [from Italy to the United States]," she writes, "served as point of identification for my first experience of cultural difference (difference not as simple distinction, but as hierarchized)." Teresa de Lauretis, "Displacing

Hegemonic Discourses: Reflections on Feminist Theory in the 1980s," *Inscriptions* 3/4 (1988): 128.

27. hooks, *Yearning,* 148.

28. Gloria Anzaldúa, *Borderlands/La Frontera: The New Mestiza* (San Francisco: Aunt Lute Books, 1987).

29. Ferguson, *The Man Question,* 165.

30. Gayatri C. Spivak, "Strategy, Identity, Writing," in *The Postcolonial Critic: Interviews, Strategies, and Dialogues,* ed. S. Harasym (New York: Routledge, Chapman and Hall, 1990), 37.

31. Rose, *Feminism and Geography,* 155.

32. Jamie Owen Daniel, "Temporary Shelter: Adorno's Exile and the Language of Home," *New Formations* 17 (1992): 35. See Meaghan Morris, "Banality in Cultural Studies," in *Logics of Television: Essays in Cultural Criticism,* ed. P. Mellencamp (Bloomington: Indiana University Press, 1990), 14–43, for a critique of any "thematics of place" that is articulated around the binary opposition of propriety and mobility.

33. David Harvey, for example, pays special attention to the connections between places and to the multiple scales of situatedness and connections in his critique of strategies of "situating" knowledge. Harvey, "Class Relations, Social Justice and the Politics of Difference," in *Place and the Politics of Identity,* ed. Michael Keith and Steve Pile (London and New York: Routledge, 1993), 41–66.

34. Rose, *Feminism and Geography.*

35. Anzaldúa, *Borderlands.*

36. B. Williams, *Upscaling Downtown* (Ithaca, N.Y.: Cornell University Press, 1988).

37. Ibid., 112.

38. Ibid., 68.

39. Geraldine Pratt, "Reproduction, Class and the Spatial Structure of the City," in *New Models in Geography,* vol. 2, ed. Richard Peet and Nigel Thrift (London: Unwin Hyman, 1989), 84–108.

40. Geraldine Pratt and Susan Hanson, "Gender, Class and Space," *Environment and Planning D: Society and Space* 6 (1988): 15–35.

41. I do not want to overgeneralize my claims about gender. I, for example, do not experience the class rupture that I describe here. On the other hand, Derek Gregory inscribes in the margins of this text: "This [class disjuncture] happens in other ways too; my own experience as a student, moving between elitist Cambridge in terms and a working-class housing estate during vacation, speaks to the possible overlapping and compounding of the different effects you posit here."

42. I recognize the difficulties associated with this class positioning. (See Geraldine Pratt and Susan Hanson, "On Theoretical Subtlety, Gender, Class, and Space: a Reply to Huxley and Winchester," *Environment and Planning D: Society and Space* 9 [1991]: 241–46.) I am trying to draw attention to the fact that many working-class women live in higher-income residential areas because of their husbands' class standings. Categories fail me.

43. Rose, *Feminism and Geography.*

44. Rosemary Pringle, *Secretaries Talk: Sexuality, Power and Work* (London: Verso, 1989), 227, 226.

45. S. K. Cho, "The Labor Process and Capital Mobility: The Limits of the New International Division of Labor," *Politics and Society* 14 (1985): 200, 201.

46. E. Klein, *Gender Politics: From Consciousness to Mass Politics* (Cambridge, Mass.: Harvard University Press, 1984).

47. Walter Hardwick, Raymon Torchinsky, and Arthur Fallick, *Shaping a Livable Vancouver Region: Public Opinion Surveys.* B.C. Geographical Series, no. 48 (Vancouver Department of Geography, University of British Columbia, 1991).

48. George Lakoff and Mark Johnson, *Metaphors We Live By* (Chicago: University of Chicago Press, 1980), 17.

49. Geraldine Pratt, "Spatial Metaphors and Speaking Positions," *Environment and Planning D: Society and Space* 10 (1992): 241–44.

# 2

# making sense of the world

One phrase that forms the nexus of this book, "making worlds through metaphor," alludes to one of the most powerful, if infrequently acknowledged, nuances of geographic thought.[1] The phrase suggests something of the terror and exhilaration of the human condition that demands that we somehow make sense of the world. It suggests at once both the primacy of personal experience, imagination, and cognition, and the risks inherent in their exercise. The construction of personal realities and their attendant geographies not only frames our personal and autonomous "worlds" but demands articulation.[2] For metaphor is the essential mechanism by which we share among ourselves those tentative expressions of our experience. They are the bridges necessarily, if tenuously, constructed over which we communicate and validate our own experience within and among our networks of kin, clan, and community (however those have been personally constructed).[3] It is metaphor that transcends the limitations of language and seeks resonance in the understanding of our fellows. Herein lies the paradox: while we "make worlds through metaphor" in the context of individual perception and experience, those metaphors are, when most powerful, resonant of our cultures.[4] That successful metaphors are embedded within and dependent on the contextual construct of culture poses some problems for geographers seeking to understand the nature of the human relationship to the world.[5] Are there fundamental proto-cultural aspects of human experience that we share through metaphors? Or are metaphors themselves culturally specific, not so much the expression of individual human experience but merely reflections or refractions of the strategies used by our individual cultures to make sense of the world? This is the fundamental theme that underpins Geraldine Pratt's paper.

Pratt suggests that in order to pursue this dilemma we must scrupulously disclose our own "positioning" in this respect. I am glad to oblige so that you may assess for yourself my comments with respect to her work. I offer the following not so much in the spirit of adherence to the now more freely admitted subjectivity of scholarship but in the belief, as I suggest below, that there are fundamental transcultural metaphors around which human experience is organized and articulated, and of these the most potent is the metaphor of landscape.[6]

It is our topographic sensibilities that not only offer a unanimity to the diversity of our human experiences across cultures but define for us our most fundamental cognitive constructs. Indeed, our first experiences as humans are spatial and presumably precursor sensory perceptions. The first knowledge we gain is topographic—the landscape of the maternal body—and this is irrespective of the cultural conditionings that later aid our interpretation of the world. Whatever reality may be, our human delimitation to three-dimensional life draws its spatial intelligence from the lessons of that initial intimate maternal landscape, as well as subsequent landscapes of individual and collective experience.[7] Upon that spatial intelligence are based our most topographic cognitive constructs: continuity and discontinuity; proximity and distance; the ability to discern both detail and generalization; a means by which to entertain constructs such as size, frequency, and directionality. Its presence has secured for all cultures not only subsistence and survival but what one geographer has described as the human "freedom and burden" of investing our lives with meaning.[8] Moreover, it serves as a benchmark for our passage through a fourth dimension, which yet defies our intellectual mastery, although we understand it experientially. The *long duree* of the landscape is a forceful, if humbling, reminder of the fragility of our own transient nature. Spatial metaphors resonate with those penumbral connotations and explain much of their power and thus their utility and potency.

While in vogue, especially in feminist scholarship, these metaphors are neither novel to intellectual discourse nor newly arrived to our battery of words and images. What I find interesting about their resurgence in this context is the way in which they reveal the relationship between the "metaphor-maker" and the landscape she inhabits. The intrigue of these revelations is, for me, central to an understanding of the relationship of people to place, specifically how humans engage the process of discovering/exploring/creating/interpreting their place(s) in the world, and it within them, while simultaneously acknowledging that they are cultural products specific to given times and places. In the spirit of that task, I will attempt to rise to the obligations of a respondent to the thoughtfully produced and commendably risky propositions that Pratt has outlined by situating my own subjectivity.

I am, as I take everyone to be, a product of the time and place of my experience. Of these it is place, more than time, that is most endemic to my reflexivity. I will therefore dispose of the former rather perfunctorily and disclose that I am a member of the "Woodstock generation," a now slightly graying cohort-member of the postwar baby boom, whose life thus far has spanned the end of the war in Korea, the launching of Sputnik, red-baiting, Howdy Doody, McCarthyism, nuclear attack preparedness training, the "Beat generation," the birth of rock and roll, the construction of a vast network of interstate highways, *American Bandstand,* independence of colonial African states, moon walks by both Neil Armstrong and Michael Jackson, white flight to the suburbs, payola, the Poor People's March on Washington, the civil rights movement (and a panoply of subsequent populist social movements based on the perhaps naive premise that the state could be a just entity), the romance of the counter-culture, the Fab Four, the second and third waves of feminism, Watts, Watergate, socialist revolutions in China, Cuba, Zimbabwe, and Zaire and the sexual revolution at home, LSD, *Saturday Night Fever* and Saturday night specials, the first Earth Day and its more recent commodifications, Guardian Angels, the rise of a crass consumer culture, the invention of the microchip and the attendant information revolution, trickle-down economics, urban cowboys, designer drugs, gentrification, the discovery of DNA structure, test-tube babies, designation of endangered species, quantum physics, sky ice, Reaganomics, twelve-step and other related support groups, vigilante television, the construction and destruction of the Berlin Wall, the fall of the "Evil Empire," urban fairy tales, two third-party U.S. political movements, union-busting, Iran-Contragate, "smart houses," halfway houses, and safe houses, supersonic transports, televangelists, fiber-optic cable, postmodernity, retribalization, rap music, and infomercials. What I am attempting to suggest in this rather playful way is that time—specifically the time or "times" in which one's human experience is played out—is transient, fluid, and often unpredictable. In some cultures—especially mainstream Anglo-American popular culture—time (or times) is presumed to take precedence as the organizing construct that best defines individual human experience. This premise argues that it is culture that primarily frames our metaphors and casts them as appropriate or fitting in our construction of reality. In this view, if we indeed "make worlds," they are worlds of only fleeting duration and remain durable only so long as their metaphoric potency prevails. Much of what resonates through a culture has little direct impact on our personal lives or our appraisals of reality. Sky ice, to select one of the eclectic events enumerated above, may betoken my life in a technological age when our capacity for creating technological wonders far outdistances our abilities to cope creatively with their residual consequences. But unless sky ice strikes me in the head and renders me unconscious as it falls in a field in which I am standing, it contributes little to my human need to make sense of the world around me. Unlike the Koori tribe portrayed in the movie *The Gods Must Be Crazy,* whose culture was dramatically affected by such an unexpected, unique phenomenon—in that case a soda bottle—in our culture there is such an abundance of literal and figurative "shit" flying through the air that I employ sky ice metaphorically more to simply mark time than to draw upon it as a source of meaning in my life. While sky ice or soda bottles—or conquests or catastrophes, for that matter—may create a contextual framework for making sense of the flux of our temporal experience, they offer little continuity with which we can satisfactorily underpin or interpret our "worlds." For that purpose we need, indeed cannot absent ourselves from, a more constant referent around which to organize our personal and shared worlds: the landscapes of place.

My full disclosure of "positioning" would be superficial if based only on the temporal dimension, for my most fundamental sense of identity is drawn from the landscape. (And, I would argue, so is everyone else's, although the "scape" may be of a different or even unacknowledged contextual sort.) I have been made to know that I come quite literally from this land, Michilmakinak, Great Turtle Island, or what most geographers refer to as North America. The creation story of my ancestry informs me how the Osauki and Mesquakie were fashioned out of the earth—indeed, those very names mean, respectively, "people of the yellow earth" and "people of the red earth" and refer to our autochthony on the shores of the Great Lakes. This landscape has shaped our cultures and communities and has given us our language, religion, political and social organization, seasonal economies, and indigenous arts and sciences. It is our greatest source of both solace and inspiration, and our culture is a rich repository of geographic lore and knowledge that is continually renewed both ceremonially and pragmatically. Place not only has profound meaning in our construction of human experience but overrides the fluidity of temporal life. The landscape of the Upper Great Lakes, sculpted by volcanoes, glaciers, floods, sea-floor spreading, and tectonic up-thrusts, is not merely the backdrop for the drama of human life. Rather, people and place are inextricably joined, and this most profound relationship to the land is told and retold in stories, songs, and oral histories, and predominates in our everyday mundane conversations, as it probably has for millennia.

In a spatial sense, then, "where I'm coming from"—to use a geographic euphemism for "positioning"—is an even more complex disclosure. The simplest way to express that dynamic relationship is, I suppose, to say simply that in my case, being a geographer is an inevitability. I have been "geographicating" throughout my entire life, in a way I suspect few of my disciplinary colleagues could even fathom. The genesis of this activity is, of course, culturally construed, and it is a happy accident that I later discovered that geography could be a profession as well as an avocation. As a product of place, I am a self-confessed "landscape junkie," a member of a traveling culture perhaps best known for its seasonal foraging jaunts and the "powwow highway" but, in truth, a culture in which little excuse is required to maintain rather constant observation and interpretation of the landscape. (Yeah, any landscape.)

The compulsion to engage continually the task of reading the landscape, however, is not merely a manifestation of the geographic imagination of a culturally conditioned "topophiliac."[9] Rather, it is perhaps the most universal human trait, albeit one that some cultures veil more successfully from the conscious cognitive operations of its members than does my own. My "positioning," then, as a respondent to Pratt's paper varies only in the particulars of time and place, not from a condition or circumstance other than time and place. If place looms larger in the space/time convergence that informs my experience than it does in that of others, it is a consequence of the sorts of landscapes that predominate in my experience.

I offer these "placial"—not "spatial"—tidbits not because I want to evoke the romance of the indigene but because Pratt's paper relies on the juxtaposition of two orders of symbolic representation, "home" and "mobility," to focus on the deployment of spatial metaphors by feminists and some social scientists to capture their "positioning" (read experiential/perceptual/intellectual locale) in relationship to their scholarship. If, as Pratt suggests, such metaphors both "open up" and "close down" thought in different ways, I feel confident that my own repertoire of experience and reflexivity should well prepare me to explore with her those vistas and canyons. I find they do not.

My interpretation of the evidentiary materials that Pratt offers both begins with and concludes at "positions" quite removed from her inquiry. The most telling intellectual distance between our interpretations is grounded in our self-selected positioning within our discipline. Although we share some tenuously held common ground as female practitioners of an inordinately androcentric discipline, I find little common ground in her work. This does not imply antagonism to her position, simply a recognition that we all relate to our intellectual covenants in somewhat disparate ways, especially in a broad synthetic discipline such as geography, which seldom adheres to a single para-digm.[10] Pratt's positioning in this respect is both more sophisticated and per-haps more conventional than is my own. Her topical inquiry is one more com-fortable with the many-tiered orders of contemporary nomothetic inquiry characterized in our discipline by intellectual angst in respect to postmoder-nity, the presumption of the supremacy of theory, and adherence to methods that bear the seal of approval by the social sciences. In contrast, my self-selected positioning within the discipline is less orthodox and perhaps more cynical. (I suspect, for example, that both the scale and order of questions that most intrigue me would find little audience among my colleagues and, further, that what for me are the more compelling aspects of the discipline are lost on most geographers.) It is the simple questions that drive my scholarship, the hermeneutic methods that best reveal for me the complexity of our discipli-nary quest to explore "Earth as the home of humanity." In practical terms, then, while Pratt's academic impact and recognition are better assured, the re-flections that I offer on the evidence she presents are founded on more expe-riential, mundane, and ideographic terms. In the polemics of human geography that seek to know "the terra incognito of both cabbages and kings," my alle-giance is definitely aligned more with the cabbages than with the kings.[11] As a devotee of the experiential geographies of the mundane, vernacular, and every-day worlds, I have a certain fascination with both how those geographies are articulated and the response they evoke within the reader. As I read Pratt's commentary on the materials she has chosen as exemplars, and the materials themselves, I am struck by an overwhelming sense of pathos.

I find it a startling prospect that Pratt's paper and the materials she cri-tiques are premised on an accepted (and acceptable?) condition of alienation. The juxtaposed notions of "home" and "travel" seem in her analysis equally im-bued with a stasis that she goes to some lengths to deny with her insistence that "geography, space, and places are not static and self-evidently familiar." While I concur that geography, space, and places are most definitively not sta-tic and self-evidently familiar, neither is the potency of our metaphoric reliance on them. Rather, I would argue that both "home" and "travel" are not the rather bleak binary opposites that contrive the geographies of alienation, which the materials suggest but, given a point of departure premised upon affinity, are metaphors of connectivity.

"Home," in the most replete sense of the word, is not about the confines of place and community; rather, it is a created place, secured not by nativity, entitlement, or endowment but by the continual and careful creation and re-creation of ties to place. My sense of place comes most dramatically not from those prior generations of ancestors who drew meaning from this land but from my own daily, seasonal, and recurrent reaffirmations of this place. The landscape that those predecessors inhabited was very different from the one I inhabit, despite the fact that they occupied the same locale. While they likely traversed it more gently than do I and my contemporaries, we are as dependent upon it as were they for our sensibilities, sacred and mundane. We, like they, are engaged in the task of making it our home. Having a "home" requires work, diligence, and a willingness to bond with a place on its own terms. Its vitality is not drawn from immutable, unchanging reliance but from interaction, commitment, and a willingness to explore the possibilities inherent in the relationship of people and place. Much of the material used by Pratt and her referents denies the potential for such comforting work. In geographic terms, an affinity to place is often described as rootedness. The rootedness to which I refer is not a taproot structure like that of our indigenous white pines, which is what I suspect most geographers intend by their use of the phrase to denote an immobile, sustaining, if confining placedness. The rootedness to which I refer is a less restrictive association to place, metaphorically more in the mode of wild ginseng: established at one locale, but connected by myriad, radial, extensive, and interconnected networks of whole societies of the species—whether ginseng or human. In this context, "travel" for the rooted is not alienation, the struggle to make a place in the world, or escape from the conditions of home, but a strategy of connecting with and interacting with other communities, conditions, and locales. Like the ginseng, we likely seek out the most amenable of these affine landscapes and establish a direct and personal relationship at distant as well as proximal locales.

What I am attempting to suggest here is that there are alternatives to the kind of geographic alienation that Pratt and her referents assume to betoken the spatial metaphors of "home" and "travel." Those alternatives, however, require a degree of moral inquiry into the complex human relationship with the landscape. Sadly, most deployers of spatial metaphors—including geographers—who are products of Anglo-American culture prefer the autonomy of alienation to the interconnectivity of affinity.[12] I suppose that this is the case because mainstream Anglo-American culture tends to foreshadow the signatory power of the natural landscape for topographies of a different sort.

The anthropologist Leslie White suggests that for analytic purposes, culture could be construed as comprising three interrelated subsets: technological, sociological, and ideological. In a similar vein, the biologist Julian Huxley identifies three components of culture: artifacts, sociofacts, and mentafacts. White and Huxley, while attempting a systematic approach to the study of cultures, emphasize the synergistic and interdependent nature of these cultural subsystems.[13] I would agree that cultures are holistic and that these subsets not only are intra-resonant but are each endowed with a topographic quality premised on the proto-cultural metaphor of landscape. "Dreamscapes," "mindscapes," and "cityscapes" are but a few of the recent barrage of neologisms based on the metaphoric fit of landscape to denote such topographic sensibilities. I would argue that, by extension, we can readily recognize the topographic qualities associated with artifacts, sociofacts, and mentafacts: the cultural (built) landscape, socioscapes, and mentascapes.[14] Further, it strikes me that the spatial metaphors that Pratt has chosen to elucidate are all derived from the latter two of these topological "scapes." It is not then so surprising that deployers of spatial metaphors nearly always resort to metaphors premised upon alienation rather than affinity, for few of us are privileged to reside or truly make our homes within the centrisms of either socioscapes or mentascapes, let alone "travel" among and between them. It is this order of spatial metaphors, the "socioscapes and mentascapes," that I would like to examine in response to Pratt's paper.

For many of us, attention to the natural landscape is eclipsed by the built landscape, and predictably, the spatial metaphors that predominate contemporary feminist writings rely almost exclusively on the cultural landscape: aspirant female professionals collide with the "glass ceiling" of workplace inequities; women's studies programs are "ghettoized" within academe; women's artistic and creative works are relegated to the "back shelf of narrow market" niches.

While such metaphors are in common currency today, their genesis dates back to at least 1660, when Mary Traske and Margaret Smith used the metaphors of colonial landscapes in their writings to challenge the patriarchy of their Boston Quaker communities.[15] Since that time women writers of the United States in particular have used the vehicle of the cultural landscape—especially the home (however contextually configured)—as the metaphoric venue by which to expose their repression, commodification, and exploitation. Some of these landscape features have taken on specific symbolic power to express or manifest women's experiences within the socioscape or mentascape. The gothic castle comes immediately to mind as the landscape icon representing the tension between women's aspirations and competencies and their susceptibility to mastery by the forces of TRUE LOVE, but the plantation as a site of resistance to social inequity and the factory as a site of empowerment and community building have also been extensively employed by female and feminist writers both to situate themselves within and to critique the socioscapes and mentascapes that configure their worlds.

Second-wave feminism in the United States was in fact ushered in on the power of landscape metaphor as Betty Friedan attempted to articulate the nameless boil bursting forth from the suburbs. While drawing on an older literary device, second-wave feminism in this country has canonized geographic metaphor, and most feminist scholarship has relied at least rhetorically on the convention as a strategy for positioning itself not with, but as, the "other."[16]

What is notable is that the canon has recently, and most especially in feminist scholarship, accomplished some referential "shifts," or what Pratt describes as having "traveled" to a new order of spatiality. I would contest her interpretation and suggest that what has happened is not anything like the linearity suggested by the term "traveling metaphors" but rather is a shift in the perceived nature of reality. The materials that Pratt has selected suggest to me that the landscape referent has been abandoned in exchange for the topography of the socioscape. The spatial metaphors these writers use are no longer connected in any sense to the natural or cultural landscape but rely nearly exclusively on the socioscape that predominates our system of spatial referents. Such a position is possible only when we have abandoned or exiled ourselves from the artifactual in favor of the sociofactual.

What is striking about the metaphors that reach beyond those of the built landscape or natural landscape to the topographic sensibilities of institutions, systems of organization, and structural contrivance is that, in their transferal, there is no position other than alienation from which to articulate relationships. That positioning has proven of some consequence in relationships among communities, especially those within postcolonial states.

When women writers couch their positioning—voluntary or involuntary—within a political analysis of perceived repression, the literature they produce resonates with metaphors of the political landscape, especially in respect to frontiers and boundaries, borderlands, and exclaves. In this tradition, which spans a variety of genres of women's writings, these positions of marginality are alternately exalted or reviled. The problematic for Pratt is whether such spatial metaphors are adequate for representing or "locating" the subjectivity of the writer. Here my reading of these metaphors departs significantly from Pratt's, taking a very different direction and denoting a very different politics of place.

Pratt's concern with metaphoric "adequacy" is of no interest to me, for I presume that the spatial metaphors struck by feminist writers either capture the essence of their experience or echo their romanticization of alienation. Let us, then, consider these in turn. I take the reliance on spatial metaphors in feminist scholarship to be strategic, in the sense that they are dependent on the reader's ability to decode the symbolic landscape as representing the socio-scape or, in some infrequent instances, the mentascape of the world they inhabit. Absent that, their power would be deflated. Consider, for example, the evocation of placelessness. Clearly assertions of placelessness are not credible. True placelessness is a total commitment that allows no accommodation to scholarly reflection, personal and professional relationships, or the mundane demands of everyday material needs. Indeed, true adherence to the dictates of placelessness is possible only for intermittent periods and then only to those bent on self-destruction or denial. Placelessness is not the sentiment of itinerant travelers or nomads; in fact, success for such people is wholly dependent on being able to quickly, accurately, and effectively read the landscape and garner an incisive sense of the place. The notion that one can construe and sustain over a long period of time such a "nonplace" seems a foolish conceit premised on some exalted notion of victimization.

Pratt is correct in her assessment that for bell hooks—or anyone else, for that matter—maintaining marginality as a site of resistance would indeed be a struggle, and one destined to failure. Marginality is always defined as a statement of relationship, not locale, and to secure marginality by definition requires acquiescence to the centrism of another position. Implicitly, then, such a posture empowers rather than diminishes the locale that marginalization concedes. Insurgencies, whether political or intellectual, that cling to the periphery reify, rather than topple, centers of power. Surely this is not what hooks intends to convey, so we must assume that her positioning is in some sense transient—the metaphor valid for the moment but untenable over time. If we accept such positioning to be but a fleeting reflection, the spatial imagery works or, in Pratt's sense, meets some test of adequacy. As Ursula Le Guin notes, "One of the worst things about the written word is that it's not allowed to change its mind."[17] Conversely, if we insist on some literal as well as figurative notion of marginality, the sentiment of the metaphor is simply reactionary.

That this is the case hints at one of the most serious critiques of feminist scholarship's deployment of metaphors of political geography and reveals the increasingly realized potential for significant tensions between feminist and indigenous women's communities in particular places, most especially postcolonial states.[18] Similarly, if we accept the notion of marginality as a site of resistance in any terms other than a rather specific socioscape, its "adequacy" is clearly questionable. Few humans have lives so easily characterized as a unidimensional state. Most of us, including (or particularly?) feminist scholars, tend to have lives much more complex and multidimensional than hooks's turn of phrase suggests. Family, community, professional, and intimate socioscapes intersect, foreshadow or recede against one another, and much of the fluidity we expect of our lives is the successful navigation of those competing socioscapes. What is perhaps most tragic about the reliance on spatial metaphors of the socioscape is that it effectively forecloses the metaphoric power of primary landscapes, natural and built, and allows us to accept the notion that our lives are dominated by these lesser topographies. Given that, it is little wonder that feminist scholarship has tended to romanticize alienation.

The romanticization of alienation is most evident in the United States, where it has reached nearly epidemic proportions, and so permeates mainstream culture that we now have support groups for virtually every nuance of exalted victimization. (I expect to hear soon about a new category of "victims" organized to bemoan their alienation from recognizable victimizations, whose recovery will demand therapeutic support groups, large doses of Prozac, and the adoption of protective legislative language or social protocols aimed at protecting their rights or entitlements.) Devotees of the doctrine of inclusive alienation internalize and personalize their sense of marginalization and find refuge only in a constructed world of the "other," where they remain perpetual victims. Regrettably, refuge becomes prison, and alienation institutionalized and, it seems, once institutionalized, also politicized. The psychology of alienation is seductive, as native communities have discovered as they struggle to free themselves from the self-imposed, as well as the superimposed, posture of victimization. In some places the politicized institutionalization of victimization has created a cleavage within native community life. In others it has forced a distancing between indigenous and other—especially feminist—communities.

Criticism of feminist perspectives by indigenous women goes directly to what Pratt sees as the use of "metaphors of exile and marginality ... to articulate a type of consciousness" or what Teresa de Lauretis calls "disidentification" to describe one of the key characteristics of postcolonial feminism. While de Lauretis may be relying on the figurative power of the spatial metaphor, indigenous women take quite literally the feminist denial of place. In interviews with hundreds of indigenous women leaders of the United States, Canada, Polynesia, New Zealand, and Australia conducted over the past three years, I have heard repeatedly how and why native women leaders have found cooperative working relationships with feminist groups and leaders untenable. These criticisms were unsolicited, and at first I believed them simply to be reflections of local dissensions or personality conflicts. Ultimately it became clear that there is a broader and more telling tension between native women's sensibilities and those of their feminist neighbors of immigrant ancestry. Likely none of the native women leaders interviewed have read or even heard of de Lauretis's notion of "marginality as location," yet they would probably agree that feminist leaders and communities have proven themselves to be displaced.[19] As one woman explained, "Most of those women can only talk about their rights. . . . Rights, rights, rights . . . they never own up to any responsibilities here."[20] Or, in the straightforward language of another indigenous woman, "The trouble in trying to work with them is that they still enjoy being victims, and we're trying to move beyond that."[21] Native women leaders made these and other commentaries on feminist philosophies in the context of their own geo-centrism. For them place is central to identity and moral conduct. Placelessness, particularly that claimed by privileged feminists who have abdicated their responsibility to place, is seen not just as a denial of responsibility and accountability but as another variant of cultural imperialism, what one Maori woman described as "the latest effort to colonize our minds."[22] To put this another way, one laughingly offered by a Native American colleague, "It's getting pretty darn crowded on the periphery." In postcolonial states, apparently few folks would choose to identify themselves with the centrisms of either the state or "mainstream" society. While feminists' metaphors of spatial alienation may communicate their own sense of distance from the postcolonial state, they send a wholly different message to women of indigenous nations—an abdication of place loyalty, the notion that they "have a real life somewhere else" or that, even after generations of occupancy, they choose to retain "one foot in the boat." Clearly feminist reliance on spatial metaphors of alienation has created a world of meaning well beyond the confines of feminist discourse. That suggests to me that there is some healing to be accomplished in this respect. While the broad outlines of communities in discord with one another regarding their identification with particular metaphors of space and place are undeniable, almost invariably native women would comment that there were women of immigrant ancestry who had proven to be exceptions to the rule, feminists with whom they felt more than a sense of camaraderie, who evinced real solidarity with indigenous communities, places, and struggles. When native women commentators would talk of these women—and sometimes communities of women—or when I would later have the opportunity to see them interact, it became clear that these women were in no sense displaced. They shared with native women a genuine fidelity to place, a sense of shared living experiences, and a sense of shared destiny that was unmistakable. What does all of this mean for our topic of inquiry?

It means, I believe, that real communities made of real people—native and immigrant—blessedly are not dependent on the machinations of scholars with respect to how we all create worlds through metaphor. They are simply engaged in the everyday work of creating a home, working out the sometimes troublesome business of joint tenancies, coming to terms with their sense of place and self, finding that alienation is untenable over the long haul, and devising strategies that allow them to find those places with which they can establish a sense of affinity. This provides some solace on the most vexing questions Pratt has raised: "who is going to care about real places . . . [and the] positive ethics of dwelling in place"? The response is simply this: the same people who have always cared for real places and engaged in the positive ethics of the politics of place; those who have come to a sense of affinity with that place and remain faithful to it irrespective of the socioscapes and mentascapes that have been superimposed on it.

## NOTES

1. See, for example, Anne Buttimer, "Musing on Helicon: Root Metaphors and Geography," *Geografiska annaler* 64B (1982): 89–96; also Yi-Fu Tuan, "Sign and Metaphor," *Annals of the Association of American Geographers* 68 (1993): 363–72.

2. See, for example, Gunnar Olsson, "Lines of Power," in *Writing Worlds: Discourse, Text and Metaphors in the Representation of Landscape,* ed. Trevor Barnes and James Duncan (London and New York: Routledge, 1992), 86–96.

3. Much of the early work of social phenomenology was premised on this experiential motif. See, for example, Ronald David Laing, *The Politics of Experience* (New York: Pantheon Books, 1967).

4. For a discussion of metaphor and metonymy in symbolic anthropology, see James W. Fernandez, ed., *Beyond Metaphor: The Theory of Tropes in Anthropology* (Stanford, Cal.: Stanford University Press, 1991).

5. See, for example, Stephen Daniels and Denis Cosgrove, "Spectacle and Text: Landscape Metaphors in Cultural Geography," in *Place/Culture/Representation,* ed. James Duncan and David Ley (London and New York: Routledge, 1993), 57–77.

6. For an alternative view, see Jonathan Smith, "The Lie That Blinds: Destabilizing the Text of Landscape," in *Place/Culture/Representation,* ed. Duncan and Ley, 78–94.

7. For a fuller explication of experiential geography, see Yi-Fu Tuan, *Space and Place: The Perspective of Experience* (Minneapolis: University of Minnesota Press, 1977).

8. This phrase, coined by Robert Sack, refers to the panoply of human spatial constructs. For a more complete catalog of such strategies, see his *Conceptions of Space in Social Thought: A Geographic Perspective* (Minneapolis: University of Minnesota Press, 1980).

9. The neologism "topophilia" is drawn from Yi-Fu Tuan, *Topophilia: A Study of Environmental Perception, Attitudes, and Values* (Englewood Cliffs, N.J.: Prentice-Hall, 1974).

10. For a full discussion of the multiparadigmic nature of human geography, see R. J. Johnston, *Geography and Geographers: Anglo-American Human Geography since 1945,* 4th ed. (London: Edward Arnold, 1991).

11. The phrase was coined by David Lowenthal in his seminal 1961 article calling for hermeneutic perspectives in human geography, "Geography, Experience and Imagination: Toward a Geographical Epistemology," *Annals of the Association of American Geographers* 51 (1961): 241–60.

12. "Alienation," of course, is an entrenched device in U.S. literary tradition. Ernest Becker notes that from as early as 1748, U.S. writers have been bemoaning the loss of "community." Becker, *Beyond Alienation: A Philosophy of Education for the Crisis of Democracy* (New York: G. Braziller, 1969). The thematic deployment of alienation in recent feminist scholarship likely draws its force from the more recent (1930s) emergence of alienation as the predominant motif of U.S. literature. The work of feminist writers of that decade (Meridel Le Sueuer or Tillie Olsen, for example) embedded the newly valorized theme of alienation in their work. What is notable is that its saliency has endured and that the theme resonates yet with feminist writing.

13. A more complete discussion of these typologies can be found in Arthur Getis, Judith Getis, and Jerome D. Fellman, *Human Geography: Landscapes of Human Activities,* 4th ed. (Dubuque, Iowa: William C. Brown Publishers, 1995), 47–49.

14. I am indebted to Michael Garrett for this insight.

15. Quoted in Claire Buck, ed., *The Bloomsbury Guide to Women's Literature* (New York and London: Prentice-Hall General Reference, 1992), 120–21.

16. See, for example, how the motif of "home" relations structures Gerda Lerner's work in the chapter titles ("The Stand-In Wife and the Pawn," "The Wife and the Concubine," "The Woman Slave") in *The Creation of Patriarchy* (New York and Oxford: Oxford University Press, 1986); Betty Friedan, *The Feminine Mystique* (New York: Norton, 1974).

17. Ursula Le Guin opens her introductory note to *Dancing At the Edge of the World: Thoughts on Words, Women, Places* (New York: Grove Press, 1989), vii, with this observation.

18. The problematic tension between Marxist and feminist theory in respect to the state is explored in Catherine A. MacKinnon, *Toward a Feminist Theory of the State* (Cambridge, Mass., and London: Harvard University Press, 1989).

19. Teresa de Lauretis, "Displacing Hegemonic Discourses: Reflections on Feminist Theory in the 1980s," *Inscriptions* 3/4 (1988): 127–44.

20. Author's interview with Koori women, Jerrinja Nunda Gundi, New South Wales, Australia, October 1991, tape OZ-3 in author's collection.

21. Author's interview with Maori women, Okaihau, New Zealand, September 20, 1991.

22. Author's interviews with Maori women, Manukau, September 30, 1991. This comment is part of a larger critique arguing that New Zealand is not a postcolonial state but that the process of colonization continues in intellectual and popular discourse. Colonialism in this context will cease only when Pakehas "get their other foot off the boat," that is, become rooted in New Zealand.

# 3

## reading marginality

I began reading Geraldine Pratt's paper in a cozy place. It was early morning, the gurgles of the coffeepot had awakened me, and I hoped that my daughter would sleep another hour as I pulled Pratt's paper under the comforter. As I lay in bed thinking about tactile places and metaphoric spaces, I realized that I am drawn to spatial metaphors—I frequently invoke notions of margins and centers in my writing—but I rarely think about their implications. Pratt's paper challenged me to evaluate this practice. What do these spatial metaphors illuminate in my own work? On the other hand, what do they hide? What assertions am I leaving unexamined?

I often present my work as a process of reinterpreting the center from the margins, both in reconceptualizing the history of industrialization and capitalist development from the hinterlands and in using gender and feminist analysis to remap existing explanations. The book that I recently completed, *The Weaver's Knot*, is about the resistance of artisans in western France to capitalist relations of production.[1] The monograph tells a deeply ironic story about a success that is, at the same time, a failure. For most of the nineteenth century, handloom weavers in the Choletais (a region south of the Loire valley around the town of Cholet) fought against merchants who tried to mechanize textile production. Their mobilization over several generations effectively blocked large-scale industrialization in the region. By the end of the nineteenth century, the Choletais was one of the few remaining textile-producing regions in France where independent, small-scale producers still controlled cloth making. The handloom weavers had won. They were poor but autonomous.

The cost of this success, however, was borne mostly by the women in their families. In the early twentieth century, as income from weaving declined, women entered the wage labor market in search of additional resources to enable their fathers and husbands to remain at the loom. This new female labor force attracted to the region a new group of entrepreneurs who had little capital to invest in machinery and factories and thus had to specialize in the cheapest and most volatile end of the fashion market in ready-to-wear clothing and shoes. This new development kept the region poor because these entrepreneurs could compete only by keeping down wages. By the time the last old weavers died in the 1930s, low-waged, labor-intensive, dispersed manufacturing—often called the "sweated trades"—had become the basis of the area's modern economy.

My book examines two margins, both of which describe power relations. The first is the location of the region on the periphery of industrial Europe. This geography poses the first set of questions for my research: How does attention to the margins transform our understanding of the center? How do we conceptualize the activity of the people in the peripheries? I argue that the defining feature of the region's supposed economic backwardness, the survival of small-scale manufacturing in the Choletais, was the result of active resistance and conscious adaptation, not passivity. The continued viability of the small-scale suggests that there were multiple roads to mass production in the nineteenth and twentieth centuries. More important, each particular configuration must be understood as one possibility, one contingent outcome of similar social struggles over technology, control, and access to markets. These struggles constitute the very process of capitalist class formation. Thus the rise of the factory system (in regions that became the core of industrial Europe) cannot be abstracted from the battles waged by weavers and other small-scale producers to retain their hold on the production process. In arresting the path of industrial development, weavers in the Choletais evaded proletarian status.

From our contemporary vantage point, the handweavers' fight seems heroic and compelling. Yet we must remain clear-sighted about the social supports that girded their role as valiant resistors. Here I specify the intimate connection between gender hierarchies and class formation. Thus the second margin in this study describes an identity or perhaps the absence of one—the inability of women to make effective claims on other household members because their activity was deemed unimportant to the social identity of the whole. In the weaving families, a paternal understanding of collective identity subsumed the interest and the welfare of women and younger, dependent men.

Elderly men defined the goals of the struggle as wives and daughters (and to a lesser extent, sons) scrambled to fill the gap between ideology and putting food on the table. Even though these weavers presented themselves as independent, dignified artisans, their ability to maintain this self-image was actually dependent on the sacrifices exacted from others. Mostly it was daughters who delayed marriages, stayed longer in their parental households, and took in piecework.

These two margins are not just analogous; they are causally connected. I believe that the second margin helps create the first. If there is a moral to this story, it centers on the broader social costs of displacing risk onto those who were not allowed to refuse. In the long run, everyone suffered from these exploitative strategies.

I would like to be able to claim that the source of my insights as a scholar derives from a feminist sensibility that pays special attention to the perspective of those who occupy the margins. But such a claim overstates my sisterhood with the women I study and understates the role of my ambitions as a scholar. In my world, centers and margins operate in a very different way than for the women of Choletais. Although I identify very deeply with them, we are not similarly located. Here my bed intrudes again. The luxury of a firm mattress and a soft comforter makes it difficult to feel truly marginal, to feel inconsequential. In the quiet of the early morning, I like my apartment. I like the fact that I have a job and that my job enables me to read in bed and think. I like the familiarity of my daughter talking and singing to herself as I stay in bed (doing my work), knowing that my job provides for us.

Claiming to be on the margins of a discipline is a very different kind of gamble than being on the margin economically or socially. The margins of a discipline can be a liberating place. One is imbued with a sense of arrogance; this margin is a "cutting edge" and may well become the new center. The fact that I feel a bond with the women I study should not cloud my vision; I shouldn't claim that their marginality and mine are somehow the same. Most important, I don't want their marginality to give romance and political purpose to mine.

Surely the women I study also experience similar feelings of well-being and connectedness, and certainly we are all aware that it is often familiarity and comfort that bind us to oppressive situations, but still, not all margins are the same. Like a cold punch to the stomach, I realized (from my safe space) that writing about the vulnerability of the women in the Choletais became the source of my security. The book helped me get tenure under conditions that I find affirming. I have a sense of being able to leave or stay. That choice, of leaving or staying—both acceptable choices—is precisely what the women I wrote about do not have. As a historian of women's lives, I need to be ever aware of this kind of contradiction between my situation and the subject of my study.

The very fluidity of spatial metaphors as descriptions of power poses dangers for feminist analysis. Although feminists do not speak in one voice, feminism as critical stance has achieved (after long battles) a legitimate place within the academy such that individual feminists can claim the authority to speak and write on the oppression of all women. While collectively we are ever aware of the deep divides between women and conscious of the need to bridge these differences, how the common bonds of womanhood are conceived and enacted has dramatic consequences. The use of margins and centers in feminist academic discourse can falsely lighten the burden of coalition building. When cut loose from particulars, marginality as a general condition attached to both femaleness and feminism can assert an all too easy analogy between many different kinds of experiences and power relations, making all forms of inequities seem alike. Geraldine Pratt's paper reminds us that geographic and spatial metaphors can hide as well as expose problems in our social relations. We have a responsibility to uncover the varied, and often contradictory, work of these metaphors.

## NOTE

1. Tessie Liu, *The Weaver's Knot: The Contradictions of Class Structure and Family Solidarity in Western France 1870–1914* (Ithaca, N.Y.: Cornell University Press, 1994).

# 4

# motion, stasis, and resistance
# to interlocked oppressions

In thinking about motion through spaces that are both real and metaphorical—and thus about motion that it-self is both real and metaphorical—we need to ask many questions. Why are we moving, who is moving, who's moving where, who is she when she gets there, whom does she find there, does she recognize them, does she recognize herself, why does she want to go there, what does she bring with her on her trip, what does she hope to gain by going there, is she going there to stay or is she going there to visit? The answers will not be the same for women who are located differ-ently. Why is it that I, for example, would go to places inhabited by other women of color?

In shifting back and forth from motion to stasis, from bases or homes to the in-between, the roads, the borders, the margins, I find the geographical metaphor of a map of oppression useful. This map contains both stasis and motion. It is a mistake to dichotomize mobil-ity and stasis as incompatible and separable metaphors in theorizing oppression and liberation.

Mobility can be used as a metaphor for resistance to oppression or as a metaphor for oppression. Oppressed mobility is coerced mo-bility. But sometimes oppressed movement also has resistant possibil-ities. Resistance can be either moving in directions that have been de-nied or forbidden or rewalking coerced paths under one's own steam and thus refashioning a sense of self. Sometimes resistant movement involves a critical consciousness, although a great deal of resistance springs not from articulations of oppression but rather from strategies of daily survival that often do not involve a reflective stance against oppression. But it isn't just a question of coerced versus spontaneous consciousness. One may also walk the same paths with different attitudes, different epistemic frameworks.

Stasis can also be a metaphor either for resistance or for oppression. Stasis conceived as a state of germination or war or maneuver—the quiet *ensimismado* (into one's self) fashioning a new sense and a new collectivity—is a resistant or liberatory metaphor for oppression. In this way I can see movement as opposition to the "if it moves it isn't cultural" that condemns colonized cultures to stagnation, lack of internal critique, and creation. Obversely, I can see stasis from this point of view as oppressive. Think, for example, of liberation movements in many Latino communities. It is easy to work in these communities politically as long as you are working in areas having to do with political tradition. But to work around issues of race, class, gender, and sexuality is a very, very hard thing to do. The success of mainstream Latino political movements would at best mean liberation for a certain small group of Latinos but neglect of the needs of the community's most vulnerable members—youth, women, gays, and lesbians.

The map of oppression is one of the possible maps of our society. It is a map with a high degree of reality. The map has been drawn by people who are shareholders in power or by others on their behalf, with a more or less hidden hand. The key to the map is that it is drawn for the power holders' benefit. Each member of the society—oppressed and oppressor—has a spot in the map. There are roads that go to and from different people's spots. But not all the roads are in good repair or open to everyone. Some roads are prescribed and some are proscribed to different people, always for the power holders' benefit. When we look at ourselves on the map through the "eyes" that draw the map, we see ourselves as tired, depressed, and quiet, except to the extent that we are obediently efficient in fulfilling the task of "our station." We are also marked in intricate and fragmenting ways that pull us apart from the possibility of personal integrity. There are complex relations between the ways in which we are tired, quiet, and obedient and the ways in which we are marked.

But each one of us occupies our place on the map in tension and resistance. When we look at ourselves and others on the map through resistant "eyes," we see ourselves both as trespassers and followers of intentions that do not mesh with the logic of obedience. Resistance has many sources; some lie in the idiosyncrasies of history, but many stem from our insertion in different and problematic collectiveness. Reading the map with resistant perception opens up the possibility of a practice of collective transformation that does not torture us into simple fragmented identities and does not abandon a politics of identity. Rather, it allows a transformation from fragmentation into complex, nonfragmented identities. In resistance we not only perceive in tension to oppression but also act. The practice in question is a motion, a walking of the map of oppression that transgresses the prescriptions and proscriptions and redraws the map in the process. One walks from place of identity to place of identity, one's own and others'. One builds stakes in each place and complicates and challenges each place and is challenged by it and its inhabitants. One is not a passerby, but no place is "home," though maybe it is a base (as in *politica de base,* or grass roots politics): a place for conflicted, hard-earned solidarity and for contestation of meaning.

What I'm suggesting, then, is a particular political practice, which includes the adoption of several new attitudes as well as a different way of living: moving in and out of communities without thinking that these are places just to pass through as tourists. I am talking about being able to work enough with other people so you gain a deep understanding of who they are, what they are thinking, where they are going, and at the same time you develop some kind of stake in their lives. In the process you might come to see yourself, to some extent, with the eyes with which they see you. To take such political action, you must be willing to adopt an epistemic attitude of being comfortable with uncertainty, moving in and out of places where you do not know what is going to happen.

As I think of issues of motion versus stasis and ways out of dichotomizing them, I think of walking and where we are walking to and from. In this connection it is helpful to recall Marilyn Friedman's distinction between community of place and community of choice.[1] Both concepts need to be complicated further. Community of place can be distinguished from community of origin, and community of choice can be distinguished from community of support and destination. Each one of these senses of *community* clarifies issues that we need to address as we answer the questions at the beginning of this essay.

Finally I would like to address the problems of home. I think that having bases is very important, but that is very different from having homes, and both are problematic. It is necessary politically to have bases because part of what needs to be changed is communities of place. The worldliness of one's politics requires that the changes not simply be in the communities of choice. Communities of choice are important for the formulation of intentions and the critique and reformulation of old intentions. It is useful to think of shifting identity points, of different emphasis given to different aspects of one's identity depending on place. In thinking about identity politics and the politics of one's identity, it is important to recognize the complexity of one's identity and the complexity of the base and then to realize that everyone has more than one base. Moving from one base to another to be able to shift identities (or aspects of identity) is very healthy.

For me motion is always for the sake of understanding and for the sake of making connections with political movement. One of the goals of movement is the formation of a heterogeneous public—a task that requires an understanding that we will not reach total agreement but rather must acquire the ability to be able to plan for each other. We must understand others' places and our own interest in them. A group putting forth its own interests is not good enough. We must work for the understanding necessary to be able to put forth a perspectival account of others' needs that is not violent (discounting, devaluing, radically distorting) but rests on communication across cultural, situational, and other "group" differences. In order for me to understand what your interests are so that I can plan in a non-self-centered way for you and you can plan in a non-self-centered way for me, a way that does not make me up, that does not engage in fantasy, it is necessary to do more than have group representation. We must have a movement that creates space for rearranging one's own identity, for making the complexity of one's own subjectivity explicit, for articulating it, for making it public.

NOTE

1. Marilyn Friedman, "Feminism and Modern Friendship: Dislocating the Community," *Ethics* 99 (1989): 15.

5

# jews, african americans, and urban space
## *constructing progressive alliances*

The several calls we have heard to make connections and to forge coalitions remind me of two recent experiences that not only exemplify the fears we all have when trying to perform political work outside our own comfortable, safe communities but also suggest how we might work across our divisions to create an alternative model for effective politics. The first experience occurred in my neighborhood in New York City, a mostly Dominican neighborhood. City schools had been trying to introduce a multicultural curriculum—the Rainbow Curriculum—and it was contested because some people were offended by a very small amount of pro-gay content. Ironically, much of the opposition came from the Latino and African American communities, even though the curriculum had been designed largely to bring the histories and experiences of people of color into mainstream education. I found it personally very painful to realize that I could not even raise this issue with neighbors in my own apartment building: *who was I to tell them how to educate their children?* And yet I knew lesbian and gay Latinos who were bravely raising the issue in the Latino community, and it became obvious to me that, as a Jewish lesbian, I could at least make connections with them and make sure that Jewish queers and progressive Jewish straights were supporting their courageous stand.

The second experience occurred at a speak-out at Medgar Evers College in Crown Heights right after the summer when Crown Heights exploded. Medgar Evers, part of the CUNY system, is a mostly third-world college. I went with great trepidation with a friend of mine, also Jewish, with that feeling you have when you go off your own home turf and onto someone else's—oh, everyone's going to hate me, nobody's going to want me—you know, *terror*. But in spite of our fear we made ourselves go. And we discovered that people were really welcoming, glad we had come.

These examples illustrate two points. The first is obvious but almost invariably neglected: there is no such thing as a representative black or a representative Jew or a representative Latino. We all have many personal identifications. The second is that there are ways to exploit these various identities so that we can begin to bring together what has been separate. One key here is to do so with humility—ready to meet, to listen, to discover, to find connections—rather than assuming that I have the answers and can tell other people how to live their lives.

Many people's lives—for example, those of people of racially mixed blood—make mockeries of orderly systems of classification. And there are many people who cross lines because of personal relationships—their lover's kids are of mixed race, for example, or they married into a different class. Others make life choices at odds with their birth communities. I am a case in point. I am a strongly identified secular Jew, a lesbian who came out in my late twenties, a child of the working and lower middle class who acquired a Ph.D. through the free public education system of New York City and who now—unlike most of those who preceded me in my bloodline—makes her living through brainwork. For still others, the people whom they look most like may have radically differing historical and cultural backgrounds. We must recognize diversity within communities; if we do not, we will fall prey to the binary representation of race so prevalent in the media and current discourse.

We can see the way this works by looking at the recent media fascination with the black–Jewish conflict. (Consider those who are black and Jewish and belong to both communities; they must find this unreal dichotomy particularly disturbing.) Why do the media lavish so much attention on isolated incidents of black anti-Semitism? It is partly because of a false image of an Edenic past: the presumed interracial cooperation during the Civil Rights movement of the 1960s. The reality is more complex. Although the movement did have considerable Jewish participation, only a small percentage of Jews were actually involved. And there were problems resulting from arrogance and lack of understanding between Jews—especially Jewish men—and African Americans. Within the Jewish community frustration and anger often arise in response to African American resentment: "We did so much for them; why aren't they grateful?"

On the other hand, many blacks lump Jews in with all whites or consider Jews as the worst of the lot of arrogant white liberals.

Exaggerated media emphasis on conflict between Jews and African Americans is partly a result of geography: the big media are centered in New York City and Los Angeles, and in New York in particular, the dynamics between the Jewish and African American communities are unique. I do not find it surprising that New York City has been the site for the construction of this African American–Jewish conflict, both real and exaggerated, for in New York City the Jewish community is large and relatively powerful, with a tightly organized orthodox, politically conservative wing that claims to represent the whole. The communities of African descent, also large, are far less organized and far more under siege. All groups in New York are competing for limited resources, and there are politicians and others who encourage them to blame and hate each other for this situation.

When you add to this equation the media machine, which supports itself on hype, you find the presentation of a stark conflict that in reality does not exist. For example, Jesse Jackson's "Hymie town" comment has been endlessly recycled in the media, while his attempts at reconciliation, which have been accepted by major leaders in the Jewish community, are hardly reported. And why do we all know the name Louis Farrakhan but not bell hooks or Patricia Williams? The media silence some voices and showcase others, thus contributing to one-dimensional portraits of strikingly diverse communities.

I think that in all such cases we must look carefully at the particular historical situation that helps elicit such media representations. Jews and African Americans are the quintessential urban people in America. They inhabit our large cities, and if the cities are going to be transformed and healed as they need to be, the two communities need to work together to find some solutions. Harping on the impossibility of such cross-cultural efforts simply condemns the cities to failure.

In addition, popular stereotypes, not coincidentally, are related in insidious ways to excuses for the failures of capitalism. Jews and African Americas have become symbols in the mass media for what ails America. Unemployment and poverty skyrocket, but the abuses of the system are blamed on Jews as archetypal money grubbers—Shylocks. And the fallout of capitalism, urban crime and chaos, is blamed on African Americans.

While these stereotypes help to deflect criticism of exploitative corporate greed, one fear of capital is that Jews and African Americans represent the possibility of progressive alliance, a possibility with historical roots. For many years the Communist Party and the NAACP were two of the few integrated institutions in this nation and provided spaces where Jews and African Americans worked together for social and economic justice. To the extent that these two communities can be set at each other's throats, the possibility of progressive alliance across lines of race, and also of class, is diminished. Currently, inflated fears of each other effectively preclude alliances and lead to strong separatist tendencies. This helps explain Farrakhan's popularity, as well as the gated communities that have become so attractive to some American Jews.

I want to suggest another way of looking at the racial and ethnic divisions in our country and, in particular, propose a different analysis of the position of Jews within this division. When race is talked about as white and black, a lot of people are left out. In earlier work responding to the writings of Nadine Gordimer, I have drawn on the image of the tripartite structure of South African apartheid—white, colored, and black—to describe the more fluid but nevertheless strongly hierarchical color scheme operating in the United States.[1] The structure of apartheid is useful to contemplate here, not because things in this country are so fixed and clear; they're not. But let me pursue the analogy as a means to get past the false dichotomy of black versus white, in which racial discussions are typically cast. South Africa has not two racial categories but three: white, black, and colored. It's the particular buffer zone of colored that I want to examine. Colored are those who will never be white but at least aren't black. Colored are those who have more access to higher status and all that implies—-better housing, jobs, education, health, leisure, safety, respect. I want to suggest that in many places in the United States, Japanese, Koreans, some Chinese, Indians, Pakistanis, Arabs, and lighter-skinned or wealthier Latinos get to be "colored." Sometimes Caribbean blacks, by virtue of their accent, their education, and the strength of growing up as the majority, also get to be "colored." And African Americans, I want to suggest, are not the only "blacks," though they are the most visible. Many Latinos are of African descent, and along with those closest to indigenous roots, are tracked in the lowest social and economic status. Immigrants from Southeast Asia hold some of the hardest, worst-paying jobs in the nation. And in the Southwest and sometimes the Northwest, where there are few African Americans, Native Americans are kept the lowest of the low, and every cruel stereotype of inferiority shows up in local racist culture.

As I've said, these categories are not totally fixed. There is a certain permeability that characterizes the class-race system in the United States, a certain amount of passing—-literally for those with skin light enough, who shed their accents, language, culture, and approximately for those who, laboring under the heavy burden of racism, through luck and extraordinary heroism and sometimes through hardness against their own people, still squeak through. Clarence Thomas rose up from poverty to hobnob with the white male club called the Senate precisely by abandoning his people's concerns.

The point of this white/colored/black classification is not to violate the hope of solidarity among people of color by dividing them but to recognize divisions that exist and must be named in order to bridge them. There are Iraqi-black conflicts in Detroit, Korean-black in Flatbush and L.A., Cuban-black in Miami—conflicts that a generation ago often were Jewish-black because they are in part the inevitable result of who owns what in whose community and who is poor and who is accessible.[2] In the swamp of classes, top down from billionaires and millionaires, who have control, power, and wealth so beyond the needs of one person, one family, that it staggers the mind, to the middle and working classes, who do the office and service work, it is women and people of color, especially immigrants, who are a replenishing, flexible pool of cheap labor. They groom their kids to escape the parents' lives, to assimilate.

It is precisely the access to better-paid jobs or lower-middle-class small-business opportunities, along with access to education for the next generation, that characterizes the experience of "colored" in the United States. It is precisely the lack of better working-class jobs and small-business opportunities, along with systematic disadvantaging and exclusion by the educational system, that characterizes the experience of "black" in the United States. Sherry Gorelick's *City College and the Jewish Poor* describes how City College was created as a path to upward mobility to distract the radical Jewish poor from the revolutionary class struggle predicted by Marx; the path of higher education was taken by thousands and thousands of poor and working-class Jews.[3] College was free for us, and there was room, if not at the top, then certainly in the middle. Where are the free colleges now? Private colleges cost more than $25,000 a year. And where is room in the middle, when even the middle is suffering? This shared economic disaster could and should unite most people across lines of color. But the illusory protection of "whiteness" offers a partial escape route toward which anyone who can scrambles. This desire to identify with whiteness, as well as bigotry and fear, blocks solidarity.

In this white/colored/black scheme, where are the Jews? Of the groups I've named as targeted by a general hatred I'll call race hate, Jews are the closest to white. Many would say we are white, and indeed a commonsense visual response suggests that many of us are. But listen to the prophet James Baldwin: "No one was white before he/she came to America," Baldwin wrote in the mid-eighties.

It took generations, and a vast amount of coercion, before this became a white country. It is probable that it is the Jewish community—or more accurately, perhaps, its remnants—that in America has paid the highest and most extraordinary price for becoming white. For the Jews came here from countries where they were not white, and they came here in part because they were not white; and incontestably, in the eyes of the black American (and not only in those eyes), American Jews have opted to become white.[4]

Now, the point is not for Jews to escape the category "white" to evade confronting our own racism, nor is it to insert ourselves artificially into a category of oppression, as sometimes happens in our progressive movements where oppression in some puny, paradoxical way confers privilege. It is to recognize a continuum where we are the closest of the coloreds to white, or the closest of the whites to colored. What I want to focus on, in James Baldwin's phrase, is "the extraordinary price of becoming white."

Many of us chose, or had chosen for us, a white path, a path of assimilation, of passing, often accompanied by extreme cultural loss. What do we know beyond or besides the now usual sources of American Jewish identity, which are, in a nutshell, religion, Israel, and the Holocaust? As the sum total of Jewish identity, this is limited. How does this restricted base help us create and strengthen an authentic American Jewish identity?

It's called assimilation. We, like others who pass or partly pass, can choose where to direct our allegiance: upward and whitening, restricting our Jewishness to that which assimilation increasingly demands—a *Jew at home, a "man" in the streets*, white people who go to Jewish church, i.e., synagogue—or we can deepen both our identity and our affiliation with the other "others," the outsiders: the coloreds and the blacks.[5]

I'm suggesting that progressive Jews recognize our position between colored and white, a source of tension but also of possibility. I can envision a powerful coalition between Jewish and Asian women against the JAP stereotype. I can also envision a nightmare coalition between Jewish and Asian men against affirmative action. The challenge is to build progressive coalitions not only among the coloreds but between the coloreds and the blacks and between these and the economically struggling whites—and then to expand still further. The issue of hate crimes, for example, can unite Jews with people of color and with lesbians and gays, and we should insist on the legal—and moral—classification of violence against women as a hate crime. That would be a powerful coalition indeed.

These are examples of the kinds of thematic relationships that can bring us to a new kind of multiculturalism. This new multiculturalism demands dynamic exchanges, new kinds of connections, new ways of perceiving, narratives that include each other. I think the threads of the conference and of this book lead me to nothing less than a refusal of false dichotomy, an increased need for fluidity, a recognition of the need to think metaphorically and analytically at the same time and of the need to refuse the false either/or of standing with one's people or with their enemies. Borders are, after all, arbitrary and shifting. Virginia Woolf wrote of women's mission to be disloyal to civilization, but given the complexity of our identities, loyalties, and material bases in a variety of communities and constituencies—a complexity that spatial metaphor can render graphically evident—we must remember that there are many civilizations to which we need to be disloyal in different ways and many loyalties among which we must negotiate.

## NOTES

1. Much of the following is excerpted from my earlier essay "Jews, Class, Color, and the Cost of Whiteness," in *The Issue Is Power: Essays on Women, Jews, Violence and Resistance* (San Francisco: Aunt Lute Books, 1992), 139–49.

2. Obviously, much of the foregoing discussion of race is intertwined with class relations. I discuss this at greater length in the earlier work, ibid., 143–45.

3. Sherry Gorelick, *City College and the Jewish Poor* (New Brunswick, N.J.: Rutgers University Press, 1981).

4. James Baldwin, "On Being 'White' and Other Lies," *Essence* (April 1984), 90–92.

5. "A Jew at home, a 'man' in the streets" was used to characterize the "modern" Jew of the European Enlightenment.

# 6

# on location

The work for my last two book-length projects, one on the politics and poetics of displacement in Euro-American poststructuralist and postmodern cultural production and one on transnational feminist critical practices, is linked by their discussions of the material conditions of postmodernity and their emphasis on historicizing the terms at use in contemporary cultural criticism. Armand Mattelart has argued that concepts and terms "represent a terrain of struggle between groups and classes."[1] In considering the circulation of terms such as *location* or *place* in relation to *displacement* or *travel,* it is important for feminists to historicize our investments in these powerful modern tropes. I am leery of a wholesale adoption of terms that have been produced through the matrix of colonial discourse, for example, or through the mystified aesthetics of elite modernisms. As metaphors of modernity, these terms compress power relations, producing particular subjects and identities under the rhetorical guise of universalism. This compression and mystification has to be countered by densely detailed historicizations so that our tools for analyzing the present are not completely eroded by the dynamics of the past.

The tension between home and away, place and displacement, local and global, etc., is nothing new. As a hallmark of modernity, developing capitalist economic organization enabled more travel in different ways, straining previous associations between place and identity, producing an ambivalent oppositional construction. The fragmentation and anomie that we conventionally attribute to modernity have given rise to discourses of nostalgia for home and unified subject po-

sitions even as celebrations of the freedom of travel have privileged the benefits of distance and separation. What I would argue is that we need more precise tracings of these oscillations between home and away as transcendental
concepts. But we can't lose sight of the structuring centrality of the dualism between place and displacement in modernity, its seeming necessity as a discourse, and its mystifying effects. Without such an understanding we cannot
recognize the continuities between modern and postmodern versions of the
place/displacement dichotomy. As Inderpal Grewal and I have argued in our
book, *Scattered Hegemonies*,[2] postmodernity must be viewed not as a radical
break with modernity but as a network of complex continuities and discontinuities. Tropes of location and dislocation participate in this network, constructing historically specific links and disparities.

It has been argued that postmodernity marks an intensification of fragmentation, disorientation, and loss of sense of place, spurring some calls for a
return to the modern as a better alternative, as a time when discernible homes
beckoned world-weary travelers. We must be careful not to imbue those lost
sites with too much nostalgia. For many of us those "places" felt more like
traps or prisons than comfortable homes. On the other hand, rejecting home
for the pleasures of the road, as it were, reveals a naive privilege as well. The
site of home/place is a complex construct, and its opposite terms—displacement and travel—are just as nuanced.

It's a rather large project, I've discovered, to begin such detailed account-
ings. What I'd like to do today is to focus on four key critical practices that
move us toward feminist deconstructive projects where modernity and postmodernity can be historically situated as sites of cultural production.

First, I'd like to question the use of structural models of center and margin
or center/periphery in feminist cultural studies. If, as Doreen Massey argues, the
"local, regional, and national are increasingly drawn into and constituted by a
logic which exists at an international level," the analytical usefulness of a binary
opposition between center and periphery is less and less obvious.[3] In classic
world-system theory, groups are presented as monolithic rather than multiply
constituted. In a world where nation-state power is eroded and transitional economic systems are formed through differentiation and flexible accumulation,
those monolithic formations can no longer account comprehensively for the
construction of subjectivities and divisions of labor. In fact, it is doubtful that
world-system theory ever adequately addressed gender diversity or the Euro-
centrism of a center-periphery hegemonic flow. Barbara Abou-El-Haj argues,
for example, that such ethnocentrism results in an overemphasis on local rela-

tions with global power brokers that ignores the complex class divisions and tensions on the local level.⁴ Nor can center/periphery models account for the terrible conditions under which some people have lived in the so-called center.

Models predicated upon binary oppositions cannot move us out of the paradigms of colonial discourse, nor can they provide us with accurate maps of social relations in postmodernity. In making this assertion, however, I am not celebrating a world cultural hybridity and heterogeneity. To put it bluntly, few of us can live without a passport or an identity card of some sort and fewer of us can manage without employment. Our access to these signs and practices is deeply uneven and hardly carnivalesque. In this context of proliferating fragmentation, power is never eliminated but differently organized and maintained. Thus, even as these deep reconfigurations of power and identity in postmodernity produce new asymmetries, historical opportunities for change, for shifts in imaginings and practices, also become possible. We need to know how to account for agency, resistance, subjectivity, and movement or event in the face of totalizing fixities or hegemonic structures without constructing narratives of oppositional binaries.

As feminists we must ask how the concept of center and periphery operates in our theories. Are we inscribing monumental identities or are we producing critical practices that will aid our efforts to analyze our diverse activities and participation in contemporary transitional cultures of modernity?

Returning to my framing of four critical practices, my second key strategy asks us to question our use of one binary formation in particular: global/local. Global/local hails us as a strategy to challenge the homogenizing globalization that modernity appears to have engendered in such pervasively hegemonic ways. Yet, as with any binary, rather than establishing an equivalence, one term is always dominant. The pitfalls of privileging the local over the global are many. Emergent fascisms, recurrent nationalisms, racisms, patriarchies, and fundamentalist religious/political movements signal the dangers of relying too heavily on ideologies of the local.

In considering the popularity of the global/local binary in contemporary cultural criticism, Inderpal Grewal and I have argued that for many critics in the United States, the global/local opposition makes "sense" because it corresponds to a specific "reality": that is, the relationship between federal and local governments in the United States. Yet for people in many other parts of the world, such a division makes no sense at all. Global/local as monolithic formation may also erase the existence of multiple expressions of local identities and concerns and multiple globalities. In this particular way, global/local binaries dangerously correspond to the colonialism/nationalism model, which often leaves out various subaltern groups as well as the interplay of power at various levels of sociopolitical agendas.

Finally, global/local oppositions usually privilege the local in such a way as to mystify the boundaries and essentialize the content of the "interior." What is lost in an uncritical acceptance of this binary division is precisely the fact that the parameters of the local and global are often indefinable or indistinct—they are permeable constructs. How one separates the local from the global is difficult to decide when each thoroughly infiltrates the other.

I would argue that feminists have great stakes in these discussions and debates, calling for more complex models of culture rather than replicating modern colonial legacies in modes of social explanation.

The third critical practice is to require that all the terms of location and displacement in modernity and postmodernity undergo historically specific analyses of the social relations that produce them. In particular, in my work I have been looking at the emphasis on displacement in modernity and the celebrations of distance and dislocation in Euro-American cultural modernisms. In my book *Questions of Travel*, I pose the terms *travel* and *displacement* not in opposition so much as in juxtaposition in order to examine the continuities and discontinuities between modern and postmodern discourses of location and identity.[5] *Travel* is very much a modern term, signifying both commercial and leisure movement in an era of expanding Western capitalism. *Displacement* refers us to the less individualized migrations that modernity has engendered. In stressing the different material and textual manifestations of displacement, however, I would resist any suggestion of neutrality or relativist hybridity. Throughout the modern era, displacement has emerged as a primary condition and trope out of the practices of economic and cultural modernization efforts and politically charged development policies. Keeping this history in mind, I use the term *displacement* to read against the grain of travel, that is, to question the modernisms of representations of movement, location, and homelessness in contemporary critical practices.

In focusing on the production of postmodern discourses of displacement in modernity, my study calls attention to the continuities and discontinuities between terms such as *travel, displacement,* and *location,* as well as between the particularized practices and identities of *exile, nomad,* and *tourist.* All displacements are not equal and cannot be reduced to the same. Yet the occidental ethnographer, the modernist expatriate poet, the writer of popular travel accounts, and the tourist may all participate in the mythic narrativization of displacement without questioning the cultural, political, and economic grounds of their different professions, privileges, means, and limitations. Immigrants, refugees, exiles, and the urban homeless also move in and out of these discourses as metaphors, tropes, and symbols but rarely as historically recognized producers of critical discourses themselves. Discourses of displacement tend to absorb difference and create ahistorical amalgams; thus, a field of social forces becomes represented as personal experience or a purely poetic practice.

Once again, feminist cultural critics must resist romanticized appropriations of the figures of exile, nomadism, and tourism in favor of historicized accounts of the social relations that produce material conditions of dwelling and displacement.

My fourth and final critical practice calls for collaborative projects that analyze the transnational configurations of power that produce contemporary genders, ethnicities, national or regional identities, and cultural locations. If Euro-American feminist practices do not acknowledge transnational material conditions, Euro-American feminist movements will remain isolated and prone to reproducing the universalizing gestures of dominant Western cultures. Notions such as "global feminism" have stood for a kind of Western cultural imperialism by eliding the diversity of women's agency in favor of a Western model of women's liberation that celebrates individuality and modernity. Anti-imperialist movements have legitimately decried this form of feminist globalizing. Yet we know that there is an imperative need to address the concerns of women around the world in the historicized particularity of their relationship to multiple patriarchies as well as to international economic hegemonies. We need creative ways to move beyond constructed oppositions without ignoring the histories that have informed these conflicts or the valid concerns about power relations that have represented or structured the conflicts up to this point. We need to articulate the relationship of gender to scattered hegemonies such as global economic structures, patriarchal nationalisms, "authentic" forms of traditions, local structures of dominations, and legal-juridical oppression on multiple levels.

Transnational feminist practices require this kind of comparative work rather than the relativistic linking of "differences" undertaken by proponents of "global" feminism; that is, they need to compare multiple, overlapping, and discrete oppressions rather than to construct a theory of hegemonic oppression under a unified category of gender.

## NOTES

1. Armand Mattelart, *Transnationals and the Third World: The Struggle for Culture* (Hadley, Mass.: Bergin & Garvey, 1983), 50.

2. Inderpal Grewal and Caren Kaplan, *Scattered Hegemonies: Post-Modernity and Transitional Feminist Practices* (Minneapolis: University of Minnesota Press, 1994).

3. Doreen Massey, *Space, Place, and Gender* (Minneapolis: University of Minnesota Press, 1994), 161.

4. Barbara Abou-El-Haj, "Languages and Models for Cultural Exchange," in *Culture, Globalization and the World System,* ed. Anthony D. King (London: Macmillan, 1991), 143.

5. Caren Kaplan, *Questions of Travel: Postmodern Discourses of Displacement* (Durham, N.C.: Duke University Press, 1996).

# PART 2

## bodies politic

The questions of theory and praxis raised by the authors of the preceding essays recur in this section, which brings together scholars who work in and across literary/cultural theory, history, African American studies, Latin American studies, queer theory, and political science. Engaging diverse geographies and historical eras, the authors focus on the intersections between social and individual bodies, reading cultural and symbolic practices as spatialized formations. By analyzing the complex mechanisms through which space is articulated, organized, and politicized, the essays elucidate the local manifestations of large-scale structural forces—industrialism, imperialism, democratization, capitalism—and show how women's relations to public space become entangled with issues of power and representation.

Mary Poovey demonstrates that with the growth of capitalism in England between the mid-eighteenth and mid-nineteenth centuries, the materiality of the body and the natural landscape were increasingly subjected to a process of displacement and abstraction—a transformation that had "profound and unexpected implications for women." This drive toward ever more refined systems of abstraction occurred as well in Saint-Domingue (now Haiti), as Joan Dayan shows in her analysis of how the increasingly intricate codification of racialized bodies—enshrined in the infamous Code Noir—underwrote the French slave system in the eighteenth century and how the "coloured" inhabitants of the colony resisted the apparati of social control through various forms of subversive play with its founding terms. Shifting to the terrains of the late twentieth century, Mary Pat Brady traces comparable connections between power, spatiality, and signifying systems. In juxtaposed analyses of drug discourses, literary texts, and queer politics, Brady considers how feminist theories might most creatively address the rapid transnational cultural alterations produced by the technologies of late industrial capitalism. The role of theory also preoccupies Joan Landes, who seeks a rapprochement between "feminist enlightenment" positions and postmodernist feminisms. Like Dayan and Poovey, Landes returns to the late eighteenth century, showing how the notions of democracy articulated during the French Revolution epitomized the contradictions inherent in discourses of individual freedom and universal human equality. Such discourses undergirded the Tanzanian nationalist movement in the 1950s, as Susan Geiger demonstrates in her analysis of the women's organizations that advanced the struggle for independence. Recalling Dayan's descriptions of subaltern women's irreverent deployment of costume and corporeal display, Geiger shows how, through the appropriation of public spaces and the subversive manipulation of performance, dress, and social networks, women transformed the landscape of Tanzanian politics.

In tracing the interactions between the state of the body and the body of the state, the authors in this section all demonstrate how political subjects may, as Geiger reminds us, "subvert the master narratives" by reconstituting spaces, both material and metaphoric—locating what Poovey refers to as "the asymmetries and contradictions" inherent in even the most totalizing of systems. Their collective analyses suggest that feminist theories must become increasingly international and interdisciplinary in order to comprehend the discursive and material practices that inform constructions of space and to resist evolving systems of domination. Such a praxis is ultimately self-reflexive, interrogating the limits of its own theoretical models even as it attempts to remap traditional terrains of power.

7

# the production of abstract space

In most accounts of capitalism, time is of utmost importance. Whether analysts of capitalism have focused on the disciplinary effects of waged labor, the periodization of capitalism, or the transformation of (what counts as) temporality itself, they have represented new conceptualizations of time as a central—perhaps even the essential—problematic of the capitalist mode of production.[1] While time's conceptual twin, space, has not been overlooked in the literature, it is in general considered less crucial to our understanding of what distinguishes capitalism as a mode of production.[2] In this essay I propose to elaborate the important work that Henri Lefebvre has begun on the spatial dimensions of capitalism.[3] My purpose is not to interrogate the importance analysts have assigned to time but simply to suggest that the temporal transformations that accompanied the consolidation of capitalism had a spatial dimension as well. More specifically, I want to suggest that thinking of capitalism as a spatial practice leads us not only to focus on the geographical unevenness of imperialism, for example, but also to think of the instantiation of abstraction as a critical component of the capitalist epistemology.

I've organized this essay into two major sections, the second of which has three parts. In the first section I'll make some general remarks about the theoretical categories I think a spatial analysis might address. The idea here is to cast the net as wide as possible, to be suggestive rather than definitive, and to prompt us all to reconsider the implications of focusing our attention on some objects and not others. In the second section I'll develop a more historically and geographically specific argument about one of the theoretical categories I've identified—what Henri Lefebvre calls the production of abstract space. In this section I'll address three topics: (1) how the materiality of the body was displaced by the production of abstract space; (2) how the increasing concentration of the English population in cities and the inequities created by the privatization of common lands mandated a new vehicle for establishing public consensus about the use of space, both public and private; and (3) how the creation of this consensus involved a contest between two representations of the new urban space. The two contestants in this discursive and political contest were the image of the social body and that of the machine. Both, as we will see, had profound and unexpected implications for women.

First, then, what theoretical categories might a historian of capitalism as a spatialized practice examine? (And let me emphasize immediately that I think that all of these topics are crucial to such an analysis.) I'll suggest four large areas. First, one might examine the *material* reorganization of the relationship between human activity and space. Here I have in mind the sixteenth-, seventeenth-, and eighteenth-century cartographic projects by which land was subjected to the "emptiness" of Euclidean geometrical representation, then rationalized and subdivided into private and crown properties amenable to legislative oversight and regular taxation; the long process of enclosure by which 6.5 million acres of common and waste lands were privatized between the seventeenth and early nineteenth centuries; the imperial march of the English into India, Africa, and the Americas during this period; the increasing concentration of the population in towns, which accelerated dramatically after 1800; the building of canals, roads, railways, and other arteries of material exchange during the eighteenth and nineteenth centuries; and the establishment and standardization of systems of money, banking, and capital investment (speculation), whose modern version began in 1688.[4]

Second, one might analyze the *textual* treatment of spatial issues in the works of apologists for (and opponents to) capitalism. Such apologies, in particular, make more visible the process of abstraction inherent in the material changes to which I have alluded. One might look, for example, at the way Locke's metaphor of the mind as a *tabula rasa* displaces a social analysis of space (such as that advanced by the Diggers, for instance) with a geometric analysis; in Locke's account, the mind, like Euclidean space, is held to be everywhere the same, uniformly subject to the same laws, and abstract in the sense of being empty—at least until stocked through the operations of the senses, particularly the eye.[5] Or one might examine the problem that spatial *distance* poses for Adam Smith (I'll return to this in a moment) or the centrality that Malthus's theory of rent assigns to the *agricultural* use of space—even in a period in which urbanization had begun to vie for critical attention.

Third, one could look closely at the specific dynamics by which what Lefebvre calls natural space was reorganized into abstract space. Since this will be my primary focus in the second part of this essay, I'll just list some of the features of abstract space. First of all, as I've already suggested, abstract space is geometric: its two-dimensionality reduces the irregularities of a natural landscape to a grid that can be mapped and subjected to mathematical laws.[6] Also, abstract space is organized by visuality, not the full range of human senses.[7] This visuality is then naturalized by a further generalization—language, whose most systematic and replicable version is writing.[8] Finally, abstract space is conceptually homogeneous: even if its various segments (or participants) are not all the same, they pass as interchangeable *because* they have been standardized and subjected to the rationalizing technologies of measurement, universalization, and monetary equivalence. In relation to things, this process results in universal equivalence. In relation to humans, it culminates in statistical persons.[9]

Fourth, one might examine the effects of these material, textual, and conceptual treatments of space on the lives of individuals. To my mind, this analysis would focus on the unevenness by which resources were distributed, including the resources of power and of space itself. It would also focus on those mediations through which material developments make themselves felt (differently) in the lives of various individuals. These mediations include everything from symbolic representations (works of art, literature, political emblems and demonstrations) to the passage and (differential) enforcement of laws governing vagrancy and loitering.[10]

I realize that I've just outlined a research agenda that could occupy countless scholars for the rest of our academic lives. My intention in sketching some of the outer limits of this field is to suggest how such inquiries could restore unity to disciplines and objects of analysis that have increasingly been separated or carelessly juxtaposed—through the New Historical use of anecdote, for example. Looking at capitalism—and postmodernism—as spatialized practices might expose the artificiality of separating materialism from textuality. It might also uncover the history of this separation and of the disaggregation and specialization of academic disciplines that developed alongside the differentiation-cum-rationalization of space. Looking at capitalism and postmodernism as spatialized practices might also provide a vehicle for getting beyond what I think of as the special-interests approach to academic inquiry and to politics. In the last decade this special-interests approach has generated mind-numbing quarrels about whether gender *or* race *or* class *or* ethnicity *or* sexual preference is *the* privileged category of analysis. In this context the advantage to looking at the social production of space is that it necessarily involves and affects every determinant of difference, *and* it restores to visibility the complex interrelationships among these differentiations (which are, after all, social productions themselves).

Now that I've made a few general—and intentionally provocative—points, let me begin to develop one small part of this research agenda. I'll focus primarily on the third area of investigation I outlined above—the dynamics of abstraction by which the capitalist configuration of space was instantiated. I'll be focusing on England as the first industrialized nation and on the period between 1750 and 1840, which most historians equate with the consolidation of capitalism. Given the constraints of space and the enormity of this topic, my analysis will seem sketchy, but I hope it will begin to suggest the kind of revision I've been describing.

In the lectures later published as *The Theory of Moral Sentiments,* Adam Smith developed a theory about what makes individuals moral and society a relatively harmonious whole. This theory suggests some of the complexities of that mid-eighteenth-century version of abstraction associated with the Scottish Enlightenment. In brief, Smith's theory combines assertions about universal truth (human nature) with statements that Smith claims to derive from empirical observation, especially of himself. We can see this epistemological mixture in Smith's discussion of what I will call specular morality: morality, according to Smith, depends upon ocular inspection, but literal seeing is always accompanied by an imaginative process that is actually a process of generalization, which substitutes for difference in kind a measurable distinction—difference in degree.[11] Through this complex amalgamation of empiricism and abstraction, the moral individual sympathizes with the pain of another because the two become, in some sense, equivalents. "It is the impressions of our own senses only, not those of his, which our imaginations copy. By the imagination we place ourselves in his situation, we conceive ourselves enduring with all the same torments, we enter as it were into his body, and become in some measure the same person with him, and thence form some idea of his sensations, and even feel something which, though weaker in degree, is not altogether unlike them."[12]

This statement, which dates from 1759, suggests how thoroughly abstraction permeated the body and regulated empiricism in the middle of the eighteenth century. It is important to notice, however, that neither the imposition of abstraction nor the effects with which it was associated were uniform—even in the works of a single writer like Smith. We see this clearly when, in the work that most historians credit with formulating the basic laws of capitalism, Smith discusses the effects of urbanization on morality. In the *Wealth of Nations*

(1776), he says that individuals remain moral as long as they either live in country villages or possess sufficient wealth to attract public attention; in both
cases, morality seems to be a function of seeing and being seen. The problem
arises when the country dweller moves to a city, for there he (Smith's paradig-
matic individual is typically figured as male) is "sunk in obscurity and darkness.
His conduct is observed and attended to by nobody, and he is therefore very
likely to neglect it himself, and to abandon himself to every sort of low prodi-
gality and vice."[13]

The fact that no equivalent problem arises when Smith imagines the
wealthy man living on his country estate suggests how uneven the process and
effects of abstraction were in his picture of capitalist society. On the one hand,
for some groups—prosperous (European) men—key abstractions displace the
materiality of the body: the morality of some men is self-regulating because
"human nature" and imagination are common to all and the physical location of
their bodies is not decisive. On the other hand, for other groups—most specifically poor men who live in cities—the body remains prominent and problematic. The physicality of the laboring population is prominent and problematic in
Smith's work because when the poor man is no longer visible to the well-to-
do, he is assumed to be immoral; he is assumed to be immoral, in turn, because
Smith considers him incapable of developing the specular morality (which is actually the ability to generalize) that Smith presents as essential to virtue and
therefore to political power.[14] By the end of the century, the physicality of the
poor had become even more prominent. In the work of Thomas Robert
Malthus, the bodies of the poor were both prominent and problematic because
they ate too much and reproduced too often for their own and the nation's
well-being.

The relationship between abstraction and materiality also runs the other
way in Smith's work. When materiality is understood not as embodiedness but
as particularization, we see that Smith treats well-to-do men as individuals,
whereas he represents the laboring poor as an aggregate, "the great body of
the people." Smith considers well-to-do individuals (men) capable of governing
their own passions, and he frees them to pursue their own self-interests; paradoxically (or perhaps logically), their freedom does not produce social chaos
because Smith claims that every (prosperous) man is motivated by the same
desire: the "propensity to truck, barter, and exchange one thing for another"
(Wealth, 13). Because poor workers cannot develop specular morality, and because the monotony and repetitiousness of their labor makes them "as stupid
and ignorant as it is possible for a human creature to become" (Wealth, 734),

Smith treats the laboring poor as an aggregate and mandates for them what is unthinkable for the well-to-do: government interference in the most intimate areas of their lives.

Initially, I want to emphasize the unevenness of the process of abstraction Smith introduces into his subject. In this case the unevenness has primarily (what we would call) class implications, although if I highlighted Smith's comparative analyses of various societies, we would see that it has racial and gender components as well. When Smith imagines working men disappearing into cities or into the more mechanical operations of the division of labor, he imagines them as simultaneously more material (in the sense of being embodied, not imaginative, creatures) and more amenable to aggregation (in the sense of being less individualized or particularized). At the same time, however, Smith is abstracting all social relations and all individuals—even, or especially, the well-to-do. Social relations become abstract in the sense that they are all reduced to versions of quantifiable (monetary) exchange, and individuals become abstract in the sense that "everyone" becomes an instance of the same, a representative of "human nature" that wants only to truck, barter, and exchange. This process of abstraction and (apparent) homogenization was also, not incidentally, the process by which what we call the economy was produced as a separate, apparently autonomous and lawful, realm of activity and thought.[15]

The second point I want to make about the displacement of the body attendant upon the production of abstract space is clearest if we move for a moment to the early nineteenth century. During the 1830s and 1840s, we see the beginning of the flood of social surveys that distinguished early Victorian Britain. For my purposes what's interesting about these surveys is how microscopically they focused on the body—not all bodies, of course, but the bodies of the urban poor.[16] Writers like James Phillips Kay and Edwin Chadwick, moreover, focused on the bodily details of these people in the context of the abstract logic that had been naturalized by 1830. As an example, I'll briefly highlight some relevant parts of what was undoubtedly the most widely read government document of the nineteenth century, Chadwick's 1842 *Sanitary Report.*

Open Chadwick's *Sanitary Report* at any page, and you'll encounter the class asymmetry we have already seen in Adam Smith's work. Whereas Chadwick identifies his middle-class informers only by name, office, and locale, the objects of the analytic gaze rise before us in excruciatingly exact detail. These detailed descriptions focus relentlessly on bodily processes; in so doing, they efface the individuality of the poor for the sake of a materiality that is amenable to both abstraction and quantification. Thus, for example, in the most frequently cited part of the *Sanitary Report,* the section entitled "Comparative Chances of Life in Different Classes of the Community," "life" is equated with longevity so that it can be separated from specific individuals, averaged, and compared mathematically in tabular form. Such abstraction has two specific spatial components. In the first place, it allows the quantified abstraction "life" (longevity) to be correlated to particular places (as well as to occupations, which have differential effects on people's mobility); in the second place, it encourages Chadwick and his informers to blur the boundary between individual people and the space they occupy. Thus we learn, for example, that in 1839 in the London neighborhood of Bethnal Green, the average gentleman or professional (who would no doubt have been relatively mobile) reached forty-five years of age, whereas the average mechanic, servant, and laborer lived only until age sixteen.[17] The point of presenting these sensational figures becomes clear in the next section of the *Report* when Chadwick assigns a monetary value to the labor lost through such statistically premature deaths and their attendant illnesses (*Sanitary Report,* 254).

If the ability to quantify the "pecuniary burden" imposed upon the nation by unsanitary conditions constitutes the explicit end of Chadwick's abstractions, then one of the means by which he pursues this goal "proves" the theoretical position with which he undertook the project. Like many of his contemporaries, Chadwick believed that poor health was the result of environment; specifically, he believed that disease was spread by "miasmas"—decaying animal and vegetable material that infiltrated the air and water and thus was concentrated in densely populated urban spaces.[18] In keeping with his environmentalism, Chadwick's descriptions tend to segue from the interiors of poor residences (with special attention given to beds and sanitary facilities) to streets (with special attention to drains and sewers) to water supplies. This descriptive logic produces a picture of cities as spatial systems of waste production and elimination, the bodily prototype for which becomes clear when Chadwick discusses the waterways that circulate throughout the city as an "arterial system" (*Sanitary Report,* 126–27). For Chadwick, human beings—especially the poor—are merely features of this giant social body. So integrally does he imagine them bound to their immediate environment that he even depicts personal hygiene and dress as extensions of their "circumstances." In one detailed vignette, for example, Chadwick describes a working-class woman whose personal appearance and temper have been "bourne down by the condition of the house" (*Sanitary Report,* 195).

Chadwick's emphasis on physical environment, as well as his insistence that residences are both the critical site of illness (and therefore targets of government inspection) *and* merely parts of a nationwide system, tends to curtail the power of the working class as a whole and of women in particular.[19] On the one hand, if the home is the center of health and if cleanliness renders the house a home, then even the poorest woman should be able to make her hearth so welcoming that her husband will be "stimulated to industry" and will shun the alehouse like the plague (*Sanitary Report,* 324). On the other hand, if the individual residence is only one part of a system that extends through streets and rivers and outlying fields, then no amount of womanly whitewashing can eliminate the effluvia that seep up through the cottage floor.

The descriptive genre epitomized by Chadwick's *Sanitary Report* privileges first-hand eyewitness accounts over the abstract theorizing so prominent in the works of Scottish Enlightenment writers like Adam Smith. Chadwick's *Report* thus seems "objective," in the modern sense of that word; it was partly on the basis of such objectivity that social economy and statistics were able to claim the status of social "sciences" as early as the 1830s. But we should not lose sight of the fact that such "objectivity," whose logical conclusion is the replacement of the human observer with a mechanical recording device, implies a set of assumptions compatible with the kind of abstraction I have been describing.[20] These assumptions include the priority of quantification over descriptions that delineate qualities; the importance of aggregation (of some groups in particular); overparticularization; and the possibility of homogenizing—rendering perfectly equivalent—all observers and everything that is observed.

The social version of homogeneity associated with abstract space currently goes under the name of "consensus." In the period with which I am concerned, the stick of coercion was occasionally lifted to hasten consensus (consider the notorious Black Acts of the eighteenth century and the repressive Six Acts of 1819), but the consolidation of modern society increasingly depended on voluntary compliance, not force.[21] Michel Foucault has discussed the displacement of coercion by incitement in terms of the creation of a self-regulating, disciplinary self, but if we think in spatial terms we can see a different facet of this process.[22] This is my second point about English society in the early nineteenth century. Once more it is helpful to begin with Adam Smith's quasi-philosophical, quasi-empirical description of the city. The problem that cities pose to virtue, you'll remember, is that their winding passageways and densely populated neighborhoods, their sheer size and complexity, literally impede vision. As the laboring poor disappear into cities, the moralizing gaze of the well-to-do cannot provide the discipline once (theoretically) available in country villages and rural communities. Given the assumption that morality is—in the first instance—a function of seeing and being seen, how can the prosperous ensure virtue in a society too spatially complex for the eye to penetrate?

In England this question assumed particular prominence in the second half of the 1790s, when a combination of economic depression, political fallout from the revolution in France, and rising poor rates made the laboring population seem problematic as never before.[23] Conceptualizing the problem of the poor as a problem of visibility—the poor were simultaneously *too* visible as a group and too impervious to oversight as individuals—helps make sense of some of the schemes advanced to solve the problem of poverty: Bentham's Panopticon, for example, which would have rendered incarcerated members of the criminal classes visible to a single, omnipotent warden, or his National Charity Company, which would have dispensed relief through a single, centralized administrative system staffed by trained inspectors and guaranteed to maximize labor and minimize dissent.[24] In addition to these relatively repressive schemes, numerous plans were offered for *inculcating* virtue in the poor during the first three decades of the century. Some, like the home-visiting scheme implemented in Scotland by the Reverend Thomas Chalmers, were specifically formulated within the problematic of visibility. According to this influential divine, a natural society was bound together by sympathy, not by coercion or legalized charity (i.e., poor relief). Because the well-to-do no longer saw the poor on a daily basis, however, the source of this sympathy had dried up, and as a consequence, the deference of the poor had withered away. To resuscitate morality and correct the "low and grovelling taste" of the poor, Chalmers commanded his clergy

> to go forth among the people; and there to superinduce the principles of an efficient morality ... to work a transformation of taste and of character ... to deliver lessons, which, of themselves, will induce a habit of thoughtfulness, that must insensibly pervade the whole system of man's desires and his doings ... infusing into every practical movement, along with the elements of passion and interest, the elements of duty, and of wisdom, and of self-estimation.[25]

The problem of how to establish consensus in a society no longer open to moralizing sight lines illuminates the context in which we should understand the early nineteenth-century debate about working-class education. In 1832, in his pamphlet on the *Moral and Physical Condition of the Working Classes ... in Manchester,* James Phillips Kay proposed a plan of education that specifically extended Chalmers's scheme of home visitation. Initially, Kay offered education as a general antidote to sloth, trade union strikes, and the kind of political-cum-economic protests that had erupted at Peterloo in 1819 and all over England in 1831.[26] In this pamphlet Kay presented a generalized program of working-class education as a supplement to free trade, which was the only instrument he trusted to bring about social harmony. By 1838 (the year before he was appointed first secretary to the Committee of Council on Education), Kay had formulated a much more detailed educational plan, which was to be instituted first in the state-run workhouses created by the New Poor Law of 1834. While Kay's scheme lacks the omniscient warden that Bentham installed in the Panopticon, his school system would have implemented many of the features we associate with utilitarianism. Because his goal was to increase pedagogic efficiency, for example, Kay insists on the importance of correctly classifying students (by age, sex, and future occupation) so that they can receive appropriate instruction.[27] Because the population of similar children in any single workhouse was insufficient for such classification, Kay suggests combining unions to support a single, purpose-built school (22). He recommends that teachers keep precise accounts to measure the productivity of each child and that any profits obtained from school gardens be returned to the school; the former was intended to encourage hard work, the latter to discourage a child's aspiration beyond the station designated by the school's guardian (24).

In Kay's plan the problem of visibility has been solved by the application of accounting: written records make virtue visible as they render labor quantifiable and diligence a matter for certification.[28] In the workhouse, which was explicitly a site of coercion (albeit "voluntarily" entered), children were to be offered this (as) freedom: an education that "inculcate[s] the great practical lesson for those whose sole dependence for their living is on the labour of their hands, by early habituating them to patient and skilful industry."[29]

Such schemes for moral "inculcation" and "habituation," like Chalmers's plan to "superinduce" habits that "insensibly pervade" a man's whole system, were undeniably designed to convert the violence of class oppression into general consensus.[30] In the logic theoretically implemented by this consensus, some places (streets and some parks and museums—on some days) were common—i.e., "public"—spaces, while other places (most notably "property") were private.[31] Ideally, working-class education was to teach the people how to behave in various places at the same time that it was to improve their "taste," that faculty of discrimination that simultaneously transcends locale and makes its presence felt in an individual's surroundings. So, at least, argues Ebenezer Elliott, the working-class poet quoted by the economist John Hill Burton in 1849:

You seek the home of taste, and find
    The proud mechanic there,
Rich as a king, and less a slave,
    Throned in his elbow chair,
Or on his sofa reading Locke
    Beside his open door.
Why start? why envy wealth like his,
    The carpet on his floor?

You seek the home of sluttery,
    "Is John at home?" you say;
No, sir: he's at the Sportsman's Arm's—
    The dog-fight's o'er the way."
O lift the workman's heart and mind
    Above low sensual sin;
Give him a home—the home of taste;
    Outbid the house of gin.

O give him taste, it is the link
    Which binds us to the skies—
A bridge of rainbows thrown across
    The gulf of tears and sighs;
Or like a widower's little one—
    An angel in a child—
That leads him to her mother's chair,
    And shows him how she smiled.[32]

In this poem we see not only how taste was both a sign of and reward for respectability, but also how intimately respectability was bound up with a "private" sphere defined as domesticity. The woman's role in the domestic sphere is so prominent, according to this logic, that she can fulfill it even when she is absent (or dead).

I have been suggesting that middle-class plans to educate the working class were symbolic solutions to the problem that cities posed to a morality supposedly based on sight. I have also argued that the consensus theoretically produced by education rationalized economic inequality by cloaking class oppression in pleas for national unity and prosperity. Having offered this general sketch of the production of abstract space, however, I now want to complicate the picture. This is my third point about English society in the early nineteenth century: while some technologies of abstraction were implemented in these decades (foremost among them, the 1834 poor law and the statistical societies of the 1830s), most projects were resisted, delayed, or even aborted. Partly this was the result of political and religious differences among the would-be reformers; sectarian disagreement about the proper role of the church in education, for example, delayed the national educational act until 1870, and political differences about the relative power of local and central governments led to the abolition of the Board of Public Health in 1854. Partly the uneven implementation of abstracting policies resulted from popular resistance; Chalmers's generally upbeat descriptions of the welcome that home visitors were likely to receive are punctuated with begrudging references to "painful repulses," for example;[33] and the 1832 Anatomy Act, which was intended to rationalize the distribution of corpses to medical schools, was greeted with widespread, unorganized violence.[34] And partly abstract space was never seamlessly installed because the very terms in which it was conceptualized created opportunities for some groups who should have been subdued to gain a modicum of power.

I'll focus on this final point, taking as an example a metaphorical contest that simmered in the 1830s. In the terms I have been using, all of the participants in this contest were on the same side: they were all apologists for—even architects of—capitalist society and abstract space. Where they differed was in the figure they offered to represent the newly urbanized, industrializing society. Some middle-class reformers—Andrew Ure is the most extreme example of this position—refurbished William Paley's metaphor of the machine to describe modern society.[35] Others—Thomas Carlyle comes to mind—resuscitated the age-old image of the social organism.[36] Both of these metaphors were offered as symbolic representations of a *dynamic* system that was too large and complex to be apprehended empirically. Both inadvertently offered justifications for middle-class women to enter discursive and literal spaces previously restricted to men.

Two texts provide a particularly clear contrast between the metaphorics of machinery and those of the social body. Charles Babbage's *On the Economy of Machinery and Manufactures* and James Phillips Kay's *Moral and Physical Condition of the Working Classes ... in Manchester* were both published in 1832.[37] Both Babbage, who was a professor of mathematics at Cambridge, and Kay, who was still a young medical man in Manchester, supported free trade and the manufacturing system; both opposed trades unions and all government interference in economic affairs. Both men also played key roles in founding statistical organizations (Babbage provoked the BAAS to create a statistical section in 1833;

Kay was a founding member of the Manchester Statistical Society, which was also established in 1833).[38] But whereas Babbage—who also invented the calculating engine—sang the praises of a social machine, Kay—the young medical man trained in physiology and anatomy—celebrated the organic qualities of a body that could regulate itself.

Like abstraction more generally, metaphors are instruments of reduction: figures of speech subdue material complexities by imposing an analytic frame that carries its own history of connotations and deployments. At the same time, however, because metaphors are neither subject to precise control nor assimilable to a single set of connotations, figures of speech also introduce semantic play into the lived experience of the material world. Metaphors open possibilities for the symbolic appropriation of physical space; such imaginative appropriation can lay the groundwork for material alterations of that space, although the power to describe by no means guarantees the power to bring about change. In the case I am discussing here, figures of speech recast either the terms in which social analysis was assumed to proceed or the object of analysis itself in such a way as to allow a group that theoretically ought to be excluded from power to discuss and participate in policy formation.

Let me briefly lay out the conceptual fields these two metaphors occupied in the 1830s. The figure of the machine imported into discussions of English society the optimism associated with both Paley's clockwork universe and the "vast extent and perfection" to which contemporaries thought England had brought the "contrivance of tools and machines."[39] In essence, according to Babbage, machines improved capacities that already distinguished "civilized" men from brutes: machines supplement muscular power, compensate for human inattention, and enhance both productivity and efficiency. In Babbage's paean to "beautiful contrivances," machines are moral agents, which counteract dishonesty; they epitomize rationalized labor, for their operations are simultaneously uniform and steady; they are the alchemists of industry, turning what men consider waste into valuable commodities (3, 15, 54, 6). While much of Babbage's text deals with literal machines and manufacturing processes, he clearly considers the machine the type for both individual humans and society as a whole. We see the former in his admiration of "the fertile invention of Mr. Brunel," which enables legless and armless operators to make shoes with the aid of mechanical prostheses (15). We see the latter in his celebration of "a New System of Manufacturing," where he imagines the division of labor and the unity of ends (both of which characterize the machine) permeating first the individual factory, then society as a whole (250). In this beautiful system, "the workmen and the capitalist would so shade into each other ... that ... the only combination which could exist would be a most powerful union *between* both parties to overcome their common difficulties" (258).

If the metaphor of the machine allowed a forecast of social harmony, then so did the figure of the social body. Ideally governed by a "sensorium"—the nerve ganglion or gland in which sensations were centered—Kay's "social body" is an organism whose health depends on the well-being of all its members. When these various parts became conscious of each other—as they would when a team of experts collected enough statistical information—the social body would improve itself, educate itself, and produce enough wealth to go around. Kay derived this model of the body from the work of eighteenth-century Scottish anatomists like Robert Whytt and William Hunter.[40] Their nerve-centered models highlighted both sympathy (which was understood as a physiological reflex) and specialization (according to organic structure and function).[41] To Kay this meant that in the healthy social body, the rich would know about and sympathize with the laboring poor, but every class would perform its special function, to which its members were fitted by design.

Kay specifically rejected the mechanical metaphor deployed by Babbage because it could not accommodate the triad that Kay considered essential to national well-being: happiness, morality, and religion.

> The social body cannot be constructed like a machine, on abstract principles which merely include physical motions, and their numerical results in the production of wealth. . . . Political economy, though its object is to ascertain the means of increasing the wealth of nations, cannot accomplish its design, without at the same time regarding their happiness, and as its largest ingredient the cultivation of religion and morality.[42]

But if the metaphor of a social body enabled Kay to attend to those interior faculties that the metaphor of the machine could not represent, the figure of the social body introduced its own problems. On the one hand, invoking a physiological model of a self-regulating organism supported Kay's position that trade restrictions should be removed. On the other hand, the figure of the social body could not be used to justify interventions that Kay thought necessary, such as home inspection and national education. By contrast, the metaphor of the machine did provide for active (if "mechanical") self-correction in the form of those "regulators" and "governors" built into every machine.[43] As Kay pointed out, however, this figure could not be deployed to build consensus where it did not already exist, for it provided no model for explaining motivation or influencing desire.

The limitations imposed by these figures upon attempts to conceptualize England's newly urbanized society only partly account for the controversy surrounding each figure. Among some groups these figures were also controversial because they admitted into the arenas of public debate and policy-making a group who theoretically belonged at home: middle-class women. Because the metaphor of the machine privileged an epistemology that was impersonal, its proponents increasingly claimed to efface all distinguishing characteristics of the social analyst—including, in some circles at least, sex. Because the metaphor of the social body highlighted intimate bodily processes, its proponents inadvertently enhanced the power culturally accorded mothers and opened opportunities for women to enter the rapidly professionalizing ranks of medicine.

A few examples of these developments will have to suffice. I'll begin with the metaphor of the machine. In the middle decades of the nineteenth century, as practitioners of the emergent social sciences borrowed from natural scientists the paradigm of mechanical observation, they were able to claim that their own work replicated the precision of recording machines. Ideally, this precision achieved that impartiality that we call "objectivity."[44] Many of the various organized efforts to render social scientific analysis exact and objective came together in 1857 with the founding of the National Association for the Promotion of the Social Sciences, also known as the Social Science Association.[45] The Social Science Association was also one of the first parliamentary pressure groups regularly to discuss women's issues and to give women a public and highly visible platform.[46] The SSA was supportive of women's issues and vocal women not only because legal reform (including the rationalization of sexually asymmetrical property laws) was one of its founders' pet projects but also because its cherished image of a dispassionate, disembodied analytic mind allowed women to slough off the sexual connotations that theoretically disqualified them from public activity. Partly because of the support of the SSA, Louisa Twining and Frances Power Cobbe gained respect for their work on poor law reform and domestic violence, Mary Carpenter found a forum for her work on juvenile delinquency, and Bessie Parkes and Barbara Bodichon were able to circulate their conclusions about women's education and employment. The response to women's participation in social investigation and public debate was predictably mixed, of course. While supporters like Lord Henry Brougham encouraged women to speak, detractors like the editors of the *Saturday Review* attacked "Lord Brougham's little corps of lady orators" as "unladylike."[47]

If the explicit analogy to scientific objectivity conceptualized as mechanical enabled one group of middle-class women to influence public policy at mid-century, then the figure of the social body even more specifically invited all women to reconceptualize their domestic labor. Placing the body—whether metaphorical or literal—at the heart of national well-being, after all, implicitly valorized the work of those routinely charged with the care of young and ailing bodies. In the late 1830s Sarah Stickney Ellis took this logic to its obvious next step when she arrogated to mothers the power to make every man what he eventually becomes: "all the statesmen of the rising generation, all the ministers of religion, all public and private gentlemen, as well as all men of business, mechanics, and laborers of every description, will have received, as regards intellectual and moral character, their first bias, and often their strongest and their last, from the training and the influence of a mother."[48] In the popular physiologies published during this decade, some medical men took violent exception to such sweeping claims for maternal influence, going so far as rhetorically to efface women even in their descriptions of breast-feeding.[49] In a period that preceded both the professionalization of medicine and the establishment of a codified link between scientific medicine and medical practice, however, directing the public's attention to the body and health was bound to direct its attention to women. In 1854, when England plunged into the badly conceived and worse-executed Crimean War, Florence Nightingale transformed women's informal care of others' bodies into an organized public service, which was soon to be professionalized and waged, as all medical work had become by the late 1850s.[50]

Florence Nightingale constitutes a fitting terminus for my comments on the production of abstract space, for Nightingale was one of the century's most outspoken proponents of the characteristic features I have associated with spatialized abstraction. A champion of statistical analysis and participant in the 1860 International Statistical Congress, Nightingale revered quantification and graphical representation, which further abstracts Euclidean space. As an advocate for the panoptical Pavilion plan of hospital design, Nightingale harped on the virtues of incessant surveillance, and as supervisor of her little nursing corps at Scutari, she extolled the importance of discipline, regimentation, and efficiency.[51] In her capacity as adviser to the 1859 Royal Commission on sanitary conditions in the Indian army, Nightingale even dreamed of institutionalizing her triumvirate of virtues (discipline, order, method) in this hitherto "uncivilized" colony.[52]

I use the example of Nightingale to remind us that simply occupying a marginal position—in this case because of sex (but not class)—does not guarantee that one will (or could) oppose the instantiation of as complex and overdetermined a phenomenon as abstract space. Indeed, the difficulty that apologists for capitalism have characteristically had with theorizing marginal and especially geographically distant spaces suggests that, in a society conceptualized according to Euclidean logic, the only way a marginalized individual can make her way into (comprehensible) discourse is by rewriting the margin as part of the center. Even if the logical outcome of the relentless expansion of the Euclidean grid that has resulted from such revision is the late twentieth-century single-world system, epitomized by instantaneous information transmission and occupied by statistical persons, I remain confident that this postmodern geography is neither seamless nor as homogeneous as it appears to be. My confidence is pinned not to some power that accrues to marginality but to the persistence—even today—of the kind of asymmetries and contradictions whose early nineteenth-century version I have outlined here.

## NOTES

1. The most canonical treatment of time and capital is Karl Marx, *Capital: A Critique of Political Economy,* 3 vols., trans. Ben Fowkes (Harmondsworth: Penguin, 1976), especially vol. I, chapter 10. On the effects of wage labor, see E. P. Thompson, "Time, Work-Discipline, and Industrial Capitalism," in *Customs in Common: Studies in Traditional Popular Culture* (New York: The New Press, 1991), 352–403. On the periodization of capitalism, see Fredric Jameson, "Postmodernism, or the Cultural Logic of Late Capitalism," *New Left Review* 146 (July-August 1984): 59–92; and Timothy Reiss, *The Discourse of Modernism* (Ithaca, N.Y.: Cornell University Press, 1982). On capitalism and temporality, see Sebastian de Grazia, *Of Time, Work, and Leisure* (New York: Twentieth-Century Fund, 1962).

2. Exceptions to this generalization include Fredric Jameson, "Cognitive Mapping," in *Marxism and the Interpretation of Culture,* ed. Cary Nelson and Lawrence Grossberg (Urbana: University of Illinois Press, 1988), 347–66; David Harvey, *The Limits to Capital* (Chicago: University of Chicago Press, 1982), especially chapters 12 and 13; and Henri Lefebvre, *The Production of Space,* trans. Donald Nicholson-Smith (Oxford: Basil Blackwell, 1991), especially chapter 12.

3. See Lefebvre, *Production of Space,* chapter 2; and Edward W. Soja, *Postmodern Geographies: The Reassertion of Space in Critical Social Theory* (London and New York: Verso, 1989), especially chapter 1.

4. On cartography as rationalization, see Mark Monmonier, *How to Lie with Maps* (Chicago: University of Chicago Press, 1991), especially chapters 3, 7; and Richard Helgerson, *Forms of Nationhood: The Elizabethan Writing of England* (Chicago: University of Chicago Press, 1992), chapter 3. On the relationship between enclosures and capitalism, see David McNally, *Political Economy and the Rise of Captialism: A Reinterpretation* (Berkeley: University of California Press, 1988), especially chapters 1 and 2. For one recent study of

imperialism that is especially pertinent to my argument, see Mary Louise Pratt, *Imperial Eyes: Travel Writing and Transculturation* (London and New York: Routledge, 1992). On early-nineteenth-century urbanization, see Eric E. Lampard, "The Urbanizing World," in *The Victorian City: Images and Realities,* 3 vols., ed. H.J. Dyos and Michael Wolff (London and Boston: Routledge & Kegan Paul, 1973), 1:3–58. On the impact of railways, see Jack Simmons, "The Power of the Railway," in Dyos and Wolff, *Victorian City,* 1:277–310; and John R. Kellett, *The Impact of Railways on Victorian Cities* (London: Routledge and Kegan Paul, 1969). On the role of money, see William M. Reddy, *Money and Liberty in Modern Europe: A Critique of Historical Understanding* (Cambridge: Cambridge University Press, 1987), especially chapters 3–5.

5. See Lefebvre, *Production of Space,* 298; and Samuel Y. Edgerton, *The Heritage of Giotto's Geometry: Art and Science on the Eve of the Scientific Revolution* (Ithaca, N.Y.: Cornell University Press, 1991), 16.

6. On the geometricization of space, see Edgerton, *Giotto's Geometry,* 11 and introduction.

7. On visuality, see Johnathan Crary, *Techniques of the Observer: On Vision and Modernity in the Nineteenth Century* (Cambridge, Mass.: MIT Press, 1990), especially chapter 3.

8. See Lefebvre, *Production of Space,* 286; and Michel de Certeau, "History: Science and Fiction," in *Heterologies: Discourse on the Other,* trans. Brian Massumi (Minneapolis: University of Minnesota Press, 1986), 199–221.

9. On standardization, see Theodore M. Porter, "Objectivity as Standardization: The Rhetoric of Impersonality in Measurement, Statistics, and Cost-Benefit Analysis," *Annals of Scholarship* 9, nos. 1–2 (1992): 19–60. On statistical persons, see Mark Seltzer, *Bodies and Machines* (New York and London: Routledge, 1992), part 3.

10. These literatures are vast. Two particularly provocative examples are Peter Stallybrass and Allon White, *The Politics and Poetics of Transgression* (Ithaca, N.Y.: Cornell University Press, 1986), especially chapter 3; and Judith R. Walkowitz, *City of Dreadful Delights: Narratives of Sexual Danger in Late-Victorian London* (Chicago: University of Chicago Press, 1992), chapters 1 and 2.

11. See David Marshall, *The Figure of Theater: Shaftesbury, Defoe, Adam Smith, and George Eliot* (New York: Columbia University Press, 1985); and Mary Poovey, "Aesthetics and Political Economy in the Eighteenth Century," in *Aesthetics and Ideology,* ed. George Levine and Carolyn Williams (New Brunswick, N.J.: Rutgers University Press, 1994), 79–105.

12. Adam Smith, *Theory of Moral Sentiments* (1759; reprint, Indianapolis: Liberty Classics, 1976), part 1, section 1, chapter 1, page 9. This is the conventional mode of citation for this text.

13. Adam Smith, *The Wealth of Nations* (1776; reprint, New York: Modern Library, 1937), 747. Hereafter cited in text as *Wealth,* with page numbers.

14. On the role of generalization in definitions of virtue, see John Barrell, "Visualising the Division of Labour: William Pyne's *Microcosm*," in *The Birth of Pandora and the Division of Knowledge* (Philadelphia: University of Pennsylvania Press, 1992), 89–118.

15. See William Letwin, *The Origins of Scientific Economics: English Economic Thought, 1660–1776* (New York: Methuen, 1963), part 2.

16. See Frank Mort, *Dangerous Sexualities: Medico-Moral Politics in England Since 1830* (London: Routledge, 1987), chapter 1.

17. Edwin Chadwick, *Report on the Sanitary Condition of the Labouring Population of Great Britain* (1842; facsimile edition, Edinburgh: Edinburgh University Press, 1965), 224. Hereafter cited in text as *Sanitary Report,* with page numbers.

18. See Charles E. Rosenberg, "Florence Nightingale on Contagion: The Hospital as Moral Environment," in *Healing and History,* ed. Charles E. Rosenberg (New York: Dawson, 1979), 116–36.

19. See Mary Poovey, "Domesticity and Class Formation: Chadwick's 1842 *Sanitary Report,*" in *Subject to History: Ideology, Class, Gender,* ed. David Simpson (Ithaca, N.Y.: Cornell University Press, 1991), 65–83.

20. See Lorraine Daston and Peter Galison, "The Image of Objectivity," *Representations* 40 (Fall 1992): 81–128.

21. See Douglas Hay, "Property, Authority and the Criminal Law," in *Albion's Fatal Tree: Crime and Society in Eighteenth-Century England,* ed. Douglas Hay (New York: Pantheon, 1975), 49–56.

22. Michel Foucault, *Discipline and Punish: The Birth of the Prison,* trans. Alan Sheridan (New York: Vintage Books, 1979), 135–69.

23. See Gertrude Himmelfarb, *The Idea of Poverty: England in the Early Industrial Age* (New York: Vintage Books, 1985), especially part 2.

24. On the Panopticon, see Michael Ignatieff, *A Just Measure of Pain: The Penitentiary in the Industrial Revolution, 1750–1850* (New York: Pantheon Books, 1978), chapters 3–4; and John Bender, *Imagining the Penitentiary: Fiction and the Architecture of Mind in Eighteenth-Century England* (Chicago: University of Chicago Press, 1987), chapter 1. On the National Charity Company, see Charles R. Bahmueller, *The National Charity Company: Jeremy Bentham's Silent Revolution* (Berkeley: University of California Press, 1981), chapters 5–7.

25. Thomas Chalmers, *On the Christian and Economic Polity of a Nation, The Works of Thomas Chalmers,* 25 vols. (Glasgow: William Collins, 1845), 14:31.

26. James Phillips Kay, *The Moral and Physical Condition of the Working Classes Employed in the Cotton Manufacture in Manchester,* 2d ed. (London: James Ridgway, 1832), 92–98.

27. James Phillips Kay, "On the Establishment of County or District Schools, for the Training of the Pauper Children Maintained in Union Workhouses," *Journal of the Statistical Society of London* 1 (1838–39): 22.

28. On the logic of accounting, see Peter Miller, "Accounting and Objectivity: The Invention of Calculating Selves and Calculable Spaces," *Annals of Scholarship* 9:1–2 (1992): 61–86.

29. Kay, "Establishment of Schools," 23.

30. See Richard Johnson, "Educational Policy and Social Control in Early Victorian England," *Past and Present* 49 (1970): 96–119.

31. For an important contribution to the conceptual distinction between "public" and "private," see John Barrell, "The Public Prospect and the Private View: The Politics of Taste in Eighteenth-Century Britain," in *The Birth of Pandora*, 41–62.

32. John Hill Burton, *Political and Social Economy: Its Practical Applications* (Edinburgh: William and Robert Chambers, 1849), 123–24. John Hill Burton was not only an economist but also Bentham's editor and Hume's biographer.

33. Chalmers, *Christian and Economic Polity*, 14:xix.

34. See Ruth Richardson, *Death, Dissection and the Destitute* (London and New York: Routledge and Kegan Paul, 1987), part 3.

35. See Andrew Ure, *Philosophy of Manufactures* (London: C. Knight, 1835).

36. Thomas Carlyle, *Sartor Resartus: The Life and Opinions of Herr Teufelsdrockh, The Works of Thomas Carlyle*, 30 vols. (New York: Charles Scribner's Sons, 1903), vol. I, book 3, chapter 2. On this metaphor, see Roy Porter, "Consumption: Disease of the Consumer Society?" in *Consumption and the World of Goods*, ed. John Brewer and Roy Porter (London and New York: Routledge, 1993), 58–81.

37. Charles Babbage, *On the Economy of Machinery and Manufactures* (London: Charles Knight, 1832); Kay, *Moral and Physical Condition*.

38. On Babbage and statistics, see Jack Morrell and Arnold Thackray, *Gentlemen of Science: Early Years of the British Association for the Advancement of Science* (Oxford: Clarendon Press, 1981), 291–92; on Kay and statistics, see David Elesh, "The Manchester Statistical Society: A Case Study of a Discontinuity in the History of Empirical Social Research," *Journal of the History of the Behavioral Sciences* 8 (July-October 1972): 280–301, 407–17.

39. Charles Babbage, *Economy of Machinery*, 3. Hereafter cited in text by page number.

40. See Mary Poovey, "Anatomical Realism and Social Investigation in Early Nineteenth-Century Manchester," *differences* 5 (Fall 1993): 6–9.

41. See Christopher Lawrence, "The Nervous System and Society in the Scottish Enlightenment," in *Natural Order: Historical Studies of Scientific Culture*, ed. Barry Barnes and Steven Shapin (London: Sage Productions: 1979), 23–28.

42. Kay, *Moral and Physical Condition*, 63–64. Here Kay is mobilizing what Boyd Hilton has called "Christian political economy," a subset of the discipline of which Chalmers was a leading figure. On Chalmers, see Hilton, *The Age of Atonement: The Influence of Evangelicalism on Social and Economic Thought, 1795–1865* (Oxford: Clarendon, 1988).

43. See Babbage, *Economy of Machinery*, chapter 3.

44. See Daston and Galison, " Image of Objectivity," 81–128.

45. See Lawrence Goldman, "The Origins of British 'Social Science': Political Economy, Natural Science and Statistics, 1830–1835," *Historical Journal* 26 (1983): 587–615.

46. See Goldman, "Origins of British 'Social Science,' " 129; Sheila R. Herstein, *A Mid-Victorian Feminist: Barbara Leigh Smith Bodichon* (New Haven, Conn.: Yale University Press, 1985), 65–66; and Lee Holcombe, *Wives and Property: Reform of the Married*

*Women's Property Law in Nineteenth-Century England* (Toronto: University of Toronto Press, 1983), 124–27.

47. Quoted Herstein, *Mid-Victorian Feminist,* 133.

48. Sarah Stickney Ellis, "The Mothers of England," in *The Family Monitor and Domestic Guide* (New York: Henry G. Langley, 1844), 12.

49. For an example of the erasure of the mother, see Thomas Southwood Smith, *The Philosophy of Health,* 11th ed. (London: Longman, Green, Longman, Roberts, and Green, 1865), introduction. See also Roger Cooter, "The Power of the Body: The Early Eighteenth Century," in *Natural Order,* ed. Barnes and Shapin, 73–92.

50. See Mary Poovey, *Uneven Developments: The Ideological Work of Gender in Mid-Victorian England* (Chicago: University of Chicago Press, 1988), chapter 6.

51. Ibid., 181, 187, 189.

52. Ibid., 184–97.

8

# codes of law and bodies of color

> Because of the inhabitants' conduct, we cannot count on
> the return of any prosperity for Saint-Domingue, since the
> terrible lesson the men have received has not been cor-
> rected. Everyone has their mulâtresse that they have brought
> up or just found, and with whom they are going to produce
> a new generation of mulattoes and quarterons destined to
> butcher our children. Here is what must happen . . . pre-
> scribe the destruction or the deportation of every free man
> and woman of color, after branding them on their two
> cheeks with an "L" which will mean *Libre*.
> —*The Marquise de Rouvray, in exile from Le Cap, Saint-
> Domingue, writing from New York to her daughter, Madame de
> Lostanges, August 13, 1793*

Those who came to Saint-Domingue in the
last years of the eighteenth century came to a country where definitions were defied as they were made, categories mixed up as more
rigorous labels were invented. Describing the ambivalence of the cre-
olizing process in Jamaica, first from the perspective of the majority,
the poet and historian Kamau Brathwaite explains: " 'Invisible,' anxious to be 'seen' by their masters, the elite blacks and the mass of free
colourdes conceived of visibility through the lenses of their masters'
already uncertain vision, as a form of 'greyness'—an imitation of an
imitation."[1] Then, turning to the white colonials, he addresses not the
troubled transparency of the masters' lenses but their mirror of pro-
jection: "White attitudes to slaves and to slavery were therefore, in a

subtle, intimate manner, also white attitudes and sentiments about themselves. . . . They simply looked into a black mirror of subordinate flesh" (179). The ambivalence that threatened the codified structures of the Jamaican colonial system was exaggerated in Saint-Domingue. Regarded as the "Babylon on the Antilles," "a second Sodom," or the most beautiful colony in the Americas by the European visitors and residents, Saint-Domingue was known for its splendor, profligacy, and greed.

Though the society boasted its castelike distinctions (*grands blancs, petits blancs,* free colored, slaves, and aristocrats, what one historian called "the oldest blood of France"), the overwhelming opposition seemed to be between whites and nonwhites.² It seemed that no matter your status, distinctions disappeared if you had white skin. As Baron de Wimpffen wrote on the eve of the French Revolution:

> The natural consequence of the order of things which prevails here, is that all those titles of honour which are elsewhere, the *pabula* of emulation, of rivalry, and of discord; which inspire so much pride, and create so many claims in some; so much ambition and envy in others; shrink to nothing, and entirely disappear before the sole title of WHITE. It is by your skin, however branded it may be, and not by your parchment, however worm-eaten, that your pretensions to gentility are adjusted.³

Yet even this categorical exclusivity was riddled with qualifications. Though small in number, the white population was divisive and contentious, changing with every new influx of "French" settlers and calling into question the meaning of national identity.⁴ The wrangling between Creole whites (those born in the colonies) and European whites, whether aristocrats or vagabonds—not unlike the discord between Creole blacks and "Congo" blacks—would determine how the French Revolution played itself out in Saint-Domingue. The conflict also infected relations between the sexes. European ladies ridiculed Creole ladies; the Creoles discounted the affectation of those polished remnants of the old regime; while the men, according to many observers, simply chose their mulatto mistresses.

## THE BLACK CODE

In March 1685 at Versailles, Louis XIV, the Sun King, presided over the completion of what would be his minister Jean-Baptiste Colbert's greatest creation: the Code Noir, or *Edict Regarding the Government and the Administration of the French Islands of America, and the Discipline and the Commerce of Blacks and Slaves in the Said Countries.* Twenty years earlier Colbert had formed the Compagnie des Indes, which sent French slavers into Africa, shipped Africans to the Americas, and returned to France with coffee, sugar, and tobacco. The most barbaric product of the Enlightenment was ignored by the philosophers and later forgotten or, more precisely, never mentioned. This discourse on methodical dispossession, a logic of conversion more horrific than the threat of damnation, has been relegated to the bowels of white thought. In three hundred years the Black Code has never been published in English, but more significantly, as Louis Sala-Molins has recently reminded his French readers in *Le Code Noir: ou le calvaire de Canaan,* "the worse refinement in wickedness, the most glacial technicality in the commerce of human flesh and in genocide" remains so difficult to find that it has vanished from historiography. "One knows about the slave trade. Also its 'abolition' in 1794. Its 'restoration' in 1802, somewhat less. But of the existence of a specific codification of what was abolished, then restored, not a trace in the common mind."[5]

The Black Code granted official recognition to an institution that had functioned for half a century without the king's seal. While it was ostensibly written to protect the planters' property (while denying the slaves' humanity), the Creole whites conspired to make it a dead letter from the moment of its emergence. Planters cooperated with the king's ordinances only if they did not oppose their customs and interests. Numerous accounts testify that in no instance was a black slave in Saint-Domingue helped by laws or regulations emanating from France. The Breton lawyer and radical critic of the colonial regime, René-Michel Hilliard d'Auberteuil, who lived in Cap Français, complained of this divorce of law from historical reality, the gap between legal prescriptions and practice:

> The Negroes of the French colonies are bound by the penal Code, and judged according to criminal regulations; the Edict of 1685 regulates the punishment that their masters can inflict on them, and establishes a kind of ratio between offence and punishment; but that does not stop Negroes from dying daily in chains, or under whip; from being starved, smothered, burned without ceremony: so much cruelty always remains unpunished, and those who exercise it are ordinarily scoundrels or persons born in the gutter of European cities; the vilest of men are also the most barbarous.[6]

The Black Code is a document of limits. Unlike the racist disquisitions that point to blacks as lacking the finer feeling of a tender heart, the Code is not

concerned with the tangled semantics of charitable servitude, lurking debauch-
ery, or the blacks' proclivities that come perilously close to romance. We read
instead sixty articles that take us into a chilling series of qualifications: prohibi-
tions that permit, limitations that invite excess, and a king's grandiloquence that
ensures divestment. What is remarkable about this text is its language. Existing
only as precepts and never in practice, the Black Code can be read as a philosophy of denaturalization or, put another way, the natural successor to Descartes's *Discourse on Methods and Meditations Concerning First Philosophy*. The
thinker of Descartes's *Meditations* in 1640 sets the stage for the 1685 edict of
Louis XIV: the making of enlightened man led to the demolition of the unen-
lightened brute.

The thinking mind's dismembering or generative proclivities dominated a
passive nature or servile body. Descartes sits by the fire. He dismembers himself. He can play with asking what remains if he takes off his ears, his arms, and
removes all his sense in his urgency to know what constitutes his identity: "Although the whole mind seems to be united to the body, I recognize that if a
foot or arm or any other part of the body is cut off, nothing has thereby been
taken away from the mind."[7] The mutilation only aggrandizes this "I" that needs
*no* senses and *no* body. Listen to Descartes's elation of discovery: "Thinking? At
last I have discovered it—thought; this alone is inseparable from me. . . . I am,
then, in the strict sense only a thing that thinks; that is, I am a mind, or intelligence, or intellect, or reason. . . . I am a thing which is real. . . . But what kind of
thing? . . . a thinking thing" (18). He sloughs off surfeit matter to get at essential
mind. What, then, does this thing do? The answer will be crucial to the assumptions that underlie the judicial regulation of blacks in the colonies. "It is a
thing which doubts, understands, conceives, affirms, denies, wills, refuses, which
also imagines and feels" (19).

Once you establish who is rational man, you can ascertain what is not.
Descartes's methodical but metaphoric dispossession becomes the basis for
the literal expropriation and divestment necessary to turn a man into a thing.
What is this thing that does not think or feel and cannot will, refuse, deny, or
imagine? The Black Code responds by inventing, by configuring, the slave whose
only rights and duties—except for the terribly ambiguous liberation of the soul
in baptism—are those shared in society by beasts and objects. Slaves are re-
claimed remnants of what Descartes has cast off: the "pieces of the Indies" or
"ebony wood" found in Africa, bought, bartered, and figured as heads of cattle,
coins, parcels of land, pieces of furniture. Think about the legality of dismem-
berment. Since slaves are construed as a special kind of property, no amount of
amputation, torture, or disfiguring can matter. The rules for controlling the

blacks and slaves in the colonies depended on the Enlightenment strategy for human ascendancy out of a fantasy of reification. Descartes's experiment with himself to establish the idea of the white universal subject is thus recovered as a collective legal experiment to produce black nonpersons in the New World.

The passage out of Africa and into the islands of America called for two kinds of stories: first, one that would create a servile body, unfit, incapable, and destitute; and second, one that promised salvation, a conversion to Christianity that would liberate the soul and give the true God to the blacks. The boon of baptism accompanied the judicial destitution of the Black Code. Degenerate but redeemable, brutalized but perfectible, the slave is recognized as having a will only insofar as it is perverted. The king, in his infinite reason, declares his concern for infinite perversion, "all the people which the Divine Providence has under our obedience."

The first eight articles of the Code establish the only true religion to be "Apostolic, Roman, and Catholic" and demand that slaves must be baptized and instructed in this religion, thus validating only the marriages of Catholics and condemning all others as partaking in "true concubinage." Like other regulations in the Black Code, the gracious dispensation of baptism and conversion was a theory that did not change practice. Numerous are the accounts of the way the needs of the market and the function of bodies replaced the desire to evangelize souls. In 1685, because of the mix of Saint-Domingue society—a few regular planters, buccaneers, noblemen, filibusters, indentured white workers, European adventurers, and slaves—the various orders, Carmelites, Dominicans, Capuchins, and Jesuits, as well as the secular clergy, were not as successful as they had been in the other French islands. And when the Code was issued, Saint-Domingue had not yet been officially recognized as French territory. No cane plantations yet existed, and according to the 1687 census, two years after the royal edict there were only 3,358 slaves to the 44,411 whites in Saint-Domingue.[8] French claims to the western third of the island were finally authenticated with the treaty of Ryswick in 1697.

Deprivation and exclusion are the basis of the Black Code: an abandonment or removal ever more severe in those articles (22–29) that "oblige" the master to feed, house, and clothe his slaves. The master can deny the slave control of his body, owning him physically, affectively, and even nutritionally. If the slave must be hungry, let him at least hunger within limits. The weekly regulated nourishment for slaves between the ages of ten and sixty amounted to "two and a half pots of manioc flour, or three cassavas each, weighing at least two and one-half pounds, or other equivalent staples, with two pounds of salted beef or three pounds of fish or other items in similar amounts" (Art. 22).

Not only are masters enjoined to feed and house their slaves, but they must also clothe them. Given the emphasis on colonial luxury and ostentation in most accounts by outsiders, this article reveals how deprivation was recast as sustenance or how literally divesting blacks guaranteed the investment in slaves. The more miserable and derelict slaves appeared, the more their outfit suited the white symbolic system. "The Masters shall be required to provide each Slave annually, two outfits of linen or four bolts of cloth at the convenience of the Masters" (Art. 25). As descriptions of slaves in Saint-Domingue in the 1780s revealed, there were many variations in slave dress, depending on whether one was a field slave or held in the more privileged position of artisan (carpenter, mason, logger, or keeper of animals) or domestic. Indeed, domestics were often turned into objects for the display of their master's extravagance; their embellishment signaled the glut of wealth on the plantation.

The Black Code designates slaves, only to negate them. Its rigorous logic does not permit the slave to play any role in the arena of law and rights. Slaves exist legally only insofar as they disobey. No juridical mention is granted for obedience. Recognition is granted only as a prohibition or corrective for insubordination. What about the slave's right to complain? In Article 26, surely one of the strangest moments in the Code, the "thing" suddenly becomes a "subject" who can deposit his written testimony (*mémoire*) with a lawyer ("our general procurator"), "which we wish to be observed for crimes and barbarous and inhumane treatment by the masters towards their slaves." Coming as it does after the rules for clothing, food, and housing, this article implies that the only "crimes" or "barbarous and inhumane treatment" of slaves involved neglect or stinginess.

But no article in the Code has meaning in itself, since the subterfuge of this regulatory benevolence depends on how the articles interrelate, how what is granted in one place is qualified in the other. The apparent concession of Article 26 is undone in Articles 30 and 31. Slaves can complain (Art. 26), but "their testimony shall only be used as a *mémoire* to help the judges clarify the matter under investigation without any presumption or conjecture or admission of proof" (Art. 30); "neither may they be civil parties in a criminal matter, except if their Masters act and defend them in a civil matter and prosecute them in a criminal matter" (Art. 31).

The Black Code was heralded as delimiting brutality. Yet the power to exceed what might be considered humane lay in the unsaid—in those places where the law falls silent—or where the language is deliberately vague or hypothetical. No limits are invoked for the number of lashes a slave can receive or for the number of hours of work that can be imposed upon him. Phrases like "corporeal punishment, even death," "let them be severely punished, even with death" were general enough to permit the severing of ears, nose, hands, and feet. What, then, were the kinds of punishment allowed and under what circumstances? Death for the slave who struck his master, mistress, or the husband of his mistress (Art. 33). Assault and battery against free persons were "severely punished by death if the person struck falls to the ground" (Art. 34). During the Old Regime in Saint-Domingue, the excessive tortures and mutilations of slaves by masters, mistresses, and overseers were frequent in spite of restrictions.

The greatest threat to the planters' property, other than overwork, starvation, torture, and sickness, was the increasing number of runaway slaves, called *maroons,* fugitives whose flight repudiated their judicial identity: "socially dead persons" deprived of freedom.[9] And when it came to the economics of slavery, the Code was unambiguous. "We declare slaves to be chattel and so do they enter into the community having no consequence other than that of something mortgaged" (Art. 44). No generality in this discourse on property. The securing of profit for the metropole and the assurance of servile "pieces of the Indies," bodies intact, healthy, and young enough to labor, account for the restrictions on gratuitous and excessive tortures, sometimes mere diversions for bored masters. Like animals on a farm or the furniture in a house, slaves must remain in colonies, in turn defined as the property of France.

## TAXONOMIES OF ENLIGHTENMENT

On January 26, 1776, the "Negro Market" was established in the Place Clugny in Cap Français on the slaves' "free" days—holidays and Sundays only— but by 1768 the marketplace opened daily. Moreau de Saint-Méry, the white Creole lawyer and historian from Martinique, described the capital Cap Français (usually called Le Cap, and today, Cap Haïtien) in his monumental *Description de la partie française de l'Isle Saint-Domingue.* Moreau de Saint-Méry's journey through the Clugny Market, the center of Creole life, calls into question the regulations of the 1685 Black Code, particularly the prohibiting of slaves' bartering, exchanging, or selling goods.[10] By the eighteenth century an amalgam of classes, castes, and colors had begun to threaten the rules for order in slave society. Marketing was one of the institutions that allowed independent transactions that contradicted the divestiture and subordination demanded by slavery.

Moreau celebrates the rich and varied products of "the colonial soil" displayed at the Negro Market at Clugny. Each section of the market was reserved for the sale of different products: vegetables, herbs, and other plants on the east side; meat (lamb, pork, and sausage) on the south; live poultry on the west and, behind the poultry dealers, millet, "Guinea grass," and "Scotland grass"; and fish and shellfish (clams, oysters, and *lambi*, or conch) on the north side. The Place Clugny, crosscut by several streets, formed intersections, or *carrés*. On either side of these intersections, harmoniously laid out, were stalls for different grains and a number of other substances that, according to Moreau, replaced bread for Negroes and even for white Creoles: cassava, sweet potato, yam, or cabbage. Flowers and fruits—including oranges, lemons, pineapple, corossol (custard-apple), papaya, and "the monstrous apricot, the insipid coco-plum"— were sold by slave cultivators from both the city and the countryside on Sundays and by retailers (*revendeuses*) on weekdays (D 1:435).

Moreau's catalogs reveal the wondrous "species" of plants, animals, and vegetables for consumption. He delights in describing "an infinity of things": the fruit of the calabash tree or gourds carved in "an ingenious or bizarre way"; the perfume of truffles stunning the gourmand from afar; two cocks making war with their sharp beaks even though their feet are bound; the "inviting smile" of the market woman. Concluding his description of the market, Moreau writes, "Everything that the island can produce for nourishing its inhabitants or for perfuming the air they breath, is in the Clugny Market, except for the commodities of colonial manufacturing" (D 1:433–36).

In 1773 the "White Market" on the Parade Ground in Le Cap was closed. Between 1735 and 1773 this market had supplied whites imported items from France: dry goods, pottery, haberdashery, china, jewels, shoes, parakeets, and monkeys. Instead of necessities, or the local foodstuffs of Clugny, this market boasted European luxuries, though it is far less fascinating to Moreau's ethnographic eye than Clugny. According to him, the market was known as the place for the fashionable tour. Women of color, especially, "cannot abide the thought of not going and showing off their luxury" (D 1:315–16). By 1773 the *gens de couleur*, especially free women of color, had steadily increased. Administrators, in closing the market, doubtless hoped to circumscribe the places these "*libres*" could display themselves, since public opinion deemed their liberty to be the telltale sign of libertinage.[11] Yet in spite of the numerous rules, ordinances, and judgments meant to redefine and restrict liberty, habitual behavior continued, as did the proliferation of irregular liberties.

The necessity to separate materially what had been constituted as two races—and, in some extreme cases, fantasized as two species—even as they mixed, meant that the very idea of *free* or *freed* had to be qualified and transformed. This "systematic abasement" worked, according to Yvan Debbasch in his *Couleur et liberté*, by power of association, a succession of images and ideas:

whoever says *libre* in white society thinks instinctively of concubinage, the spectacle of the great city, and the *mulâtresse*-courtesan.[12] The ideal of European beauty, once exported to the colonies, like outmoded goods in a Creole market, faced the fact of "misalliances" that debunked the myth of the undesirable Negro. In 1770 there were about 6,000 emancipated people of color; in 1780, 12,000; and by 1789, 28,000. The generative increases doubtless reminded white ideologues of what they kept trying to conceal or constrain in their laws, statutes, and memoirs.

Moreau records the words of a traveler to Le Cap who overheard a high-class white lady exclaim, when she saw three *mulâtresses* in skirts of muslin garnished with lace: "Look at these rotten pieces of meat! They deserve to have their lace cut flush with their buttocks and to be sold on the fish table in the Clugny Market!"[13] Yet when Marianne and Françoise, two women of color, spoke sharply about a white woman, their chastisement is chronicled, though their words are not. Their punishment—its form and the place chosen for display—demonstrated to such women where (and to whom) they belonged. On June 9, 1780, the Council of Le Cap condemned them to be shown in the Clugny Market, affixed to a pole by an iron collar placed around their necks. They were to remain there from seven in the morning until ten at night, with a placard in front of them bearing these words: "Mulâtresses insolent toward white women." The council's order proved the power of white justice to denude what some deemed objects of luxury. Not only were *people of color* forever excluded from *becoming white,* but these women, like the thousands of slaves in Clugny, would be forced to relive the shame of their origins as flesh for sale in the marketplace. But ingenuity outsmarted the law. Marianne and Françoise went into hiding, and the council had to be satisfied with carrying out their judgment in effigy.[14]

In less than a century the promise of "same rights, privileges, and immunities as persons born free" had been perverted. Louis XIV in the Black Code had expressed the wish "that the merit of acquired liberty" would "produce . . . the same effects that the happiness of natural liberty produces in our other subjects" (Art. 59). That such happiness was impossible, that the boon of "natural liberty" became the doom of "acquired liberty," would be the story of the *libres* of Saint-Domingue. In Saint-Domingue the term *gens de couleur* (people of color) was used interchangeably with *sangs-mêlés* (mixed blood) and *affranchis* or *libres* (emancipated or free). Of the people of color, only one-third were black, so the term became synonymous with *mulatto,* although, like *affranchis,* it actually applied indistinctively to mulattoes born free and freed slaves and thus to every member of the category called *libres.*[15] Though in France and sometimes in the colonies, *mulatto* was used to denote all persons neither black nor white, in Saint-Domingue it most often referred specifically to the offspring of a white and a *négresse* in a genealogical scale of minute gradations of blood and nuances of color.

Since "concubinage" with slaves had created the discoloration of blacks so feared by whites, in 1773 a royal edict modified Article 9 of the Code, which had legalized marriage for interracial liaisons (if the white man was unmarried). Not only did this revision forbid marriage with a person of color, but it abolished the emancipation that could stem from such an alliance. And since there were numerous cases of whites marrying women of color (about three hundred white planters had married women of color by 1763),[16] those whites guilty of *mésalliance* had to suffer the curse of color and descend into the purgatory assigned to *affranchis*. These "degenerated" whites, who formed yet another intermediate category between whites and people of color, were evicted from public life.

The techniques of degradation depended on social segregation and judicial inequality, all of which read as if they were castigated for the sin of blurring the "demarcation line" between castes (that is, between colors) in Saint-Domingue. The ritual of naming, so central to enslavement, was now brought to bear upon the free people of color. If naming slaves confirmed them as white property while it symbolically stripped slaves of their past identity, the new onomastics reminded *libres* of their origins. In 1773 the administrators in Saint-Domingue forbade mixed-bloods from taking the name of a white, whether their natural father or the one who freed them: "The name of a white race usurped can cast doubt on the status of persons, throw confusion into the order of inheritance, and ultimately destroy this insurmountable barrier between Whites and people of color that public opinion has established, and the wisdom of government maintains."[17] Further, no longer owned but free, they were now to bear names that reverted to another kind of freedom, forever distinct from that of European subjects: their past in Africa. With the birth of their children, natural mothers "must give them a surname drawn from African idiom, or from their trade and color, but never can it be that of any white family in the colony."[18]

The law requiring that names bear no trace of mastery but instead metonymize servitude, was matched by directives intended to strip away the trappings of acquired taste. The many ordinances concerned with removing external embellishment were intended to signal a fundamental inferiority masked by finery. "The luxury of mulâtresses," lamented Moreau de Saint-Méry, "has gone beyond the limits. . . . Luxury consists, nearly entirely, in a single object, clothing."[19] To remind these women of their servile origins and to curb their "insolence," a number of laws were passed to symbolize "simplicity," "decency," and "respect." In 1775 the attorney general of Le Cap tried to "restrain the excessively dazzling luxury of the *filles publiques*" (prostitutes, though male visitors and even Moreau warned they were *not* what the European term denotes). A statute in 1779 determined dress codes for people of color for "the purpose of morals"[20] and thus regulated what could be worn or purchased on moral or religious grounds. The mask of virtue disguised the ever-increasing necessity for racist segregation. A white Creole, Madame Laurette Aimée Mozard Nicodami, writing her memoirs of Port-au-Prince in the early years of revolution, recalled the heady context between Creole ladies "humiliated in their claims by mulâtresses, *femmes publiques*." Desiring a distinguishing mark that would place them on another level than these courtesans, white women presented their woes to the Superior Council of Le Cap: "At the Cap they issued an order that forbade this degraded class from wearing shoes. They then appeared in sandals, with diamonds on the toes of their feet."[21]

The free coloreds in Saint-Domingue were three times more numerous than the *affranchis* in the remaining islands of the French Antilles. By 1789 free coloreds owned one-third of the plantation property in Saint-Domingue, the slaves, and one-quarter of the real estate property and also competed in commerce and trade.[22] Yet no gift of liberty or surfeit of affluence could remove the contamination of blood. Strict reminders of the stain became ever more necessary as bodies of color began to emerge, to lose the visible mark of inequality, and fade gradually into areas reserved only for enlightened whites. Girod de Chantrans, writing in 1782, caustically observed: "It is now time to declare [free coloreds] free; since nature often enjoys flinging ridicule in these kinds of dealings by producing a slave much whiter than the Provençal who buys him."[23] These "new whites" had to be recolored, inventively darkened, and the resulting "onomastics of color" depended on a fiction of whiteness threatened by what one could not always see but learned to fear and always suspect: a spot of black blood.[24]

How could people tell if a "suspect" was colored? Could an expert eye apprehend the stages of discoloration? The attempt to categorize, name, label, and classify the degrees of color between the extremes of black and white resulted in fantastic taxonomies of a uniquely Antillean enlightenment. Once it became necessary to classify the amount of blood that determined racial identity, as well as an appearance of color that had to be named, the system of differentiation generated phantasms of color, spectral entities of a new species. The naturalist George Louis Leclerc Buffon dedicated his *Histoire naturelle* to

Louis XV, as intriguing a correlation as Sade's reference to the reign of Louis XIV at the beginning of *The Hundred and Twenty Days of Sodom*. If Sade's fiction referred to Louis XIV and his formulation of the Black Code for the Antilles, Buffon's natural history, read carefully by the next Louis, might well have resulted in the king's decision formally to issue his 1771 "Instructions to Administrators" in the colonies, the new code of restrictions meant especially for the *gens de couleur*. If Buffon complained about the difficulty in separating men from animals—especially from the orangutans Linnaeus named nocturnal men—and called for more rigorous categorization, the administrators of the Old Regime saw the naturalist's theoretical problem literalized when their symbolically loaded hierarchies began to break down.

Buffon's descent "by nearly insensible gradations from the most perfect creature to the most unformed matter, from the best organized animal to the most brute mineral" and his celebration of these "imperceptible nuances" as "the great work of nature," once applied to the successive generations of blacks with the traits and colors of whites, required a new typology. Buffon recognized that the "arbitrary" must enter into any "general system" or "perfect method."[25] But this way of thinking, once exported to the Antilles and experimented on persons in the colonial laboratory, resolutely ignored Buffon's caveat. Instead, the project of certifying place, position, and rank in a chaos of contradictions became a colonial obsession, and systems of classification, backed up by repressive laws, became more urgent as the visible, economic, and traditional proofs of distinction vanished. An artificially induced regression was summoned in order to take away from the *gens de couleur* everything that made them appear white: an invented taxonomy that was scientifically spurious but mathematically exacting. It was no longer a question of proving men to be beasts in order to justify slavery but one of demonstrating how these men, even if freed, were still slaves with a damning defect of blood.

With each new generation, those who used to be closer in appearance to apes, or so the ideology of natural bestiality went, because of successive misalliances, looked more and more devilishly like apparitions of men. These appearances haunted whites. As colors faded and hair, eyes, and other varied and arbitrary traits entered the schema, new divisions had to be made and other names invented that referred to any category, class, or genus *except* human. The epistemology of whiteness, absolutely dependent for its effect on the detection of blackness, resulted in fantasies about secret histories and hidden taints that would then be backed up by physical, explicit codes of law. Such a system not only displaced the human element from the hybrid offspring of colonial coupling but became a desperate attempt to redefine whiteness. Moreau de Saint-

Méry's taxonomy of color in his *Description de la partie française de l'Isle Saint-Domingue* is crucial to this analysis.

For Moreau, Saint-Domingue was a "colored locality," and he reproduced ghosts of the place, a fable of enlightenment that would not only be used by those who called themselves whites but internalized by the *clairs,* or light-skinned residents, of the Antilles. Let us turn briefly to Moreau's attempt to systematize the conundrum of color. Moreau's taxonomy operates on two fronts: color and blood, what ostensibly can be observed and what is invisible. Something like a racialized body and soul dichotomy, the distinctions brought forth are chimerical, as fantastic as what Moreau ridiculed as the superstitions of Creole and African slaves. He presents eleven categories of 110 combinations, ranked from absolute white (128 parts white blood) to absolute black (128 parts black blood), pushing the invisibility of color differentiation to such extremes that even he must admit indecipherable genetic effects.

In Saint-Domingue it took a universally applicable concept of blackness, and as it turned out, a fairly rarefied one, to underpin both a sense of racial superiority and the privileges or arrogations that were supposed to stem from it. What became known as "the law of reversion" certified the futility in trying to remove blackness—even "the least molecule of black blood"—by successive alliances with whites. In Moreau's system, the concept of blackness (like that of bestiality in other natural histories) had to be reinforced, made absolute and ultimately unchangeable against the prima facie evidence of fading color. The strategy was to call this idea blood. As a metaphysical attribute, blood provided a rational system for the classification and distribution of a mythical essence: blood equals race. Once the connection was made, color could be referred to, but now it denoted blood. Finally, the word *color,* like *blood,* is fictitious, signaling—especially in extreme cases, like Moreau's example of "8,191 parts white opposed to one part black"—what is not observable: not fact, but ideology.

Stranger than any supernatural fiction, and surely one of the most remarkable legalistic fantasies of the New World, the radical irrationality of Moreau's method demonstrates to what lengths the imagination can go if driven by racial prejudice. The figures of blackness imagined by the white colonialist exposed how unnatural were the attempts to sustain "natural" distinctions between races of men. This kingdom of grotesques would resonate in later supernatural "fictions," rooted quite naturally in the need for racist territoriality: Bronte's Heathcliff, not "a regular black"; the blood taint lurking in Dracula's not-quite-right white skin; or Mallarmé's blooded *"femme stérile,"* his Hérodiade.

How does Moreau's color continuum work? If we want to know what happens when a *mamelouque* sleeps with a mulatto, or a pure-blooded Negro with a *sacatra,* or a mulatto with a *négresse,* Moreau provides the result, figures mathematically in eleven tables with titles like "Combinations of White," "Combinations of Negro," "Combinations of Mulatto," "Combinations of Quarteron," and so on through "Marabou." (Note that the thirteenth and fourteenth sets of combinations with "*Savages and Caribs of America,* or Western Indians," and "*Oriental Indians*" do not concern me here.) The "misallied" couple is the foundation for Moreau's combinational romance: a father and a mother of different colors (unequal in degree of blood) appear in each operation, or "combination," as Moreau terms it. Here, then, is his first example of one of the eleven lists of possible nuances, based on a common denominator, the white man:

Combinations of White
From a White and a Négresse, comes a Mulatto.

| | |
|---|---|
| Mulâtresse | Quarteron. |
| Quarteron | Métis. |
| Métis | Mamelouque. |
| Mamelouque | Quarteronné. |
| Quarteronné | Sang-mêlé. |
| Sang-mêlé | Sang-mêlé, |
| | that continually approaches white. |
| Marabou | Quarteron. |
| Griffone | Quarteron. |
| Sacatra | Quarteron. |

D 1:86

In order to get the color of the offspring, we must always divide by two the additive color obtained by two parents. For example, one white + one *mulâtresse* = 0 + $1/2$ divided by 2 = $1/4$, a *quarteron,* or one-quarter black. The stable figure in every combinatorial sequence is the male (whether white, Negro, mulatto, *quarteron, métis, mamelouque,* or other), and he chooses from among the supply of female specimens, as shown in the above table. Note that even though the example comes from the table "Combinations of White," the child is articulated in terms of blackness—that which is feared in oneself and treated with contempt in others—rather than in terms of the desirable whiteness.

After these charts of what Moreau calls "distinct classes, as regards the nuance of skin in individuals who form the population of the [French] part of Saint-Domingue," Moreau describes a few types in terms of physiognomic traits (skin color, hair texture, and facial features) and also explains how many different ways there are to produce mulattoes (twelve ways), *quarterons* (twenty ways), *métis* (called *octoroons* in Louisiana and other islands of the Americas, the product of six combinations), and so on. "Of all the combinations of White and negro," Moreau insists, "it is the Mulatto who unites the most physical advantages; of all these crossings of races it is he who retains the strongest constitution, the most appropriate to the climate of Saint- Domingue" (D 1:90).

In order to make himself "more intelligible" in this habitat of "denominations drawn from color," Moreau turns to rigorous mathematical calculations, giving numerically the *possible* range of combinations, figured with the exact parts black to white. For example, "The 20 combinations of the Quarteron offer from 71 to 96 parts white and from 32 to 57 parts black." There are always new admixtures and changing nuances, though the names themselves do not denote the yellows, reds, browns, whites, or blacks of the people of Saint-Domingue. The differences are, after all, *insensible* in a climate where even "the skin of the European . . . takes on a yellowish [or sallow] tone," or as some noted, a brown tint (D 1:100). Moreau then returns to the rigor of numbers to define what is rapidly becoming indefinable. These numbers tell a very different story than Moreau's less than precise representations. The person named is an amalgam of parts, the product of an illicit mixture of blood quanta.

But what about the majority of people in Saint-Domingue, the slaves in Moreau's *Description?* Immediately after his introduction to the white population of Saint-Domingue and before discussing the *affranchis,* he turns to Negro slaves, both African and Creole. After describing the individual nations and their traits, as well as what he calls "the negro character" and "magic and sorcery," he turns to the overwhelming preference of African women for black, not white, men. "Neither their behavior with whites, nor the advantages which that brings them, even the possible freedom, for themselves or for their children, can hold them back.... Nor can their concern about the punishment that white pride and jealousy can make so severe." Even if they "more or less happily hide this inclination, their preference for black men wins in the end" (D 1:79).

The production of variously shaded and lightened people of color, Moreau implies, was less an acquired habit than a coercion made possible and sustained by slavery. Whiteness, therefore, meant something very different to those he calls "slaves from Africa." But even slaves born in America and creolized retained their sensitivity to color and to those whose skin and ways of thinking suggested either privilege or perversion. Blacks also invented names for whites who were not-quite-right whites, not because of color but because of status: *petits blancs* or *blanchets* ("little whites") as opposed to the true whites, the wealthy *grands blancs* or *blancs-blancs* (meaning something like "whiter than white").[26]

In "Varieties in the Human Species," along with accounts of giants, dwarfs, and porcupine men, Buffon tells the story of Geneviève, a "white *négresse*" born to "perfectly black" parents in the island of Dominica in 1759, though Buffon assures his readers that such curiosities could be found in Cuba or Saint-Domingue as well. Geneviève exemplifies those "deviations," variously called *blafards* (pale-colored or wan), albinos, Dondos, or white Negroes, typed by Buffon as "sterile branches of degeneration" rather than "a stock or true race in the human species." Using the same argument as that applied to mulattoes, he then turns to sterility, the lack of generative possibilities in males, as further proof of what he calls this "degradation of nature." When the female, fertile specimens reproduce, however, their children return to "the primitive color from which their fathers or mothers have degenerated." The curse of blackness, when denatured into whiteness, can be made intelligible only in terms of defilement, rot, imbecility, or a ghastly bestiality: hands so poorly formed that "one must call them paws"; hair described as wool, fur, or down. Buffon implies what Moreau and other theorists of color would later emphasize: mulattoes (and the different nuances "degenerated" from whiteness) are as weird or monstrous as the *blafards* who have issued from blackness (*OC* 5:206–7).

Such corporeal surprises, Buffon concludes, "do not form a real race." Like the anomalous Geneviève, they can never be part of "the race of blacks and whites," with their generic characteristics passed on from generation to generation. Instead this figure of reproductive variety is a trick of nature, or as Buffon puts it, a "monster by default." What matters here is that Buffon's elucidation of the proliferating changes possible, in terms of the "nuances and limits of these different varieties," resembles the nearly infinite rarefactions of color and appearance in Moreau's taxonomy.

Uncontrollable concubinage and licentiousness, as we have seen, were considered by some as heralding unholy mixtures, what the superior of the missions, writing to the governor of Martinique in 1722, called a "criminal conjunction of men and women of a different species," giving birth to "a fruit that is a monster of nature."[27] One grotesque offshoot of coital combination, in fact, what could be seen as a literalization of the trope of crossbreeding, is the "pied Negro," dappled with spots or stains of white and black. A Monsieur Taverne of Dunkerque sent Buffon his account of a pied *négresse*, Marie Sabina, born in October 1736. Taverne explains that in spite of the English legend at the bottom of her portrait, which claims her to be the offspring of two Negro slaves, he suspects that she issued from "the union of a white and a *négresse*," and a question of honor (according to Taverne, the mother's) resulted in the false genealogy. Buffon answers Taverne's letter with his astonishment at the portrait, a marvel of nature, but focuses on proving that she has Negroes for parents. The proof lies again in expelling *real* whiteness from anything faintly redolent of black blood.

If whites were threatened with moral deformation when they misallied with blacks, blacks also found themselves surprised into whiteness. Not only did offspring after many generations revert to the original blackness, but in the case of the white Negroes, they issued from the loins of mothers with a very dark skin. What did it mean when the skin started to alter, sometimes in "marks" or "stains" large or small, "and with nuances that varied from reddish to milky white"? How did "Negroes," aware, as Moreau implies, that "the deep black of the skin is a beauty," react to the phenomenon of being stained white?

All the attention to bodies, to skins like copper or bronze or complexions dull and chalky, must have preoccupied the vision of blacks as well as whites in Saint-Domingue. Some blacks feared lightening in much the same way that whites feared the black stain: invisible but *sensed* as moral deterioration. Yet what whites feared as an internal transformation or a demonic lapse was physically, externally visited on blacks, described in passages on white Negroes, pied Negroes, and albinos as literally breaking out in spots, splotches, or stains (*taches*). White "natural historians" were obsessed with these wonders. The bodily change signifies something much more subtle than the racist stories about couplings between Hottentot females and orangutans. White and black skin combined—nature wronged—generated monsters, what Derek Walcott much later would deem "prodigies of the wrong age and color." Or so an ideologue might reflect. These observations seem fantastic, but no matter how strange they appear, they are natural. As Buffon warned about ghosts, "The prejudice with respect to spectres, therefore, originated from nature; and such appearances depend not, as philosophers have supposed, solely upon the imagination."[28]

But what about those reactions that did get written down? Can we know, for example, what Frances, the Negro cook of Colonel Barnet of Virginia, must have thought when at "about the age of fifteen years she observed that those parts of her skin near her nails and her fingers gradually became white. In a short time after, her mouth underwent the same change; and from that period to her fortieth year, the white has been gradually extending over her whole body"?[29] The ghosts, creatures of the night, and vampires without skin who formed part of the population of Saint-Domingue suggest that what was called superstition might well have been a revelation of what white enlightenment was really about. Out of what white priests, superstitious planters, or prudent administrators projected on those they made slaves, blacks told stories, sometimes shaped by their own legends, but always reinvented in the New World.

## NOTES

A longer version of this essay appeared in *New Literary History* 26 (1995): 283–308. Joan Dayan's presentation at the "Making Worlds" conference drew on material that forms the basis of this essay.

1. Kamau Brathwaite, *Development of Creole Society in Jamaica 1770–1820* (Oxford: Oxford University Press, 1971), 22; hereafter cited in text.

2. The diversity in terms of class and social status is much more complex than I can analyze here. Charles Frostin, in *Les révoltes blanches à Saint-Domingue aux XVII et XVIII siècles (Haiti avant 1789)* (Paris: Editions de l'Ecole, 1975), has begun the necessary work in deconstructing such divisions as *petits blancs, grands blancs,* slaves, and free coloreds. As he demonstrates, the categories of whiteness were themselves more vexed than has been allowed, especially in the 1700s, as more white workers, adventurers, and individuals of ill-defined and varied activities left France for Saint-Domingue.

3. Francis Alexander Stanislaus, Baron de Wimpffen, *A Voyage to Saint-Domingue, In the Years 1788, 1789, and 1790,* trans. from unpublished manuscript by J. Wright (London: printed for T. Cadell, Jr., and W. Davies; Successors to Mr. Dadell in the Strand; and J. Wright, opposite old Bond Street, Piccadilly, 1797), 63.

4. According to Moreau de Saint-Méry, who gives figures for Saint-Domingue in 1789, there were 39,000 whites, 27,500 free colored, and 452,000 slaves. François Girod, in *La Vie Quotidienne de la Société Créole* (Paris: Librairie Hachette, 1972), warns that these official figures "tended to inflate the numbers of whites, to diminish those of 'people of color,' and to minimize the figures of slaves for obvious fiscal reasons" (10).

5. Louis Sala-Molins, *Le Code Noir, ou le calvaire de Canaan* (Paris: Presses Universitaires de France, 1987), 241. Confronting what he takes to be a neglect nearly as pernicious as the Code itself, Sala-Molins introduces the Code to his readers as if a fairy tale in six parts, told for the pleasure of the "little Frenchman grown big." Note that the only English translation I have found is in an appendix in Howard Justin Sosis, *The Colonial Environment and Religion in Haiti* (Ph.D. diss., Columbia University, 1971). Sala-Molins demonstrates its inaccessibility by noting how, were you so inclined, you might locate and read the unreadable. Fully transcribed in Labat, evoked in Raynal, and listed in the *Encyclopédie* under "Code," it is otherwise ignored. I first read the Code in a collection that included each king's added rulings and edicts, *1699–1742: Recueils de reglements, edits, déclarations et arrêts . . . conçernant le commerce, l'administration de la justice, la police de colonies françaises de l'Amérique . . . avec Le Code Noir et l'addition au dit Code* (Paris, 1745), 220 pages. Note that the 1685 Code was only a dozen pages, while its 1770 edition,

according to Sosis, though it contained the same number of articles, requires more than 400 pages in the same size print (Sosis, 111–12).

6. René-Michel Hilliard d'Auberteuil, *Considérations sur l'etat present de la colonie française de Saint-Domingue* (Paris: Grangé, 1776–1777), 1:143.

7. René Descartes, *Meditations on First Philosophy*, trans. John Cottingham, with an introduction by Bernard Williams (Cambridge: Cambridge University Press, 1986), "Second Meditation," 59; hereafter cited in text.

8. Frostin, *Les révoltes blanches à Saint-Domingue*, 138.

9. Orlando Patterson, *Slavery and Social Death* (Cambridge, Mass.: Harvard University Press, 1982), 5.

10. Médéric-Louis-Elie Moreau de Saint-Méry, *Description topographique, physique, civil, politique et historique de la partie française de l'Isle Saint-Domingue* (Philadelphia: Chez l'auteur, 1797), rpt. ed. B. Maurel and E. Taillemite (Paris: Société de l'histoire de colonies français, 1958); hereafter cited in text as *D*. Moreau de Saint-Méry, was born at Fort Royal, Martinique, on January 13, 1750. In Cap Français he practiced law and became a member of the *conseil supérieur* of the colony, during which time he began his collection of laws, published in six volumes, *Lois et constitutions des colonies françaises de l'Amérique sous le vent de 1550 à 1785*. His ethnographic histories of the French and Spanish parts of the island of Saint-Domingue are the best accounts of the Creole culture before the revolution. For about four years (October 14, 1794, to August 23, 1798) he remained in Philadelphia, where he opened his own bookstore and printing press and published these two important works: *Descriptions topographique et politique de la partie espagnole de l'isle Saint-Domingue (1796)* and *Description topographique, physique, civile, politique et historique de la partie française de l'Isle Saint-Domingue*.

11. Gabriel Debien, *Les esclaves aux Antilles françaises (XVII–XVIII siècles)* (Basse-Terre: Société d'histoire de las Guadeloupe; Fort-de-France: Société d'histoire de la Martinique, 1974), 371.

12. Yvan Debbasch, *Couleur et liberté: Le jeu du critère ethnique dans un ordre juridique esclavagiste* (Paris: Librairie Dalloz, 1967), 101.

13. Moreau de Saint-Méry, *Notes historiques*, quoted in Pierre de Vassière, *Saint-Domingue* (Paris: Pettin et Cie, Libraires-Editeurs, 1909), 318.

14. Judgement of the Council of Le Cap, cited in Antoine Gisler, *L'Esclavage aux Antilles françaises (XVII–XIX siècle): contribution au problème de l'esclavage* (Fribourg, Switzerland: Editions Universitaires, 1965), 95–96; and Jacques Thibau, *Le Temps de Saint-Domingue* (Paris: Editions Jean-Claude Lattès, 1989), 210.

15. Frostin, *Les révoltes blanches à Saint-Domingue*, 71.

16. Carolyn Fick, *The Making of Haiti: The Saint-Domingue Revolution from Below* (Knoxville: University of Tennessee Press, 1990), 19.

17. Arrêt of 22 January, Council of Port-au-Prince, cited in Gisler, *L'Esclavage aux Antilles françaises*, 95.

18. Jean Fouchard, *Les Marrons de la liberté* (Port-au-Prince: Editions Deschamps, 1988), 257.

19. Moreau de Saint-Méry, *Lois et contitutions* 1:105, cited in Debbasch, *Couleur et liberté*, 96.

20. Debbasch, *Couleur et liberté*, 96, cites Moreau de Saint-Méry, *Lois et constitutions*, 5:855–56.

21. Madame Laurette Aimée Mozard Nicodami Ravient (1788–1864), *Mémoires d'une créole de Port-au-Price* [1844] (Paris: A la Librairie-Papeterie, 1973), 24.

22. Trouillot, "Motion in the System," 331–88.

23. Justin Girod de Chantrans, *Voyage d'un Suisse dans différentes colonies d'Amérique*, ed. Pierre Pluchon (Paris: Librairie Jules Tallandier, 1980), 166.

24. Debbasch, *Couleur et liberté*, 69–71; for a discussion of the "legal assumption of race as blood borne," see Cheryl Harris, "Whiteness as Property," *Harvard Law Review* 106, no. 8 (June 1993): 1707–91.

25. George Louis Leclerc Buffon, *Oeuvres complètes de Buffon* (Brussels: Chez Th. Lejeune, Libraire-éditeur, 1828–1830), 1:72; hereafter cited in text as *OC*.

26. Frostin, *Les révoltes blanches à Saint-Domingue*, 71.

27. Lucien Peytraud, *L'Esclavage aux Antilles françaises avant 1789* (1897); rpt. *Edition et Diffusion de la Culture Antillaise* (Paris: E. Kolodziej, 1984), 1:249.

28. Buffon, *A Natural History of the Globe, of Man, of Beasts, Birds, Fishes, Reptiles, Insects and Plants*, ed. John Wright (Boston: Gray and Brown, 1831), 134.

29. Ibid., 185.

9

# specular morality, the war on drugs, and anxieties of visibility

> Land is becoming extinct, and all this will be developed.
> —*Livia León Montiel*

> What would it mean—what difference would it make—to think of capitalism as a spatial practice?
> —*Mary Poovey*

By noting that "land is becoming extinct," Livia Montiel invokes naturalizing rhetoric to describe Arizona's on-going capitalization.[1] Pointing to the "killers" of land, developers and state zoning commissions, she also registers her awareness of the production of space. For Montiel, dead land is developed land, and developed land transforms relationships. Montiel subsequently explains that she hopes her children will maintain a few acres of her family's *rancho* as a "little piece of land for them to reunite from time to time."[2] By suggesting that space serves as a link between legacy, memory, and relationships, Montiel proposes an important concept: space is produced by and produces sociality.

As Cindi Katz explains, "Social power is reflected in and exercised through the production and control of space."[3] But rarely, of course, is social power immediately connected to what typically gets referred to as "the landscape." Nonetheless, the construction of space is a structural element of the contemporary political economy. Spaces are produced—shopping malls, universities, public housing projects, militarized national borders, corporate headquarters, factories, national wilderness areas—and their construction produces changed so-cialities. Capital consistently abandons spaces, constructs spaces, reconstructs other spaces, and decimates existing spaces. This process creates and destroys jobs, directs the flow of capital from one region to another, enhances the mon-etary value of one space or another, creates hierarchies of desirability, changes power relations, and affects social interaction. Of course, decisions about the production of space hardly exist in a vacuum, nor does control belong com-pletely in the hands of a few power brokers. Alternative productions and op-positional conceptions of space resist and attend to corporate and govern-mental efforts to dominate and control the production of space. Picket lines, community theaters, *nichos,* crisis care centers, barrio murals, independent bookstores, and food cooperatives exemplify the production of alternative spaces.

Contemporary interrogations of the relationship between space and so-cial power have begun to expose their imbricated connections. Understanding these enmeshed relationships requires a complex untangling and diligent un-masking of a series of ideological and cultural practices that have reduced space to a background, a stage on which social interactions take place, or have hidden spatial practices altogether. For example, American literary history, broadly considered, is frequently described in terms of spatial practices. An-thologies begin with travel narratives that are as much about "the land discov-ered" as about the writer and the culture from which she or he emerges.[4] The selections then grow alongside accounts of the territorial expansion of the U.S. government; exploration narratives accompany "settlement" accounts. What is interesting to me about much of this literary practice is not the linkage be-tween site, movement, and text but rather the degree to which capitalism as a spatial practice goes underexamined even as the very literature being dis-cussed often offers a response to this practice, a qualified intervention rather than a celebration.

Because these literary histories tend to start with the East Coast and move West, even when they harshly critique the accompanying movements of troops and terror, they further solidify the hegemonic linkage between capital-ism and territorial expansion. This practice suggests that the "natural" literary history of the United States is one that starts with the East and ends tri-umphantly with the West. Indeed, the very insistence of anthologies and liter-ary histories on a geographic progression implicitly assimilates literary produc-tion into the spatial practices of capitalism. The creation of a geopolitical map of the United States accompanied by a geoliterary map of U.S. cultural pro-duction finally serves once again to disguise capitalist spatial practices. This may explain, at least in part, the virtual exclusion of Chicano and Chicana literary productions from these anthologies and histories: this literature, from its very inception, has contested both the naturalness of the geopolitical map and the completeness of the geoliterary map.

Clearly, then, the production of space does not take place apart from the production of knowledge, of texts, or even of urban myths. Race (and racism), gender (and patriarchy), class (and elitism), sexuality (and heterosexism) inform spatial decisions from the mundane to the spectacular. Yet studies of this production are only beginning to incorporate these categories.[5] And it is here, I believe, that an antidisciplinary feminism, committed to serious antiracist, antihomophobic, and antielitist politics, can make an impact.

What does such a critique of space, one that acknowledges the significance of intersectionality (as formulated by Kimberlé Crenshaw) and the need for an oppositional consciousness (as theorized by Chela Sandoval), begin to look like?[6] In the discussion to follow, I argue that such a critique benefits from a commitment to interdisciplinary approaches. An interrogation of questions of spatiality ought also to understand the shifting relationships between gender and the process of concretizing difference. By this I mean that feminist scholars should take up issues not traditionally aligned with feminist inquiry, as well as those more typically marked out for a feminist examination. Mary Poovey's provocative suggestion that capitalism be studied as a spatial practice, particularly her turn to the deployment of visuality in spatial practices, provides the opportunity to bring together seemingly disparate and contradictory spatial practices. My hope is that the discussion here will both broaden the field and suggest ways to pay further attention to the still largely unspoken race/class/sexuality nexus.

Contemporary feminist interrogations of the production of space occur at the same time that the conceptual epistemologies of space are being transformed by the technology of late capitalism. With the ratification of NAFTA and the pending establishment of globally organized trade, worldwide bureaucratization and reorganization of national boundaries, regions, and zones around the ideology of free trade will undoubtedly accelerate a new organization (and, by extension, production) of space. This reorganization of spatial management proceeds with undeniable rapidity, entailing not simply the creation of an international bureaucracy to "manage" trade but also the folding of distance and time into a new concept of spatiality whose coordinates are no longer land and water masses but satellites, microchips, and fiber-optic cables.

In other words, attention to space arises at the very same time that the manner in which space is commodified, abstracted, and fetishized is changing.

Understanding such shifting cartographies and attendant epistemologies requires close attention to a variety of discourses, to the prevailing winds of political economy particularly, as multinational corporate policies continue to effect massive technological changes. Since "the new global economy" entails an entrenched international division of labor, tests the tenacity of nationalist politics, and forces continuing renegotiations of political power relations according to the terms of financial capitalism, critical feminist attention to the production of space needs to be inter- (and anti-) disciplinary in scope and nature.

Interdisciplinary feminist critiques enable us to follow the trajectory of discursive practices that accompany, inform, and produce the construction of spaces. Such critiques also mean taking into account the valences of social habits and institutions, crunching numbers, and paying attention to public policy. The critical issues worth exploring require engaging with, in Jenny Sharpe's words, "the shifting scenes of the aggressive territorial expansion of modern colonialism,"[7] as well as the genealogies of surveillance and coercive state systems, and the production at the local level of alternative discourses and significatory systems. It matters not simply whether we attend to spaces but also how we attend to them and which we focus upon. As Elsa Barkley Brown asks, for instance, what happens to the vernacular and academic understandings of sexual harassment if its presumed site is not simply the professional suite but also the home, where domestic workers have often been subject to sexual harassment?[8] Add the field of agribusiness, where migrant workers are frequently raped or abused, and sexual harassment no longer emerges as simply a late-twentieth-century middle-class "woman's issue." Paying attention to location, so that specific sites pressure the production of knowledge, changes the valences of available information.

Disciplinary studies too easily erase multiple subject positions, as well as the political and economic conditions pertinent to the production of knowledge within the discipline.[9] Interdisciplinary studies, with a sense of the inextricability of economic relations and academic knowledge production, hold out the possibility of developing an effective critique of the material/discursive construction of space. Studies focusing on the production of space often entail compartmentalized disciplines such as geography, political science, urban planning, history, architecture, and anthropology. By crossing and contesting the boundaries of such compartmentalized knowledge, and utilizing the tools of feminist and literary theories, as well as literature, a feminist critique of the relations of power and spatiality may begin to expose "the hegemonic structures of our theoretical models." Interdisciplinarity may prevent critical work from once again "serv[ing] an institutional function of securing neocolonial relations."[10] In other words, the feminist spatial work to be done cannot afford to be caught up in compartmentalized battles over disciplinary approaches to knowledge or boundary disputes over the difference between the material and the discursive.[11] To the extent that these conversations can reveal more productive forms of knowledge, then such discussions need to take place, but not at the expense of re-establishing hierarchies that simultaneously fragment and homogenize information, perhaps unintentionally mirroring capital's system of producing space.

## THE VISION THING

The unfolding and nuanced links between social power and the control and coordination of space suggest multiple avenues for exploration. As I have been arguing, the study of spatiality may best be served by an interdisciplinary approach that extends beyond simply using the tools of different disciplines and attempts instead to make connections between academic activity and political and ideological power structures. Such a mandate requires utilizing methods that open up new ways of performing analysis. Mary Poovey's examination of the relationship between visuality and capitalist spatial practices moves toward a particularly suggestive method, one that I want to expand upon by discussing the spatial practices of drug discourses, literary production, and queer politics.

As Poovey explains it, anxiety over the excessive visibility of the poor as a class and their invisibility as individuals prodded early capitalist theorists to propose a series of schemes to heighten the visibility of individuals by quantifying them and measuring their behavior while at the same time containing their visibility along gender and class lines. In other words, early capitalist theorists attempted to map people, to abstract them in the same way land had been abstracted and reconfigured according to the terms of Euclidean geometry. Poovey calls this "specular morality." Morality becomes a function of "seeing and being seen."

The dominant ideology of visuality portrays vision as objective and truthful, as if it were unmediated. Visuality's "transparency" and "impartiality" emerge out of the seemingly "objective" project of Euclidean geometry and give credence to specular moralities. Various Anglo cultural practices reinforce this ideology. For example, metaphors of knowing are often visual ("I see your point," "I can't picture that," "What is your perspective?"), suggesting a naturalized collaboration between visuality and epistemology. Similarly, the linkage between seeing and knowing is further reinforced by the turn to cartographic metaphors for descriptions of arguments and theories ("map out," "lay out," "establish the perimeters," "challenge the boundaries"). What gets hidden by this ideology is the interpretive process linked to visuality. At the same time, sight becomes privileged as the transcendent form of knowing.

"Ocular inspection" undergirds specular moralities and, according to Poovey, relies upon "an imaginative process that is actually a process of generalization" and interpretation. This process is applied to both spaces and people. For example, conceptualizing space, treating it as abstract, entails denying differences (between one space and another). This abstraction process homogenizes everything, thereby rendering differences *invisible*. But specular morality simultaneously suggests that differences are apparent. Therein lies the kind of contradictory structure that makes such a discourse of visibility so powerful. In other words, the process of abstraction erases differences in order to create a homogeneous unit while at the same time arguing that this homogeneous unit serves as a kind of objective truth against which differences can be visibly apprehended and measured. This double operation—the denial of difference accompanied by a belief in the truth of heightened visibility—enables the spatial/ocular practices of the political economy.

Ironically, discourses of visibility structure spatial practices while remaining largely hidden. Various specular moralities were structured into the creation of larger societal institutions, such as educational systems, according to Poovey. Because contemporary institutions, including prisons, public housing, and schools, emerged in part from the practices of specular morality, the current impact of various specular moralities cannot be underestimated. These scopic regimes, in Martin Jay's phrase, are literally built into designs directing the gaze, framing events and people, and signifying status. More than a question of how a building looks or where a person's gaze travels within a given space, scopic regimes prescribe who looks, where, when, and especially how.[12] Yet another way to say this is that if spatiality structures sociality, visuality is one mediator of the interanimating spatial/social alliance.

## SEEING THE WAR ON DRUGS

Feminists' attention has not tuned in to what in the contemporary United States is typically called "the war on drugs."[13] In an issue too complex to discuss here, contemporary cultural analysts, in general, have tended to ignore the impact of substance abuse and the drug wars on public policy and cultural production. But such silence becomes increasingly impossible as critical attention takes the production of space more and more seriously. Additionally, this is a field begging for feminist analysis—from the gendering of drug addiction to the redefining of "feminine" sites such as the home to the pathologizing and crimi-nalizing of women of color. My focus here is on the way discourses about drugs "make space." And by extension, I suggest some of the impacts such space-making practices are having on women.

The contemporary drug wars exemplify the spatial/ocular interplay de-scribed by Poovey. Specular moralities structure drug discourses. In turn, dis-courses about drugs drive contemporary constructions of space. The spatial/ocular ideologies driving the discursive practices of the drug wars manifest themselves in a variety of arenas. Any analysis of them would entail exploring the intermeshed relationships between public policies, film, literature, music, capital accumulation, media portrayals, narratives of economic crisis, and inter-national relations. My point here is to suggest the kind of interventionist analy-sis that might productively emerge from careful attention to issues of visibility within the production of spatiality.

Perhaps more than any other current spatially productive formation, drug discourses presume the transcendence of the visible. Law enforcement de-scriptions of drug arrests abound with verbs like *act, seem,* and *appear,* which serve as tropes alluding to the transcendence of the visual. In this arena, spec-ular morality relies on uninterrogated categories such as race and gender as well as on the assumed justice of criminalizing the drug trade. For example, in his conclusion to a description of a Houston drug bust, Customs Officer Nigel Brooks explains the impact of arresting Blanca Dominguez, who "did not act like a teacher on a sabbatical" and therefore "alerted" inspecting officers so that "the long arm of the law [could reach] across continents to dismantle a drug smuggling organization which had started in South America and stretched through North America to Europe and Asia."[14] Government publications en-couraging citizen participation in the "war on drugs" explain that people should be "on the lookout" for "suspicious" vehicles, persons, and behavior. Similarly, instruction manuals for immigration and customs officers assure new officers that, given time and the wisdom of experience, they will develop an instinct for detecting "criminals" based on appearance and behavior.[15] The interpretive process that turns a person into a suspicious character remains mystified in these publications and necessarily so. For while a discourse of visibility justifies surveillance practices, the raced and gendered markings that underpin this dis-course remain unspoken.

But if discursive practices usually mask the race and gender tropes struc-turing drug discourse, these tropes do occasionally become blatantly obvious, often around issues of surveillance. For example, in a *Customs Today* description of new heroin networks, M. Cordell Hart argues for the "accuracy" of the film

*Year of the Dragon.* Hart critiques what he understands as the aesthetic limitations of the film but urges his readers to see it because it shows "the general problems law enforcement and intelligence personnel have in dealing with the names and mindset of Oriental criminals." Here Hart clearly assumes the validity of a racist portrayal of Asians and Asian Americans in order to further rationalize the racialized tropes underpinning the ethnic surveillance network his essay lauds. Hart suggests that solutions to this "burgeoning heroin threat" include the "highly capable database for sorting and tracking ethnic Chinese" developed in Seattle; New York's "Oriental suspects' database"; a computerized tracking system developed by a nineteenth-century British railway engineer and now used by all "federal agencies concerned with Oriental names"; and personnel instruction "instill[ing] an understanding of Orientals."[16] Anxiety about how to manage the invisibility of drug-trading suspects drives Hart's essay toward a specular morality that clearly relies upon long-standing racial tropes.[17]

The racialized policing of nonwhite populations has also developed via federal funding for the "Weed-and-Seed" antidrug program. Local and federal agencies have developed extensive databases cataloging the activities of virtually every black and Latino youth in major urban areas. Collusion between national intelligence organizations and state and city police agencies may make it possible, according to labor historian Mike Davis, to maintain surveillance over the most intimate of activities among entire populations. The "drug war" has expanded and justified developing mass surveillance techniques, enabling police to look forward to technology that will allow them to "put the equivalent of an electronic bracelet on entire social groups."[18] Surveillance practices undeniably change the experience not only of public spaces but also of those more typically thought of as private. What is at stake here seems to be an effort to make it impossible for certain people, particularly young men of color but increasingly women as well, *ever to be invisible.* Yet the goal of such drug-war-sanctioned ocular/spatial practices clearly has nothing to do with *subjectivity.* It is not the particular experiences of men and women of color that interest these containment systems but their enforced, inescapable bodily visibility.

If these current ocular/spatial police practices tend to focus on young, nonwhite men, it should also be clear that the ideology supporting this focus is linked to an entrenched patriarchal practice. For while African American and Latino men are disproportionately criminalized, justifications for this practice reach back toward a pathologizing of single mothers and the ideological construction of the nuclear family. Former Reagan administration official Charles Murray took full advantage of this strategy when he proposed "drug free zones" that would refuse housing to "welfare mothers" and the "pregnant teenager smoking crack."[19] Further reinforcing this strategy, Hollywood-funded and -distributed films like *Boulevard Nights* and *Boyz N the Hood* clearly link drug addiction and trafficking to pathologized single mothers.[20] The end result of a scopic regime that draws upon the productive ideology of welfare moms and dark male bodies is a largely citizen-sanctioned governmental commitment to high-tech surveillance systems and criminalization policies that reconstruct, remap, and redefine social space.

In addition to funding the surveillance systems currently transforming spatiality, the war on drugs informs the construction, policing, maintenance, and fluidity of the boundaries of nation-states, contemporary immigration policies, and the solidification and further racialization of the urban-suburban dyad. National borders obviously emerge out of all kinds of ideological tangles and constructions. The drug war has justified shifting definitions of sovereignty. It has served as Bill Clinton's justification for a military invasion of Haiti, just as it conveniently served to justify George Bush's invasion of Panama. The United States has been pushing drug interdiction treaties on countries throughout the world, resulting in agreements like the 1986 Anti-Drug Abuse Act, which formed a joint U.S./Bahamian military task force enabling the United States to police the air and sea space around the Bahamas and to search vehicles with impunity. Similarly, drug discourse prompted the U.S. House of Representatives to essentially redefine the geopolitical definition of *borders* when it passed an amendment mandating that U.S. military forces "seal land, air, and sea borders" within forty-five days. Surveillance blimps suspended a thousand feet above-ground and stationed every few hundred miles along the U.S.–Mexico border epitomize this militarization. These blimps ostensibly scour the terrain for low-flying airplanes. More frequently, however, they appear as both expensive tools to spot straggling migrant workers and as yet another military experiment. In turn, drug transportation networks have constructed elaborately engineered tunnels that effectively move drugs out of sight while literally under the nose of the blimps' radar screens.

Drug discourses also serve to redefine *home* and *prison*. People moving into publicly funded housing in Chicago, for example, must submit to random searches for drugs. Signing a lease essentially means acquiescing to an open search warrant. Similarly, prisons are developing as a new spatial formation. With 3.5 million people now in the criminal justice system, the majority of them locked up, prisons have become a significant location. Sixty percent of the federal inmates have been incarcerated for drug-related offenses, and not coincidentally, since 1980 the federal prison population has expanded by 168 percent.[21] Increasingly, women fill the jail beds. The relationship between the high rate of incarceration in the United States and the social production of prison space merits further analysis. Given the fact that people of color are disproportionately housed in prisons and public housing, the drug war's transformation of civil rights, as a spatial discourse, would bear much more critical attention.

The symbolic capital utilized by contemporary real estate developers relies on enemies, real and imagined.[22] The "dangerous criminals" constructed by drug discourses more than adequately provide these. The producers of fortressed housing, shopping, and entertainment centers deploy specular morality, wildly wielding the tropes emerging from drug discourses. But at stake here, in a discursive ocular/spatial practice structured by racism and sexism, is the production of symbolic capital that may reinforce whiteness as a form of property, at least in part by erasing from visibility the largest percentage of participants in the drug market—white men and women.[23]

Specular moralities, drug discourses, and the production of space merge to form a question that should be undertaken across disciplines: to what degree have drug addiction and interdiction, the drug war, taken on a structural relationship to systematic uneven development? What is the structural relationship between contemporary political/global economies and the drug/law enforcement industries? Economists and policy analysts note that given the size of world sales of illegal drugs (anywhere from $300 billion to $500 billion annually), we must consider them to be a serious force in the world economy.[24] Given that the U.S. government budgeted close to $13 billion for drug interdiction, prosecution, and detection in the last year of George Bush's term and that Bill Clinton's crime bill may be his government's largest "new domestic spending initiative," feminist theoretical attention needs to turn toward the drug wars.[25] If drug discourses directly affect the production of certain kinds of space (such as prisons) they also certainly affect the production of other kinds of spaces (such as schools, low-income housing, and hospitals). The escalation of the drug wars and substance abuse itself, perhaps, occurs along almost the same spatial/temporal coordinates as the escalation of the international division of labor, the entrenchment of multinational corporations, and the solidification of U.S.-supported police-state regimes. In any case, feminist considerations of "spatial matters" that move beyond lip service to antiracism and antielitism will need to turn to fields often considered "male," like the drug wars.

## INVISIBILITY AS AN "UNNATURAL DISASTER"

While government policing policies have intensively sought to make it impossible for some sectors of the population to be invisible to their surveillance mechanisms, many people have simultaneously disparaged invisibility as a source of oppression. I am interested now in examining the linkages between two seemingly disparate and contradictory anxieties of visibility—state-sponsored ocular/spatial practices and the quest for visibility that operates as a theme for many contemporary writers and activists. An examination of both ought to suggest some of the spatial dimensions of what, for many, counts as a largely discursive rather than material issue.

In the winter of 1992, California Governor Pete Wilson's veto of a bill protecting gay and lesbian civil rights sent huge crowds into the streets of Los Angeles and San Francisco. In L.A. thousands of protesters frequently blocked traffic while chanting, "We're here, we're queer, get used to us, we're fabulous!" The crowds' assertion of longevity invoked *visibility* as a strategy of oppositionality as the largely white gay male protesters asserted their unapologetically visible presence in public spaces. Such a strategy directly combats one of the mechanisms of oppression that, as Judith Butler points out, "works not merely through acts of overt prohibition, but covertly, through the constitution of viable subjects and through the corollary constitution of a domain of unviable (un)subjects—*abjects,* we might call them—who are neither named nor prohibited within the economy of the law."[26]

Butler's comments echo the arguments of women of color who, since the 1970s and particularly since the publication of groundbreaking anthologies like *This Bridge Called My Back,* have been pointing out how invisibility serves as a strategy of containment. Mitsuye Yamada notes the link between silence and visibility when she suggests that raising one's voice in protest entails a recognition that "invisibility is not a natural state for anyone."[27] Further emphasizing the link between voice and visibility, Gloria Anzaldúa describes the alienated space the female writer of color may find herself in: "Unlikely to be friends of people in high literary places, the beginning woman of color is invisible both in the white male mainstream world and in the white woman's feminist world, though in the latter this is gradually changing. The *lesbian* of color is not only invisible, she doesn't even exist. Our speech, too, is inaudible. We speak in tongues like the outcast and the insane."[28] Visibility and voice become inextricably linked as means of protest and survival. Such strategic demands for visibility evocatively contradict state-sponsored efforts to increase surveillance and control peoples' visibility. Demands for visibility invoke specular morality in part perhaps because the process of making space is at least initially a visual process.

For many contemporary fiction writers as well, issues of visibility remain central motivators because visibility and representation suggest the ideological problematics of colonialism and class stratification. For example, the narrator of Merle Hodge's *Crick Crack Monkey* alludes to the relationship between representation and authority: "Books transported you always into the familiar solidity of chimneys and apple trees, the enviable normality of real Girls and Boys who went a-sleighing and built snowmen, ate potatoes, not rice, went about in socks and shoes from morning until night and called things by their proper names. . . . Books transported you always into Reality and Rightness, which were to be found Abroad."[29] When subsequently asked about this novel, Hodge notes that "we never saw ourselves in a book, so we didn't exist in a kind of way and our culture and our environment, and our climate, the plants around us did not seem real, did not seem to be of any importance."[30]

Like Hodge, Dorothy Allison and Terri de la Peña also draw on their experiences of invisibility. Allison explains that having read widely, she still found no representations that corresponded to her own experience: "I was ashamed of the reflections of me that appeared in most literature. The vast majority of people writing fiction in this country *don't know* what it's like to be trash." Noting that the sheer invisibility of Chicanas in literature partly motivated her turn to writing, de la Peña ruefully comments on her own first novel: "I wrote [*Margins*] because I wanted to read it, because I couldn't find anything like it."[31]

Questions of visibility and invisibility arise as systems of representation align with hegemony to reinforce power structures. In her analysis of the relationship between literary studies and the British rule of India, Gauri Viswanathan argues that literature has been deployed as a means to gain cultural hegemony and deflect representations of colonizers as ruthless and exploitive in order to paint them as descendants of an admirable and knowledgeable race who deserve to conquer and rule. Viswanathan's work suggests that literature works to reify colonial authority.[32] Within the U.S. context, the relationship between literary representations and state power has begun to come under increasing scrutiny. Still, the degree to which (white) middle-class identity is mediated through literature and subsequently sanctioned by the state could bear more examination. It may be that a crucial component to recognizing oneself as middle class includes being able to find one's reflection in literature. Such literary sanctioning may then enable a kind of political and symbolic capital that makes obtaining financial capital and spatial control easier.

It is in these terms of representation as a "political force" that women writers, particularly women of color and white women from the working classes, take up the issue of discursive visibility. As critical legal theorist Kimberlé Crenshaw suggests, "At least one important way social power is mediated in American society is through the contestation between the many narrative structures through which reality might be perceived and talked about."[33] The available narratives, particularly those with the widest circulation, clearly, if sometimes intangibly, have a political impact. The "welfare mother" narrative, for example, continues to be deployed as politically efficacious. In this light, more work needs to be done on the relationship between narratives *about* women of color and the spaces allotted *to* them.

Crenshaw argues that the availability of narratives directly influences the production of civil rights law: "Underlying the legal parameters of racial discrimination are numerous narratives reflecting discrimination as it is experienced by black men, while underlying imagery of gender discrimination incorporates the experiences of white women." The particularities of black female subordination are suppressed as the terms of racial and gender discrimination law require that we mold our experience into that of either white women or black men in order to be legally recognized.[34] Clearly, civil rights law has widely transformed the production of space even as it has failed to eradicate U.S. versions of apartheid and discrimination. So the attention that writers, particularly women of color, have begun to give to issues of visibility and the production of narrative is neither politically naive nor unsubversive.

Narrative invisibility, or as Crenshaw puts it, "a political vacuum of erasure and contradiction,"[35] is largely being combated by the production of new narratives. As de la Peña says, "I didn't *see* myself in literature." She subsequently wrote a novel that textualized an experience similar to hers.[36] Narratives produced by women of color intend, in some sense, to collide with the overdetermined but readily available narratives *about* women of color produced by patriarchal and racist cultural practices that simultaneously invoke these narratives to justify the production of spaces.[37] De la Peña's *Margins,* for example, links visibility to oppression and argues that to fight oppression one must insist on visibility. It also lays out a critique of the spaces Chicana lesbians must negotiate.[38]

*Margins* is set on the west side of L.A., mostly in Santa Monica, a region more typically represented as white and wealthy. De la Peña, in a sense, re-populates Santa Monica with Chicanas and Chicanos. In doing so, she argues for the retextualization of neighborhoods that have survived, however gingerly, freeway construction and gentrification. She also rewrites an L.A. script that usually locates "authentic" Chicanos in East Los Angeles and the San Gabriel Valley. This move disrupts the symbolic system that has obliterated Santa Monica's Chicano/a history. The novel also explores both the production of queer spaces (ranging from texts to bars) and the relative unavailability of these spaces to Chicana lesbians. In this sense, *Margins* clearly reveals a means to remap the terrains of power. "Resistance to oppressors," Norma Alarcón notes, "is in effect resistance to the future as it is represented by them."[39] As *Margins* suggests, resistance writers may need to reclaim the sites of past oppression in order to reimagine a new future.

Yet if de la Peña's novel, like *Crick Crack Monkey* or *Trash*, interrogates the production of the "real" as authorized by textual narratives and promotes visibility as a strategic response to oppression, feminist critics cannot assume that this provides a far-reaching spatial solution. I would contend that visibility is politically powerful. But the emphasis on visibility cannot be seen as completely distinct from the ocular/spatial practices currently utilized by governments and corporations. Put another way, gaining access to new narratives, while empowering, can only be one step in the process of rebuilding what Audre Lorde refers to as "psychic landscapes."[40] Indeed, narrative and activist visibility may force reconceptualizations of people of color or activist communities and may in that sense succeed in redirecting symbolic capital. Redirection of such capital may be empowering, or it may just result in further commodification both of the texts and bodies of people of color in a marketplace that constantly seeks new and exotic others for fetishizing. Additionally, naively celebrating visibility may serve to direct attention away from the currently oppressive uses to which federal and local police agencies are putting it, because here social power is clearly being constructed in such a way as to promote the assumption that no space goes unsurveyed, and hence nobody goes unnoticed.

My point, then, in bringing together the ocular/spatial practices of the drug wars and invisibility/visibility as a charged political trope is to suggest the various disjunctures existing within the same framework. The drug wars define and produce space in such a way as to enhance a bodily visibility that mystifies, even makes invisible, particular subjectivities and refuses difference. Such a production of visibility stands in compelling contrast to the demands for visibility by various activist communities. These demands tend to distance themselves from the productive uses to which state power puts surveillance. At the same time they seem to long for the academy/state sanctioned power that narrative visibility may provide. What I find missing in so many of the celebrations of visibility is a careful critique of the uses to which literature/narrative visibility has been put by the state and its disciplinary apparatuses like the academy. Too quickly new texts (including film, rap, novels, and zines), as oppositional as their narratives may intend to be, are recuperated and reinscribed within capitalism's machine for producing marketable, consumable otherness. The production of queer spaces, often a hallmark of visibility activists, poses no radical possibilities for social transformation if such visibility and attending spaces merely reify existing power structures.

A feminist critique of the production of space holds out the enticing possibility of crossing disciplinary boundaries and also utilizing them in order to critique and change the direction of social power that, in Cindi Katz's words, "is reflected in and exercised through the production and control of space."[41] Understanding the multiple ocular/spatial functions of surveillance networks as operating alongside, and perhaps enabled by, the contemporary claims for visibility that deny connections to surveillance systems may be one way to intervene in the continuing production of oppression via the concretizing of difference. A transformed, antidisciplinary feminism that attends to both the space-making practices of public policy and the too easily utopian claims of visibility activists might finally begin to remap the terrains of power.

## NOTES

1. I would especially like to thank Ann Brigham, Alycee Lane, and Sonnet Retman for their comments and assistance with earlier drafts of this essay. The Livia Léon Montiel quote is part of her *testimonio* in *Songs My Mother Sang to Me: An Oral History of Mexican-American Women,* ed. Patricia Preciado Martin (Tucson: University of Arizona Press, 1992).

2. Ibid., 23.

3. Cindi Katz, "Growing Girls/Closing Circles: Limits on the Spaces of Knowing in Rural Sudan and US Cities," in *Geography of the Life Course,* ed. Janice Monk and Cindi Katz (New York: Routledge, 1993), 88.

4. A brief list of anthologies would include those published by Norton, Harper, and Heath. Similarly, major literary histories, including the *Columbia History of American Literature,* the *Columbia History of the American Novel,* and the *Cambridge History of American Literature* (edited by Sacvan Berkovitch), implicitly rely on this geographical narrative to sustain their literary narratives.

5. Spatial studies have been flourishing in multiple fields, though possibly geography and urban planning have done the most to call attention to spatial issues. In any case, spatial studies have largely concentrated on what could be called "class issues" or "gender issues" to the detriment of an analysis that also incorporates race and sexuality as space-making categories. Although I could point to any number of works where an analysis of race, as well as class, for example, would have transformed the project, it might be more productive to point to some essays where such analysis is being usefully carried out. For example, Norma Alarcón discusses the relationship between geopolitical locations, race, gender, and representation in "Anzaldúa's *Frontera:* Inscribing Gynetics," in *Displacement, Diaspora and Geographies of Identity,* ed. Smadar Lavie and Pat Swedenborg (Durham, N.C.: Duke University Press, 1993). José Saldívar's "Américo Paredes and Decolonization," in *Cultures of United States Imperialism,* ed. Amy Kaplan and Donald Pease (Durham, N.C.: Duke University Press, 1993), 292–311, provides a suggestive dis-

cussion of the dimensions of racial politics and the construction of the U.S.-Mexico border. See also Richard Thompson Ford, "The Boundaries of Race: Political Geography in Legal Analysis," *Harvard Law Review* 107 (1994): 1841–1921.

6. Kimberlé Crenshaw, "Whose Story Is It, Anyway? Feminist and Antiracist Appropriations of Anita Hill," in *Race-ing Justice, En-gendering Power,* ed. Toni Morrison (New York: Pantheon, 1992), 402–40; Chela Sandoval, "U.S. Third World Feminism: The Theory and Method of Oppositional Consciousness in the Postmodern World," *Genders* 10 (Spring 1991): 1–25.

7. Jenny Sharpe, *Allegories of Empire: The Figure of Woman in the Colonial Text* (Minneapolis: University of Minnesota Press, 1993), 29.

8. Elsa Barkley Brown, Presentation at University of California Humanities Research Institute, Irvine, California (Spring 1994).

9. For useful critiques of academic knowledge production as a disciplinary practice, see Ali Behdad, "Traveling to Teach: Third-World Critics in the American Academy," in *Race, Identity, and Representation in Education,* ed. Warren Crichlow and Cameron McCarthy (New York: Routledge, 1992); and Edward Said, "Orientalism Reconsidered," in *Literature, Politics and Theory,* ed. Francis Barker et al. (London: Methuen, 1986), 210–29.

10. Sharpe, *Allegories of Empire,* 29, 19.

11. Judith Butler, *Bodies That Matter: On the Discursive Limits of "Sex"* (New York: Routledge, 1993), suggests a way to think past the material/discursive binary. Instead of a radical constructivist position, she proposes "the notion of matter, not as site or surface, but as *a process of materialization that stabilizes over time to produce the effect of boundary, fixity, and surface*" (9). Such a contention enables her later question, "What does it mean to have recourse to materiality, since it is clear from the start that matter has a history (indeed, more than one) and that the history of matter is in part determined by the negotiation of sexual difference?" (29). Thus, no radical disjuncture can be found between the discursive and the material—in some sense they realize each other. It might also be useful to begin to think about the questions of materiality and discursivity along the lines of Donna Haraway's theoretics. In other words, to begin to ask what *counts* as material or discursive, when, and why.

12. Martin Jay, "Scopic Regimes of Modernity," in *Vision and Visuality,* ed. Hal Foster (Seattle: Bay Press, 1988), 3–23. The specular moralities to which I am referring are mostly those initiated in part by Cartesian perspectivalism. Although postmodernism has by and large disrupted the grip of this particular scopic regime, I would argue that it remains a force, particularly in terms of police-state surveillance networks.

13. For a useful survey of contemporary feminist concerns both inside and outside the academy, see Johanna Brenner, "The Best of Times, The Worst of Times: US Feminism Today," *New Left Review* 200 (July-August 1993): 101–59. I'd like to thank Laura Pérez for bringing this essay to my attention.

14. Nigel Brooks, "The Revenue Nose," *Customs Today* 27 (Summer 1992), 18.

15. See, for example, *Guide for the Inspection and Processing of Citizens and Aliens by Officers Designated as Immigration Officers* (Washington, D.C.: U.S. Department of Justice,

Immigration and Naturalization Service, 1982) and *Immigration Detention Officer Handbook* (Washington, D.C.: U.S. Department of Justice, Immigration and Naturalization Service, 1987). See also any of a number of U.S. government-supplied drug interdiction flyers distributed to the public.

16. Like most of the authors in *Customs Today,* Hart feels no responsibility to verify that Asians and Asian Americans, specifically the Chinese, are actively involved with the heroin trade. M. Cordell Hart, "Chinese Organized Crime and Drug Smuggling: The Newest Threat," *Customs Today* 24 (1989): 39. But Ian Dobinson disputes U.S. government assertions that large "ethnic" syndicates control or direct heroin trade. Ian Dobinson, "Pinning a Tail on the Dragon: The Chinese and the International Heroin Trade," *Crime and Delinquency* 39 (July 1993), 373.

17. For a compelling discussion of early journalistic deployments and developments of racist stereotypes of the "inscrutable Oriental," see Rachel Lee's "Journalistic Representations of Asian Americans and Literary Responses from 1910–20," in *An Interethnic Companion to Asian American Literature in English,* ed. King-Kok Cheung (New York: Cambridge University Press, 1996).

18. Mike Davis, "Uprising and Repression in L.A.," in *Reading Rodney King/Reading Urban Uprising,* ed. Robert Gooding-Williams (New York: Routledge, 1993).

19. Charles Murray, "Drug Free-Zones," *Current* 326 (October 1990): 23–24. That such depictions and attitudes display themselves in drug arrest situations ought to be no surprise. My thanks to Mike Murashige for directing me to this essay.

20. William Chambliss, for example, documents one such scene: "While the suspect is being questioned one policeman says: 'I should kick your little Black ass right here for dealing that shit. You are a worthless little scumbag, do you realize that?' Another officer asks: 'What is your mother's name, son? My mistake . . . she is probably a whore and you are just a ghetto bastard. Am I right?' " William Chambliss, "Don't Confuse Me With Facts: Clinton 'Just Says No,' " *New Left Review* 204 (March-April 1994): 118.

21. Chambliss, "Don't Confuse Me," 114.

22. The significance of enemies fueling funding is all too well illustrated in Iowa Sen. Tom Harkin's modified budget amendment, which transferred defense funding to law enforcement under the telling slogan "From Star Wars to Drug Wars." Harkin's amendment was modified and endorsed by a huge number of "liberal" Democrats, including Pennsylvania's Harris Wolford. See *Congressional Quarterly* for March 22, 1994, pp. S3423ff.

23. Cheryl Harris, "Whiteness as Property," *Harvard Law Review* 106 (1993): 1709–91, suggests a useful point of entry. Harris discusses the rhetorical and cultural tropes that promote a notion of whiteness as a legalized form of property to which one may make a claim, and which one may protect. The relative disproportion of arrests of white drug users suggests another way in which whiteness protects a person from forced entry into the criminal justice system.

24. Rosa Del Olmo, "The Geopolitics of Narcotrafficking in Latin American," *Social Justice* 20 (Fall-Winter 1993): 5.

25. Ronald Brownstein, "Federal Crime Bill Swells With a Spending Bonanza," *Los Angeles Times* (May 1, 1994): A1.

26. Butler, *Bodies That Matter,* 20.

27. Mitsuye Yamada, in *This Bridge Called My Back: Writings by Radical Women of Color,* 2d ed., ed. Cherrí Moraga and Gloria Anzaldúa (New York: Kitchen Table/Women of Color Press, [1981] 1983), 40.

28. Gloria Anzaldúa, "Speaking in Tongues: A Letter to Third World Writers," in *This Bridge Called My Back,* ed. Moraga and Anzaldúa, 165.

29. Merle Hodge, *Crick Crack Monkey* (London: Heinemann, 1970), 61.

30. Simon Gikandi, "Narration in the Post-Colonial Moment: Merle Hodge's *Crick Crack Monkey,*" *Ariel* 20 (October 1989): 19.

31. Dorothy Allison and Terri de la Peña, quoted in Kate Brandt, *Happy Endings: Lesbian Writers Talk About Their Lives and Work* (Tallahassee, Fla.: Naiad Press, 1993): 11–12, 244.

32. Gauri Viswanathan, *Masks of Conquest: Literary Study and British Rule in India* (New York: Columbia University Press, 1989).

33. Crenshaw, "Whose Story Is It," 403, 404.

34. Ibid., 404.

35. Ibid., 403.

36. Personal communication, April 29, 1992.

37. For a different and provocative perspective on visibility, see Lisa Walker, "How to Recognize a Lesbian: The Cultural Politics of Looking Like What You Are," *Signs* 18 (1993): 866–90.

38. Terri de la Peña, *Margins* (Seattle: Seal Press, 1992).

39. Norma Alarcón, "What Kind of Lover Have You Made Me Mother?: Towards a Theory of Chicanas' Feminism and Cultural Identity Through Poetry," in *Women of Color: Perspectives on Feminism and Identity,* ed. Audrey McCluskey (Bloomington: Indiana University, Women's Studies Program Occasional Papers Series, 1985), 93.

40. Audre Lorde, quoted in Katie King, "Audre Lorde's 'Lacquered Layerings': The Lesbian Bar as a Site of Literacy Production," in *New Lesbian Criticism,* ed. Sally Munt (New York: Columbia University Press, 1992): 51–74.

41. Katz, "Growing Girls," 88.

JOAN B. LANDES

10

# bodies in democratic public space
## *an eighteenth-century perspective*

From the outset during the revolutions of
the eighteenth century, modern democracy produced a discourse
and a practice of gender difference even as democrats embraced the
universal principles of human equality and individual freedom. Gender, in turn, was caught in the webs of modern politics, marked by oppositions between individual and community, private and public, particularity and universality. Certainly the struggle for women's rights
was influenced everywhere by specific historical circumstances. Broadly
speaking, however, the relationship between gender and democracy
was in the past and remains today a paradoxical one: the democratization of public life created opportunities for the participation of
women in public life, and in theory democratic ideals posited equality
between the sexes. Yet the democratic tradition has been acutely attentive to the difference between men's and women's bodies and
committed to a division between public and private life in which
women are assigned a domestic rather than a political role.

An investigation of the question of gender and democracy immediately calls forth two (routinely opposed) strains in recent feminist theorizing. On the one hand, there is the feminist/postmodernist
claim of absolute performativity, whereby (to quote Bonnie Honig's
formulation) "nothing is ontologically protected from politicization."[1]
On this view, neither the intimate terrain of private, domestic life nor
even the body—nor, for that matter, the dichotomizing implications
of gender discourse—is free from the risks accompanying action. On
the other hand, the feminist/enlightenment demand for universal rights
and equality reverberates in every struggle for women's rights.[2]

I want to propose, however, that there is value in both postmodernist and enlightenment feminist insights, and that this is best seen once the problem of gender and democracy is situated in relationship to public sphere theory. In this essay I will draw on my previous work on women in the age of the French Revolution in order to highlight how women's participation in (and exclusion from) the new democratic public spaces of the 1790s were bound up intimately with issues of power, interest, discourse, style, and representation.[3] I do not intend to untangle all of the complexities of gendered democracy, although I do hope to identify some of the stakes involved in creating a world in which gender would no longer be a barrier to equality. I ask the reader's forbearance, too, as I juggle historical illustrations alongside arguments from contemporary political and feminist theory.

Having tried and executed the king in January 1793, republican France faced the "metaphoric and material" task of constructing a political body composed of the people, the new democratic sovereign. Significantly, the representatives of the new nation chose to represent the new popular sovereign as a female, Liberty, even as they excluded women from the full rights of citizenship in the new republic. The French were not alone among modern political nations in choosing a female representation of the republic. Elsewhere, too, the choice of a female goddess was dictated by a republican refusal of the taint of absolute monarchy. Yet by representing the nation and its highest values in female form, they risked the possibility that women might enter the new public spaces opened up by revolutionary action or, to paraphrase Linda Orr, that women might give back to Liberty a physical shape, a "social referent" wholly at odds with the abstract, juridical body of the nation.[4] At many points during the revolution, at moments of popular militancy as well as in the everyday course of political club life, women made their claims to citizenship palpable, and various factions of the revolutionary movement at times welcomed women's political participation. Moreover, as a result of revolutionary family legislation, fathers granted autonomy to their children; daughters and sons achieved equal rights of inheritance; and wives as well as husbands were able to sue for divorce. These reforms in the civil law introduced further paradoxes concerning the status of women: a simultaneous increase in civil status and a denial of political rights. Impressed by these circumstances, the historian Lynn Hunt sees the emergence of domestic ideology in France as a political and cultural response to the need to justify systematically the continuing exclusion of women from politics "while they were admitted to many of the legal rights of civil society."[5] Whereas Hunt underscores the powerful role of collective fantasy and the political unconscious in the process of gender exclusion, with good reason she holds out considerable hope for the realization of the democratic potential of liberal theory and politics.

But if the problem of gender and democracy is not intractable, its political consequences bear special consideration. The record of women's rights during the revolution is conditioned by the fact that women never wholly succeeded in undermining the new gendered boundaries of public and private life nor in redressing a central feature of the new polity: the standing of all women (irrespective of class or race) as secondary, passive subjects under law. Though they could not vote or sit as representatives in the assemblies, many women did nonetheless manage to perform the role of citizen, overriding at least temporarily the constraints imposed on their sex by republican morality and laws. Militant women's discordant, egalitarian actions expressed the contingent, fragile, yet expansive possibilities within the political practice of democracy. To that extent, as members of a newly democratic polity, the women's actions during the revolution (like the men's) constantly enlarged and tested the very limits to sovereignty set by the representatives of the nation. Whereas in the past, authority was anchored in god, king, and tradition, democracy established a new source of authority in the republic—what the political theorist Hannah Arendt regards as the specifically political capacity for change: an openness to change, resistance, and creativity.[6] Similarly, Claude Lefort contends that within a democratic polity, "without the actors being aware of it, a process of questioning is implicit in social practice, . . . no one has the answer to the questions that arise, and . . . the work of ideology, which is always dedicated to the task of restoring certainty, cannot put an end to this practice."[7] Thus, Arendt's and Lefort's esteem for democracy and Hunt's appraisal of liberalism are important reminders that whereas the opening of democratic public space in France (like other modern Western societies) was accompanied by a strict partitioning of space into gendered territories, we need to know how in given instances women (and men) responded to the disparities between formal equality and actual discrimination.

A further perspective on the universal promise of democracy derives from Jürgen Habermas's reconstruction of the democratic potential of the liberal public sphere (the sphere of informal civil associations and spaces—cafes, reading societies, museums, concerts, libraries, political clubs and societies, the press, and bookstores), whose principles include equality, accessibility, generality, and critical reason.[8] Habermas conceives of the public as a discursive sphere in which consensus is achieved through a series of speech acts within free, open, uncensored public spaces. Within the region of social discourse, he believes, a public body is created wherein the differential rights of private individuals cease to matter. But here, too, we need to know whether the liberal public sphere affected any lessening of the barriers of gender.

By Habermas's own admission, the eighteenth-century liberal public sphere only partially achieved its stated goals of equality and participation. But he sees this as a limitation of an actually existing society, not of the model of a universal public according to which preexisting social inequalities are bracketed. In practice there are strong requirements for admission to this club as to any other. Even if property does not become a topic for discourse, class position and literacy remain the precondition for participation in the bourgeois public sphere, and during the revolution censorship and political control by the dominant factions worked to undermine earlier-won freedoms.

More generally, because the liberal public sphere and the conditions for publicity presuppose a distinction between public and private matters, Habermas's civic body is ill equipped to consider in public fashion the political dimension of relations in the intimate sphere. Equally disabling is the expectation that all those who engage in public discourse will learn to master the rules of disinterested discourse. Under ideal conditions, then, the members of a theoretical public are to behave according to the bourgeois liberal principle of abstract equality. Just as the laws of the market assume a certain forgetfulness concerning the real existence of property, so too the laws of the public sphere are predicated on the principle of disinterestedness and on the observance of the norms of reason, not power; rationality, not domination; and truth, not authority. Still, Habermas never asks whether certain subjects in bourgeois society are better suited than others to perform the discursive role of participants in a theoretical public.

I have argued elsewhere that Habermas's formulation effaces the ways in which the bourgeois public sphere from the outset has worked to rule out all interests that would not or could not lay claim to their own universality.[9] The notion of an enlightened, theoretical public reduces to "mere opinion" (cultural assumptions, normative attitudes, collective prejudices, and values) a whole range of interests associated with those actors who would not or could not master the discourse of the universal. Moreover, the structural division between the public sphere, on the one hand, and the market and the family, on the other, means that multiple concerns come to be labeled as private and treated as improper subjects for public debate. Habermas overlooks the strong association of women's discourse and their interests with "particularity," and conversely the alignment of masculine speech with truth, objectivity, and reason. Thus he misses the masquerade through which the (male) particular is able to posture behind the veil of the universal.

A question arises as to whether a universalistic discourse model can satisfy conditions of genuine equality. I have suggested that the values of universality and reason are offset by the role they play within a system of Western cultural representation that has eclipsed women's interests in the private domain and aligned femininity with particularity, interest, and partiality. In this context the goals of generalizability and appeals to the common good may conceal rather than expose forms of domination, suppress rather than release concrete differences among persons or groups. Moreover, by banishing the language of particularity, the liberal public sphere jeopardizes its own bases of legitimation in the principles of accessibility, participation, and equality. Style and decorum are not incidental traits but constitutive features of the way in which embodied, speaking subjects establish the claims of the universal in politics. In a contemporary context Jane Mansbridge makes a similar point, observing how styles of deliberation may serve as masks for domination and render mute the claims of members of disadvantaged groups.[10]

It could be said, furthermore, that the representation of power in the democratic public sphere is premised on the fiction of a neutral but embodied (because natural) subject, an individual capable of subjecting passion and interest to the rule of reason. Only men's bodies are deemed to fulfill the ideal requirements of this contained form of subjectivity. In contrast, women seem to inhabit bodies that, rather than guaranteeing their political liberties, are marked by physically distinctive sexualities and irrational, hence apolitical, qualities. Dorinda Outram has argued this point specifically in relation to the French Revolution, stating that "much of the political culture produced by the Revolution was aimed, whether successfully or not, at redistributing various attributes of the king's body throughout the new body politic."[11] Outram maintains that middle-class men created and filled new public spaces with attributes of heroic dignity. "Bodily dignity, as well as political and moral virtue, gave the right to rule" to such men, who sought to remain stoical, self-contained, and dignified even in the face of death.[12] Women, on the other hand, were constrained from achieving the kind of personification based on the successful, public display of physicality because the latter for them always involved potential humiliation. Likewise, women's ideal roles of mother and wife did not conform well to an intense involvement with self nor to a resolutely fixed heroic image of Stoic calm.

Whereas Outram implies that gender roles in modern democratic polities were constructed in such a way as to disadvantage women, Carole Pateman extends the point in *The Sexual Contract*. She posits a gendered body seemingly prior to all social experience. Not unlike Simone de Beauvoir, for whom immanence is a universal condition of femaleness, at least in its threateningly pregnant shape, Pateman sees women's bodies as decidedly different from men's, and at odds therefore with the requirements of individuality in modern contract theory. In contrast to the older, classical patriarchy where the father "denies any procreative ability to women, appropriates their capacity and transforms it into the masculine ability to give political birth," in Pateman's view:

> In modern patriarchy the capacity that 'individuals' lack is politically significant because it represents all that the civil order is not, all that is encapsulated in women and women's bodies. The body of the 'individual' is very different from women's bodies. His body is tightly enclosed within boundaries, but women's bodies are permeable, their contours change shape and they are subject to cyclical processes. All these differences are summed up in the natural bodily process of birth. Physical birth symbolizes everything that makes women incapable of entering the original contract and transforming themselves into the civil individuals who uphold its terms. Women lack neither strength nor ability in a general sense, but, according to the classic contract theorists, they are naturally deficient in a specifically *political* capacity, the capacity to create and maintain political right.[13]

It would seem, on this account, that the problem of women and modernity is not a consequence of the cultural or social exclusions in a society otherwise committed to formal equality. Pateman in particular situates inequality directly on the female body, from which there seems to be no possibility of indifference or escape. She remains deeply skeptical that the principles of universal civic equality can extend to women. For Pateman, "Civil society (as a whole) is patriarchal" and the civil sphere gains its universal meaning in opposition to the private sphere of natural subjection and womanly capacities.[14] I have been arguing, however, that even under conditions of extreme gender dichotomy or denial of formal political rights, women have never been entirely absent from the modern public sphere.[15] Furthermore, inequality is not simply a consequence of any given society's failure to guarantee full participation in the civil and political sphere or to achieve freedom and equality for all its members. We also need to consider how the abstract discourse of universal rights may privilege the traits belonging to certain rights-bearing subjects by illicitly positing only one "particular" subject—typically the male—as the embodiment of universal reason.

The problem of the masculinism of seemingly universal rights is well documented in recent studies of the French Revolution. Especially before the Jacobin repression of October 1793 banning women from club membership, some

women and men demanded political rights for women, and women partici-
pated in the articulate, mobilized citizenry.[16] Militant female citizens demanded
the right to bear arms, in self-defense or against the nation's enemies, and the
right to sanction laws. At times women appeared to exercise the vote, a right
that they formally lacked. For example, during the summer of 1793, when the
constitution was being accepted, large numbers of women from Paris and the
provinces wrote to the Convention that "although the law deprives them of
the precious right of voting for the acceptance of the Constitution," they ad-
here to it.[17] More commonly women joined in collective demonstrations, often
with the application of force; they petitioned the authorities; and they made
their presence known in clubs, section assemblies, popular societies, festivals,
street demonstrations, on bread lines, and at the markets. They frequented the
galleries of the Convention and appeared at revolutionary tribunals and exe-
cutions. The most militant among them practiced a politics of intimidation,
unrelenting surveillance, and control—through either legal or insurrectionary
means. Women also became particularly adept at inciting action through the
use of words. As Dominique Godineau notes, "Women made it their work to
jolt masculine apathy. They took on the role of 'firebrands': 'if they began the
dance, the men would follow.'"[18] As a consequence of these actions, revolutionary women helped to legitimate and dramatically expand the newly
achieved popular sovereignty and to challenge the assignment of women solely
to the private sphere. The full extent of their involvement in the revolutionary
movement is manifested in a series of key episodes: the women's march on Versailles in October 1789, women's participation in armed processions of the
spring and summer 1792, the organized insurgency of women in the Society of
Revolutionary Republican Women in May–October 1793, and women's participation in the opening demonstrations of the insurrections of May 1795.

The meanings of French revolutionary women's actions are emblematic of
democratic theorists Habermas's and Arendt's insistence on the potential of
words to generate power, a potential that needs to be distinguished from either violence or force. Indeed, Arendt locates power not merely in the associational space but also in the competition for excellence that occurs among actors who are by definition moral and political equals.[19] She deems action to be
the only sphere in which individuals may distinguish themselves, even to the
point of "greatness"; they do so through word and deed when they narrate the
distinctive story of their own lives.[20] Through storytelling, men "create their
own remembrance,"[21] and so for Arendt the polis is "a kind of organized remembrance."[22] Paradoxically, however, the greatest female political philosopher
never entertained the idea that women also had stories to tell, actions that

might "create their own remembrance" and work to disrupt the hegemonic, stabilizing discourses of men.

I want to conclude with two such remembrances of women whose stories are intertwined with the history of the revolution, Madame Roland and Charlotte Corday—both self-described revolutionaries, both victims of the Terror, who appear to have gone willingly to their deaths. Although Jean-Marie Roland was later to take his own life upon hearing of his wife's execution in Paris, initially he successfully avoided capture even after being charged with arrest during the crackdown against members of the Girondin circle in the late spring of 1793. Refusing the opportunity to escape with her husband, Madame Roland stayed behind, determined to denounce the illegality of his arrest by addressing the Convention on his behalf. She may have been animated by her success of the preceding December, when she had cleared her name and won public applause before the bar of the Convention, where she had been summoned to answer charges of participation in a royalist conspiracy. Still, it is surprising that Madame Roland would opt for another such public appearance, as even in the regular meetings of the Girondin, which took place at her home in the years 1791–93, she had gone to great lengths to avoid any participation in the discussions. In marked contrast to the *salonnières* of earlier decades, she seated herself apart. Preoccupied with sewing or writing letters but nonetheless alert to all that was said, she remained silent, offering these men a forum in which to speak without the intrusions of a female voice.[23] Yet her struggles for virtuous self-control even in the private sphere, though they may have won her respect among this close circle of men, did not protect her from public calumny. She remained the special object of abuse by members of the increasingly influential Montagnard faction and especially Jean-Paul Marat, who likened her in his popular sheet *L'Ami du Peuple* to Lucrezia Borgia, the female poisoners Brinvilliers and Voisin, and the hated Marie Antoinette herself.

Given how jealously Madame Roland had guarded her carefully fashioned private role of virtuous femininity, her determination in a moment of crisis to address the Convention once again was doubly risky: she was placing not only her life at stake but also her reputation, in that a public appearance might work to confirm rather than dispel Marat's accusation of her scheming political nature. As it turned out, Roland never had a chance to address the Convention, whose session had adjourned under pressure from the Commune. Instead of seeking shelter with a friend, she chose to return home, where she was arrested. As she explained in her *Memoirs,* "she had a naturally strong aversion for anything inconsistent with a straightforward course of action. To escape from injustice would have cost her greater effort than to face it squarely."[24] She may also have held out hope that in the unlikely event of her own arrest and trial (as were to happen), she would win a reprieve from the Revolutionary Tribunal, which until then, she believed, had only guillotined enemies of the revolution.

In the end it was her willingness to die in the name of the principles of the revolution that elevated Madame Roland's place in history. On her ride to the scaffold, she is famously reported to have cried, "Oh liberty, what crimes are committed in your name!" Yet even these apocryphal words might not have been uttered had she persisted in her conviction to take a lethal quantity of opium or starve herself to death in her prison cell. Instead she was persuaded by her friend Louis-Guillaume Bosc to go through with the actual execution as an example of political rectitude to the rest of the nation. On his advice she chose the path of martyrdom, and according to Dorinda Outram, in death she succeeded in transcending the potential humiliation that plagued her and other women who would display their physicality within the public realm. Even more than her friends who did take their own lives in hiding from the Terror, Madame Roland's "achievement of execution . . . point[ed] up her capacity to use more than one register of a heroic role, and to amalgamate in herself the totality of those potential roles, just as she could amalgamate within herself both chastity and unchastity. In reconciling the disparate elements of her physical self-consciousness, Mme Roland succeeded in becoming a heroine at last . . . [and] to attract a mythology and historical attention out of all proportion to her actual influence on events."[25]

Charlotte Corday's assassination of Jean-Paul Marat inspired a veritable cult around her by Catholic antirepublicans and aroused deep contempt among revolutionaries for Corday in particular and for public women in general. But her reputation goes beyond this deed and also rests on her execution in 1793, which immediately fostered a myth. Against the protestations of eyewitness medical men, it was reported that the executioner's assistant held up and slapped Charlotte Corday's severed head before an assembled crowd of the people. According to Daniel Arasse, "When he slapped, it appeared to blush at the indignity. A scandal erupted. Public anger led to a similar response at the highest level. The inhumanity of the act, and the lack of respect shown to the victim contributed to the indignation, but Corday's reddening cheeks did much to diminish people's confidence in the humane efficiency of the machine," that is, of the guillotine, whose legitimacy was based on the assumption that it was a more humane method of execution than had been practiced under the old regime; its supporters claimed that once the blade fell, death was instantaneous. The horror thus produced, Arasse explains, was the "guillotine's monstrous creation, a head that can think without a body, but think, or so we might suppose, one thought only, 'I think, but I am not.' "[26]

It is of more than passing interest that the blush of this young virgin's dead head was an important source of the wreckage wrought upon what Arasse terms the enlightened philosophic machine of the guillotine. It was, as well, a wellspring "of all the concern which the guillotine aroused in the middle class about physical invasion and shame. Nor [is it accidental] that the authorities should have tried to discredit ... Corday's claim to virginity in an attempt to destroy her capacity to represent these concerns." As Dorinda Outram points out, "In actual form the story is also a parallel ... to the classical legend beloved of the middle class (the severed head of Medusa, still active after death, causing consternation to all who see it)."[27] Whatever irrational and mythical excesses attached to her action, Corday herself drew upon a very bourgeois concept of heroic Stoicism. Like Madame Roland, and even more so her male contemporaries, she was a careful reader of Plutarch's *Lives*, an admirer of Brutus and Cato, who had sacrificed personal emotions and ties in order to achieve political actions on behalf of the Republic. Marat's supporters portrayed Corday as a deceptive female. (Her letter of supplication, which gained her entrance to Marat, appears in David's famous homage to the politician, although Corday herself is absent from this representation.) Yet Corday drew upon a very bourgeois, masculine version of public virtue—heroic Stoicism—and not on traditionally feminine feelings of sensibility.

Of course, neither of these women escaped being tarred by their humiliating association with the grotesqueness, immorality, and indecency of public women. Nor was either woman's body ever a site of indifference—in Corday's case the special mark of femaleness, a blush, was said to repel even the moment of physical death. And in each case their movements, posture, and actions—even at the zero point of all public spaces, that of public execution—generated their own forms of authority. Despite the pull of competing representations of femininity to which each subscribed and were equally subject, both Corday and Roland struggled to achieve a kind of heroic death modeled on masculine virtue. In doing so, they aimed to reconcile the opposing roles available to virtuous men and women and to find an honorable path to public action as women.

These examples are at best extreme illustrations of the way female bodies are marked. At the same time they remind us of the strategies by which individual subjects attempt, through words and actions, to resist this marking even under the direst circumstances and thereby to author their own stories, which, in Arendt's sense, are the very stuff of public life. More generally, a cursory consideration of the democratic public sphere of revolutionary France illustrates the extent to which, through their gendered performances of citizenship, women made use of the language of universal rights and sometimes managed to disturb the categories of truth and nature to which masculine privileges were anchored.

## NOTES

1. Bonnie Honig, "Toward an Agonistic Feminism: Hannah Arendt and the Politics of Identity," in *Feminists Theorize the Political,* ed. Judith Butler and Joan W. Scott (New York: Routledge, 1992), 225.

2. For the purpose of contrast and in order to underscore its historical indebtedness to enlightenment strains of feminism, I term this second position "feminist/enlightenment." However, I respectfully follow Seyla Benhabib—one of today's most persuasive feminist theorists of universalism—who underscores the difference between her own position and earlier formulations. She argues that "a post-Enlightenment defense of universalism, without metaphysical props and historical conceits is still viable. Such universalism would be interactive not legislative, cognizant of gender difference not gender blind, contextually sensitive and not situation indifferent." Seyla Benhabib, *Situating the Self: Gender, Community and Postmodernism in Contemporary Ethics* (New York: Routledge, 1992), 3.

3. Joan B. Landes, *Women and the Public Sphere in the Age of the French Revolution* (Ithaca, N.Y.: Cornell University Press, 1988), and "Jürgen Habermas: The Structural Transformation of the Public Sphere: A Feminist Inquiry," *Praxis International* XII, no. 1 (April 1992): 106–27.

4. Linda Orr, *Headless History: Nineteenth-Century French Historiography of the Revolution* (Ithaca, N.Y.: Cornell University Press, 1990), 16.

5. Lynn A. Hunt, *The Family Romance of the French Revolution* (Berkeley: University of California Press, 1992), 202–3.

6. See, for example, Hannah Arendt, *On Revolution* (New York: Viking Press, [1963], 1965). Bonnie Honig, cited above, offers an insightful reading of the performative dimension of Arendt's theory of politics.

7. Claude Lefort, *Democracy and Political Theory* (Cambridge, U.K.: Polity Press in association with Basil Blackwell, 1988), 19.

8. Jürgen Habermas, *The Structural Transformation of the Public Sphere: An Inquiry into a Category of Bourgeois Society,* trans. Thomas Burger with the assistance of Frederick Lawrence (Cambridge, Mass.: MIT Press, [1962], 1989).

9. Joan B. Landes, "Jürgen Habermas."

10. Jane Mansbridge, "Feminism and Democracy," *The American Prospect* 1 (Spring 1990): 126–39.

11. Dorinda Outram, *The Body and the French Revolution: Sex, Class and Political Cul-*

*ture* (New Haven, Conn.: Yale University Press, 1989), 4. Lynn Hunt clarifies another dimension of this matter, asking: "Where was the new center of society, and how could it be represented? Should there even be a center, much less a sacred one? Could the new democratic Nation be located in any institution or any means of representation? . . . French revolutionaries did not just seek another representation of authority, a replacement for the king, but rather came to question the very act of representation itself." Hunt, *Politics, Culture, and Class in the French Revolution* (Berkeley: University of California Press, 1984), 88.

12. Outram, *Body and the French Revolution*, 121–23.

13. Carole Pateman, *The Sexual Contract* (Stanford, Cal.: Stanford University Press, 1988), 96.

14. Indeed, she insists that "liberty and equality appear as universal ideals, rather than the natural attributes of the men (the brothers) who create the social order within which the ideals are given social expression, only because the civil sphere is conventionally considered on its own. Liberty, equality *and* fraternity form the revolutionary trilogy because liberty and equality are the attributes of the fraternity who exercise the law of male sex-right. What better notion to conjure with than that 'fraternity' is universal and nothing more than a metaphor for community" (Ibid., 113–14).

15. Mary P. Ryan, *Women in Public: Between Banners and Ballots, 1825–1880* (Baltimore: Johns Hopkins University Press, 1990), makes a similar point regarding women's presence both as symbols and actors in the North American context.

16. Darline G. Levy and Harriet B. Applewhite, "Women, Radicalization, and the Fall of the French Monarchy," in *Women and Politics in the Age of the Democratic Revolution,* ed. Levy and Applewhite (Ann Arbor: University of Michigan Press, 1990), 81–107; Levy and Applewhite, "Women and Militant Citizenship in Revolutionary Paris," in *Rebel Daughters: Women and the French Revolution,* ed. Sara E. Melzer and Leslie W. Rabine (New York: Oxford University Press, 1992); Dorinda Outram, "Le langage mâle de la vertu: Women and the discourse of the French Revolution," in *The Social History of Language,* ed. Peter Burke and Roy Porter (Cambridge: Cambridge University Press, 1987), 120–35.

17. Dominique Godineau, "Masculine and Feminine Political Practice during the French Revolution," in Levy and Applewhite, *Women and Politics,* 69.

18. Ibid., 75.

19. Arendt seems to take for granted the conditions of slavery, labor, and gender division of labor, which are the basis for the equality between free propertied male subjects in the sphere of the polis. On Arendt's antimodernism, see Hanna Pitkin, "Justice: On Relating Public and Private," *Political Theory* 9, no. 3 (1981), 327–52; Seyla Benhabib, *The Reluctant Modernism of Hannah Arendt* (Thousand Oaks, Cal., Sage Publications, 1996); George Kateb, *Hannah Arendt: Politics, Conscience, Evil* (Totowa, N.J.: Rowman and Allanheld, 1983).

20. "Action can be judged only by the criterion of greatness because it is in its nature to break through the commonly accepted and reach into the extraordinary, where whatever is true in common and everyday life no longer applies because everything that

exists is unique and sui generis." Arendt, *The Human Condition* (New York: Doubleday, [1958], 1959), 205.

21. Ibid., 208. On storytelling, see Melvyn A. Hill, "The Fictions of Mankind and the Stories of Men," in *Hannah Arendt: The Recovery of the Public World*, ed. Melvyn A. Hill (New York: St. Martin's Press, 1979); Elisabeth Young Bruehl, "Hannah Arendt's Storytelling," *Social Research* 44, no. 1 (Spring 1977), 183–90; Seyla Benhabib, "Models of Public Space: Hannah Arendt, the Liberal Tradition and Jürgen Habermas," in *Habermas and the Public Sphere*, ed. Craig J. Calhoun (Cambridge, Mass.: MIT Press, 1992).

22. "It assures the mortal actor the reality that comes from being seen, being heard, and, generally, appearing before an audience of fellow men, who outside the *polis* could attend only the short duration of the performance and therefore needed Homer and 'others of his craft' in order to be presented to those who were not there." Arendt, *The Human Condition*, 198.

23. As Dorinda Outram observes, "Mme Roland's continual emphasis in her *Mémoires* [composed entirely in prison during the months before her execution] on her private, domestic, solitary life, even during Roland's two ministries, come straight out of her efficient internalization of the idea that women can only have a public existence in as much as they wield corrupt power. When she was finally arrested and imprisoned in Sainte-Pélagie, she found with a degree of shock explicable only on those lines, that the authorities had taken little care to segregate her from the ladies of easy virtue (revealing phrase) also held within its walls." Outram, *Body and the French Revolution*, 147. In the following remarks, I am greatly indebted to Outram for her discussions of both Roland and Corday from the perspective of heroic stoicism and the female body. For further amplification of some of these issues, see the excellent account of Roland's life by Gita May, *Madame Roland and the Age of Revolution* (New York: Columbia University Press, 1970).

24. May, *Madame Roland*, 259.

25. Outram, *Body and the French Revolution*, 149.

26. Daniel Arasse, *The Guillotine and the Terror* (London: Penguin, 1989), 37–38, 39.

27. Outram, *Body and the French Revolution*, 121, 63.

11

# sightings, sites, and speech
# in women's construction of a
# nationalist voice in tanzania

> We were furious when the Government said that we could
> not wear *sare* [matching cloths, as uniforms] the day Mwa-
> limu [Julius Nyerere] returned from UNO. He pacified us
> by telling us that the *buibui* [full-length black garment worn
> by Muslim women as head-to-foot covering] we had put on
> for the occasion was a uniform itself.[1]

During a brief period in the 1950s (1955–
59), women in the British Trust Territory of Tanganyika, and especially
Muslim women in Dar es Salaam, the capital, and in other urban centers, claimed a place and a voice at the public sites of speech created
in a historic moment of anticolonial nationalist movement. In so doing, they positioned themselves physically and vocally as a community
to be seen and heard, constructing themselves as conscious political
actors and shaping major aspects of what would become Tanzania's
particular form of nationalism. I cannot say that their voices and actions permanently transformed Tanzanian gender relations; nor did
their construction and expressions of nationalism ensure gender
equity in the "postcolonial" state. But to dismiss their voices and actions as insufficiently transformative or radical to warrant attention is
to reinscribe their absence from the meta-narrative of Tanzanian nationalism and from Tanzania's historical record.

Attending to the voices, actions, and presence of predominantly

Muslim, predominantly illiterate female Tanganyikan nationalists of the 1950s requires complicating, and in some cases rejecting, a number of current scholarly, including feminist, theoretical generalizations and understandings. Few of us would carelessly project onto *all* women of the 1950s a characterization based on our understanding of U.S. middle-class white women during that decade. By the same token, we have been alerted to the distortion produced when Muslim women are stereotyped as everywhere and always passive, confined, and oppressed. Yet new theoretical tendencies toward universalization and ahistorical generalization about women seem to emerge as quickly as the old ones are challenged and discredited.

Theories and generalizations involving the relationship between women and nationalism are, not surprisingly, of particular concern to me. Recognizing that I am overgeneralizing to make a point, I see recent studies of women's relationship to nationalism and nationalist movements falling into three categories.[2] The first identifies women as primary and particular victims of "nationalistic" excess (especially rape).[3] In its recent formulation and incarnation (roughly, since the breakup of eastern Europe and the Soviet Union beginning in 1989), this focus responds to the current tendency to characterize all extremist political conflict and rhetoric, including "ethnic cleansing" and civil warfare, as "nationalism," and nationalism therefore, by definition, as reactionary and evil.[4]

A second and more theoretically au courant approach emphasizes the historical as well as contemporary use of "woman" as objectified symbol or icon of the masculinist, modernist nation.[5] One debate about representations of women and their relationship to constructions of nationalist gender ideology centers on the extent to which women in different social and political settings have used and/or internalized such representations to defend their interests or advance their own political and other purposes.[6]

A third approach—one seemingly closest to my own—seeks to analyze and explain women's historical *participation in* nationalist movements. In recent formulations of non-European nationalisms, where nationalism and modernization are closely associated if not conflated, emergent groups identified as "middle class" and Western educated—invariably small and vulnerable subsets of women—are most frequently associated with the nationalist movements of their respective countries.[7] Sometimes, notably in the important work of Partha Chatterjee, the "representationist" and "participationist" approaches are combined in analyses that relate the necessity for (in this case Indian) women to represent *and* maintain something called "traditional (specifically Hindu) culture" in the face of vituperative Western attacks and the modernizing, civilizing performance of this nationalist function by middle-class Indian women.[8] How-ever, with few but significant exceptions, when women are identified as partici-pants in nationalist movements, they are portrayed as mobilized, if not co-opted, by male leaders and creators of particular nationalist movements, who are in turn often (if unintentionally) portrayed as ciphers for hegemonic West-ern nationalist thought via the colonial experience.[9]

Each of these approaches is theoretically distinctive and each draws on nationalist stories and histories best suited to a particular thesis about the relationship between women and nationalism. What these approaches have in common, however, is also striking. The first formulation of woman's relationship to nationalism stresses her dehumanized and helpless (material) embodiment; the second, her dehumanized (iconic) transcendence. In the third formulation, "real" women receive attention; but they are women who are "drawn in" to nationalist struggle by men, or they are inevitable products, not shapers, of nationalist thought and movement.

Writing on "woman" as absence, marker, and body is, at present, theoreti-cally sexier than writing about women as presence, actors, and bodies. And given the current scholarly criticism of white Western feminists' "positionality," privilege, and "power" vis-à-vis (other) women (i.e., women who are not us) as an end in itself, it is a lot safer.[10] What, then, can I say about the women who proudly claim to have created a nationalist movement in Tanganyika in the 1950s—a movement in which women were neither raped nor elevated/mar-ginalized to the status of nationalist symbol, and which, at least in its formative years, did not involve significant participation by middle-class women? Posed in this way, the dilemma is similar to that identified by Margaret Somers, who notes that a hegemonic "theoretical schema of class formation" has required for its maintenance rejecting as "deviant" all workers who did not replicate the particular form of revolutionary behavior predicted by the theory.[11] In other words, a theory of the relationship between women and nationalism, and espe-cially a feminist theory of that relationship, that identifies women *and* national-ism only in places and historical contexts that confirm current theoretical formulations must define as deviant both the Muslim nationalist women of Tan-ganyika and the country's nationalist history.

But if the dilemma strikes me as similar, so too does Somers's "way out." Somers charts this exit via her concept of "social narrativity." She writes:

> Above all [social] narratives are constellations of *relationships* (con-nected parts) embedded in *time and space,* constituted by what I call *causal emplotment.* Unlike the attempt to explain a single event by

placing it in a specified category, narrativity precludes sense-making of a singular isolated phenomenon. Narrativity demands that we discern the meaning of any single event only in temporal and spatial relationship to other events. Indeed, the chief characteristic of narrative is that it renders understanding only by *connecting* (however unstable) *parts* to a constructed *configuration* or a *social network* (however incoherent or unrealizable). In this respect, narrative becomes an epistemological category.[12] (Emphasis in original)

In the remainder of this essay, I want to plot the connecting and connected social narrative of Tanganyikan nationalist women into the history of what was then Britain's underdeveloped (by its own neglect) "trust" territory. This narrative, which establishes the presence, actions, and voice of women, is, of course, circumscribed by and embedded in the larger one, which must, therefore, be sketched in outline form.

The aftermath of World War II in Tanganyika, as in much of colonized Africa, was characterized by a crisis in European colonial rule, both for colonial administrators on site and for the governments of the various metropoles. On the one hand, there was increasingly criticism of imperial rule from within the metropoles; on the other, an increasing determination to hang on to power by making colonies pay for themselves. In the case of Tanganyika, always a lesser trinket (a U.N. Trust Territory, not a "real" colony) on Britain's imperial charm bracelet, making the territory pay for itself meant imposing increasingly harsh agricultural regulations and controls, initiating large and, as it turned out, ill-designed schemes to increase cash crop production for export, and attempting to modernize the mechanisms of indirect rule through appointed chiefs and councils in order to dress continuing colonial overrule in more acceptable garb.

Not surprisingly, however, the postwar period was not simply a time of ferment and crisis of confidence for the colonizers; it was a time of increasing anticolonial discontent and growing self-confidence on the part of the colonized. By the early 1950s these dialectical forces had opened up an unsettled and ambiguous space—a space that the Tanganyika African National Union (TANU) founder and future president, Julius Nyerere, marked and claimed for but did not (indeed, could not) fill with nationalist politics in 1954.

It is important to understand that the space opened up for nationalist activity was new, relatively undefined, and hence very much under construction at the point of women's occupation. Nyerere's role as an astute, thoughtful, Western-educated leader was crucial to the formulation of Tanganyika's nationalist ideology. But as Benedict Anderson reminds us, ideologies do not *cre-*

*ate* nationalism, nor can they fill existing political spaces with nationalism. That is, nationalism has never simply been about "self-consciously held political ideologies" but has necessarily involved "the large cultural systems that preceded it, out of which—as well as against which—it came into being."[13] Referring specifically to Tanganyika's nationalist origins, historian John Iliffe notes, "No state—especially no colonial state—creates a nation. A state creates subjects. The subjects create the nation and they bring into the process the whole of their historical experience."[14]

The social narrative (i.e., "constellations of relationships embedded in time and space") of urban, predominantly Muslim women drew on a "large cultural system" and "historical experience" shaping Tanganyikan nationalism in particular and extremely important ways. I came to my own understanding of this narrative in the process of modified and directed life history interviews with more than eighty TANU women activists, conducted in Tanzania in 1984, 1988, and 1992.[15]

Where does the women's narrative begin? In a very real sense, Muslim women's initial recognition as a *significant* presence in Tanganyika's nationalist political space was an accident of history, achieved less by their occupation of a particular site than by their "sighting" in that space. As the statement by Halima Hamisi that begins this essay reveals, the *buibui* worn to express the modesty of the Muslim wearer under "normal" circumstances could also serve as a "uniform" when worn by women acting collectively and in unison.

Nearly all accounts of women's nationalist participation in Tanganyika begin, and many end, with a reference to John Hatch, then Commonwealth officer of the British Labour Party, whose "where are the women?" query to TANU's all-male Central Committee in June 1955 is widely understood to have, in effect, caused the formation of a TANU Women's Section almost overnight. At that time Hatch was touring "British Africa" on behalf of his party, which was sympathetic to African nationalist aspirations and anxious to play a major role in an orderly decolonization process. Asked by TANU officers who thought (rightly) that his appearance would lend legitimacy to the party, Hatch agreed to address a TANU meeting in Dar es Salaam on June 1 and was impressed to find an attentive and enthusiastic crowd of some 15,000 to 40,000 persons gathered at Mnazi Moja, an open, parklike plaza in central Dar es Salaam.[16] He was particularly surprised to see "several rows of black-veiled Muslim women" within the "vast sea of dusky faces and white clothes."[17] When the rally was over and he met with an all-male group of TANU Central Committee members, Hatch "happened to mention the lack of women members of TANU, a universal weakness of all African nationalist parties in their early years."[18] When the committee members responded disingenuously that they had a "women's section,"[19] Hatch replied that he would like to meet its leaders.

Were I to limit my discussion of women's participation in the nationalist movement to John Hatch's reconstruction of his visit—and his narrative rendering of events already figures in Tanganyika's dominant nationalist narrative—I would note the importance of his gaze (after all, he saw the women at the rally), his support of TANU and Nyerere, and his influence on male TANU committee members. In so doing, I would reiterate the existing nationalist narrative in which Hatch, the British (Western) agent, shapes (the modernist, masculinist party) TANU through his prior meeting with and positive impressions of Nyerere, influencing not only the party but also, by his (white) presence, the party's importance and credibility in the eyes of heretofore dubious and suspicious Tanganyikans. Most importantly, for my purposes, I would reiterate a narrative in which Hatch, by questioning his TANU hosts about a women's section, becomes inadvertently responsible for its creation. And finally, were I a dedicated deconstructionist, I might also elaborate on Hatch's representation of what he "saw" at the event to which TANU leaders actually *brought him to be seen:* that is, "several rows of black-veiled Muslim women" amid a "vast sea of dusky faces and white clothes." Orientalist objectification/otherization indeed!

But what if Hatch's narrative is interrupted, challenged and replaced by that of Bibi Titi Mohamed, the woman whom TANU committee member Sheneda Plantan hastily identified to the other TANU committee members as the "leader" of the nonexistent women's section and then summoned to TANU headquarters for a meeting with Hatch? How might a different social narrative refuse the anonymity of the women in Hatch's sight and (to use Somers's words) emplot the connecting parts to a "constructed configuration or a social network" of nationalist stories in which *women's response* to historical accident, *not* the accident itself, effectively narrates Tanganyikan women's relationship to nationalism?

When Sheneda Plantan (Bibi Titi's brother-in-law) came to her home to ask Titi Mohamed to meet John Hatch as the leader of the TANU women's section, and asked her third husband, Boi Suleiman, to permit her to go, Bibi Titi was thirty years old. Having already bought a TANU membership card from Plantan (card number sixteen, as she proudly remembers), Bibi Titi agreed to go but insisted that her good friend Tatu Binti Mzee be invited as well so that she wouldn't be "alone." Bibi Titi's narrative of the momentous events of June 1 and 2 was related to me in 1984 with a keen recognition of the irony and humor in the situation not found in the usual accounts:

Then [following the rally] there was a party for John Hatch at the TANU office—it was a small house. It was at that time that I became a leader. Before the party, at his hotel, John Hatch said, "I see there were a lot of people at Nyerere's meeting today. About 20,000 people." Nyerere wasn't there then; he was at his home in Butiama. Hatch continued, "A lot of people came, but do you have a women's section? Or are the women just called to listen and then to leave?"

Well, the TANU leaders replied, "Oh yes, we have a women's section," and Hatch said, "I want to meet their leader." "Ah," they said, "you will be able to meet her tomorrow. We will organize a party for you at the TANU office so that you can see her."

But the fact is, they didn't have a woman then! You understand? Everyone had locked their wives away [in the house]. No one wanted to take his wife and say, "This is my wife, this is the one," or even to say, "She is not my wife." Everybody refused. "Then what shall we do?" they asked themselves.

Then Sheneda [Plantan] said, "I will go and collect Titi," "Bwana, ha! Titi is married," they replied. "But her husband is my friend. I'll talk to him and she will come." So Sheneda came to me. He met with Boi, my husband. And he said, "Tomorrow, John Hatch, the person who spoke yesterday will be invited to the TANU office. He wants to see some of the women. I have come to ask you if your wife can meet John Hatch." Boi said, "Take her, she is there. At what time will you come to collect her?" Sheneda said, "John Hatch is coming at four; I will come at three for Titi."

Well, I told Sheneda that he should go and collect Tatu Binti Mzee as well so that there would be two of us, and he agreed. Tatu and I are related because we share the same grandmother with my stepbrother. We shared the same father. Tatu Mzee's mother and my brother's mother were sisters. So I'm related to Tatu through my half-brother. Sheneda went to Binti Mzee and spoke to her and she agreed, so he came back and told me.

So tomorrow we were going! I prepared myself, and when it was three, Sheneda came. He collected me in his car and also Binti Mzee. I'm sorry I can't show you the picture that was taken. I don't know where I've put it.

Well, we [Titi Mohamed and Tatu Mzee] were taken to the TANU office. At four exactly, Dossa [Aziz] arrived. We didn't know him. Perhaps he was one of the leaders, we thought, because before I had gone to the other women, the beginning was like that. Anyway, he introduced us to John Hatch, saying, "This is Bibi Titi binti Mohamed, leader of the women's section."

But I was not a leader of that section—not even the "vice"! Do you hear? Ohoo! John Hatch took my hand and said, "I pray to God that you will be able to undertake this work without difficulty. You know, if women wanted to cause riots, they could do so. You should be polite." He spoke like this and like that.

John Hatch talked a lot. Then he took hold of my friend's hand. So I sat there. We had a little tea party. Then he went away, and from then on, I was told that I would be the chairman of the women.

How could this be possible, to be elected chairman of the women just here? They said that the committee would meet, and it met. They held a discussion and decided to write a letter to my husband asking him to allow me to be part of the TANU committee so that I could encourage the other women. And my husband gave his permission. That's how I joined the TANU leadership.[20]

Bibi Titi's narrative credits John Hatch with creating the circumstances under which TANU leaders needed to say that the party had a women's section and therefore a woman leader of that section. And she credits her brother-in-law, Sheneda Plantan, with coming up with her name and convincing her husband that he should let her meet Hatch and become a TANU leader. But she also emphasizes not only the amusing (to her) way in which TANU was "caught" without women or a women's section to show to Hatch but, more importantly, her awareness that TANU could not make her a leader of the women nor could it create a women's section. These could only happen when and if women themselves agreed to use their strong relational and associational networks for TANU politics and agreed as well to confirm her leadership.

At the time she was summoned to meet John Hatch, Bibi Titi Mohamed, like most Muslim townswomen, considered herself essentially a "housewife" and confined her public activity to the culturally sanctioned realm of women's *ngoma* (dance) groups. Although she had achieved local popularity within this realm as lead singer in the group Bomba, her reputation in this regard could scarcely have prefigured her rise to political prominence. Nor would anyone have predicted her mercurial success as an organizer. Nevertheless, on July 8, 1955, Bibi Titi held the first meeting of the TANU Women's Section, at which four hundred women joined.[21] By October 1955, just three months later, Oscar

Kambona, then the organizing secretary-general for TANU, reported to the Fabian Society that Bibi Titi Mohammed had enrolled five thousand women members and, "though only semi-literate," was "inspiring a revolution [in] the role of women in African society." Kambona went even further, proclaiming confidently, "The problem of the emancipation of women at a later date has, in this way, been disposed of." [22]

Kambona's eagerness to declare the emancipation of women complete was premature and unfounded. Nevertheless, his rhetoric accurately captured the sense of initial astonishment with which the fledgling TANU leadership reacted to the rapidity and extent of women's nationalist mobilization. Although not politically prominent in any formal sense that would have brought them to the attention of TANU or colonial officials, many of the women Bibi Titi's presence and leadership brought in to the nationalist movement were what Karen Sacks has called "centerwomen," that is, "women who initiate and sustain informal ... social networks, and who are often keystones of family and kinship networks as well. They tend to initiate activities that maintain group cohesiveness. People expect them to know the events, opinions, and needs of those in the network, and to use that information for their shared wellbeing." [23]

Tatu Mzee, who accompanied Bibi Titi to the meeting with John Hatch, was one such centerwoman, and sought out others in the course of political mobilization. She explained,

> We tried to keep in mind what type of people to look for. We looked for *lelemama* [dance] groups and beer brewers because these were the groups that had many people. And through these groups we could spread propaganda about our organization. . . . That was the first idea because [the women themselves] had formed societies . . . and we could encourage their people and those people could go and encourage other people. We were with Bi Mgeni. Mgeni Ndombe Saidi, Binti Saidi [deceased]. There was one woman leader in Gerenzani area, another in Temeke, another in Ilala and in Kinondoni [all "suburbs" of Dar es Salaam]. But we had to start with Dar es Salaam. We got them from different clubs like *lelemama*. We used to pick those who were courageous.
>
> We worked through many [musical] organizations, such as *tarab*, and *ngoma* [dance groups] like *lelemama*, and religious groups. Gombe Sugu [a Dar es Salaam Zaramo-initiated *ngoma* group] tried to pull us very fast [was very aggressive politically]. I was in Roho Mgeni with Titi. We were both singers. We cooperated with the group Al Watan. [24]

Women emphasized that they were far more active than TANU's male leaders or men generally in organizing and mobilizing both women and men for the nationalist cause. It was primarily women who undertook house-to-house canvassing, often at the risk of being accused of "looking for men." It was women who mobilized communities and neighborhoods for mass rallies and visits from the TANU leadership and who raised money locally and pawned their rings and bracelets for Nyerere's trips abroad, for his court case in 1958, and for headquarters expenses and staff salaries.[25]

Women purchased their own TANU membership cards and sold them to others, frequently holding and hiding cards for their husbands and others who were either forbidden to join TANU if they were civil servants, or afraid they would lose their jobs if caught with membership cards. Although the women did this on their own initiative and to protect men from reprisals, by 1962 Julius Nyerere was already reshaping the historical record to place the initiative for women's membership and TANU activism in the hands of their husbands. In his inaugural address as independent Tanganyika's first president, he assured men who had failed to participate in the nationalist movement that it would not have been sensible, nor was it necessary, for civil servants, employees of commercial firms, and mission workers who stayed away in the 1950s to "throw up their jobs and join TANU." "Many of them, however," he stated inaccurately, "persuaded their wives to join instead."[26]

Women in Moshi and in Mwanza housed TANU leaders when they visited their areas, and in the case of a few property-owning women, offered houses for use as local TANU offices. They also fed TANU visitors, "guarded" Nyerere, and in Moshi even set up decoy guards to mislead TANU antagonists regarding Nyerere's whereabouts. A TANU activist in Moshi, whose mother was Masai and father Chagga, translated for Nyerere when he went to Masailand to address people in that area. Women strategized and "taught" their fellow women about TANU and raised others' consciousness as well.[27]

Women's narratives also reveal the extent to which they constructed, reproduced, and solidified Tanganyikan nationalism through performance. Like the selling of TANU cards, the performance of nationalism was largely women's work. As TANU activists, women performed and paraded nationalism, writing, singing, and popularizing song lyrics praising the party and leaders, urging people to join, extolling freedom and unity, and marching exuberantly at a kind of shuffling jogger's pace to and from meeting places and alongside Nyerere and other leaders when they rode in slow-moving vehicles. Moreover, far from being incidental, performance was fundamental to Tanganyikan nationalism. That the colonial administration understood this is clear from their attempts to limit and control public performative aspects of nationalist politics.

British administrators were especially frustrated by their inability to prevent women from organizing visible, colorful, and exciting signification of popular support for TANU. By 1955 the nationalist movement was offering people specific forms of engagement, entertainment, and spectacle along with the politics of freedom. There was no possibility of charging TANU with the ritual violence associated in the colonial mind with Mau Mau to the north in Kenya. Indeed, administrators frequently seemed caught between wanting to dismiss the significance of TANU's popular appeal by characterizing people's, especially women's, enthusiasm as only superficially political and primarily responsive to the attractions of mass spectacle on the one hand, and viewing it as dangerous on the other.

Evidence of the latter view became apparent as TANU gained membership and strength. For example, in 1957, in response to the increasing popularity of displaying TANU support and membership through dress, the administration passed a public order making it a violation for any person to wear a "uniform or distinctive dress which signifies association with any political organization or the promotion of any political object" in a public place or to a public meeting, and setting a fine of up to one thousand shillings or up to six months' imprisonment, or both, as the penalty for contravention.[28]

Meanwhile, TANU was benefiting enormously from the appeal of uniformed members of the party's women's section, choirs, and youth league, who were identified and identifiable to visiting TANU leaders, to people gathering to see and hear TANU national leaders for the first time, and to colonial officers who wished they were not there. Like the women's section, a TANU youth section was specified in the 1954 constitution, but the reality and functions of the youth league eventually formed in 1956 were produced by its membership, who became the self-appointed guardians and greeters of TANU dignitaries, as well as the TANU "police" in charge of crowd control.[29] The district commissioners now found themselves saddled with responsibility for preventing nationalist "entertainment," banning "distinctive dress ... which signifies ... association with your political organization," and reminding local TANU leaders that permission to organize an assembly or procession stipulated that no drum could be beaten before or after a meeting and that no meeting could be held near any local court.[30]

Similar reminders about drums and uniforms flowed from the district officers and police, while infractions persisted. On November 21, 1958, the assistant superintendent of police, Kigoma District, wrote to the TANU district chairman, Ujiji, "It has been noticed recently that members of the TANU have been wearing distinctive dress signifying association with TANU. I particularly refer to the green dresses worn by lady members at the Kigoma Railway Station on the 15th November." Reminding the TANU district chairman of the order prohibiting uniforms, he went on to point out lamely that the Kigoma Railway Station catered to the general public and that

> the assembly of large crowds interferes with the right of free access of the public and also causes obstruction to traffic.
>
> Would you please in future confine your reception or farewell committees to between 20 or 30 persons. Should you so desire, a larger demonstration of affection or loyalty can easily be arranged at some pre-arranged or more suitable venue on application to this office.
>
> I believe it to be correct that a similar point was recently put to your president and other Members of your Central Committee and they accepted it.[31]

This particularly polite assistant superintendent of police was quite right. On March 19, 1958, the commissioner of police in Dar es Salaam wrote to the TANU president, drawing his attention to Government Notice No. 20 of January 11, 1957, and pointing out that the sashes bearing reference to TANU, worn by stewards at a TANU meeting held at the airport on Sunday, February 16, 1958, "may well be interpreted as a breach of that notice" and that any future application for a meeting should state that "stewards will be present to assist," and that if they wished to identify such persons as officials, a further note should say that the identification will take a particular form, "e.g., Identification of officials—Blue Rosette. . . . These identification aids should be in the form of a small and distinctive band, i.e., BLUE ROSETTE, OR BLUE ARMBAND. Will you please issue the necessary instructions to your branches."[32]

The struggle continued. On January 3, 1959, "some 100" TANU members went to the Kigoma Railway Station to say good-bye to two TANU visitors, Mr. G. Mlay and Miss Anna Gwasa, in direct defiance of previous orders.[33]

In addition to trying to limit the size of TANU groups and ban the signification of support through dress, the administration insisted that TANU seek permission to use a loudspeaker or megaphone or to sing songs at TANU meetings. Moreover, the song lyrics had to be approved in advance.[34] Miserly concessions were sometimes made. At a meeting of the district officer of Kigoma with TANU committee members from the district, the TANU chairman requested that the police waive the rule requiring the words of every song to be submitted before each meeting on the grounds that the repertoire was very small and the songs were always the same.[35] And on September 23, 1959, W.J.W. Bowering, the D.C. Kigoma, wrote to the TANU district chairman to say that it wasn't necessary to give fourteen days' notice for using a megaphone or for permission to sing songs and that monthly subscriptions could be collected in public from members who had already paid, but that it wasn't possible to waive the order concerning submission of copies of songs to be sung at meetings: "However, if the songs are the same each time as the Committee assert it would suffice to give a complete copy of all the songs signed by the Chairman or Secretary. The songs should be numbered and future applications could read for example: 'TANU Youth League singing songs 1,2,3, and 5.' "[36]

The TANU central leadership did not create the various performances and significations of nationalist political culture put to the service of party mobilization and membership, and performance and signification produced nationalism as surely as Nyerere's speeches. Moreover, women were central to these aspects of nationalism, and their presence and importance were established through them.

Like many popular expressions of nationalism, performance and the wearing of identical dress to signify membership and support were appropriated by the postindependence TANU government bureaucracy and put to the service of the one-party state. Nyerere came to rely on them throughout his career. One of his first acts as president was to establish a Ministry of National Culture and Youth, but instead of noting the significance of popular nationalist performance to his own success as a nationalist leader, Nyerere took the popular intellectual's position that colonialism had destroyed Tanganyika's cultural forms and practices. "Of all the crimes of colonialism there is nothing worse than the attempt to make us believe we had no indigenous culture of our own, or that what we did have was worthless—something of which we should be ashamed, instead of a source of pride."[37]

TANU women, and in fact many men and women in the countryside, would have been surprised to learn that colonialism had alienated them from their cultural practices. On the other hand, this view was understandable coming from a Western- and mission-educated man. Moreover, Nyerere clearly had his fellow educated Tanganyikans in mind when in the same address he asked:

> How many of us were taught the songs of the Wanyamwezi or of the Wahehe? Many of us have learnt to dance the 'rumba', the 'waltz' and the 'foxtrot'. But how many of us can dance, or have even heard of,

the *Gombe Sugu,* the *Mangala,* the *Konge, Nyang'umumi, Kiduo* or *Lele Mama? . . .* [and how often do those Western dances] really give us the sort of thrill we get from dancing the *mganda* or the *gombe sugu*—even though the music may be no more than the shaking of pebbles in a tin? It is hard for any man to get much real excitement from dances and music which are not in his own blood.[38]

The government soon became preoccupied with the belief that it was necessary to promote and control the integration of "ethnic cultures" into a "national culture."[39] If centralized control were not the issue, Nyerere might have acknowledged that he owed his own awareness of Gombe Sugu and *lele-mama* and Mganda to TANU women.

Forty years have passed since the women I spoke with first came together to listen, discuss TANU, march, organize, and gather again with dedicated regularity. Nevertheless, these activists of the 1950s clearly constituted in the 1980s, during the time I was recording their life-history narratives, what Maurice Halbwachs has called "affective community," that is, a group that aids each other's memories because its members remain in harmony with each other. "There must be enough points of contact so that any remembrance they recall . . . can be reconstructed on a common foundation. [The] reconstruction [of past events] must start from shared data or conceptions. Shared data or conceptions . . . are present . . . because all have been and still are members of the same group."[40]

Time after time, the women's narratives included a litany of relational ties and networks formed through *ngoma* (dance), rotating credit union, and other women's groups, and of the names of remembered women, including those deceased. Shared data and conceptions—what Halbwachs might call collective memory—characterized the activists' recollections of their nationalist activities as expressed and reconstituted in their life histories. From these it is therefore possible to plot a collective biographical narrative of the larger whole—including the 5,000 women who by October 1955 had become card-carrying TANU members.[41] In their constructions of the present, as well as in their reconstructions of their political involvement of the 1950s, the women offered social narratives about a "large cultural system" in which "ordinary" (illiterate, frequently self-identified as Swahili, Muslim) women played a critical role.

Through TANU activism, women became intentional political subjects. As Kathleen Berry indicates,

In subjectivity, both history and the future are given connection through the subject's intentionality. Intentionality signifies self-determination, not in the overblown sense of liberal individualism, but in the everyday action of life. *When intentionality is marked by consciousness, women's subjectivity is political.* To the extent that women reclaim their history through their own intentionality, their history will be socially constructed and self-determined.[42] (Emphasis in original)

I am not arguing that Muslim women were *singularly* responsible for Tanganyikan nationalism, but I am arguing that recognizing their narrative presence, actions, and voices changes our understanding of nationalism in Tanganyika and subverts the master narrative that traces Tanganyikan nationalist history from the acts of "proto-nationalist" men through TANU modernizers and the ideological importance of Nyerere to independence.[43] Far from being victims, pawns, or symbols in the development of nationalist movement, TANU women activists constructed and embodied significant aspects of Tanzanian nationalism and continue to do so today.

## NOTES

1. Interview with Halima Hamisi, Amani Street, Dar es Salaam, October 23, 1984.

2. Scholars who would include within the nationalist framework movements involving armed struggle and claiming revolutionary, anticolonial objectives (for example, those in Mozambique, Guinea Bissau, Angola, South Africa, Vietnam, Zimbabwe, Cuba) would argue for a fourth category and hence a fourth, more transformative relationship of women to nationalist movements. Although a great deal of feminist work produced in the 1970s and 1980s supported an optimistic view of women's impact on gender transformations and predicted their permanence, and while the verdict on South Africa certainly remains out, recent work shows a slippery slide back to prerevolutionary gender norms and roles in many instances, whether for internal, external, or a combination of both reasons. For a sensitive and thoughtful examination of Mozambican women's achievements and struggles to the late 1980s, see Stephanie Urdang, *And Still They Dance* (New York: Monthly Review Press, 1989). See also Sonya Kruks, Rayna Rapp, and Marilyn Young, eds., *Promissory Notes: Women in the Transition to Socialism* (New York: Monthly Review Press, 1989).

3. See, for example, Silva Meznaric, "Gender as an Ethno-Marker: Rape, War, and Identity Politics in the Former Yugoslavia," in *Identity Politics and Women: Cultural Reassertions and Feminisms in International Perspectives,* ed. Valentine M. Moghadam (Boulder, Colo.: Westview Press, 1994), 76–97.

4. There is a precedent and trajectory for this focus in a large body of feminist work identifying women primarily as the victims of war, revolution, and other manifestations of physical strife. A number of the essays in Judith Stiehm, ed., *Women's and Men's Wars* (Oxford: Pergamon Press, 1983); and Sharon Macdonald, Pat Holden, and Shirley Ardener, eds., *Images of Women in Peace and War: Cross Cultural and Historical Perspectives* (Madison: University of Wisconsin Press, 1988), illustrate this point.

5. See, for example, Anne McClintock, "'No Longer in a Future Heaven': Women and Nationalism in South Africa," *Transition* 51 (1991): 104–23. This focus on woman as representational object also has both feminist and nonfeminist traditions in scholarship concerned with "woman" as "mother," "justice," "witch," "whore," "earth," or "bearer of the culture." See Lynn A. Hunt, *Politics, Culture and Class in the French Revolution* (Berkeley: University of California Press, 1984), and *Eroticism and the Body Politic* (Baltimore: Johns Hopkins University Press, 1991).

6. Temma Kaplan's "Female Consciousness and Collective Action: The Case of Barcelona, 1910–1918," *Signs* 7 (Spring 1982): 545–66, is among the most often quoted. See also Julia Wells, "Why Women Rebel: A Comparative Study of South African Women's Resistance in Bloemfontein (1913) and Johannesburg (1958)," *Journal of Southern African Studies* 10 (October 1983): 55–70.

7. See, for example, Margot Badran, *Feminists, Islam, and Nation: Gender and the Making of Modern Egypt* (Princeton, N.J.: Princeton University Press, 1995).

8. For one of several articulations of his thought, see Partha Chatterjee, "Colonialism, Nationalism and Colonized Women: the Context of India," *American Ethnologist* 16 (1989): 622–33. For an excellent study of the multiple positions imposed on *and* claimed by different segments of the population of Indian women, see Mrinalini Sinha, "Reading Mother India: Empire, Nation, and the Female Voice," *Journal of Women's History* 6 (1994): 6–44.

9. An exception is Kumani Jayawardena's important *Feminism and Nationalism in the Third World* (London: Zed Books, 1986). My own greater familiarity is with scholarship on nationalist movements in Africa, a scholarship that began in the late 1970s when there was still greater hope that nationalist movements in Africa were capable of transforming colonial political and economic legacies. No doubt there are many powerful examples from other continents. See Susan Geiger, "Women and African Nationalism," *Journal of Women's History* 2 (1990): 227–44. See also Cora Ann Presley, *Kikuyu Women, the Mau Mau Rebellion, and Social Change in Kenya* (Boulder, Colo.: Westview Press, 1992). A collection that shows both the range and limits of postmodernist approaches is Andrew Parker, Mary Russo, Doris Sommer, and Patricia Yaeger, eds., *Nationalisms and Sexualities* (New York: Routledge, 1992).

10. For a perfect example of the extent to which critique of others' positions has become a thriving scholarly industry, see Kirk Hoppe, "Whose Life Is It, Anyway?: Issues of Representation in Life Narrative Texts of African Women," *International Journal of African Historical Studies* 26 (1993): 623–36. For an excellent response to Hoppe, see Heidi Gengenbach, "Truth-telling and the Politics of Women's Life History Research in

Africa: A Reply to Kirk Hoppe," *International Journal of African Historical Studies* 27 (1994): 619–27.

11. Margaret R. Somers, "Narrativity, Narrative Identity, and Social Action: Rethinking English Working-Class Formation," *Social Science History* 16 (Winter 1992): 592, 595.

12. Ibid., 601.

13. Benedict Anderson, *Imagined Communities: Reflections on the Origins and Spread of Nationalism* (London: Verson, 1991), 12.

14. John Iliffe, *A Modern History of Tanganyika* (Cambridge: Cambridge University Press, 1979), 486.

15. I add the qualifiers "modified" and "directed" to the basic definition of a life history as an account of a person's life told to another person who records it, to make explicit the extent to which my interest in women's participation in politics and TANU in the 1950s influenced the life history interviews and content. The women who recounted their experiences to me did so precisely because I expressed direct interest in their political activities and thinking. With few exceptions, interviews were conducted in Swahili and I was accompanied by a fluent or native Swahili speaker and assisted in the transcription and translation of interview tapes. Funding for various periods of research in Tanzania came from the Graduate School and College of Liberal Arts at the University of Minnesota, from Fulbright, and from the Social Science Research Council. I am indebted to dozens of Tanzanians for their support and assistance, but most especially to M. W. Kanyama Chiume, without whose personal political networks, continuous encouragement, and practical assistance and advice I never could have undertaken my work.

16. In his first published account, Hatch estimated the crowd at 15,000. In his second, he had revised his impression to between 20,000 and 40,000 people. See John Hatch, *New From Africa* (London: D. Dobson, 1956), 55, and *Two African Statesmen: Kaunda of Zambia and Nyerere of Tanzania* (Chicago: Henry Regnery, 1976), 104.

17. Hatch, *New From Africa,* 55.

18. Hatch, *Two African Statesmen,* 107; see also Judith Listowel, *The Making of Tanganyika* (London: Chatto and Windus, 1965), 263. Hatch's observation wasn't particularly original. Kumari Jayawardena begins her introduction to *Feminism and Nationalism in the Third World* with the following quote from Bhikaiji Cama of India, who at a meeting of the Egyptian National Congress held in Brussels in 1910 stated: "I see here the representatives of only half the population of Egypt. May I ask where is the other half? Sons of Egypt, where are the daughters of Egypt? Where are your mothers and sisters, your wives and daughters?" (*Feminism and Nationalism,* 1).

19. The TANU Constitution of July 1954 called for a women's section, but nothing had been done to establish one by the time of Hatch's visit eleven months later.

20. Interview with Bibi Titi Mohamed, Temeke, Dar es Salaam, October 1984.

21. The figure is from D. Z. Mwaga, B. F. Miran, and E. F. Lyimo, *Historia ya Chama cha TANU 1954 Hadi 1977* (Dar es Salaam: 1981) Chuo Cha CCM, Kivukoni, 113.

22. Oscar Kambona to Fabian Society, October 18, 1955, FCB (Fabian Colonial Bureau) Papers, 121, Rhodes House, Oxford. Unlike the majority of Dar es Salaam women

of her generation, who had no formal education, Bibi Titi attended four years of primary school before being withdrawn for the customary period of seclusion in preparation for marriage. She neither spoke nor read English at the time Kambona characterized her as "semi-literate."

23. Karen Brodkin Sacks, "What's a Life Story Got to Do with It?" in *Interpreting Women's Lives: Feminist Theory and Personal Narratives,* ed. Personal Narratives Group (Bloomington: Indiana University Press, 1989), 91.

24. Interview with Tatu Mzee, October 18, 1984.

25. Interviews with Halima Hamisi, Dar es Salaam, October 23, 1984; Mwamvita Mnyamani, Buguruni, October 26, 1984; Salima Ferouz, Magomeni, September 26, 1984.

26. Julius Nyerere, *Freedom and Unity/Uhuru Na Umoja* (London: Oxford University Press, 1966), reproducing December 10, 1962 "President's Inaugural Address," 180.

27. Interviews with Halima Selengia Kinabo, Moshi, October 1988; Mwamvita Salim and Zainabu Hatibu, Moshi, October 1988; Elizabeth Gupta, Moshi, October 1988; Kanasia Mtenga, Moshi, December 1988; Pili Juma, Mwanza, November 1988; Mwajuma Msafiri, Mwanza, November 1988; Agnes Sahani, Mwanza, November 1988.

28. Ref. No. A6/5/32, March 20, 1958, R. W. Smith, District Commissioner, Kigoma, to District Secretary, TANU, Ujiji. Tanzania National Archives (hereafter cited as TNA) A6/5 TAA (Tanganyika African Association), Kigoma, citing Government Notice No. 20 on November 1, 1957, "Political Uniforms Prohibition," Sections 2 and 3.

29. Iliffe, *Modern History of Tanganyika,* 532.

30. R. W. Smith, D. C. Kigoma, to District Secretary, TANU, Ujiji, March 20, 1958, Ref. No. A6/5/32; N. D. Morant, Commanding Officer, Police, Kigoma District, to R. H. Missozi, Branch Sec., TANU, Mwangongo, January 7, 1958, Ref. No. A. 24/9/84, TNA A6/5 Kigoma.

31. Asst. Superintendent of Police, Kigoma District, to Dist. Chairman, TANU, Ujiji, November 21, 1958, Ref. No. S/14, TNA A6/5, Kigoma.

32. Commissioner of Police, Dar es Salaam, to President, TANU, Dar es Salaam, March 19, 1958. Ref. No. S/15/3/185. TNA A6/5 Kigoma.

33. Officer I/C Police, Kigoma District, to District Chairman, TANU, Ujiji, January 5, 1959, Ref. No. S/14, TNA, A6/5, Kigoma

34. S. G. Pierce to Kashindye, District Sec., TANU, Ref. No. KIS/A.24/24/41, June 25, 1959, re TANU meeting to be held at Usagara ground, Ujiji, Kigoma District, June 29, 1959, TNA A6/5 Kigoma.

35. Notes of a meeting with TANU Committee, September 9, 1959, TNA A6/5.

36. W. J. Bowering, D. C. Kigoma, to District Chairman, TANU, September 23, 1959, re September 9, 1959, meeting, and police officer's reply concerning Youth League songs, copy No. KIG/A/8/2, S. G. Pierce, Officer I/C Police, Kigoma District, to D. C. Kigoma, September 18, 1959. TNA A6/5.

37. Nyerere, *Freedom and Unity,* 186.

38. Ibid.

39. For a recent exploration, see Helena Jerman, "How I Feel to Be a Tanzanian," *Suomen Antropologi,* March 1993, 31–41.

40. Maurice Halbwachs, *The Collective Memory* (New York: Harper & Row, 1980), 31.

41. Oscar Kambona, Organizing Secretary-General of TANU, to Fabian Society, October 18, 1955, FCB papers 121, Rhodes House.

42. Kathleen Barry, "Biography and the Search for Women's Subjectivity," *Women's Studies International Forum* 12 (1989): 569. Emphasis in the original.

43. The formal associations generally followed Western organizational models. As the immediate precurser to TANU, the most fully studied and described is the (Tanganyika) African Association (TAA); others include the Tanganyika African Welfare and Commercial Association and the African Commercial Employees Association. A variety of worker organizations, cooperative societies, and tribal unions are also identified for their (usually proto-nationalist) role.

ANGELIKA BAMMER
MINROSE GWIN
CINDI KATZ
ELIZABETH MEESE

PART 3

# the place of the letter:
# an epistolary exchange

[Editors' note: In order to promote experimental and interactive productions of feminist texts, we asked four conference participants to create a written dialogue about their own works before and during the conference. We created a panel of scholars whose work ranged widely in perspective and in historical focus but seemed to us to share a concern with locating narrative and material spaces of resistance. All seek to understand the influential role that displacement has in metaphoric and material imaginings and in productions of space and subjectivity. We sent each of the panelists copies of abstracts the others had written about their ongoing projects and asked Elizabeth Meese to initiate the letter exchange. The four correspondents adapted this into an impressive conference presentation. Imagine, four women, spacing themselves randomly in the audience, reading to each other, and to all, the letters they had written over the preceding three months.]

## AN INTRODUCTION, ELIZABETH MEESE

Here to perform a process of exchange and, in some instances, drift, exhibiting our own alienation (or displacement in the making) with respect to our individual projects and the rubric under which we come together: "Making Worlds: Metaphor and Materiality in the Production of Feminist Texts."

So, a beginning:

I am a bricoleur, making something—a presentation, a bricolage—from something else, an exchange of letters (about fifty pages, single-spaced) among four strangers. In bricolage, as Derrida puts it, one takes something whose truth-value one "criticizes, conserving . . . all these old concepts, while at the same time exposing . . . their limits, treating them as tools which can still be of use. No longer is any truth-value [or rigorous meaning] attributed to them; there is a readiness to abandon them if necessary if other instruments should appear more useful. In the meantime their relative efficacy is exploited, and they are employed to destroy the old machinery to which they belong and of which they themselves are pieces."[1]

As the bricoleur in search of a method of presentation, I wrote to the panelists. "I have a certain responsibility, but also a certain privilege—the right to set the tone, to construct the narrative thread (order) of our exchange. Now there are ways to decentralize this function, and it is a responsibility and a privilege I would happily give up. We could simply read bits from our letters in the order in which they were written (this gives prominence to chronology in an obnoxious way, I think) or along some thematic lines (which also seems fairly arbitrary). Or we could, à la John Cage, select an order at random. That is, each of you could mark the parts of your own letters that you would like to present. You could assign a number to each part. Then we could "order" the bits from the four of us at random, by drawing lots. Obviously this would disrupt the timeliness of the exchanges—responses might come before instigating comments, comments might exist without any responses, and vice versa. But conversation is like this, and it makes sense to me (since nothing about order makes much sense to me except the capriciousness of the orderer and her scheme)."

As you will see, we elected to engage the tyranny of chronology, the pretense of the narrative thread to order our exchange. Thus we begin with my first letter to the panelists.

"Everything is written in the white spaces between one letter and the next. The rest doesn't count."[2]

July 14, 1993

*Dear Cindi, Angelika, and Minrose,*

*I received your position papers a while ago from the very efficient group of conference organizers. I couldn't make myself read them, partly because I have been struggling with my own work (trying to launch a new project), partly because it's summer and all work is hard (I live on a lake outside Tuscaloosa and like to enjoy it), and perhaps mainly because I have grave reservations about any synthesizing role these days.*

The conference title, "Making Worlds: Metaphor and Materiality in the Production of Feminist Texts," suggests that metaphor and materiality are different, that they are used in "making worlds," that worlds are "made," that is, constructed, and not "found" or inherited. The metaphorical and material construction of worlds are/may be different.

Since I work with writing, I have great difficulty telling the difference between material space and metaphorical space, difficulty not necessarily restricted to text. The minute someone tells me about the place they live, we are both working in the realm of metaphor. So, you say, perhaps you should go see for yourself. Well, the minute I articulate to myself what it is that I've seen, the very categories I use in order to process or understand what I've seen place me in a metaphoric field. There seems to be no way of escaping it.

In order to reach a point where we can speak to one another, I want to respond to your statements with some questions.

Is there a special grammar, syntax, rhetoric of material space? If space is produced, in what sense is it "real"? How or when is it ever non-metaphorical? In this context, what is a "room of one's own"? One I own (not the bank)? One I occupy (no one else is allowed in without an invitation)? Because it is "mine," does that make it "disalienating"? No bad dreams allowed? No television? No newspaper? What about the brain's production of sensations, the role of the unconscious in the claiming of territory?

Does writing, as a political act, have the same valence as other forms of political activism—marching, demonstrating, lesbian avenging? How is the way a writer "creates space" (what does that mean?) in a literary text reflective of a specific (material?) context within which the writer writes or dreams? How will the reader know this? What constitutes a subversive space? Spivak's caution in "French Feminism in an International Frame" relates nicely here: "However unfeasible and inefficient it may sound I see no way to avoid insisting that there has to be a simultaneous other focus: not merely who am I? but who is that other woman? How am I naming her? How does she name me? Is this part of the problematic I discuss? Indeed, it is the absence of such unfeasible but crucial questions that makes the 'colonized woman' as 'subject' see the investigators as sweet and sympathetic creatures from another planet who are free to come and go; or, depending on her own socialization in the colonizing cultures, see 'feminism' as having a vanguardist class fix, the liberties it fights for as luxuries, finally identifiable with 'free sex' of one kind or another."[3] Does the attempt at *assessing another woman's text always require a sort of negotiation? How is stepping inside the web of context and experience affected by cybernetics? Is there a sense in which we could say that when we communicate electronically, we are all in the same net, sharing the same cyber-space? Would we then describe that shared space in ways that reflect other contexts and experiences and cultures?*

*Well, this is precisely the mess that I must have anticipated in my resistance to thinking about what we are all doing. Anyone see a way that we can think together about any of these questions? I am eagerly awaiting the next round of correspondence.*

> *Metaphorically yours,*
> *Elizabeth*

*August 15–19, 1993*

*Dear Angelika, Cindi, and Elizabeth,*

*I, too, find this assignment a bit daunting, not because I don't want to write to you, but because a letter like the kind I like to write to friends and colleagues whose work I'm interested in sounds nothing like what I think I'm supposed to produce for this piece of conference writing. I'm afraid that either my letter will sound like a conference paper, or it will sound like a real letter, which—believe me—sounds nothing like a conference paper. I guess the challenge of this assignment for me is to find a way to write to you that is real to me and that interests you. I am, in fact, as interested in how this whole process is going to unfold as I am in what we end up producing.*

*Elizabeth, I like the way you've gotten us started, particularly with your comments about the difficulty in telling the difference between materiality and metaphor. Even what is foregrounded as "materiality"—for example, the Weimar Republic in Angelika's work or the East Harlem of Cindi's young girl subjects—is at least somewhat constructed by language. In the work I've just initiated I'm interested in how women's stories draw us inside material/metaphorical spaces of resistance. So, yes, I think some women's writing is highly political, in the sense that their stories give narrative frames— a sense of concrete being—to women's very different but somehow connected struggles. They draw us inside those material/metaphorical spaces of resistance. Donna Haraway says that feminists "need an earth-*

wide network of connections, including the ability partially to translate knowledges among very different—and power-differentiated—communities."[4] My question at the outset is just how political is women's literature in this respect? Can women's writing about our vastly diverse cultural experiences take us as feminists into shared spaces we've been unable to attain and maintain in our communities? Is it possible that the very process of reading allows a kind of absorption of cultural experience which is not possible except in very intimate relations among women? Can what Biddy Martin and Chandra Mohanty call "the pleasures and terrors of interminable boundary confusions" among women play themselves out productively in the writing, reading, and teaching of texts?[5]

What I've been trying to think about this summer is how feminist reading of women's stories—being drawn into other women's narrative spaces when we are invited—may indeed be one way of traveling difference that can really make a difference. In a nutshell, I'm exploring a literary strategy that I've come to call "space travel." I'm interested in such a spatial model for reading women's stories—a literary strategy of travel that brings us into one another's spaces and allows us to be there in ways that may alter subjectivity and thereby problematize positionality—in ways that allow us to reposition ourselves imaginatively.

Now, if this were a real letter to friends, I would think I had already done more than enough talking about what I'm up to. I'd want to ask about your lives, your work. Angelika, I'm interested in what you have to say about "the here and now," and Cindi, how your project leads to a more "grounded" notion of difference. I think I'm trying to get at the same thing—to think about how we can be more precise, damn it, about our differences, our positions, our identity politics, but at the same time be able to flow between, to make some inroads into spaces we can share, spaces we want to share. How easily difference can become translated into distance. How much we have yet to learn about traveling difference. As you say in (Ex)Tensions, Elizabeth, we need to find "a space from which difference can speak and be spoken with respect, a space where we can write and/or speak with one another rather than for or against each other."[6]

I'm at a point in this letter now where I want to go in at least five different directions at once. And there are all of Elizabeth's questions still looming. Instead of making a decision, I went out and cleaned the backyard of dog debris—a chore that always clears the cobwebs (and sinuses). I ate a couple of crackers and threw some clothes in the washer. I'm worried about this letter. I don't think I'm doing it right. Or is there a right way to do it? I am selfish enough to hope you're having the same problems. It would make me feel better.

Here's another plunge.

However we figure feminist community (or whether we believe such a thing exists), entering and being absorbed into the actual spaces of women's stories may lead us to a more palpable, more substantive sense of how difference moves in a variety of patterns through our lives and imaginations. I guess the real question is how do we understand difference as tangible but fluid. Nancy K. Miller says we need new metaphors for difference, but she's not sure what they would be.[7] I think that's because we need to conceptualize difference as a nebulous entity—a fluid space full of potential but not form, which changes shape with each story that is told, each life that is lived. In our ongoing attempts to release difference, as Audre Lorde would say, from its inscriptions of power and privilege, there's a need to allow our material differences to create their own identities, their own metaphors.[8] But the wonderful thing about metaphor is that it can be fluid; it exceeds representation. Because we are different, metaphor may, in some situations, be the only way to enter one another's materiality.

Hmmmmm. If there is a relationship between cultural context and women's senses of and portrayals of spatiality—and I think there is—then reading/entering these material spaces in women's texts may indeed become an act of crossing boundary in feminist consciousness, of releasing our differences to take shape and speak to one another. These are spaces of resistance. I'm thinking of particular physical spaces: the bathroom in which the girl Bone in Dorothy Allison's Bastard out of Carolina is beaten by her stepfather, who will later rape her, the nine-by-seven-by-three-foot garret in which the slave Harriet Jacobs lived for seven years.[9] As one of Elizabeth's questions indicates too, the difference within a text itself may reflect these fluctuations, this simultaneous gathering of identity and opening of borders, as in Sandra Cisneros's The House on Mango Street.

Let me give an example: the in and out spacings of The House on Mango Street. The short narrative sketches of this text take on the contours of the tightness of the house itself—so many people, so little space in the Latino quarter of Chicago. But there's play here. Creativity and rich culture inside these boundaries. Motion and expansiveness. Girls skip and hop and sing:

> Skip, skip
> snake in your hips,
> wiggle around
> and break your lip.[10]

Inside this space, this house, this street, there's motion within compression, ebb and flow like an inflatable balloon. To enter this space—this place—is to be swept into the rhythms of jump rope, song, giggles, running, play—a series of dexterous negotiations of tight, tight spaces. (I'm reminded here of what Houston Baker says about the "blues matrix" of African American cultural experience—subtle, refined, nimble motion within the confinement and rigidity of the dominant culture—pushing those borders out.)[11] Girl spaces, girl talk. (Cindi, I wonder how this corresponds with the girls you interviewed. Is this what you mean by "produced space"?)

Then there's the squeeze. Girls grow up, get hips, get beaten, get raped, get married. Esperanza gets out, but not before she is raped by a man with a sour mouth and dirty fingernails who calls her his "Spanish girl." She/we are still in border space, the in and out space of the jump rope. The space of resistance and return. (Elizabeth, in answer to your question, I see this space as the place where resistance is enacted, is in process. Yes, I guess I do think that resistance always occurs within a space of some sort.) A misstep, a stumble can mean disaster. Esperanza sees her life as a negotiation of the spaces between Mango Street and the rest of the world. She knows that she can get away only to come back again and again to the house on Mango Street.

Esperanza's story leads me to think about how original home space holds us, no matter what clean, swept-out houses we come to create for ourselves. This is why we keeping traveling, negotiating, moving the borders back and forth. Our cultural homes may differ. Cisneros describes herself as the daughter of a Mexican father and a Mexican-American mother. Her borders are literal and, as in the case of Gloria Anzaldúa and many other Chicana writers, linguistic. But many of us as women, as feminists—for one reason or another—share this negotiation between leaving and coming home. In a sense we are always doing both. Skipping from one side of the rope to the other and back again; as the chant goes, "Yes, no, maybe so. Yes, no, maybe so."[12]

This is what I mean by traveling other women's spaces (which often results in exploring shared space) in narrative texts. In a more general way, I think María Lugones's directions for what she calls "world"-traveling are helpful here, particularly her suggestion that we need to be "open to self-construction."[13] I'm trying to involve myself in a kind of spatial reading that opens me, and whoever may read what I'm writing, to this kind of destabilization.

The metaphor of travel is itself fraught with difficulties. Lugones herself points out that historically women of color have been forced to travel (materially and metaphorically, I'm assuming) into the world of the dominant culture, whether they wanted to or not. I just read Janet Wolff's article entitled "On the Road Again: Metaphors of Travel in Cultural Criticism." She points out that such metaphors of travel, like those used by James Clifford, Edward Said, and Fredric Jameson, are tainted with gender bias, simply because many women have never had the same access to travel as men. Metaphors of unrestrained mobility therefore work to maintain androcentric perspectives.[14] Likewise, bell hooks critiques conventional concepts of "travel" in terms of race and points out that, from certain positions—including her own as an African American woman—"to travel is to encounter the terrorizing force of white supremacy."[15] She writes about what she has had to go through to travel—from one side of her hometown to the other, from one side of the globe to the other. I wonder, though, about "travel" through reading. Gloria Anzaldúa, for instance, says she always was reading with a flashlight under the covers when she was a girl.[16] Frances Murphy Zauhar confesses to having grown up with her nose in a book and cites what she calls "other pernicious examples of excessive female reading" (my emphasis . . . I love that term).[17]

Is it possible, then, that some women are particularly adept at "traveling" through reading, hence, at rematerializing the metaphor of travel???

But as I think about all this, I feel I should also interrogate "reading"— and the implications of the disproportionate exclusion from literacy of women and other groups in the United States—not to speak of the world. Obviously, to write about writing and reading is itself exclusionary. This brings me to a screeching halt for now.

I'm really looking forward to seeing/meeting you all. And having finished this finally, I am looking forward to the next exchange.

Best regards,
Minrose

*P.S. Now, on October 11, as I edit this material for the actual presentation, I am also fascinated by the way that this short exchange of letters has destabilized my own thinking. For example, as Angelika and Elizabeth will later point out, the concept of "community" needs more careful attention and interrogation. Iris Young, for example, critiques communal politics of homogeneity, suppression, and exclusion. She finds that the privileging of face-to-face relations in the ideal of community creates "a model of social relations that are not mediated by space and time distancing." Such an ideal dematerializes its conception of interaction, "for all social interaction takes place over time and space."[18] I am now wondering whether reading may offer to feminist community that mediation of time and space. Surely there is some alternative between such extremes: "the ideal of community," which suppresses difference, and the alternative model offered by Young—the impersonal city, which offers countless spaces for the expression and interpretation of difference.*

*August 16, 1993*

*Dear Elizabeth, Minrose, and Cindi,*

*I like the idea of a letter exchange of this kind, the chance to shift registers and create a frame that marks our various places of speaking and address in their evolving configurations. I particularly like the way it creates a different space of conference writing, a space for writing differently where the public form of address is mediated privately. My pleasure at this frame and the attendant lack of the usual writing anxiety conference papers instill makes me realize the degree to which—several decades of feminist and other attempts to produce alternative cultural practices notwithstanding—I continue to experience the space of academic writing as a space of control in which I feel myself interpolated in the Althusserian sense ("Hey, you!"): asked to perform or at least show my credentials.*

*I begin our exchange, then, with pleasure at the invitation to create together a textual form that corresponds to our situation: a multidirectional, layered letter exchange in which we can simultaneously speak and listen to one another. And so, as we exchange our letters, our work for the conference begins.[19] At issue, at least for me, is the ongoing need to create livable spaces in language, spaces where "I," "you," and "we" together can exist in my, your, our lived, historical particularities. Perhaps because language is arguably one of the most controlling worlds that we (at least we in Western* culture) inhabit, this issue of space in language—language as a site of struggle, I guess—is central to my work. Perhaps this is the one obsession that we who work with literature share.

In our forum, however, we will be taking "language" more broadly to mean not just verbal communication but cultural forms of representation in general: the myriad ways in which we express and situate ourselves in relation to others within social contexts. Here's where we enter interdisciplinary terrain. I am embarking on a project located on that terrain: a study of two women, one a writer (Else Lasker-Schüler), the other a visual artist (Hannah Höch), that will be a blend of cultural history and social biography. Both women were active as artists in Germany during the Weimar Republic: Lasker-Schüler emigrated to Palestine in 1933; Höch remained in Germany throughout the Nazi years. I am interested in the relationship between the worlds they created and deconstructed in the forms and performance of their work and the worlds in which they were living. How did they situate themselves in relation to these worlds, aesthetic, social, and political? How did they—and others for them—construct their identities and define their work in relation to such categories as gender, sexuality, art, politics, or nation? What were the implications and consequences of their different choices—and lack of choice—in relation to each of these categories? My analysis assumes that in each instance their negotiations of any one of these constructions are at once metaphorical and material: Lasker-Schüler's androgyny, fanciful costuming, and masculine pseudonyms; her mythologized staging of her relationships with men; her life-long bond with her mother and passionate love for her son; her relationship to her Jewishness, her father, and her German homeland both while in Germany and later in exile; Höch's cross-dressing and public persona as the only woman in the Berlin dada group; her bisexuality and the relative silence in art history about her long-term lesbian relationship with the Dutch writer Til Brugmann in favor of her much-discussed relationship with her dada compatriot Raoul Hausmann; her decision to stay in Germany during the Nazi years; and her view of art and/as politics.

My interest in utopian possibilities—the emergence over time of what the German Jewish philosopher Ernst Bloch calls the Not-Yet—is still keen.[20] Increasingly, however, I am more concerned with marking as precisely as possible the specific coordinates of the heres and nows in which this process materializes. My interest is thus defined more by the first part of the conference title, "Making Worlds," or as I have reframed it from the beginning, "Making—and Un-making—Worlds." Perhaps that is why, as you,

Elizabeth, point out, in my prospectus on Höch and Lasker-Schüler, "the connections . . . to metaphor and materiality are not clear." You are right: to me it is the boundaries between them that aren't clear.

Which isn't to say that I see no difference between language ("metaphor") and matter ("materiality"). During a recent visit to Israel I was actually able to see and physically be in the places where Lasker-Schüler had lived. Being there, being able to link her poetic metaphors to material sites, made her words and images more resonant. And out of that resonance new questions emerged for me. I found myself wondering what this land (still Palestine in the 1930s, when Lasker-Schüler first arrived) had looked and felt like to her then. What kind of home did this Mediterranean, Middle Eastern world, with its dry brightness and stark contrasts, provide someone raised as she had been in the gray coolness of west-central Europe? What did Jerusalem as it was then mean to an artist like her, formed in the crucible of bourgeois German culture and the bohemian avant-garde of 1920s Berlin? What did going (or was it "coming"?) to Palestine mean to this German Jewish woman who had constructed a poetic persona (Jussuf, prince of Thebes), a language ("I write in Hebrew," she maintained, even though the words she used were German), and a mytho-poetic world in which her identity was, in her words, "Hebrew"? The "land of the Hebrews," as she called it, was her spiritual home.[21] Yet not until she was forced to leave Germany when the Nazi terror began did she discover that the very world she had always rejected as not hers ("The language of this cool land/I can not,/And I can not keep its paces./Even the clouds that pass by/These, too, I can't read.")[22] was a home she carried into exile with her in the form of memories, longings, and dreams, images, and language.

Making and unmaking worlds happened contrapuntally in her case: Else Lasker-Schüler "unmade" Germany in her writing while it physically was her home; she re-wrote it as home in exile when her imaginary homeland—the Hebrewland of her poems—felt foreign in its materiality. Whichever place she lived in, she felt out of place: home—the place of (be)longing—was the other, the place where she was not. How much did this "othering," both of place and of her self, have to do with gender? Here opinions diverge.[23] Certainly gender cannot be considered apart from concepts of ethnicity and race as they were cast at the time in terms of national(ist) agendas.

This, finally, brings me to a question that has been dogging my work of late: the "woman" or "gender" question. More and more I find myself approaching, or reassessing, a given project with questions like: How important is the issue of gender here? Is it a necessary category? How or why not? I don't come to this set of questions via the philosophical path of subject deconstruction. Rather, I come to it by a much more material (as it were) route as I find myself thinking about bodies in history and their fate and the fact (unarguable, it seems to me) that gender can be incidental at times. For that reason, the work I have been doing on displacement, cultural identity, and home has been framed less by gender per se than by a notion of history in which gender is a, but not the, defining variable.

Neither my dilemma nor my solution is, of course, new. Both theoretically and practically, the question of the relative weight to assign gender in a given case has been the challenge of feminist work from the outset. Perhaps this is why many of us find ourselves institutionally relocating from time to time, periodically redrawing our professional and intellectual maps, changing places depending on our projects. For the place from which we embark is likely to have a critical effect on the project's outcome, defining not only the questions we ask but the ways we see our conclusions. I have been reading texts written by German, Austrian, and Swiss women during the 1970s and 1980s for an essay to be included in a cultural history of German women's writing. One of the striking features of the writings I am working with, taken as a body of work, is the degree of violence (mostly physical abuse of girls or women) enacted in the plots and graphically detailed in the narratives. Reading from a women's studies perspective, I arrive at what seems like an obvious interpretation: the texts, I conclude, portray the pervasive violence against women in social contexts of male dominance. Yet from another perspective—a German studies perspective, say—another reading, equally feasible, presents itself to me. From this perspective, the gender violence of these texts is a displaced reflection of another history of violence that has been particularly difficult for German women to deal with, namely, Nazi Germany.

If the space of analysis is defined in feminist terms, I interpret what I see within a gender grid. If I shift my critical position to another interpretive paradigm (German or cultural studies, say) what I see not only changes but signifies differently. To think gender historically thus must mean recognizing and acknowledging the degree to which it is at once a constant factor and a constantly variable one.

The usefulness and consequences of a gender-defined model (as of any model, at that) need to be critically reviewed—and if need be, adjusted or even temporarily set aside—each time we set out to apply it. This takes me to Cindi's research and my discovery of the exciting new work on the complex relationships between place and identity being produced by scholars in (cultural) anthropology and (social) geography. I am struck by the difference that a different accountability makes, by the fact that (if I am an anthropologist, say) whom I talk to and as whom I talk can matter in concrete ways that literary scholars can get away with ignoring. For a geographer like you, Cindi, it must be a fact, not a question to debate, that the meanings of spaces and thus, by implication, the spaces themselves are constructed within a variety of meaning-giving systems (political power, cultural tradition, economic exigency, psychological need) that are simultaneously fictive (in the sense of being both made and un- and re-made) and real (in the sense of having measurable consequences). The problem, then, as I see it, is not that we metaphorize reality and take our metaphors for real but that we are often insufficiently attentive to the fact that our metaphors have real, i.e., material, consequences.

Materially yours,
Angelika


August 29, 1993

Dear Elizabeth,

It's getting down to the wire on responding to your letter before the first of September, as the organizers have requested. While I usually can't muster the proper adrenaline to write until a deadline is closer (preferably 'til it's past), I'm determined to do this today and quickly because I'm leaving the country for three weeks about two minutes after the semester begins, so there's no time to breathe, let alone dally.

You ruminate about the conference title, wondering whether it means that metaphor and materiality are different, in a way that suggests that you think they are not. A little later you say that since you work with writing, it is difficult for you to discern a difference between material and metaphorical space. I gather from this that you are saying, because most conventional ways of knowing are expressed—at least in the last instance—in words, everything becomes metaphor. But this sort of linguistic turn—where language eats all—forecloses the ventilation of meanings I think would be useful.

Although we geographers hardly have a corner on space—and, in fact, "our" unproblematic way, traditionally, of using spatial terms has left them open for plundering—my sense is that while many of us have tried to learn from literary discourses, there's been little reciprocity. Little sense that there might be something to learn about location, position, place, displacement, and the like from those who deal with these notions from outside the linguistic arena. It seems we could all profit from subjecting some of these well-worn metaphors to scrutiny; that doing so could loosen some new meanings and aerate our ideas and possible practices. That kind of aeration seems to be a real possibility of the conference, even though (or perhaps because?) I've already gotten uncharacteristically testy, offensive/defensive. Perhaps it was something I read?

You talk about "making worlds" and question whether they are made rather than found. Why can't they be both? I'm a materialist. The world is out there, and there is no knowledge outside experience, but neither is there a world apart from the knowing subject. The whole world is produced (I think for similar reasons as why, for you, there's no difference between metaphor and materiality)—because there is no knowing the world apart from our subjectivity, and the act of apprehending constructs the world. This construction does not negate the materiality of the world, of space and nature (I don't question the existence of gravity or, for that matter, produce it, though I exert my own little force); it just says that worlds exist for us as social constructions. Worlds are found and inherited as well, of course, not made from scratch by each of us each day. But as with written texts that are made anew with each reading, despite the fixity of what's written on the page, each of us constructs something new with each interaction.

Your questions concerning context seem unduly black-and-white. Why can't we study the diversity of women's experiences in relation to their context (both material and metaphorical), but necessarily in and through our own material and metaphoric contexts? The latter (the role of the investigator's subject position) is usually ignored, if not mystified, in most social science. Yet feminist and poststructural theories have taught us we are all situated, not fixed or timelessly stuck somewhere, and the somewhere can be specified in time and space as well as in class, sexuality, race, and gender. On the differences between a spatialized feminist politics and a feminist politics of space: by the former I meant all the ways that space and spatial relations are imbricated and implicated in oppression and liberation; whereas by a feminist politics of space I mean of politics that concerns itself explicitly with space and spatial issues, such as access to particular environments, the sites of violence against women from the bedroom to the street, or the location of particular services and facilities that, for example, constrain rather than enable a parent's participation in the wage labor force.

On translating between metaphors and materialities of space: who knows how well we can do it? What I had in mind and was barking about above was a kind of opening up of "both sides"—the metaphors of space themselves and the seemingly unproblematic relations upon which they are based. Both might be invigorated by the process. A couple of weeks ago I was reading a short piece on language that talked about refreshing metaphors by thinking them through literally and working forwards and backwards from there. The author suggested that it enlivens the metaphors and makes one think about their sources. The slippage is precisely what I am interested in because it seems there are transformative possibilities in the cracks and fissures of language and other forms of practice. (That's why I study everyday life—I'm interested in ruptures within the routine. Some of them might be critical.)

The question juxtaposing real and produced makes no sense to me. How does the production of space obviate its "realness"? I guess what you are saying is that if we produce our spaces, does it matter what is "really" out there. I hope what I said above about producing/finding and the spatialized politics/politics of space makes clear that by produced I don't mean dreamed up. Although dreaming the world is certainly one way of producing it, it's only one of the ways. I am more concerned with shared productions and knowledges, not with the individual or idiosyncratic worlds in each of our heads. The world we produce is, of course, metaphorical, but it is not just that. It is nonmetaphorical when some of the population cannot walk certain streets and others can, when some have access to property/land and others don't, when you go to sit down and your butt hits a horizontal surface. A chair is not just a metaphor; private property isn't either; neither are spaces in which the violence of some members of the population is tolerated and even encouraged; or to be more positive, neither are safe or special places like lesbian bars or shelters for battered women.

Exploring what a "room of one's own" is might be another productive and interesting exercise at the conference. Certainly nothing in my conceptualization of "disalienation," which is a project, requires a particular notion of ownership or exclusive occupation or excludes bad dreams, the unconscious, or the tentacles of other productions of space that reach us electronically or otherwise. Virtual reality is a whole new world; the ether still seems to belong to no one, but I'm always struck by how when things are constructed as belonging to no one, like the night, like public space, like e-mail, they work in ways that exclude particular someones. That is why the four tasks of "reconquest" that I outlined seemed apposite to developing a new spatialized politics.

The practical reconquest of space entails, at the very least, understanding how space is used by different social actors; interrogating the dynamics by which space is produced both structurally and in the course of everyday life; renegotiating socio-spatial relations to build a politics of space that is concerned with access, difference, and the production of space and place; and excavating sites of critical rupture in the arenas of everyday life to construct a transformative spatialized politics. I use Marxist and feminist theories to try to identify and develop the key theoretical and practical underpinnings of such a "reconquest" under contemporary socio-spatial conditions.

I draw on Jameson's invocation of the urban planner Kevin Lynch, in which he notes that urban "disalienation . . . involves the practical reconquest of a sense of place."[24] The project of disalienation—as promulgated by Lynch and Jameson—has obvious material and metaphorical implications. These rarely have been explored. Much less have their significance for a feminist politics of space been addressed. At the same time, the spatial metaphors deployed by feminists and other subaltern theorists have been successful in delineating the contours of cultural contest, suggesting sites of possible rupture, but have relied on problematic notions of space and geography. Most troubling among these, spatial metaphors seem to assume a fixity of space in order to let everything else float.[25] The resulting geographical constructions of difference remain discursive, with little connection to practical projects of "disalienation" such as struggles to resist gentrification, to "make home," to decolonize, or to replant a city street or vacant lot. I'd like to think through what material, social practices might be entailed in cognitive mapping. Perhaps this can come out of a feminist interrogation of metaphors and materialities of space. Or am I hoping for too much to come out of this conference?

Enough! I look forward to hearing from you and the others. I suppose my "position" requires me to be

Materially yours,
Cindi

*Dear Minrose, Cindi, and Elizabeth,*

*Cindi's letter both heightened and helped clarify a reaction I'd had to Minrose's letter earlier, although it was then still more vague and inarticulate. What I have been feeling is a sense of discomfort (that is now frustration) with the degree to which we seem to be circling well-trodden ground—the metaphor/materiality terrain—without pushing ourselves and each other further. Our claims and quibbles seem too obvious and too abstract to yield much energy. When I got to the place in Cindi's letter challenging Elizabeth's inference that there is no difference between metaphor and materiality (a point you reiterate several times in different words), I distinctly felt that something had gone wrong. Or at least, I thought, if this is the point at which we get stuck, we won't have learned much that is useful.*

*I would think that we could take the fact that "there is a difference between metaphor and materiality" as an operating premise, one on which we could all agree. Cindi reminds us that "the world is produced." Agreed. But you yourself introduce the critical term "produce" here. That language in the broadest sense, namely, forms and structures of representation, articulates and thus makes conscious and, in so doing, makes our worlds is also, I think, unarguable. In other words, both the means of representation and the things they represent are real. At the same time they are also material, in the sense that, to paraphrase Mao Tse-Tung, ideas become a material force when they take hold in the minds of people.[26] So why continue to belabor the point? I think we agree on the framing coordinates. Yet if we are seeking common ground, it is not terribly productive, it seems to me, to hover at the level of axioms. Where it gets interesting and productively unsettling is when we get down to the ground on which each of us stands and we talk about what all this ("metaphor" and "materiality," say) means to each of us when we do our actual work. How do we map our field of work metaphorically? Does this change—over time, according to the project? What follows from the metaphors we use? Or perhaps, instead of narrowing our scope, we need to broaden it historically and comparatively. Do some of us rely on metaphors more than others, and is that discipline-based? Is it true that travel, place, and displacement have become central metaphors in cultural and feminist studies these days? If so, why and since when? Is there a common connection between the currency of these metaphors and the current state of debate about "identity" and "identity politics"?*

On the other hand, I wonder if this metaphor/materiality debate isn't sidetracking us now. Rereading our letters, my sense is that it is neither "metaphor and materiality" nor "making worlds" (the two named foci of the conference title) that seems most to compel us in our work (and, perhaps, our lives), but the relationship between "traveling" and "community." Whether it is travel (Minrose's term), displacement (my term), the "reconquest of space" (Cindi's term), or the movement through cyber-space that fascinates Elizabeth, we are thinking about mobility and place. And, in that context, of community. So I suggest that we regroup and move on.

We could begin by taking up some of the assumptions floating around, such as the idea that travel is a privileged activity in which only some (those with the requisites of time and money) engage while the rest stay involuntarily put. You, Minrose, raise the issue of the biases (gender, race, and class) with which the metaphor of travel is tainted. While I agree to a point, I think that this is again an example of the way in which we are constrained by the cultural weight of our own metaphors. For as soon as we think of the movement from one place to another not in terms of travel (with all the class connotations of that world) but in terms of the kind of traversal of space that migrant workers, immigrants, refugees, and people forced into exile undergo, it becomes evident that we all travel, albeit in significantly different ways. A question for us as feminists is, how do these experiences of travel—displacement through traversal of space—affect women particularly and differently. How do pleasure and danger, comfort and survival, notions of identity and community shape this experience in gender-specific terms?

Questions like these were on my mind last fall when I was in London for a week and finally had a chance to visit the Freud Museum in Hampstead. I went looking for traces of what must undoubtedly have been a wrenching experience of displacement and loss of home for this Austrian Jewish family in England in 1938. Yet when I got there, what struck me was the reassuring feeling of home the house conveyed, not the feeling of loss I had anticipated. How had this happened? Who arranged this? And for whom? The descriptive tablets in the museum tell us that prior to Sigmund Freud's arrival his son Ernst and his housekeeper, Paula Fichtl, set out to recreate as precisely as possible the look and feel of the apartment in Vienna he had had to leave. The same furniture, the same artifacts and books were put in the exact same places here as there. His friend Marie Bonaparte had procured the house and paid for the move. Later that fall I visited the Nietzsche house in Weimar and again found a place made by

women for a man: Nietzsche's sister, Elizabeth, commissioned and super-
vised every detail of the house's interior design, installation, and maintenance, and if I remember correctly, another woman (whose name I neglected to write down) gave the money that made it all possible.

This brings me to the relationship between travel and community and
the many implicit, and insufficiently examined, assumptions that govern our
discussion in this regard. One of these is the assumption that they are virtually opposite poles on a spectrum of mobility and stasis: travel is being
mobile, community means staying put. Implicitly this puts mobility and community at odds, sets them in opposition. Yet this is neither always nor necessarily so. Often it is precisely the traveling that makes community possible
over time: the trips undertaken to be with family or friends at special times
to keep from losing touch, to participate in celebration; the calls made and
the letters sent; the special occasions remembered and commemorated,
the shared familial or community rituals. Roger Rouse makes this point in
his essay on Mexican migration and the social space of postmodernism:
community for the migrant workers he discusses is not a place "here" or
"there" but a network of multiple and constantly changing links between
here and there.[27] What Rouse leaves unexplored is the question of who creates and tends this web of community: who writes the letters, makes the
calls, remembers the birthdays, arranges the visits? This, I suspect, is where
gender comes in as a critical variable.

Finally, I am very uncertain about the notion of reading as "world-
traveling" that you, Minrose, propose as a vehicle for (social? personal? political?) transformation. Erich Auerbach, both in Mimesis (1946) and in an
essay written in the early fifties, "Philosophy and Weltliteratur," makes a
similar case, even if his choice of metaphors is different. As Maire and
Edward Said put it in their translators' introduction to this latter piece,
"Weltliteratur ... transcends national literatures without ... destroying
their individualities.... [It] is a concert among all the literatures produced
by man about man."[28] A profoundly and, in Auerbach's case, poignantly ide-
alistic belief, compelled by his refusal to relinquish his faith in the humanis-
tic potential of Western culture, the very culture in the name of which Nazi
policies had a decade earlier denied his right as a Jew to exist. Conceptually, this is much the same as what María Lugones says when she writes
that "those of us who are 'world-travelers' have the distinct experience of
being different in different 'worlds' and ourselves in them."[29] Good enough.
Yet while I understand and empathize with their impulse to (re)constitute
community through reading (both of them exiles/expatriates in different

ways: Lugones, an Argentinean, living in New Mexico and New York now; Auerbach, a German Jew, exiled to Turkey before he came to the United States), I wonder what this means in concrete terms. How, to paraphrase Minrose, does this flow from (women) writers to (feminist) readers pull us into (narrative) spaces that strengthen (feminist) community?

Reading alone is not transformative, I believe, beyond—perhaps—the individual. The move from one person reading (and we rarely read collectively these days, except in virtual spaces) to many people world-changing is a complex process of multiply-mediated translations. How this happens and what gets translated is a matter to be investigated carefully in each instance. Change, then, is negotiated in the links between material realities and the forms of representation in which those realities are made conscious in language. And so I'm right back where we began and where I said I didn't want to end: with metaphor and materiality!

On that note and in the interest of sending this off, I remain for now,

        Skeptically yours,
        Angelika

                                        September 19, 1993

Dear Cindi, Elizabeth, and Angelika,

Now that I have Angelika's lost letter and a second one, as well as Cindi's response to Elizabeth, I'm ready to give this another shot, though I must say I do so with a certain amount of trepidation. I am wondering whether the very form of these exchanges does not tend to foster oppositional debate rather than collaborative exchange, and whether this is the mode of dialogue that is most helpful to us as we all struggle with the implications of our own work. As Angelika says of the materiality/metaphor debate, "If this is the point at which we get stuck, we won't have learned much that is useful" from one another. Perhaps it would be helpful to discuss positionality—our own standpoints vis-à-vis the epistemologies we are drawing upon and the directions we are moving in. In these letters I feel that our own materialities, our own positions, become veiled because that's what this strange epistolary genre of academic letter exchange (not to speak of the academic worlds we live in) seems to be demanding of us—to be talking heads. Perhaps my resistance to this bifurcated format derives from a profound sense of what Diane Freedman has called a "paradigm

shift" in the past two to ten years in feminist theory and literary criticism—
a move toward more, much more, personal, collaborative, almost oral writing in literary and cultural studies.[30] More on this issue of positionality as
I write.

Before I heard from Angelika, I had drafted a short response to Cindi,
which said in part that it seemed to me that to render something
metaphorical—to conceptualize the material—does not diminish it by removing it from the realm of the material but may instead work to enlarge
our sense of its materiality. It's not a matter of "reducing" a material experience such as starvation to "words alone." For example, in his autobiographical novel Black Boy, Richard Wright writes over and over about
being hungry—really hungry—but he also writes about his "hunger" for
something to fill the terrible emptiness that he feels intellectually, emotion-
ally, and socially.[31] To focus on how material experience may be translated
into metaphor is not, I think, to diminish or ignore the hunger in the belly;
nor is it to ignore the political and moral issues raised by the presence of
physical hunger. It is to say that "hunger"—of the intellectual, emotional,
and social sort that Wright felt growing up as a poor African American boy
in the Deep South of the twenties—is also real, material to him (and, I
think, becomes so to the readers of his text). Nor am I saying that hunger
and "hunger" are the same thing. But I am thinking that the line between
them is less than distinct and that one form of "hunger"—young Richard's
loneliness, fear, isolation, despair—enlarges our sense of how many forms
hunger may take. As Adrienne Rich writes in one of her "Tracking Poems":

> remember: the body's pain and the pain in the streets
> are not the same but you can learn
> from the edges that blur O you who love clear edges
> more than anything watch the edges that blur[32]

Angelika, I hope this commentary goes beyond what you call the obvious interchanges between metaphor and materiality and moves into the
realm of your specific and very difficult questions about how metaphors actually do become material forces: "Which metaphors, applied in what context, by and to whom?" Again the question of position emerges. It's important, I think, that both Wright, whose stomach was often knotted with
hunger as a boy, and Rich, whose body has been ravaged by arthritis, are
the ones creating these "edges that blur" between metaphor and materiality—hunger and "hunger," "the body's pain" and "the pain in the streets."
Because they are subjects in the material realities they render as

metaphorical, *their metaphors are laden with a materiality that clings to those metaphors in such an inevitable way as to raise questions about what is what. (Of course, these are not* their *metaphors either, in the sense that they didn't create them out of thin air; such terms were and are certainly in circulation within the arena of representation.) This leads me into the arenas of "identity" and "politics" (and "identity politics") vis-à-vis the metaphors of travel, place/displacement, space. I'm far from saying this with certainty, but it seems to me that the inquiry and "aeration" (Cindi's term) of the metaphors we employ may need to involve an analysis of our own identity politics and what Angelika might call our "translation" (what I would call our "reading") of the metaphor/materiality relation, as well as other questions we are exploring.*

*Take my own notion of reading. Angelika, you say that you "don't see how reading anything per se is politically, materially transformative." Well, yes. There is no guarantee that reading "per se" is transformative in every case or even in a few. Nor is transformation reliant on reading. But I'd certainly venture a bet that some of the most important transformations in both personal lives and cultural histories have hinged on writing and reading (and certainly "translation"—literal and analogical—as well). I know this at a personal level for all sorts of reasons. Some women have always written to save their own lives, as Dorothy Allison says she does, and women have always read books to save their own lives.[33] Virginia Woolf, Alice Walker, Hélène Cixous, Barbara Christian, Paula Gunn Allen, and countless others write about women's connections via writing and reading and other forms of creativity.*

*Now, what does all this mean in concrete terms? It means that, yes, I think that something is going on here that is connected to women's experience; yes, I think it's often something that is different from other kinds of experience—"a . . . defining variable," as Angelika says in her first letter. I am, as I said, interested in how cultural space and gendered space converge in the narrative spaces of women's writings—how feminist readers who "think spatially," who are willing to try to travel to the interior cultural configurations a text may contain, may be able to read certain of these texts from positions that are neither inside nor outside those configurations but somewhere in their interstices. I think that this form of reading may result in the problematizing of positionality through the dislodging (that's probably too strong a word), through the subtle shifting of identities, and therefore may have political implications.*

*So it isn't just a case of traversing someone else's spaces; it's a case of that space becoming mobile and traveling within you. And for white middle-class feminist academics like myself, it may be a case of trying to leave "home" if "home," as Biddy Martin and Chandra Mohanty would say, is an illusory configuration based on the repression of difference. All too often, Martin and Mohanty write, "the white middle-class feminist's mode of adding on difference without leaving the comfort of home" has resulted in the continued marginalization of other women.[34] But as you say, Angelika, we never travel unencumbered. I guess it boils down to the fact that I'm not sure we ever remain "still ourselves" in the sense that the very identities and representations of identity you describe so eloquently seem to me to be always fluctuating, always, as Kristeva would say, "subjects-in-process."[35] Oddly, I think, you seem to be implying that the self/other binarism stays in place regardless of the changes each part of that binarism undergoes in the process of "travel." But isn't there a difference, as James Clifford says in "Traveling Cultures," in "being there" and "getting there"?[36] By that I mean isn't it possible—even probable—that the self/other binarism will itself become dislodged and transformed in this whole process into . . . something else, a borderland?*

*Though this is not a process limited to women, I find it compelling to think about in terms of material connections among women and the way those connections are conveyed in narrative. Much of my work has been on women's relationships, especially as they relate to race. This has much to do with growing up among women in the segregated, explosively racist South of the late fifties and early sixties. It also has to do with my teaching in women's studies, my readings in feminist psychoanalytic theory, and my lesbianism. Women's spaces have many resonances for me. My interest is not so much to ascertain how women's experiences are different from men's within certain cultural milieus, but the dynamics (and difficulties) of women's exchange with other women in male-dominated culture. The shared spaces. The contested spaces. I guess my belief in reading as a site of change comes from my own early necessary "travel" through reading—and not just "travel" but almost complete merger in the books I read, which were for the most part novels about girls and women doing exciting things (often traveling, which I could not do). Cixous says that reading can become "a journey into the self,"[37] but for me reading is and was a transformation of self, and one that has occurred over and over throughout my life. Such "travel," whether through reading or through exchanges like this, makes me over, again and again, and enables me to transform the material spaces I walk in and, more important, to be open to their transformations of me. I think* of such transformations as common occurrences rather than the wishful thinking of an idealist, and I believe they have much to do with many women's relational identities. Cindi, you write that you are "more concerned with shared productions and knowledges, not with the individual or idiosyncratic worlds in each of our heads." Like you, I am interested in "shared productions and knowledges," but I am also completely fascinated by "the individual [and] idiosyncratic worlds in each of our heads." Doesn't the latter make the former possible?

> Tiredly yours,
> Minrose

September 20, 1993

Dear Minrose, Cindi, and Angelika,

> "The madness of power resides in its idea that it can control fiction, that is to say, the imaginary expression of desire. The madness of fiction is to believe that it doesn't."
> —Luisa Valenzuela[38]

I have two things to write to you about: (1) in response to Minrose's question—my own work, and (2) a response to the letters that have come in during the last month.

(1) A piece of my own work
### WHAT THE DREAMER DREAMS
"Pigs dream of acorns and geese dream of maize."
> —Hungarian proverb quoted by Ferenczi in Freud's Interpretation of Dreams[39]

The brain is a storehouse (like the furniture store) of dream material. There, whatever was, IS. Affect bonded to image. Nothing lost in the archive. It's like playing Faceball 2000. If you run over sometimes secret buttons, doors open, providing entry to hidden storage places. At first you don't always know what they contain, but once you discover them, they are yours. You don't usually forget them again.

I envy those people whose grandparents lived long enough into their grandchildren's adulthood that they staked a claim on some bytes of con-

scious memory. Most of my memories involve small figures who lurk somewhere behind the screen. But even these memories I'm glad to have: of my
grandmothers—the one, with her black dog Betsy, who killed a chicken
every Sunday for dinner, and the flashy French-Canadian granny, who slid
out her bottom false teeth to make us scream—and of my grandfather in
his overalls riding his tractor. That one grandfather died before I was born
compels me to invent him. Similarly, I want to reinvent my dead father so
that I can know him better now that I am older and have more versatile
ways of understanding this man who said so little that it was always important, and a little strange, when he spoke.

"Society often forgives the criminal; it never forgives the
dreamer."

—Oscar Wilde[40]


### The Grandfather Dream

The German grandfather, who died before I met him, was born a
dreamer. Whenever I asked about him, that's what they said: "He was a
dreamer." Nothing more, like that was nothing much. My mother's tone,
when she described her husband's father, made this (pre)occupation sound
inconsequential.

Dreamer = "goodfornothing"

He lived on a farm in North Dakota. He was a farmer (most Midwestern grandfathers were farmers). Those men didn't say much. They ate
ice cream from big cardboard drums and had weak hearts. When others
were talking, they looked off into the far distance, out toward the river bottom land.

Dreamer = farmer

When my father died, I found a watch fob and one cuff link with or-
nate M's on them. "No good," said the mother, by which she meant, "not
gold." "They were his father's. He got them for selling insurance, a contest
or something." Farmers who are dreamers also sell insurance. They have to.
Remember Willy Loman? This was not steady work.

Dreamer = insurance salesman

A few years ago I found my father's birth certificate. It said: "Mother's
Occupation—Homemaker" (meaning Mother?); "Father's Occupation—
Carpenter" (meaning Dreamer?).

Dreamer = carpenter

I wondered. Did he dream what he made or make what he dreamed,
out there in Rugby, North Dakota, where, according to Fodor's (not)Com-

plete Guide *to the U.S. of A.*, you can stand at the *Geographical Center of North America, west of Devils Lake on U.S. 2.* Some special magnetism must have made that old man dream, or maybe it was the memory of some other geographical time, how the seconds click by on another farm in that country that became unmentionable. (War's enough to turn anyone outside in.)

"You go to bed and you never know what you're going to see."
—Sixteen-year-old girl[41]

*It's not so much what I see as it is what happens to me, the traps my dreams set for me. They're more exciting than an "action thriller." I do as much running as Tom Cruise in* The Firm. *When we work for money, we all work for "The Firm," don't we? Some Firm or other. My dreams tell me that much anyway. I dream my failings, never or rarely my successes. They are a workout, a trial run to prepare for success. A-N-T-I-C-I-P-A-T-I-O-N. Homework for life in the fast track. One of my favorite lines in fiction is from a novel called* Maiden. *The character twitches out of bed early every morning "for fear that the day would get the drop on her."[42] I read this when I was a new assistant professor at Rutgers, a place representative of an inappropriate level of aspiration for a Wayne State Ph.D. I knew they all knew I didn't belong there, that I was another example of the department chair's madness. So I knew what it meant for the day to get the drop on me.*

*I wonder what people who aren't like me dream. Did Grandfather dream of winning cuff links, or did he dream of losing his farm, the death of his father and mother, the black forests that he left in Germany? I finally went to Rugby, North Dakota, to see what I could see there, to find out if I could understand my father better or maybe only remember him better. I read the Yellow Pages, which had huge sections for things I never think of: (1) aerial spraying, (2) potatoes, (3) farm equipment, (4) fertilizers, (5) grain elevators, (6) auctioneers. (I wondered if that last one was a recent addition to the fixtures of the prairie. And the grain elevators at the main intersection downtown—bigger than any of the few blocks of stores.) North Dakota is an unremarked treasure, the sky bigger than the ground (I used to think you had to go to Montana for that), the horizon is so low. The dirt is blacker than black. Fertile because it's so black.*

*I cried on Route 2 going into Rugby. Was it Peter Gabriel singing his heartland song on the CD player? Was it that I didn't know any answers— whether my grandfather died there, how my father got to Indiana, where they lived in Rugby, which one-room school he had gone to—or was it because my father had to leave such a strangely beautiful place and I never knew it before? North Dakota doesn't resemble Michigan. What did my father think of this new place, the place where I grew up? When does one form an attachment to the distribution of space, the look of a landscape? Elizabeth Hampsten speculates, "I expect one's sense of place is deeply psychic; I doubt we are moved by or drawn to mountains, deserts, rivers, woodlands, coastlines, or amber waves of grain alone and in a vacuum, but imperceptibly respond to them in combination with whatever human circumstances connect us to them."⁴³ North Dakota can't be forgotten. Perhaps there were resemblances to more than Minnesota, where my father also lived, but to those Michigan lakes—the expanse from the shore of a big lake and the spread of that big open land—that my father, a link in the chain of immigrant transplants, felt, or that I might feel, ignoring the climate and the specific varieties of trees, at the lake where I live in Alabama.*

(2) My response to your last letters

    *I wondered if our comments with respect to metaphor and materiality couldn't be grouped into four categories: (1) the representation of "reality," the latter like the Lacanian Real that we never really get at and are able to approach only through modes of representation; (2) the reality of representation, or I should say, the reality effects of representation, because it seems that we learn our sense of reality through representation (socialization, domiciles, neighborhoods), that it pretends in various ways to offer us versions of reality; (3) the representation of representation, or the "meta" discourses in which we speak of representation (the novel speaks of the novel); and (4) the reality of reality, the stumbling block in all our discussions because we don't want to let go of the realness of the real, and yet we aren't able to get at it through means other than the symbolic, that is, representational systems and languages (I include images, numbers, etc., here).*

    *About desires to enter another space through reading: the page of a book, like the computer screen, is a frontier through which we enter a nonspace space, the space that isn't "really" there. It is safe space, which the actual, material spaces in which many people live is not. The primary danger of this metaphorical space, the space of the text or the screen, is psychological (something we often resist including in our discussions of material reality, because the immateriality of the unconscious suggests an approach that is contrary to the belief in agency that often accompanies material feminism).*

    *While it would be all too comfortable were I to convince myself that*

*"reading" (and I don't differentiate between literature and theory, a spe-
cious distinction when one gets out on the borders) is an effective means of
political intervention, I really don't believe that. I do think that reading and
writing can be political. What I find interesting in the space travel theory of
reading is the change in subjectivity and positionality. There, I think, is where
political change can begin. In this respect I offer the following observations.
From a Kenyan writer:*

> *Five days later—or exactly six weeks after the banning of
> NGAAHIKA NDEENDA [I WILL MARRY WHEN I WANT]—I
> was in cell 16 at Kamiti Maximum Security Prison as a political
> detainee answering to a mere number K6,77. Cell 16 would be-
> come for me what Virginia Woolf had called A ROOM OF ONE'S
> OWN and which she claimed was absolutely necessary for a
> writer. Mine was provided free by the Kenya government.*
> *—Ngugi wa Thiong'o[44]*

*From an Egyptian feminist:*

> *As a writer, I am often invited to international conferences, and I
> must say that I hate this division between Eastern and Western
> feminists. Because, in fact, many women in the West are quite
> backward and many women in the East are very progressive,
> and vice versa, so the division between East and West is ambigu-
> ous and misleading. And when I attend such international meet-
> ings I am frequently asked a question by Western women that I
> know is well intentioned but, even so, is grounded in assumptions
> that are quite racist: "You have come from an impoverished,
> backward country. How can we help you?" It is always assumed
> that we women of color need assistance and that so-called First
> World women must help us. And so we often hear, "How can we
> help you?" We usually respond by saying, "Well, you can help us
> by fighting here in your country against the same system that is
> oppressing us all."*
> *—Nawal el Saadawi[45]*

*Finally, I don't know what to say about the transformative capacity of
reading. Reading can but doesn't necessarily change the individual reader,
regardless of gender. What that individual then does about the political context (local to global) in which s/he or others live is how change occurs. (I am*

reminded of Spivak's insistence that political stands are taken in the old way.)

That's all for now,
Elizabeth


October 10, 1993

Dear Elizabeth, Angelika, and Minrose,

It is the dreariest day I can remember—I've had soup, done wash, am wearing socks. I still feel clammy. The warm Tucson air will feel good tomorrow. Yesterday the trees luminous in the sharp fall sunshine made the prospect of going quite another thing (is this the materiality of space?)—today it's only the idea that I feel committed to writing one more "installment" before I go that's holding me back. I theoretically have wanted to write this for over a week now and have managed not to. In the midst of doing other things—mostly reading—I've thought of things I wanted to say, but when I have tried to harvest them, I've felt lethargic and distracted. It struck me today, as I was folding the towels and remembered that Minrose mentioned crackers and the wash as detours around her first letter, that maybe our collective hesitations and resistances had come to roost in me.

I alternately appreciate (and mostly agree with) so much of what each of you has said, and then feel somehow cornered by it into Literary Studies 101. Did I seem that crude? Interdisciplinarity all of a sudden seems a lot harder. I don't think we have much disagreement on the differences, similarities, and mutual infusions between metaphors and materialities, and I agree with Angelika that if that is where we stop, it won't have been a productive journey (without much to commend even looking out the windows on the way). But to push this (spatial) metaphor further, I already like looking out the windows and had hoped for more—to visit each other in contiguous (as well as textual) space. As Angelika (and I thought I) said, it seems crucial to this project to understand why spatial metaphors are being deployed at this historical moment, by whom, to what ends, and with what implications. And to go back and forth between the metaphorical and material spaces we have constructed to see how they entail, expand, reflect one another. Said's work on Orientalism in general and Zionism in particular is illuminating in this regard. He carefully examines how historically and geographically specific "worlds" and texts produce, reinforce, enable, even require one another. (More recently Mary Louise Pratt has examined similar relationships in the constructions of nature, race, and empire.[46]) My interests are in the interstices of these domains where we might uncover the tensions and contradictions between these metaphoric and material constructions and undermine their mutual determinations. Spatial metaphors are often deployed in feminist theory to work in the opposite way; rather than scrutinizing the entailments that produce and reflect oppressive relations, they are seeking/attempting to carve out a liberatory space, a space of betweenness, a home on the borders. Either way, it seems careful scrutiny of the relationship between metaphors and materialities of space promises, at the least, new insights on each and, more ambitiously, paths toward a newly or differently invigorated politics.

In my reading of your statements and letters, I felt particularly close to Angelika's project. My work shares many common concerns with displacement and a search for the in-between, though in a different—ethnographic—terrain. I share Minrose's concern with producing common grounds from which to speak as situated but connected subjects, and Elizabeth's concerns with representation. I thought in the little time I have scrunched this endeavor into, I would try to outline some of these concerns more specifically with reference to my work in Sudan and East Harlem and try to make some responses to specific things each of you has said.

My research is broadly concerned with the relationship between culture and political economy, specifically addressing the production and exchange of knowledge under specific historical and geographical circumstances with a view to examining the practices of everyday life as critical, wherein rupture is immanent in the routine. The stuff of my work is prosaic—what children know about their environment and how they use this knowledge in their work and play, and more loftily how they construct their (spatialized) identities and produce spaces infused with their agency. First I looked at these questions in rural Sudan in a village undergoing transformation as a result of its inclusion in a state-sponsored agricultural development project and then (now) in East Harlem New York, where industrial restructuring and urban disinvestment are displacing working-class Latino kids in frighteningly similar ways as in Sudan. In both sites children are being marginalized and deskilled, not learning what they need to know in the world in which they are coming of age.

The work has involved a series of displacements—material and metaphorical. To do it I traveled and lived for a year in a mud house in a

Sudanese village. I was immersed in this world, but I traveled others—the Spain of Don Quixote and the Russia of Tolstoy—with nightly visits from "the world" courtesy of the BBC. My sense, then, of people's lives is rooted in my own experience, my various ways of knowing them. It's my sense, to be sure; I do not speak for those with whom I worked but about them. As in all relationships, they invented themselves for me, told me what they wanted me to know. So I am not claiming some fundamental truth rooted in "the real" of privileged authenticity, but my sense of their lives is not intermediated. It's situated in a historical geography I shared for a time, discovered in heat, dust, a particular kind of light. A smell can bring it back. It is different from reading about others' experiences (although it can be shared with others only by my intermediation—you read here about my experiences). Work in the spaces of others has a peculiar tension around its particular materiality, its historicity, its geographic specificity, the ways these intersected with my biography, and the particular privilege, baggage, and responsibility of being able to make that happen.

I recognize that I constructed "the field," dropping the grid of my study on knit-together places and cordoning them off, and my foreignness (traveler status) enacted but also enabled my intrusion. (I'm leaving aside for now the obvious and well-interrogated power relations in such endeavors.[47]) Displacements are the way I approach the social construction of the space/site/field as multiply determined and determining and situate my self and my project in it. The social matrices of these spaces and knowledges intersect in real (metaphoric and material) ways. The initial displacement (to Sudan) had, of course, all kinds of beginnings in and connections to my biography that I won't discuss here, but going to an African village to learn about resistance and reproduction was not something I undertook lightly or naively—the politics were serious.

I thought the things I wanted to see would be in starker relief in a setting undergoing such profound imposed changes in its political economy and cultural ecology, and I thought those changes posed particularly daunting political challenges. I saw/constructed continuities between my concerns about capitalist social relations and those of the people with whom I worked. I took seriously that capital was indeed global and confronted, made sense of, and produced by multiply-positioned actors who were situated in specific (and knowable) ways—that in this there were ties between my political concerns and those of the people in the village where I worked. I don't elide the differences between my struggles and theirs (indeed, determining which ones were significant remains an underbelly of the work), but neither can I ignore the similarities. Moreover, I cannot deny that (metaphorically) I was already there—implicated in the colonial and imperial projects of my country. Still I felt queasy—why the need for high relief brought about by distance and acute difference?

One of the ways I worked through this difficulty was to situate my subjectivity more explicitly within the problematic to connect political struggles in my everyday life with those of the kids confronting an altered field of meanings/possibilities. An obvious area of connection was my struggles centered on the production and exchange of knowledge and my attempts to alternately/simultaneously alter/stay afloat in the dominant discourse; but I also concentrated on my participation in the larger collective struggle to dismantle the power relations associated with capitalism, patriarchy, racism, and heterosexism. Locating some common ground helped me to understand their struggles and needs better, and establishing critical intersections in our material social practices led me to work more explicitly at exposing the machinations of the oppressive social relations they confronted. I neither attempted to elide the subjectivities of those with whom I worked (and their possibilities for consciously appropriating their knowledge to change their circumstances) nor tried to grandiosely construct my project as speaking for them. (Minrose, this seems similar to your setting up a space to speak with one another rather than for or against.) I don't want to suggest an easy slippage or equivalence between our struggles—they are different in deep and profound ways—but any successful politics of change will necessarily move between such (and other) subject positions, and this seemed a way to enact that possibility.

Still this wasn't enough. I wanted to live where I worked and work where I lived, to connect this politics to one closer to home. In another displacement (fictive and real; material and metaphoric) I began to work in East Harlem, where the pernicious effects of "global economic restructuring" (such a banal and mystifying term for such gut-wrenching political-economic shifts) were producing dislocations in children's everyday lives similar to what I saw in Sudan. The prospect of meaningful work was no brighter for these kids than for children in Sudan, and the reasons for this were of a piece with what was occurring in Sudan. These sites—Harlem and rural Sudan—are usually constructed as so different that they are rarely considered in the same frame. Exploring the differences and similarities between the material social practices of identity construction and the production of space in both settings (as well as my own interpolation in both) situates and connects disparate and often inchoate struggles on the grounds of a shifting global capitalism, and makes possible multiply-positioned responses, new spaces of betweenness that make clear that the global is instantiated in the local and the local infuses the global. Someone at a conference I attended recently called this "glocal," but it sounds too much like a sugar substitute.

I call this transnational project "seditious eruptions," inspired by a lovely quotation from Louis Gabriel Gauny about how sedition first erupts in the desert and then moves to the city.[48] In material and metaphoric ways this has been my own trajectory and, I hope, is reflected in the movement of my work.

I've gone on too long. I look forward to meeting you all.

Seditiously,
Cindi

### A POST:SCRIPT

We may seek to return to matters as prior to discourse to ground our claims about sexual difference only to discover that matter is fully sedimented with discourses on sex and sexuality that prefigure and constrain the uses to which that term can be put. Moreover, we may seek recourse to matter in order to ground or to verify a set of injuries or violations only to find that matter itself is founded through a set of violations, *ones which are unwittingly repeated in the contemporary invocation.*

—*Judith Butler*, Bodies That Matter: On the Discursive Limits of "Sex"[49]

May 25, 1994

Dear Minrose, Cindi, and Angelika,

It's summer again, and I'm at home. My study, where I write, has recently been reconfigured, so I can say that, literally, I have moved into a new writing space. The study has been remade, its elements supplemented and reconfigured. I didn't completely escape the old ones. The container of space is the same—walls, floor, and ceiling still where they were. The components, however, occupy different positions, and some new pieces have been added, some old ones recycled, moved into other people's writing spaces. This seems like the way the lexicon changes, yet doesn't, like the protocols of *writing. Some views remain the same; others don't. The bricoleur at work once more.*

*The conference was for me a satisfying experience on several counts. The setting afforded a most wonderful place to get together with people whose work I have admired but with whom I had spent little or no time. The response to our group presentation was terrific, and the ex/changes concerning my own work were both moving and encouraging, the effects of which I am about to discover, moving into a summer of writing. I hope that each of you also benefited.*

*There is something quite odd about the notion of a postscript. Of course, a postscript can never be post script, I realize as I sit here writing to you again. Post other writing, post conference, post last summer, but not post script. There might be no such thing as a postscript, as though the signature or the pre-text were all, as though I could end writing, speak from beyond or after it. But I'm still in language. I'm still scripting.*

*Right now I'm working on the notion of critical fictions, claiming that, at best, these are what writers write. They are no less useful because they are fictions, and the story that these fictions might be otherwise is the biggest plot of all. This is not to say that we should all give up criticism and begin to write novels, since, in my view, most fiction isn't critical and thus is part of the plot. Well, what else would you expect from me?*

> *Continuing, fictionally yours,*
> *Elizabeth*

*June 9, 1994*

*For Angelika, Cindi, and Elizabeth, from Minrose*

*Travel*

> *Tonight her feet are planted on rocks*
> *at the edge of San Pablo Bay. Under*
> *a jacket she touches the hand*
> *of a dark-haired woman. The sun leans across*
> *the Golden Gate Bridge, threads a needle of light*
> *all the way in to shore. She is farther out*
> *than she ever dreamed of, and wider.*

When I was a girl, she says, Memphis
was the farthest place in my mind.
On hot nights I used to pull
my nightgown up to my chest and
dream of Memphis until I could not tell
where I was, or where the smell of mimosa
came from. I would wake up in the night
with my head down by the window at the
foot of the bed and my legs pointed to
the head, and I would not know how
I got that way, or why the katy-dids
had stopped their singing and the air
held nothing but heat.

She says: when I first saw California
on a map in school, it looked alone and
afraid. I thought no wonder they have
earthquakes. They're out there where
everything can be washed away, where nothing
is on solid ground. Now I see
how the land goes in and out
and the tide stays. The tidal pools
make here and there seem like the same
place, and succulents with pink buds
grow from rock and sand.

Across the bay today, under a leaking
umbrella at Haight and Ashbury she
looked for the pond where they
took off all their clothes and
said it was a new space in time.
She read about it 20 years ago
from a borrowed book in a basement
apartment in Tennessee where she
lived for three years with a baby
allergic to mold and mildew. One night
she dreamed her breasts were grazing the
California grass. The next day she

*signed up to learn how to tie-dye*
*in a free class at the Y.*

*She says: my mother married*
*a traveling salesman. He went all over,*
*and only came home on weekends, hot and*
*smelling like grease. He would fall down*
*on the sofa and sleep all day, his face*
*turned in. While he slept we would*
*trace the lines gliding down the back*
*of his neck like rivers to the sea. All*
*he ever wanted was for us to be quiet and*
*let him sleep he was so tired from*
*traveling, we never knew how far. He liked*
*his biscuits flat and the bottom of his*
*cornbread burned. On Saturday night my*
*mother would shell field peas for him until*
*her nails turned blue. When Monday*
*came and he left again, she would*
*wander around the apartment singing,*
*I hear*
*you calling me,*
*lovely Vienna so gay,*
*so free.*
*City of love*
*and sparkling*
*wine, you're such*
*a part of*
*this heart*
*of mine.*

*This woman's mother ended up traveling*
*south to the state asylum. Later she*
*died in the back of an ambulance on a*
*journey to no one knows where. When*
*this woman watches the sun*
*set over the map's crease, she*
*thinks of the return*
*to the other side,*

*the freighter from China*
*she saw coming into the harbor*
*this morning, the way Vienna*
*might look in spring.*


*July 12, 1994*

*Dear Cindi, Elizabeth, and Minrose,*

*In May, right after I returned from Germany, several days after my mother's death, I wrote a postscript to our letters that never materialized in print. Rereading them after the conference, after we had actually, finally, met—had sat and talked, shared food, spent time together—our words on paper seemed strangely abstract. What now, in this rereading, seemed only minimally present in our letters in written form (indeed, in mine, almost absent) was precisely what had so powerfully informed our collective experience of our exchange when, at the conference, we spoke them: the insertion of bodies into language.*

*It is that experience of our embodied presence, performing what had been disembodied words, that stays with me most keenly in memory. I remember the way we positioned ourselves in the room: spread out so that we each had our own space but could see one another well. I remember the feel of air from opened windows, each of you in a different corner of the room, the four of us standing, holding our letters in our hands. I remember the audience—the women and some men—in clusters of chairs rearranged (no longer neatly in rows), looking at us, us looking at them, gazes traveling. I remember our voices, reading aloud, making connections palpable. I remember the energy in the room, the shadowed light, the mood of anticipation.*

*No doubt, these postscript reflections were strongly influenced by my recent experience of physical loss (my mother's death), the still vibrant memory of another room of shadowed light and the knowledge, forged in that room, of the impossible and necessary links between the articulate and the sensate, words and bodies. Elaine Scarry's brilliant study of* The Body in Pain *had offered perspectives for understanding. In the space that language vacates, she proposed, the body resides. So perhaps, I thought, as letters demonstrate, the inverse is also true: where bodies are absent, language can fill in. When both, language and bodies, come together— intelligible and palpable one to the other, connected in mutual engage-*

ment—something rare and powerful occurs. I felt it that day at the Making Worlds conference when you—Elizabeth, Cindi, and Minrose—and I stood and spoke our letters and listened and, in listening, understood things about our words that our letters, just read, had left suspended.

In May I wrote this postscript (that I am rewriting again now) and somehow, somewhere, it got lost in my computer. Lost in virtual space. As if to rebuke me for my joy in materiality. And so I write it again, and end it as I ended my first letter in this exchange,

Materially yours,
Angelika Bammer

August 8, 1995

Dear Elizabeth, Angelika, and Minrose,

Still at the same desk, now worlds away from those first letters. Somehow I remember being cold and damp as I forced myself to write the second one—the first one I was vaporizing with heat and anger on my front porch. That was two years ago. Now I sit two days after an interminable heat wave broke, and the clear air feels like a miracle. As I write I wonder about why I have to start with weather talk—is this just the elevator part before I get to work?

Is this work? I think not, although I keep slithering away from Penny's requests to write a postscript . . . and yet I have such good feelings about our—our what? project? (too intentional), collaboration? (too conspiratorial), letters? (too disembodied), relationship? (we were too fleeting)—and our crisscrossing. I have spoken about its inception and unfolding many times, often to suggest that it be emulated as a way of having an open-ended airing of something. The political really was more charged by being so personal, and I keep having hopes that other as yet subterranean troubles might be scratched at this way. When I suggest an exchange of letters, everyone thinks it sounds great but no one—including me in my various editorial board incarnations—has actually gone for it. I think I'm a little scared to try it because I don't want our exchange to become an exercise, something mechanical. A conference ingredient for the twenty-first century: three panels, a plenary, six paper sessions, and a chain letter. . . .

One of the things I savor most about our exchange was how indeterminate it was—there's so much determined indeterminacy these days that participating in something without really knowing where it was going was exhilarating, if a bit daunting. Our dance of entailments did really just unfold, and much of my pleasure in it is the memory of its motion from the vantage point of knowing its outcome. I like moving in the space of our interchange so that my own feelings in its midst get churned up and reflected on from the moment of their happy ending—our meeting in Tucson and the presentation of our letters. I like talking of our different reactions, how Angelika ripped open the letters like they were messages from an illicit lover, while I put them aside, unread missives of resentment and loathing. How when I met all of you I liked you so much I could no longer imagine my initial anger and cut so much of it from my presentation (this says something discomfiting about how I can bark at strangers but not so easily at people I know), while each of you, of course, left intact your responses to it. I like the spatiality that was produced by this and other performative aspects of our exchange; the ricocheting of our letters spoken in space, and the ways it resonated with the spatiality of the letters—the written and unsaid, the said and unwritten. I love that it was Angelika, the "literary theorist," who used the space of the room to give a material form to our metaphorical positionings. I appreciated the conversation that ensued. Maybe it was something we said? Or was it the way we said it? Of course, these cannot be separated—at that moment we somehow managed to perform metaphor and materiality as double helix—and that was the point all along.

Getting there—if only in retrospect—was more than half the fun. The only disconcerting part is that "there" has become here, and this may be it. In the flush of the conference (now who's having a love affair?) it felt like we might somehow keep going, but without its structuring episodes (of which this is the last), we have not. I do delight in knowing each of you that little bit, and when I come across things you write, they feel like presents. Presence.

> Until the next crisscrossing,
> Cindi

## NOTES

1. Jacques Derrida, *Of Grammatology*, trans. Gayatri C. Spivak (Baltimore: Johns Hopkins University Press, 1976), xviii–xix.

2. Giorgio Pressburger, *The Law of White Spaces*, trans. Piers Spence (New York: Pantheon Books, 1992), 38.

3. Gayatri C. Spivak, "French Feminism in an International Frame," in *In Other Worlds: Essays in Cultural Politics* (New York: Methuen, 1987), 150.

4. Donna J. Haraway, *Simians, Cyborgs, and Women: The Reinvention of Nature* (New York: Routledge, 1991), 187.

5. Biddy Martin and Chandra Talpade Mohanty, "Feminist Politics: What's Home Got to Do With It?" in *Feminist Studies/Critical Studies,* ed. Teresa de Lauretis (Madison: University of Wisconsin Press, 1986), 193.

6. Elizabeth Meese, *(Ex)Tensions* (Urbana: University of Illinois Press, 1990), 28.

7. Nancy K. Miller, *Getting Personal* (New York: Routledge, 1991), 36.

8. Audre Lorde believes that it is not our differences that separate us, but our refusal to recognize them and those distortions that come from misnaming and ignoring them. See *Sister Outsider* (Freedom, Cal.: Crossing Press, 1984), 122.

9. Dorothy Allison, *Bastard Out of Carolina* (New York: Dutton, 1992); Harriet Jacobs, *Incidents in the Life of a Slave Girl,* ed. Jean Fagan Yellin (Cambridge, Mass.: Harvard University Press, [1861] 1987).

10. Sandra Cisneros, *The House on Mango Street* (New York: Vintage, 1989), 51.

11. See Baker's discussion of African American cultural space and "the economics of slavery." Houston A. Baker, Jr., *Blue, Ideology, and Afro-American Literature* (Chicago: University of Chicago Press, 1984), 1–14.

12. Cisneros, *House on Mango Street,* 51 (see also the description of Cisneros at the end of this Vintage edition: "The daughter of a Mexican father and a Mexian-American mother, she is nobody's mother and nobody's wife"). A revised portion of this discussion of Cisneros's *House on Mango Street* is included in my article "Space Travel: The Connective Politics of Feminist Reading," *Signs* 21, no. 4 (Summer 1996): 870–905.

13. María Lugones, "Playfulness, 'World-'Travelling, and Loving Perception," in *Making Face/Making Soul: Haciendo Caras,* ed. Gloria Anzaldúa (San Francisco: Aunt Lute, 1990), 400–1.

14. Janet Wolff, "On the Road Again: Metaphors of Travel in Cultural Criticism," *Cultural Studies* 7 (1993): 234.

15. bell hooks, "Representing Whiteness in the Black Imagination," in *Cultural Studies,* ed. Lawrence Grossberg, Cary Nelson, and Paula Treichler (New York: Routledge, 1992), 343–44.

16. Gloria Anzaldúa *Borderlands/La Frontera: The New Mestiza* (San Francisco: Aunt Lute Books, 1987), 65.

17. Frances Murphy Zauhar, "Creative Voices: Women Reading and Women's Writing," in *The Intimate Critique,* ed. Diane P. Freedman, Olivia Frey, and Frances Murphy Zauhar (Durham, N.C.: Duke University Press, 1993) 105–6.

18. Iris Marion Young, "The Ideal Community and the Politics of Difference," in *Feminism/Postmodernism,* ed. Linda J. Nicholson (New York: Routledge, 1990), 305.

19. *The American Heritage Dictionary of the English Language* (New York: American Heritage Publishing Co., 1969) defines this work as comparing views, consulting together, and settling differences "for mutual benefit." See "conference" and "confer": 278–79.

20. See my previous work on the potential and hazards of utopian thinking, *Partial Visions: Feminism and Utopianism in the 1970s* (New York and London: Routledge, 1991).

21. *Herbräische Balladen* (Hebrew Ballads), which appeared in several different versions between 1913 and 1920, is perhaps Lasker-Schüler's most famous poetry collection. It predates her first visit to Palestine in 1934. Her prose work, *Das Hebräerland* (The Land of the Hebrews), was published in 1937, the year of her second visit to Palestine. Her third Palestine visit, in 1939, became permanent exile when her request for a return visa to Switzerland was denied.

22. *"Ich kann die Sprache/Dieses kühlen Landes nicht,/Und seinen Schritt nicht gehen./ Auch die Wolken, die vorbeiziehn, Weiß ich nicht zu deuten"* (English translation mine). From the poem "Heimweh" (Homesickness), published in 1910 in the Expressionist journal *Die Fackel*.

23. Two studies of Lasker-Schüler published in 1985 propose significantly different answers to this question. Jakob Hessing's *Else Lasker-Schüler: Biographie einer deutch-jüdischen Dichterin* (Else Lasker-Schüler: Biography of a German-Jewish Poet) (Karlsruhe: Loeper Verlag) foregrounds her Jewishness, while Judith Kuckart's *Im Spiegel der Bäche finde ich mein Bild nicht mehr: Gratwanderung einer anderen Ästhetik der Dichterin Else Lasker-Schüler* (Frankfurt/Main: S. Fischer) puts the emphasis on gender. For a historical overview of the shifting trends and emphases of Lasker-Schüler scholarship, see Calvin Jones, *The Literary Reputation of Else Lasker-Schüler: Criticism 1901–1993* (Columbia, S.C.: Camden House, 1994).

24. Fredric Jameson, "Postmodernism, or the Cultural Logic of Late Capitalism," *New Left Review* 146 (July-August 1984): 89.

25. Neil Smith and Cindi Katz, "Grounding Metaphor: Towards a Spatialized Politics," in *Place and the Politics of Identity*, ed. Michael Keith and Steve Pile (London and New York: Routledge, 1993).

26. Mao Tse-Tung, "Where Do Correct Ideas Come From?" in *Four Essays on Philosophy* (Peking: Foreign Language Press, 1968), 134.

27. Roger Rouse, "Mexican Migration and the Social Space of Postmodernism," *Diaspora* 1, no. 1 (Spring 1991): 7–23.

28. Erich Auerbach, *Mimesis* (Bern: A. Francke, 1946); Auerbach, "Philosophy and *Weltliteratur*," trans. Maire and Edward Said, *Centennial Review* 13, no. 1 (Winter 1969): 1.

29. María Lugones, "Playfulness," 396.

30. Diane Freedman, *An Alchemy of Genres* (Charlottesville: University Press of Virginia, 1992), 44. Examples of this more personal style are Nancy K. Miller's *Getting Personal;* Elizabeth's *(Sem)Erotics* (New York: New York University Press, 1992); Jane Tompkin's "Me and My Shadow," all of bell hooks' works; the new anthology from Duke called *The Intimate Critique: Autobiographical Literary Criticism*, ed. Diane P. Freedman, Olivia Frey, and Frances Murphy Zauhar (Durham, N.C.: Duke University Press, 1993); Gloria Anzaldúa's *Borderlands/La Frontera;* Patricia Williams's *The Alchemy of Race and Rights* (Cambridge, Mass.: Harvard University Press, 1991); and, of course, the work of Audre Lorde, Adrienne Rich, and Minnie Bruce Pratt, to name but a few.

31. Richard Wright, *Black Boy* (New York: Harper & Row, 1945).

32. Adrienne Rich, No. 9 of "Contradictions: Tracking Poems," in *Your Native Land, Your Life* (New York: Norton, 1986), 111, lines 9–14.

33. In her preface to the short story collection *Trash* (Ithaca, N.Y.: Firebrand, 1988), Dorothy Allison writes: "I write stories. I write fiction. I put on the page a third look at life at which I've seen in life—the condensed and reinvented experience of a cross-eyed working-class lesbian, addicted to violence, language, and hope, who has made the decision to live, is determined to live, on the page and on the street, for me and mine."

34. Martin and Mohanty, "Feminist Politics," 12.

35. Julia Kristeva, *Desire in Language,* trans. L. Roudiez (New York: Columbia University Press, 1980), 120.

36. James Clifford, "Traveling Cultures," in *Cultural Studies,* ed. Lawrence Grossberg, Cary Nelson, and Paula Treichler (New York: Routledge, 1992), 99–100.

37. Hélène Cixous, *Readings,* trans. Verena Conley (Minneapolis: University of Minnesota Press, 1991), 131.

38. Luisa Valenzuela, in *Critical Fictions: The Politics of Imaginative Writing,* ed. Philomena Mariani (Seattle: Bay Press, 1991), 82.

39. Sigmund Freud, *The Interpretation of Dreams,* trans. James Strachey (New York: Avon Books, 1965), 165.

40. Oscar Wilde, "The Critic as Artist," quoted in Isobel Murray, *Oscar Wilde* (Oxford University Press: 1989), 274.

41. Adam Phillips, *On Kissing, Tickling, and Being Bored: Psychoanalytic Essays on the Unexamined Life* (Cambridge, Mass.: Harvard University Press, 1993), 20.

42. Cynthia Buchanan, *Maiden* (New York: Pocket Books, 1973), 41.

43. Elizabeth Hampsten, *Mother's Letters: Essays* (Tucson: University of Arizona Press, 1993), 39–40.

44. Ngugi wa Thiong'o, *Decolonizing the Mind: The Politics of Language in African Literature* (London: James Currey, 1986), 64.

45. Nawal el Saadawi, Untitled piece in *Critical Fictions: the Politics of Imaginative Writing,* ed. Philomena Mariani (Seattle: Bay Press, 1991), 155.

46. Mary Louise Pratt, *Imperial Eyes: Travel Writing and Transculturation* (London and New York: Routledge, 1992).

47. I have dealt with these questions elsewhere. See Katz, "All the World Is Staged: Intellectuals and the Projects of Ethnography," *Environment and Planning D: Society and Space* 10, no. 5 (1992): 495–510; "The Expeditions of Conjurors: Ethnography, Power, and Pretense," in Diane L. Wolf (ed.), *Feminist Dilemmas in Fieldwork* (Boulder, Colo.: Westview Press, 1996), 170–84; and "Playing the Field: Questions of Fieldwork in Geography, *The Professional Geographer* 46, no. 1 (1994): 67–72.

48. Cited in Kristin Ross, *The Emergence of Social Space* (Minneapolis: University of Minnesota Press, 1988), 21.

49. Judith Butler, *Bodies That Matter: On the Discursive Limits of "Sex"* (New York: Routledge, 1993), 29.

# PART 4

## a different script:
## constructing moral geographies

Like the correspondents in the previous
section, the authors in "A Different Script" refuse the distinctions of
metaphorical and material. Representing a broad range of interests—
religious studies, queer theory, Native American studies, architecture, anthropology, women's studies, English, African studies, and history—they ponder the role of boundaries in ethical claim-making by
examining the politics of inclusion and exclusion inherent in the fashioning of value-laden worlds. Through a relational reading of Katie
Cannon's *Black Womanist Ethics* and Sarah Hoagland's *Lesbian Ethics*,
Janet Jakobsen considers the implications of geographical metaphors
for feminists confronting a world of "moral multiplicities." She argues
that feminists have avoided using the geographical metaphor of
boundaries because it connotes separation and essentialism. She suggests, however, that this misses the ways in which the recognition
of boundaries exposes relational possibilities and creates space for
building alliances across difference. Contemporary essayist Nancy
Mairs, viewing the world from the "waist-high" perspective of the
wheel chair to which her multiple sclerosis has confined her, analyzes
the ways metaphors have been used to label and dismiss her bodily
existence, while suggesting that the very construction of voice is
grounded in material conditions. Using words, drawings, and pho-
tographs, Rina Swentzell shifts these meditations onto a different terrain by summarizing the cosmology of Pueblo Indians, who believe in
the interconnectedness of everything in the universe—human beings, other animals, plants, the earth. Echoing Youngbear-Tibbetts's

focus on affinity over alienation, she sees this interactive cosmology, with its interplay of "masculine" and "feminine" elements, as a site for the moral focus on relationality among Pueblo peoples. Fran Mascia-Lees and Patricia Sharpe reflect on the history, locations, and theoretical implications of their own collaborative work, in which they attempt to literalize metaphors in order to expose their limitations. Finally, in an alternative take on the idea of speech acts, Luise White considers two seldom mentioned spaces—those of silence and the imagination. Noting that the privileging of speech over silence in African studies and women's studies marginalizes many aspects of African women's lives, White argues for the possibilities of silence and the creation of imaginary terrains as strategies of resistance and agency.

12

# feminist ethics in a world
# of moral multiplicity
## *dimensions and boundaries*

[I sit down to write this paper after talking to my friend Julie, who is in Lesbian Avengers, Atlanta. She has just been to a meeting to discuss cross-racial alliances in queer politics. The specific purpose of the meeting was to address recent moves by the Christian Coalition in Georgia to organize in African American Christian churches. We discuss how the construction of queer politics and certain failures of cross-racial alliance have made resistance to the ideological separation of race and sexuality more difficult. I turn to the question of making worlds.]

The breakup of unitary and universalist modern moral reasoning has led to a recognition that moral claims are made within a social world of moral multiplicity. The question for ethical theory, then, is how to make and respond to moral claims within this world of multiplicity if overarching claims will no longer suffice. Without an overarching unity, the moral world is marked by diversity and complexity—diversity created by differences within and among persons and a correlative complexity created by multiple crisscrossing power relations and the resultant contradictions.

For the purposes of this essay, I am particularly interested in the complexity—in part because in feminist theories we tend to talk about diversity more frequently, but also because the ways in which we talk about diversity are often so unsatisfactory precisely because they elide complexity. This diversity and complexity point to the necessity of recognizing the partiality of any single moral voice or vision, including any single feminist vision.[1] My particular question is, In these times when alliance politics are both extolled and necessary, how do we go about making these alliances? More specifically, if part of making alliances is making moral claims on one another, how do we understand each other's claims and respond to them without appealing to an overarching moral framework?

I will pursue this question through a brief consideration of the use of geographic metaphors in ethical theory and then through a relational reading among three ethical voices, Katie Cannon's *Black Womanist Ethics,* Sarah Hoagland's *Lesbian Ethics,* and my own feminist and lesbian voice.[2] I pursue this reading in part because these texts are rarely read together. I think one reason the texts are read separately is a disciplinary boundary—*Black Womanist Ethics* as a religious studies text is frequently ignored outside religious studies.[3] Another reason is, I think, the common separation made between issues of race and issues of sexuality and the difficulties in reading multiple and crisscrossing differences together. In fact, one of the few references I have seen that ties these two texts together is a footnote reference to *Black Womanist Ethics* in Sarah Hoagland's description of *Lesbian Ethics* in the recent "Lesbian Issue" of *Hypatia.*[4]

## GEOGRAPHIC METAPHORS IN ETHICS

Not surprisingly, geographic metaphors have begun to be used in feminist ethics as a way of theorizing moral multiplicity. In the follow-up volume to *In a Different Voice,* Carol Gilligan uses the geographic metaphor of "mapping the moral domain" to describe the relationship between gendered voices.[5] Gilligan employs the mapping metaphor by describing two ethical perspectives, the justice perspective (articulated and enacted primarily by men) and the care perspective (articulated and enacted primarily by women), as two dimensions on a map of the moral domain.[6] Using this metaphor, Gilligan establishes the two perspectives as rooted in the universal bases of all moral experiences in the same way that dimensions underlie any and all particular mappings.[7]

At first, for many reasons I was very suspicious of the mapping metaphor. Perhaps my greatest suspicion with respect to Gilligan's invocation of geography is the question of whether she uses the mapping metaphor to reify given locations and even oppositions. In particular, Gilligan depends on a naturalized version of geography in order to naturalize the two perspectives and the difference between them. The moral domain is out there waiting to be mapped, its parameters established by the dimensions of universal experience. In asso-

ciating gender with underlying dimensions, gender difference becomes fundamental in relation to any other form of marking distinctions on the map. Moreover, this naturalization of geography allows Gilligan to naturalize morality into
voices or perspectives/visions.

What if, however, we think in terms of both a denaturalized morality and
a denaturalized geography? In order to denaturalize morality, rather than speaking in terms of voices or perspectives, I want to focus on and in some sense literalize the language of "making" moral claims. Morality is not simply found out
there in the structure of the universe. Nor is morality simply inside us ready to
be spoken in our "voice." Rather, moral voices are produced by the labor of
moral agents within a particular time and space. The geographical, historical,
and social location of particular communities all influence the labor that a given
community undertakes and the moral voice(s) which that community produces. Similarly, geography is denaturalized if it is understood not as the underlying context, the dimensions upon which we speak/act/write our moral selves
and communities, but as part and parcel of the activity of constructing or con-
stituting—making—ourselves and our social "worlds."

When thinking of "worlds," I want to acknowledge another geographic
metaphor, that of "world"-traveling. Introduced by María Lugones in her article
"Playfulness, 'World'-Travelling and Loving Perception," it is important as a denaturalized conceptualization of "worlds" and of morality.[8] Thus, the world of
moral multiplicity that I have described may be better thought of as a set of
"worlds" in Lugones's sense, complex worlds with different powers vis-à-vis
each other. The conjunction between " 'world'-travelling and loving perception"
in the title of her text implies that to undertake a project of relating across
"worlds," of forming alliances across differences (what I am here conceptualizing in terms of moral claim-making and response), certain relational skills are
required. Where I read the particularity of her text in relation to the one that
I am constructing here is that Lugones argues that in the United States these
skills are necessary for survival for women of color in a situation where
"world"-traveling is imposed upon them, whereas white/Anglo women can
self-consciously learn them.

In the project of learning these relational skills, I have found another geographic metaphor to be particularly helpful—that of boundaries. The way we
enact and act in relation to boundaries contributes to how we make our
worlds and our moral claims. Boundaries also influence how we participate in
alliances—how we can respond to the claims of our allies. (Again, this reacting
and enacting frequently happen at one and the same time. It is not simply that
we find boundaries in our social worlds and then act, but that even as we act in

relation to those boundaries, we are also enacting them and possibly changing them in various ways.) Once again, the metaphor of boundaries proves most useful if denaturalized. Edward Said has usefully articulated cultural boundaries in terms of shifting historical constructions.[9] Thus, boundaries can be read as subject to agency (negotiation, defense, abandonment, remembering) and as permeable, rather than reified, coherent, monolithic, and ontological. On this reading, boundaries become a site of struggle, a place of conflict, and a place of agency.

If we take up Said's suggestion to think of boundaries as permeable and subject to agency, then moral questions turn on such factors as where these boundaries lie; what type of "worlds" they construct; how the boundaries are constructed and maintained; and when, where, and how (in what manner) we are able to cross or raise these boundaries. What do the spaces that depend on particular boundaries look like? What is it like to live in those spaces? What is it like to be moral in such spaces? How are the spaces related to other social spaces? I address these issues by reading *Black Womanist Ethics* and *Lesbian Ethics* with these questions in mind, particularly reading for the points of complexity—where in a sense the texts overlap—in relation to the question of what types of boundaries are enacted by these texts.

## BLACK WOMANIST ETHICS AND LESBIAN ETHICS

In reading these texts relationally, I want to briefly consider my own relational position by reading my own text for the boundaries of my position as white/Anglo, feminist, and lesbian reader. I also want to question my processes of identification in order to denaturalize the activity of relational positioning. I want to acknowledge both my identification as a lesbian reader with *Lesbian Ethics* and the racial difference between myself as a white/Anglo reader and *Black Womanist Ethics*. I also want to acknowledge the complexities invoked by the boundaries I have just acknowledged. In part I find certain relational connections come to the fore in reading *Black Womanist Ethics,* including my connection to Christianity as a dominant religious system in the United States— although, again, this connection is not simple because African American and Euro-American Christianity are very different religions and *Black Womanist Ethics* represents an active participation in religious tradition, a participation that I resist. Perhaps more importantly, I read *Black Womanist Ethics* in the context of the active process of having become allies with women, some of whom would also identify as lesbian and some of whom would not, who identify as womanist, and these alliances are part of the process that I bring with me when

I read myself into *Lesbian Ethics* and ask, "How am I relationally implicated in reading these two texts?" Thus the boundaries enacted in my reading of these texts are not just the simple ones of identification and difference but the more complex boundaries of relational interaction.

There are some structural similarities between these two texts. Both texts include a critique of dominant culture ethics in the United States, as well as a construction of new values. Both texts point out the ways in which dominant ethics legitimate capitalist economics, inculcating the virtues of capitalist success (frugality, delayed gratification, etc.). Both texts are particularly critical of the emphasis on "free choice" in dominant ethics, an emphasis that is often disempowering when acting under conditions of oppression. Both texts specify the social location and conditions, particularly the conditions of labor, under which new values are produced. At this point of specificity, the two texts diverge in both their critical and constructive moves.

In *Black Womanist Ethics,* Katie Cannon critiques white standards of femininity.[10] She is also critical of the way in which dominant white ethics (particularly white Protestantism) contribute to domination through the co-construction of whiteness and racism. Drawing on black women's literary traditions, particularly the life of Zora Neale Hurston, Cannon delineates three sets of virtues that are alternatives to dominant ethics—invisible dignity, quiet grace, and unshouted courage (17).[11] Cannon argues that black women carry a particular responsibility for both the survival and enrichment of the black community. This responsibility is based on a vision of community relatedness. Responsibility for the community issues into responsibility to act on behalf of social reform. Thus responsibility for the survival and enrichment of the community delineates the particular moral labor that is taken on by black women.[12]

In delineating black womanist ethics, Cannon is making a claim for specificity, a claim that does not, however, dissolve the possibility of moral relationships with those who don't share the womanist perspective. First she indicates an openness to "others who care" (5–6), who can learn about and from the richness of black women's moral labor without reading womanist ethics as prescriptive for all of moral life. Second, in a complex move Cannon claims both specificity and universalism, acknowledging the contribution of black women's struggles to universal struggles for human dignity and wholeness. She places the ground of her universal claims in the black church tradition, a unique, syncretistic religion that was created by slaves who were able to combine West African religious survivals with colonial Christianity to make a religion "truly their own" (17). Thus Cannon's making of universal claims must be distinguished from both enlightenment rationalist universals and the revealed universals of

Euro-American Christianity. This difference is based on a narrative understanding of truth that allows for multiple truths and "difference without domination."[13] These universal claims must always be read in relation to the concomitant specificity that Cannon maintains throughout her text. In recognizing this particularity, it is not necessary for feminists or even nontheological womanists to enter Cannon's truth structure in order to respond to her claims—in order to participate in the struggle for womanist and human dignity.

Sarah Hoagland, alternatively, is not at all interested in making any form of universal claim in *Lesbian Ethics*. Hoagland adopts a separatist stance that refuses to grant meaning to heterosexualist relations in which women are subordinate and lesbians are erased as incomprehensible. Adopting this stance does not, however, dissolve the possibility of morality. It opens the door to an alternative ethics grounded in lesbian community, which enables agency, in contradistinction to dominant ethics, which controls agency. The new values of what Hoagland calls "autokoenony," of a self both autonomous and in relation, provide an alternative to the bifurcated feminine and masculine virtues of heterosexualism. Such a move also does not render lesbian ethics either amoral or apolitical. Rather, the separatist stance adopted by Hoagland is a specific politics, a refusal to contribute in any way to the system of heterosexualism that structures lesbians' (and women's) oppression.

## READING FOR BOUNDARIES

In reading these two texts for boundaries, particularly at the point of intersection between race and sexuality, the point at which the texts might overlap, the boundaries between race and sexuality appear to create a relational silence. *Black Womanist Ethics* is basically silent on issues of sexuality. I would argue, however, that this particular exclusion is mutually constituted with the particular form of inclusion of women of color, including African American women, in *Lesbian Ethics*. I want to make clear that my critique of this mutually constitutive inclusion and exclusion is not a critique of these two particular authors and texts but rather of the way in which this problem is symptomatic of some deeper issues. These two theorists are in many ways leaders in articulating relational complexities. Elsewhere in her writing, Cannon is strongly critical of "heteropatriachal familialist ideology" and "compulsory heterosexism."[14] Hoagland is one of the few lesbian or feminist ethicists to acknowledge Cannon's text. How is it, then, that these two texts were produced with this particular relational silence?

The answer can be understood by exploring the ways in which the inclusions and exclusions of these two texts are mutually constitutive. In particular I want to explore the ways in which the form of inclusion that occurs in *Lesbian Ethics*—specifically the ways in which certain boundaries are enacted—may contribute to the constitution of exclusion that occurs in *Black Womanist Ethics*. Sarah Hoagland is in one sense extremely suspicious of enactments of boundaries; she refuses to define *lesbian*, arguing that such definitions are defensive enactments of an ethics of control within the structure of heterosexualism. This refusal of definition is one of the many textual points that resist an essentialist reading of this text. It has also proven to be a point at which those who might otherwise find themselves at the margins of lesbian ethics can build relational possibilities—for example, Elisabeth Däumer's reading of the text in relation to bisexuality.[15] Yet throughout the text boundaries that distinguish lesbian ethics are enacted. One obvious point is through Hoagland's invocation of separation, specifically from heterosexualism. Separatism is not the particular issue that interests me, however, because Hoagland presents a performative understanding of separatism, a conceptualization of separatism that resists a reified boundary.[16]

I am more concerned about the particular form of inclusion of diverse lesbians that Hoagland enacts. In other words, I am concerned with how the drawing of inclusive boundaries, while an important step in recognizing differences within lesbian communities, may elide the complex relationships among the various communities within which lesbians move and act. Since the publication of the book in 1988, critiques have been made along these lines, specifically by María Lugones, who suggests that multiple forms of separation and separatism should be acknowledged in order to recognize different communities in which lesbians live, and Hoagland has shifted her analysis in response to these criticisms.[17] Yet even in the introduction to *Lesbian Ethics* that Hoagland provides in the Fall 1992 "Lesbian Issue" of *Hypatia,* traces of a singular lesbian community within which difference is contained remain. I would like to suggest that this problem is in part the result of the dominance of (and dominant understandings of) another spatial metaphor in theorizing lesbian community—that of the closet and coming out. Hoagland states in beginning her section on differences:"So what are the possibilities of lesbian communities? One is diversity, for we emerge from everywhere—Palestine and Israel, Argentina and Cherokee Nation, China and India."[18] Her language then shifts from that of lesbian communities to that of living "in community," a form of living in which each individual is one among many. Some of this is a shift from the noun of *communities* to the adverb of living *in community.* Yet it can also be read as the dominant story of coming out; we as lesbians emerge from (not within) our various communities, which we leave in order to live in community with each other, where we are one among many. My concern is that this scenario, in its failure to theorize the ways in which we live within differing communities even while we live as lesbians—we may both come out and stay in various communities—is part of what creates the mutually constitutive exclusion and inclusion, in other words, the silence at the intersection of the two texts.

This silence has particular potential dangers associated with it for lesbians, although different dangers for white/Anglo lesbians than for women who would identify as womanist and lesbian. By creating a dominant story of what it is to enter lesbian community that involves coming out of another community or tradition, it becomes particularly difficult, is in fact a form of silencing, for lesbians who are living and acting in multiple communities. How is it that by enacting (performing) the story of coming out as a dominant lesbian story, we make it less safe for those lesbians whose stories are those of coming out (of the closet) and staying in (various communities)? The dominance of the scenario of coming out and the silences (as well as the visibility) it produces may also contribute to the public perception of a connection between lesbian (and gay) communities and certain forms of race and class (and gender) privilege. If in order to be publicly visible in lesbian community, we have to come out—of the closet, but also of our diverse communities—then the public perception of lesbian community is likely to be monolithic. This perception is particularly dangerous given current attempts by the Christian Coalition, among others, to mobilize homophobic sentiment specifically in African American Christian communities based on the claim that lesbian and gay communities are distinct from the concerns of African Americans. Thus the Christian Coalition is depending on a strong boundary between issues of race and sexuality—a boundary that belies the lives of African American lesbians but a boundary that can also be performed/enacted by an uncritical use of the spatial metaphor of coming out.[19] The goal of my critique is not so much to question Hoagland's text as to question the central role that the politics of "coming out" has taken on in mainstream lesbian and gay activity.

My concern in reading for boundaries is to provide a language for thinking about how we enact them, whether textually or materially. In creating texts, we are also creating communities that have particular boundaries, so that the question of boundaries is not just to read for them but to understand how it is that we make worlds and remake worlds in relation to understanding how it is that moral claims are made from one world to another. Thus the limits, as well as the possibilities, that become apparent when reading for boundaries demonstrate some of the various tasks presented by moral claim-making and response in multiple worlds. It is not simply a matter of mixing things around differently, being more inclusive, recognizing diversity by hearing each other or trying harder. Rather, it is a matter (literally?) of making worlds and of making worlds differently. Responding to each other frequently implies remaking our own worlds, including remaking the boundaries that form our movements and communities, not just moving these boundaries or changing their shape but changing how we act in relation to them. Are they remembered, forgotten, or enacted? There is no singular form or set of actions that can address all differences. I have read only two texts, and the complex moral task presented by moral multiplicity will undoubtedly be further apparent in other essays in this volume.

## NOTES

1. Angelika Bammer, *Partial Visions: Feminism and Utopianism in the 1970s* (New York and London: Routledge, 1991).

2. Katie G. Cannon, *Black Womanist Ethics* (Atlanta: Scholars Press, 1988); Sarah Lucia Hoagland, *Lesbian Ethics: Toward New Value* (Palo Alto, Cal.: Institute of Lesbian Studies, 1988). Hereafter cited in text with page numbers in parentheses.

3. See, for example, Rosemarie Tong's recent survey of "feminine and feminist" ethics, which includes a chapter (chap. 9) on lesbian ethics but fails to consider black womanist ethics. Tong, *Feminine and Feminist Ethics* (Belmont, Cal.: Wadsworth Publishing, 1993).

4. Sarah Hoagland, "Why Lesbian Ethics?" *Hypatia* 7 (1992): 195–206.

5. Carol Gilligan et al., eds., *Mapping the Moral Domain* (Cambridge, Mass.: Harvard University Press, 1988); Carol Gilligan, *In a Different Voice* (Cambridge, Mass.: Harvard University Press, 1982).

6. Gilligan makes her claim for an association between ethical perspective and gender based on a "focus phenomenon." She reads her data as showing that while men and women are aware of both perspectives, men are more likely to focus on the justice perspective, while women are more likely to focus on care. For a summary explanation of the focus phenomenon, see Carol Gilligan, "Moral Orientation and Moral Development," in *Women and Moral Theory,* ed. Eva Feder Kittay and Diana T. Meyers (Totowa, N.J.: Rowman and Littlefield, 1987).

7. Gilligan argues that the two universal experiences that lead to the two perspectives are the experience of injustice and the experience of abandonment.

8. María Lugones, "Playfulness, 'World'-Travelling and Loving Perception," *Hypatia* 2 (1987): 3–19.

9. Gilligan, I think, shies away from the metaphor of bounded communities and chooses the dimensions metaphor because boundaries are so often taken to imply separation and only separation, thus threatening one of the primary norms of the care perspective—nonseparation.

I also have suspicions, overdetermined by the current theoretical climate, about the language of boundaries. This language has been problematized in current critical discourses because invocations of bounded communities or selves can tend to invoke clearly separated and internally coherent identities, a clarity and coherence that is belied by the internal diversity of categories such as "women," "feminism," "womanism," or "lesbian." Edward Said's interpretation of boundaries helps to avoid some of these problems, so that the explanatory power of reading for boundaries is not lost to overly simplistic critiques of essentialism. Edward Said, "Representing the Colonized: Anthropology's Interlocutors," *Critical Inquiry* 15 (1989): 205–26.

10. Hoagland makes a similar critique of "femininity," although she doesn't specify the standards of femininity that she critiques as white racial standards for womanhood.

11. Here Cannon draws on Mary Burgher, "Images of Self and Race in the Autobiographies of Black Women," in *Sturdy Black Bridges,* ed. Roseann Bell et al. (New York: Anchor Books, 1979), 13.

12. It is important to note here that the "relationality" described by Cannon is different from the "relationality" that is taken to be the hallmark of Carol Gilligan's ethic of care or different voice. While Cannon's relationality is grounded in a community of struggle, relationality as understood by the women in Gilligan's study is grounded in particular relationships between individuals.

13. James Evans, "African-American Christianity and the Postmodern Condition," *Journal of the American Academy of Religion* 58 (1990): 219.

14. Katie G. Cannon, "Roundtable Discussion: Christian Ethics and Theology in Womanist Perspective," *Journal of Feminist Studies in Religion* 5 (1989): 92–94; Cheryl Clarke, "Lesbianism: An Act of Resistance" in *The Bridge Called My Back,* ed. Cherríe Moraga and Gloria Anzaldúa (Watertown, Mass.: Persephone Press, 1981), 128–37; and Adrienne Rich, "Compulsory Heterosexuality and Lesbian Existence," *Signs* 5 (1980): 631–60.

15. Elisabeth Däumer, "Queer Ethics; or, the Challenge of Bisexuality to Lesbian Ethics," *Hypatia* 7 (1992): 91–105.

16. On performative self-constitution, see also Judith Butler, *Gender Trouble* (Routledge: New York, 1990).

17. María Lugones, "Hispaneando y lesbiando: On Sarah Hoagland's *Lesbian Ethics,*" *Hypatia* 5 (1990): 38–46.

18. Hoagland, "Why Lesbian Ethics?" 201.

19. Since writing this essay, I have further explored the efforts of conservative Christian movements like the Christian Coalition and the Traditional Values Coalition to form cross-racial alliances. See Janet Jakobsen, *Working Alliances: Diversity and Complexity in Feminist Ethics* (Bloomington: Indiana University Press, 1997), and "The Body Politic v. Lesbian Bodies: Publics, Counter-Publics, and the Uses of Norms," in *Differing Horizons: Feminist Theology and the Role of Theory,* ed. Rebecca Clapp and Sheila Davaney (Minneapolis: Fortress Press, 1997).

## 13

# the view from waist high

In biblical times physical and mental disorders were thought to signify possession by demons. In fact, Jesus' proficiency at casting these out accounted for much of his popularity among the common folk (though probably not among swine). People who were stooped or blind or subject to seizures were clearly not okay as they were but required fixing, and divine intervention was the only remedy powerful enough to cleanse them of their baleful residents.

Theologically as well as medically, this interpretation of illness now strikes us as primitive, and yet we perpetuate the association underlying it. A brief examination of "dead" metaphors (those that have been so thoroughly integrated into language that we generally overlook their analogical origins) demonstrates the extent to which we equate physical vigor with positive moral qualities: "keep your chin up," we say (signifying courage), "and your eyes open" (alertness); "stand on your own two feet" (independence) "and tall" (pride); "look straight in the eye" (honesty) or "see eye to eye" (accord); "run rings around" (superiority). By contrast, physical debility connotes vice, as in "sit on your ass" (laziness), "take it lying down" (weakness), "listen with half an ear" (inattention), and get left "without a leg to stand on" (unsound argument). The way in which the body occupies space and the quality of the space it occupies correlate with the condition of the soul: it is better to be admired as "high-minded" than "looked down on" for one's "low morals," to be "in the know" than "out of it," to be "up front" than "backhanded," to be "free as a bird" than "confined to a wheelchair."

Now, the truth is that, unless you are squatting or six years old, I can never look you straight in the eye, and I spend all my time sitting on my ass except when I'm taking it lying down. These are the realities of life in a wheelchair (though, in view of the alternatives, "confinement" is the very opposite of my condition). And the fact that the soundness of the body so often serves as a metaphor for its moral health, its deterioration thus implying moral degener- acy, puts me and my kind in a quandary. How can I possibly be "good"? Let's face it, wicked witches are not just ugly (as sin); they're also bent and misshapen (crooked). I am bent and misshapen, therefore ugly, therefore wicked. And I have no way to atone.

It's a bind many women of my background and experience, not just the ones with disabilities, have historically found themselves in by virtue of their in- carnation in a sociolinguistic system over which they have had relatively little power. (Notice how virile the virtues encoded in the examples above.) Female bodies, even handsome and wholesome ones, have tended to give moralists fits of one sort or another (lust, disgust, but seldom trust). As everyone who's read the *Malleus Maleficarum* knows, "All witchcraft comes from carnal Lust which is in Women insatiable." If a good man is hard to find, a good woman is harder, unless she's (1) prepubescent, (2) senile, or (3) dead, and even then, some will have their doubts about her.

It's tricky enough, then, trying to be a good woman at all, but a crippled woman experiences a kind of double jeopardy. How can such a woman con- struct a world that will accommodate her realities, including her experience of her own goodness, yet remain comprehensible to those whose worlds are founded on premises alien or even inimical to her sense of self?

Disability is at once a metaphorical and a material state, evocative of other conditions in time and space—childhood and imprisonment come to mind— yet "like" nothing but itself. I can't live it or write about it except by conflating the figurative and the substantial, the "as if" and the relentlessly "what is." Let me illustrate with a recent experience. Not long ago my husband and I went to a luncheon honoring the Dalai Lama, held at a large resort northwest of Tuc- son. Although we were not participating in the five-day workshop he had come here to lead, we found ourselves in the hallway when the meeting room dis- gorged the workshop participants—all fourteen hundred of them—into a nar- row area further constricted by tables laden with bells, beads, and brochures. And let me tell you, no matter how persuaded they were of the beauty and sa- credness of all life, not one of them seemed to think that any life was going on below the level of her or his own gaze. "Down here!" I kept whimpering at the hips and buttocks and bellies pressing my wheelchair on all sides. "Down here! There's a person down here!" My only recourse was to roll to one side and hug a wall.

Now, postmodern criticism, feminist and otherwise, makes a good deal of the concept of wall-hugging, or marginality, which is meant to suggest that some segment of the population—black, brown, yellow, or red, poor, female, lesbian, what have you—is shouldered to the side, heedlessly or not, by some perhaps more numerous and certainly more powerful segment—most frequently wealthy, well-educated Euro-American males.

Regardless of the way marginality is conceived, however, it is never taken to mean that those on the margin occupy a physical space literally outside the field of vision of those in the center, so that the latter trip unawares and fall into the laps of those they have banished from consciousness unless these scoot safely out of the way. "Marginality" thus means something altogether different to me from what it means to social theorists. It is no metaphor for the power relations between one group of human beings and another but a literal description of where I stand (figuratively speaking): over here, on the edge, out of bounds, beneath your notice. I embody the metaphors. Only whether or not I like doing so is immaterial.

It may be this radical materiality of my circumstances, together with the sense I mentioned earlier that defect and deformity bar me from the ranks of "good" women, that has spurred me in the past, as it no doubt will in the future, to put the body at the center of all my meditations, my "corpus," if you will. Not that I always write *about* the body, though I often do, but that I always write, consciously, *as* a body. (This quality more than any other, I think, exiles my work from conventional academic discourse. The guys may be writing with the pen/penis, but they pretend at all times to keep it in their pants.) And it is this—my—crippled female body that my work struggles to redeem through that most figurative of human tools: language. Because language substitutes a no-thing for a thing, whereas a body is pure thing through and through, this task must fail. But inevitable disappointment does not deprive labor of its authenticity.

And so I use inscription to insert my embodied self into a world with which, over time, I have less and less in common. Part of my effort entails reshaping both that self and that world in order to reconcile the two. We bear certain responsibilities toward each other, the world and I, and I must neither remove myself from it nor permit it to exclude me if we are to carry these out. In a life bound by permissions (I have to weigh every act in terms of whether I can or can't perform it) and obligations (I must overcome inertia in order to make the smallest gesture), I can't become a "hopeless cripple" without risking moral paralysis; nor can the world, except to its own diminishment, refuse my moral participation.

But is a woman for whom any action at all is nearly impossible capable of right action, or am I just being morally cocky here? After all, if I claim to be a good woman, I leave myself open to the question: Good for what? The most straightforward answer is the most tempting: Good for nothing. I mean really. I can stand with assistance but I can't take a step; I can't even spread my own legs for sex anymore. My left arm doesn't work at all, and my right one grows weaker almost by the day. I can't put on or take off my clothes, and I'm having more and more trouble raising a fork or a cup to my lips. (It is possible, I've discovered, though decidedly odd, to drink even coffee and beer through a straw.) I can no longer drive. I lack the stamina to go out to work. If I live to see them, I will never hold my own grandchildren. These incapacities constitute a stigma that, according to social scientist Erving Goffman, removes me from normal life into a "discredited" position in relation to society.

From the point of view of the Catholic Church, to which I belong, however, mine must be just about the ideal state: too helpless even for the sins other flesh is heir to. After all, parties aren't much fun now that I meet the other revelers eye to navel, and getting drunk is risky since I can hardly see straight cold sober. No matter how insatiable my carnal lust, nobody's likely to succumb to my charms and sully my reputation. But I am, by sympathy at least, a Catholic *Worker,* part of a community that wastes precious little time fretting about the seven deadlies, assuming instead that the moral core of being in the world lies in the care of others, in *doing* rather than *being* good. How can a woman identify herself as a Catholic Worker if she can't even cut up carrots for the soup or ladle it out for the hungry people queued up outside the kitchen door? Physical incapacity certainly appears to rob such a woman of moral efficacy.

Well, maybe moral demands should no longer be placed on her. Perhaps she ought simply to be "excused" from the moral life on the most generous of grounds: that she suffers enough already, that she has plenty to do just to take care of herself. This dismissive attitude tends to be reinforced when the woman lives at the height of your waist. Because she "stands" no higher than a six-year-old, you may unconsciously ascribe to her the moral development of a child (which, in view of psychologist Robert Coles's findings, you will probably underestimate) and demand little of her beyond obedience and enough self-restraint so that she doesn't filch candy bars at the checkout counter while you're busy writing a check. (God, I can't tell you how tempting those brightly wrapped chunks are when they're smack up against your nose.) "Stature" is an intrinsic attribute of moral life, and the woman who lacks the one may be judged incapable of the other.

I'm exaggerating here, of course, but only a little. Beyond cheerfulness and patience, people don't generally expect much of a cripple's character. And certainly they presume that care, which I have placed at the heart of moral experience, flows in one direction, "downward": as from adult to child, so from well to ill, from whole to maimed. This condescension contributes to what Goffman calls "spoiled identity," though he does not deal satisfactorily with the damage it inflicts. Without reciprocity, the foundation of any mature moral relationship, the person with a defect cannot grow "up" and move "out" into the world but remains constricted in ways that make being "confined to a wheelchair" look trivial.

And so I would say that while it is all right to excuse me from making the soup (for the sake of the soup, probably more than "all right"), you must never—even with the best intentions, even with my own complicity—either enable or require me to withdraw from moral life altogether. So much for carrot cutting, then, or any other act involving sharp instruments. But wait! One sharp instrument is left me: my tongue. (Here's where metaphor comes in handy.) And my computer keyboard is . . . just waist high. With these I ought to be able to concoct another order of soup altogether (in which I'll no doubt find myself up to my ears). In other words, what I can still *do*—so far—is write books. Catholic Workers being extraordinarily tolerant of multiplicity, on the theory that it takes all kinds of parts to form a body, this activity will probably be counted good enough.

I've chosen to title my book *Waist-High in the World* not simply because it describes my physical location but because, in resonating with "knee-deep," it reflects the enthusiasm I feel for rolling out into fresh political, moral, and spiritual terrain.[1] Poet Mary Oliver has written that the "one question" we need to ask is "how to love this world."[2] The world to which I am a material witness is a difficult one to love. But I am not alone in it now, and as the population ages, more and more people—a significant majority of them women—may join me in it, learning to negotiate a chill and rubble-strewn landscape with impaired eyesight and hearing and mobility, searching out some kind of home there. Maps render foreign territory, however dark and wide, fathomable. I mean to make a map.

## NOTES

1. Nancy Mairs, *Waist-High in the World* (Boston: Beacon Press, 1997).

2. Mary Oliver, "Spring," in *New and Selected Poems* (Boston: Beacon Press, 1992), 7. See Mairs, *Waist-High in the World*.

14

# a feminine world
## *pueblo spaces*

In Pueblo Indian cosmology existence is an interconnected unity. Through the thousands of years of living in the desert climate of the Southwest, the Pueblo people developed a mode of thought that assumes the oneness of human beings with the land, with the earth, and with all other living beings. This assumption of the interconnections of all things leads to a strong focus on mutuality and relationality. Relationships with the sun, moon, plants, and other animals are accepted facts of life. People regularly talk with plants, animals, rocks, clay. Because everybody and everything deserve respect and consideration, it is possible to have cross-communication with plants, rocks, and animals, as happens in Pueblo dances and ceremonies. Pueblos believe in an inclusive and, hence, feminine world. Their world view acknowledges that even opposite forces, such as cold and warm, dark and light, male and female, are necessary for the health of the whole. It is a philosophy that includes, considers, and nurtures all aspects of the whole.

Physical spaces are also envisioned as explicitly feminine in that they include opposites and are concerned with relationships and kinships. The cosmos is conceived as spherical, with the upper half being the basket sky and the lower half the earth bowl. One is heavy, the other light. One is male, the other female. Both are needed for a balanced whole.

Male and female are parts of that self-fertilizing whole. The father sky provides the mother earth with light and rain via the movement of the sun and clouds in the sky. Life emerges out of the mother, who

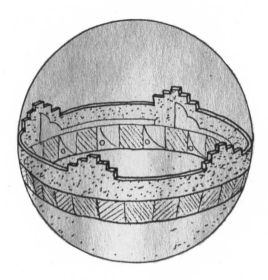

Figure 14.1  Earth Bowl. Illustration by Rina Swentzell.

is the source, but the father is needed for movement, without which stasis and death would occur. The emergence myth, or the birthing story, of the Pueblo people illustrates how the people visualize their emergence out of the womb of the mother and entry into the middle place between the earth and sky, where they know both mother and father.

According to the myth, the people emerged from life in the dark under-world at the north place and walked south, searching for the center or the middle place. When they felt that they had arrived at the center of the universe, they asked for confirmation from water spider and rainbow. Water spider spread out her legs, forming a semi-sphere. The spot directly under her belly was the center. Rainbow arched over the area and determined that the spot directly under the highest point of his arch was the center.[1] After the center was confirmed, the people dug a small hole in the ground at the spot. This hole, or *nansipu,* which is still found in every Pueblo village, is only about one foot deep and half a foot wide. It is the vulva of mother earth, the center of the cosmos. All life revolves around this female opening.

Once the center is established, the space around it is ordered. Shrines, or other female openings into the earth, are established in the four directional mountains to mark the far boundaries of the pueblo—the physical space within

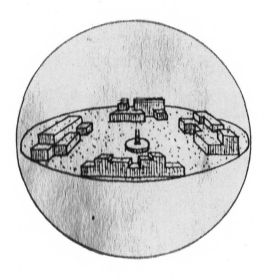

Figure 14.2 Conceptual model of Pueblo town. Illustration by Rina Swentzell.

which the people live. These mountain shrines acknowledge the masculine mountains, which contain the feminine valley spaces. They also symbolize the connection with the underworld while providing points at which the breathing of the mother earth is acknowledged. The hills surrounding the pueblo are also acknowledged by other shrines that recognize the importance of plants and other animals in human existence. Significantly, unlike "positive," or masculine, elements such as posts, fences, or walls, these boundary markers are "negative," or feminine, spaces: small holes, oftentimes almost undetectable, which mark areas that remind human beings of their interconnectedness to every other part of existence as well as to life in the underworld. Connection between the dark inner and light outer worlds, below and above, is also acknowledged.

Within the Pueblo village, spatial organization is similar. The nansipu, or central negative space, is located within the plaza, another feminine space, which contains the human activity of the community. The plaza is where people meet, where many of the ritual dances and ceremonies occur, and where the sky meets the earth. It is a meeting and containing space.

The plaza spaces are bounded by the male structures or buildings. These interconnected housing units are often built in stepped, mountainlike forms

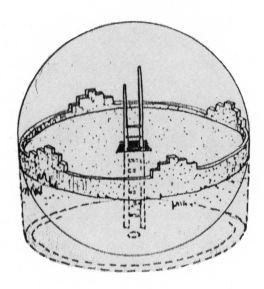

Figure 14.3 Kiva model. Illustration by Rina Swentzell.

bounding the valleylike plaza areas. Again, the male structures contain and hold the feminine spaces. The house interiors are thought of as wombs. They are dark and warm.

Further, within the plaza space is also located the *kiva,* or community structure. Here the organization of the cosmos is reiterated and the interplay of masculine and feminine spaces and symbolisms is restated. The kiva contains a nansipu, a dirt floor to symbolize the earth, and a ceiling with vigas interwoven with smaller branches to symbolize the all-covering father. The ladder, or male symbol, enters the symbolic womb through the opening on the top of the structure. The interior is dark, warm, and often moist because water is sprinkled on the dirt floors.

The acceptance of sexuality, or the coming together of opposite forces as a natural part of the cosmos, is restated in dances, dance costuming, pottery form and design, and basketry. For instance, in one of the Tewa basket dances, the male dancers hold long zigzag sticks representing lightning while dancing toward the women, who hold baskets with yarn representing hair in front of them. This bringing together of opposing forces in a harmonious manner is a continuing statement of Pueblo cosmology.

The act of separating and splitting is seen as unnatural and undesirable.

Figure 14.4 Mother and Child. Sculpture by Roxanne Swentzell, 1989.

Thus the spiritual pervades all experiences; science is not separated from magic, medicine from herbal knowledge and psychic/seasonal environment, sexuality from the sacred, or art from craft. Life is not divided into higher and lower categories such as mind over matter. Indeed, the ideal person in the Pueblo world is the *gia,* or mother, a considerate, caring, gentle, and creative person. Even men who have attained ultimate respect are labeled gias. Men in that world, then, do not work toward being patriarchs but rather toward becoming matriarchs, who operate not on principles of dominance but on those of kinship.[2]

There is, of course, no concept of a God—male or female. The entire world is a working, moving whole that has essential volition and breath. It moves without domination by any person, God, or gods. Communal celebrations occur cyclically and seasonally in order to feel the interconnectedness and unity of human life with the land, plants, rocks, and other animals. Physical spaces and built structures are seen as living, breathing entities that are a part of and affect the flow of life. Although they are acknowledged, as are all living beings, to contain male and/or female qualities, the overall whole or cosmos is ultimately perceived as feminine, moving with the principles of spirituality, wholeness, interrelatedness, harmony, and balance.

## NOTES

1. For a similar emergence story that was related to anthropologist Elsie Clews Parsons in the early-twentieth century, see Parsons, *Tewa Tales* (New York: American Folk-Lore Society, 1926; reprint edition, New York: Kraus Reprint Co., 1969), 9–15.

2. For a more extensive discussion of gias, see Rina Swentzell and Tito Naranjo, "Nurturing: The *Gia* at Santa Clara Pueblo," *El Palacia* 92, no. 1 (Summer-Fall 1986): 34–39.

FRANCES E. MASCIA-LEES

PATRICIA SHARPE

15

# locked in or locked out or holding both ends of a slippery pole
## *confusion of metaphors, collaborations, and intellectual travesties*

In thinking about space as metaphor and as actuality in our work and in feminist writing more generally, a natural place to begin seemed to be the Albany branch of Borders, the chain of book superstores owned by K-Mart that have recently proliferated. The name *Borders* might appear to echo a geographical metaphor that, although it seems contradictory or at least ironic to say so, has had a central place in feminist and subaltern theory—that of the margin, the interface of two cultures as a locale of displacement from which to speak a multiple vision. In actuality, the name refers not to a postmodern intellectual condition but to a locatable origin or author: Tom Borders, founder of the original academic bookstore in Ann Arbor, Michigan. At the mall in Albany or Westchester, the name takes on the appearance of a metaphor that speaks to the problem of figuring out, as ideas and disciplines transmogrify, which ideas belong together, which fields adjoin or butt up against each other: shelf by shelf stand women's studies, queer studies, men's studies, birth and infancy, mysticism and occult. As intellectual fashions shift, as the political connotations of names, fields, and topics change and are manipulated, borders take on new contours, follow new rifts and fissures in the intellectual landscape.

At Borders, our book, *Tattoo, Torture, Mutilation, and Adornment: The Denaturalization of the Body in Culture and Text,*[1] is placed discreetly away on the somewhat recherché anthropology shelf between ethnographies like Bronislaw Malinowski's *Argonauts of the Western Pacific* and Margaret Mead's *Coming of Age in Samoa,* an accident of alphabetical geography. Its cover photograph, depicting a mural at the Smithsonian entitled "Soft-Tissue Modification," which portrays practices of altering the body from around the world—Chinese foot binding, African scarification, Japanese tattoo, New Guinea nose rings, Sara lip plates—suggests this placement (see fig. 15.1).

Yet the book contains no ethnographic description of these exotic practices, despite what one might think, given its title and the cover photograph. Like many contemporary writers, we could not, in good conscience, use an illustration to show simply what people look like with bound feet or manipulated skulls. After all, the shifting terrain of bookstore shelves is a sign of underlying tectonic shifts: we are, we have been told repeatedly, in the midst of a "crisis of representation." In the social sciences this crisis has been tied to the post–World War II changes in global power relations that have undermined faith in totalizing frameworks like Marxism and models of stability like functionalism that dominated social analysis earlier in this century, holding First and Third Worlds in place.[2] We are in a period of questioning the adequacy of descriptive modes, and there is active debate about how social life might best be mapped. A similar self-consciousness about metaphors and representation underlies this book, raising questions about whether such stylistic innovation can offer a more useful Baedeker or whether it simply draws attention to the artificiality of all atlases and gazetteers.

Perhaps nowhere else in the social sciences has this critique raged so strongly as in anthropology, where the crisis of representation has been variously termed "the postmodernist turn," influenced as it is by poststructuralist theory or "the new ethnography," suggesting the revision anticipated by the incorporation of such theory into ethnographic practice. The appearance of two books in 1986—James Clifford and George Marcus's edited collection, *Writing Culture: The Poetics and Politics of Ethnography,* and George Marcus and Michael Fischer's *Anthropology as Cultural Critique*—marked the beginning of widespread recognition of the need for questioning the role of the anthropologist as privileged voyager from the "civilized" to the "primitive" and reexamining the traditional ways in which anthropologists have portrayed non-Western peoples.[3] This concern with representation manifested itself in two interrelated ways that were reflected in the subtitle of the *Writing Culture* volume: "the poetics and politics of ethnography."

The focus on poetics has led to an almost wholesale borrowing of literary techniques in the writing of new ethnographies. New ethnographers experiment with polyvocality, intertextuality, and juxtaposition, and they frequently

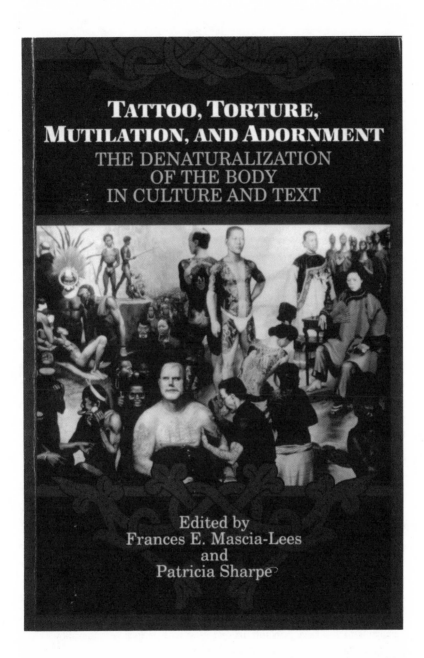

Figure 15.1  Cover of *Tattoo, Torture, Mutilation, and Adornment: The Denaturalization of the Body in Culture and Text,* © 1992 State University of New York Press. Reprinted by permission of the publisher.

include some self-conscious commentary on form within their texts, marks of the modernist novel rather than the traditional ethnographic account.

Such techniques are, however, not employed for purely aesthetic reasons. Far from it. Underlying this search for new modes of representation is a profound questioning of the politics of anthropology's past: How have anthropological writings constructed or perpetuated myths about non-Western people? How have these myths sustained Western hegemony? These questions have focused recent critiques within anthropology on classic forms of ethnographic writing, exposing how ethnographic rhetorical styles encode and reinforce the ethnographer's authority, producing representations that have been taken as truths about other cultures rather than as the partial, subjective constructions that many see them as today. This exposure has opened new possibilities for ethnographic writing in the present. And it is through such new forms of writing, it is claimed, that anthropologists will be able to avoid the ills of the past. The aim of much experimentation in anthropological writing is to expose within the ethnographic account the partial, constructed, dialogic, politically charged nature of ethnographic representation.

Thus, interestingly, while turning to postmodern theory for new insights, anthropologists have made a modernist move, analogous to Picasso's at the start of the century. As he flattened the picture space to draw attention to the paint on canvas that constructed the illusion of a family of clowns on a beach, so they are trying to expose and destabilize the realist illusion of ethnography by drawing attention to the manipulation of media—whether words, tropes, photographic images, or graphs and charts—that brought it about.

In *The Predicament of Culture,* for example, James Clifford uses a photograph of Franz Boas composing a suitably unspoiled image of "An Indian woman spinning yarn and rocking a cradle with a cord tied to her foot" (see fig. 15.2).[4] Boas and his colleague George Hunt hold up a blanket in the background to block out the white picket fence that would make it evident that a boundary between civilized and native exists *within* this woman's world rather than at its edge. Clifford uses the photograph as emblematic of the postmodern strategy that we have been describing: he expands the frame of the anthropologist's depiction to include the researcher and his cultural milieu, thus highlighting the interaction and manipulation that underlie ethnography.

Like Clifford's *The Predicament of Culture,* our *Tattoo* book is less actual ethnography than meditation on it. It looks not at what it has meant for people in other cultures to transform their bodies but at what it means that our culture has described and understood these practices as it has. Our cover image, like Clifford's picture of Boas, is emblematic. It is not used to show what it

Figure 15.2   Indian woman spinning yarn and rocking cradle. Photograph by O. C. Hastings. Courtesy American Museum of Natural History, New York, negative 11604.

seems to illustrate—soft-tissue modification. That was the aim of those who placed the mural it depicts in the Smithsonian. Our purpose was to turn the lens on our culture, to analyze the Western creators and consumers of this exhibit in the physical anthropology room of the Natural History Museum where it is found.

In our introduction to the book, we discuss the mural as an instance of the role exoticizing has played in Western ideas about cultural difference.[5] We point to the forefronting of the white sailor whose outward gaze suggests that the other cultural variants depicted take place in memories of his travels, in imagination. We note the exclusion of white women from the mural, women whose body modifications in the 1940s and '50s, the period of the mural's painting, certainly would have qualified as soft-tissue modifications: pancake make-up, bright red fingernail polish and lipstick, girdles, push-up bras, and stiff-permanented hairdos. We suggest that the mural, like Joseph Conrad's *Heart of Darkness,* equates the exotic "other" with the unspeakable within the white

Western male unconscious.[6] The white Western woman, by contrast, represents a purity that demands this repression and denial of the other: she becomes whited sepulcher in contrast with an uncivilized site of "horror." Thus, we conclude, Conrad's story and the mural both exempt the white woman and her body modifications from scrutiny in order to construct the exotic and thereby to affirm her normality. The purpose of our *Tattoo* book, then, is to bring the white woman into the picture in order to disrupt the relationship between the Western male mind and the body of the exotic other.

In keeping with the postmodern injunction to turn the critical lens on the West, more specifically, to put the researcher in the picture, we include a family story in our analysis of the mural as representation, describing Fran's visit to the museum with her teenage son, his horrified reaction to the mural, and her failed attempts to lessen his revulsion. "Look," she said, "the juxtaposition here of a white sailor with these exotic body modifications is trying to show us that what they do to their bodies is not so different from what we do to ours, things we think are OK. It's saying that all cultures use the body as a ground for inscribing significant meaning." Her son was not convinced. To him, the practices shown were mortifications, violations to the integrity of the body. In the book we go on to problematize both his response and Fran's professional reading of it:

> Whether one reads in the mural a disruption of ethnocentric attitudes or a reinforcing of the notion of the "other" as exotic or horrific, the underlying message seems surprisingly the same: that the unadorned, unmodified body is an unspoiled, pure surface on which culture works. Either way, this message dehistoricizes and decontextualizes the body. It ignores the particular meaning that both the body and the specific modifications to which it is subjected have for the people being represented. It resolves all bodies into the Western notion of the body as prior to culture and, thus, as natural.[7]

This metaphor of the body as ground is itself highly culture bound, as the work of some anthropologists like Marilyn Strathern has shown. She suggests that among the North Mekeo of Papua New Guinea, for example, conceptualizations of the body do not allow for the idea that things are done to it. For them the body is neither subject nor object.[8]

The traditional anthropology that could accept so essential and real a notion of the body was one in which geography, too, was not, first and foremost, metaphorical. It involved arduous travel as well as acceptance—even physical ingestion—of the unfamiliar and the—not only metaphorically—distasteful.

Field work was an essential rite of passage in which the anthropologist neo-phyte was expected to "bleed from every orifice." Thus, within the field—or rather, to avoid metaphorical confusion, the discipline—the anthropologist's body was, like the native's, seen as an essential ground, the proving ground of professional knowledge, even as that same body and its functions and desires were to be kept absent from the ethnographic text, creating the illusion of objectivity.

But wait a minute. Should we really avoid metaphoric confusion? This ap-parently flippant aside could offer a shortcut to Eldorado, a direct route to the thesis of this paper: that confusion—metaphoric, textual, or actual—is a crucial and effective postmodernist feminist strategy. Although stylistic or methodo-logical innovations cannot guarantee more accurate or politically enlightened and effective representation, as we have tried to show in our various critiques of postmodern ethnography, that doesn't mean that they can't be eye opening, revealing both new territory and new perspectives.[9] Much of what recent fem-inism has attempted is not improved orienteering but *dis*orientation. For intel-lectual travelers to see the actual terrain, not some presupposed mental image of it, may require putting down the guidebooks, spinning like dervishes, putting one ear to the ground and cocking the other.

We suggest that the feminists who use metaphors to the most revolu-tionary effect are those who hopelessly mix them up. The confusion created through this mixing is akin to the confusion created through the blurring of identity that we play with in our collaborative writing, a strategy Naomi Schor has called female travesty: the blurring of difference within difference.[10] We have found our collaborative writing, our intellectual travesty, to act as a pow-erful form of resistance to the myth of the lone scholar, traditionally the male academic working in search of the "truth." It allows us to disrupt notions of unitary subjectivity and to experience ourselves as multiplicitous as we take up each other's intellectual positions. Indeed, it is our own form of border cross-ing: we can manipulate our images so as to refuse an absolute definition from outside, shifting from one image to another just as we shift from singular to plural pronouns and back again, until bewildered colleagues call us by each other's name and students refer to us as Frat and Pan.

Mixing metaphors, like blurring identities and boundaries, can act as intel-lectual travesty. If feminist awakening and resistance demands bringing dead metaphors—those slumbering Frankenstein's monsters of accumulated assump-tions—to light, how do we then deal with and diffuse their power? Susan Son-tag's interrogations of the discourses surrounding tuberculosis and cancer in *Illness as Metaphor* are instructive.[11] Her strategy of juxtaposing the nineteenth-century mythology of consumption with the contemporary portrayal of cancer as psychologically self-induced or morally deserved brilliantly exposes the kinds of magical thinking that underlie explanations of terrifying and uncontrollable disease. Yet her conclusion—that we must resist the impulse to mythologize, that only through sticking to the truth about cancer will an unmediated experience of the disease be possible—is naive. Sontag's distrust of metaphor is understandable, of course. She must have resented the implication that her own cancer could be seen as self-inflicted or her fault. Her illness, however, is never mentioned in the book, a failure to put herself "in the picture" in the interests of traditional philosophical objectivity, which also excludes objective reality.

By contrast, again and again in our work we have sought a different objectivity by exposing our engagement with an issue. We have treated the drive to analogize as an unavoidable strategy of understanding, one that must be consciously manipulated. Eschewing "bad" metaphors, whether of boundaries and centers or closeness and distance, offers no protection. What we must break with is the interdiction on mixing metaphors. It is a form of cultural regulation, or border maintenance. Why are students taught this in basic writing courses? Because mixed metaphors are often those used unthinkingly, metaphors that have lost all vitality and vividness, in other words, metaphors that function as part of ideology. When we mix them, we reveal contradictions in ideology. Thus these habitual metaphors are a site where cultural assumptions can be exposed. Can we dismantle the master's house with the master's tools? Yes, we would say, at least if we use them incorrectly.

We hold that metaphor must be deployed strategically to direct attention at once to the social construction of subjectivity and to the social construction of fact, of embodiment, of the real. Along with others in this volume, we wish to disrupt any comfortable separation of the material and the textual or of the real and the metaphoric. Intertwining the metaphoric and the literal is, like mixing metaphors, an essential tool for the feminist cultural critic. It is a strategy we have adopted in much of our work: following out the implications of the use of metaphors in contemporary critical theory by literalizing them, and thus exposing the hidden cultural assumptions they contain. In our essay "The Marked and the Un(re)marked: Tattoo and Gender in Theory and Narrative" in the *Tattoo* volume, for example, we begin by questioning why the body has recently been the site of obsessive theoretical focus.[12] To interrogate Foucault's metaphor of history as inscription on the body, we turn to actual bodily marking and to narratives about it—from a canonical treatment like *The Scarlet Letter* to the trashy B-movie *Tattoo*. By literalizing the image of body marking and contrasting this with stories that use it metaphorically and symbolically, even as they suggest the impact of such marks on individual people, we expose the tenacious convictions about gender that underlie both stories of marking and those of erasure, since "a simple reversal of binary terms cannot bring about a truly recursive picture"—that is, one "in which ground can be seen as figure in its own right." Either imposing or removing a mark from a woman could represent the imposition of a restrictive, unitary femininity. And underlying the several stories we present lurks the "conviction in the metaphoric thought of the West that it is the male body which does not lie."[13] This leads us to the conclusion that the apparently undifferentiated body alluded to in much postmodern theory is a male body. If males in the present moment can reclaim the body—traditionally seen as feminine—it is apparently because it is newly understood as cultural construct. The body, once seen as stripped of any connection to actual flesh, can be claimed as male.

But aren't the two postmodern feminist strategies we are describing—blurring boundaries and putting oneself into the picture—contradictory? Doesn't the strategy of mixing metaphors or identities, which we are suggesting as a feminist tactic, undermine the equally important one of situating the writer within a text to undermine authorial control? Is contradiction another useful feminist strategy? To be honest, we must confess that blurring, confusing, dodging, and masquerading may well be new forms of protection, ones we feel we need as compensation for the risk involved in the new forms of exposure that putting ourselves into the picture entails. Thus our book's cover photo is a sort of double bind, a cover(up) for a complex of motivations enabling us at once to exploit and to criticize exoticism. Borders thinks it's anthropology; Albany's lesbian bookstore files it on the "kinky and dangerous" rack. But can these strategies—of positioning and fixity on the one hand, and confusion and slipperiness on the other—coexist? And what is at stake or at risk for the feminist writer in employing either or both?

To rethink the metaphor of positioning for this book, we turned to Donna Haraway's now classic article "Situated Knowledges."[14] We had been struck by the image of the *flaneuse* in recent feminist writing, denied by Janet Wolff and brought into view by Anne Friedberg's unearthing of evidence for the mobile female gaze in the modern period.[15] We began to wonder whether we could sketch out a contrast in the images of bodies in space in feminist texts between fixity (or situatedness) and mobility, or in the case of our own writing, between situatedness and fluidity in authorial identity. Such a tension also exists among feminist film theorists between those who insist on female spectatorship as fixed—like Mulvey and Doane—and those—like de Lauretis—who stress women's ever-changing position and process of identification.[16]

In rereading Haraway, however, we were embarrassed to discover how in memory we had reduced and simplified her concept of situatedness. (Does some law of conservation of mental energy inevitably convert the slippery and subtle into the unitary and graspable for better storage and retrieval?) In fact, Haraway's doctrine of "embodied objectivity" assumes the split and contradictory self. She escapes essentialism by advocating not *being* but *positioning*. "Feminist embodiment," she stresses, "is not about fixed location in a reified body, female or otherwise .... objectivity cannot be about fixed vision when what counts as an object is precisely what world history turns out to be about." We are less interested here in Haraway's argument about objectivity than in the fact that she makes it with metaphor—a deliberate jumble of conflicting images that constantly pulls the reader up short and exposes buried assumptions vividly. Her reenvisioning of the metaphor of vision itself is dazzling, but even more striking for our purposes is the metaphoric feat that leads her to it. She writes: "In our efforts to climb the greased pole leading to a usable doctrine of objectivity ... we have alternatively, or even simultaneously, held on to both ends of the dichotomy: ... radical constructivism versus feminist critical empiricism. It is, of course, hard to climb when you are holding on to both ends of a pole.... It is, therefore, time to switch metaphors."[17]

No doubt it is also hard to catch a feminist sliding down—or is it up?—such a pole. Although the analogy of contemporary writer of cyborg theory and Bloomsbury sophisticate may seem far-fetched, we discern a similarity between Haraway's strategy and Virginia Woolf's characteristic chameleon shifts that have led critics like Rachel Bowlby to identify her as the quintessential modernist *flaneuse*.[18] Woolf opens her long, divagating pilgrimage to understand the relationship between women and fiction with her conclusion: what is needed is a room of one's own and a fixed income of 500 pounds a year. The rest of her fascinating, frustrating essay is, she says, simply a record of her meandering and vexed progress to this conclusion—being shooed off the grass and barred from the library, observing the comfort of male scholars in their lush dining rooms and the poverty of women gnawing stringy prunes in theirs. Repeatedly she sets up metaphoric oppositions, only to diffuse or confound them, shifting their underpinnings. In her intellectual ramblings nothing is secure: "I thought how unpleasant it is to be locked out; and I thought how it is worse perhaps to be locked in."[19]

Can we situate ourselves without being locked in, without being trapped in a characterization that belies our multiplicity? Can we reveal our embarrassments and errors, our desires and investments, our contradictions and confusions, without being locked out?

To explore the limits of the risks we could take in self-revelation, we set out on a fieldwork experiment into the darkest wilderness of desires and predatory natives: the American suburban shopping mall. In an article entitled "The Female Body in Post-modern Consumer Culture," we analyzed the mall store Units and its interesting mixture of postmodern and liberal feminist concepts in its address to the female buyer.[20] As in much of our work, we were interested in literalizing contemporary critical theory. In asking what women might find appealing in Units' postmodern use of space, its particular address to them as buyers, and its unusual sales practices, we sought to assess the promises and the perils for women of an emerging postmodern consumer culture. We began our analysis with Fredric Jameson's call for a political postmodernism that involves "a global mapping on a social as well as a spatial scale," but we chose not to stand, as cartographers traditionally have, at too great a distance from our object of study.[21] Rather, we submitted to the ritual of being dressed like mannequins for display in the Units' store window. The extent of the risk of such self-revelation was revealed while wriggling out of a bandeaux, the piece of cloth meant to complete the Units outfit. Who should stroll by while we were engaged in this significant fieldwork but our academic dean, in whose imagined eye we felt caught like preteens with nothing to do but try on clothes together in the mall.

"It's research," Fran insisted.

"They're costumes," Pat said when we wore our Units' outfits to deliver the paper and projected images of ourselves trying them on in the store to dramatize the need for researchers to keep themselves "in the picture."

It was fun, risky, and even significant scholarship, we thought, but also easily dismissed, as we learned when *Social Text* rejected the paper, calling its topic "trivial."

Ironically, not long after, we ourselves were accused of such border maintenance by a self-declared feminist, Vicki Kirby, who undertook to critique our article addressing the current "crisis of representation" in anthropology. In it we urge politically sensitive anthropologists to think beyond the changes in writing and style that new ethnographers seem to propose as adequate solutions for addressing the relations of power in the anthropological enterprise. We suggest that anthropologists take their lead instead from feminist researchers who frame research questions according to the desires of oppressed groups and choose work that others want and need. This celebration of feminism over postmodernism left her out, Kirby claimed. She saw herself as both and us as unitary: we were Anglo-American feminists who lacked an appreciation of Continental philosophy and the Australian feminist variant Kirby espoused.[22]

Kirby deplored what she saw as our naïveté in calling for an ethnographic practice attentive to what the research subjects "want and need." According to her, we had resurrected Malinowski's misplaced belief in the possibility of grasping the native's point of view, a claim rooted in a nostalgic faith in the unitary Cartesian subject. In reply to Kirby, we argued that all human contact involves guesses about what others want and need, some more sensitive than others, some more attentive, and we sought to defend Malinowski.[23] His words, that he wants to "make clear to traders, missionaries, and exploiters what the Natives really need and where they suffer most under the pressure of European interference," are clearly rhetorical and political, reflecting active critical engagement against some forms of Western exploitation.[24] There is no representational practice—ethnographic or otherwise—that can escape the larger power relations in which it is embedded, or the disorienting slipperiness and tangle underfoot entailed in trying to get anywhere with language. Still we argued for the utility of a self-conscious politics as compass, perhaps a constantly recalibrated one, recreated and reformulated as the magnetic fields of ideology and institutions are negotiated. We resented the implication that this measured claim could be dismissed as naive. Indeed, to disrupt her view of us as flat-footed feminists blind to the play of the signifier, we adopted the pose of three ugly stepsisters to her Cinderella, the princess entitled to enter the master's house of poststructural theory. To disorient her in her turn and interrogate her charge, we metamorphosed stepsisters into a three-headed Cerberus, listing the most contradictory aspects of our collective identity as coauthors. Kirby had gotten us wrong, we said, and we used our reply as an opportunity to reveal who we were, to situate ourselves. We wanted to show that as collaborators we had embraced contradiction, multiplicity, and play. "Ha, ha," we thought, "that was fun." But another embarrassment was in store: "I could see," said our *Signs* editor, "how very angry you were."

Were we? And was that all we were? What of the disagreements out of which that response grew? Fran read and reread Kirby, saying, "Oh, she may have gotten us there," while Pat left her copy in a sealed envelope for a month, then took it to the bathtub and mingled its arguments in soothing steam. Angry or not, we certainly were deliberately manipulative in our response, and the images by which we situated ourselves were partial and self-serving, reflecting our best efforts to recover from this challenge to our authority, clearly not the goal of the original injunction to put the writer into the text in order to limit his or her mystique. Our use of linguistic play in this piece highlights how even such supposed correctives as self-revelation and positioning can be used to reinforce authority and in the service of driving argumentation. Our strategy seemed successful; at least our friends reassured us that we put Kirby's criticisms to rest. But we couldn't be smug for long.

Our next article would focus on a very upsetting situation where we both felt strongly about the politics and people on all sides. In writing about it, we tried to construct an ethnography in which we were situated and engaged, but to do so less oppositionally than in our response to Kirby. We sought to reflect our multiple and shifting sympathies and commitments. In the writing, we used novelistic vignettes, which we enacted in performance when delivering the paper, to elicit the audience's sympathetic identification in evaluating accusations of sexual harassment. These were brought by a group of twenty students calling themselves the Defense Guard who accosted and encircled three teachers and one student at the college where we teach. We juxtaposed our fictionalized portrayals of various participants in the situation, including ourselves, with more "distanced" analyses of the claims of discourses competing in the academy today: humanism, postmodernism, and feminism. Echoing a challenge we heard in our students' protests, we asked readers to reflect on their own allegiances to these discourses and to think through the contradictions they can place on students.

While we admittedly sought to elicit empathy for ourselves through personal exposure in this piece, as we had in our response to Kirby, here we also attempted to do the same for most of the other people and positions involved in this contentious situation. In doing so, we tried to create an ethnography of the type we had advocated in theory: one that expressed our understanding of what the various participants wanted and needed. In it we acknowledged the inevitability of strategic manipulation and the partial-ity of all accounts: "Our struggle has been to leave some raw ends dangling, to balance coherence with ambiguities, to situate ourselves while writing an analysis that is more than personal therapy. But the difficulty of that struggle is a reminder that all writing of necessity entails multiple decisions and erasures, manipulation and control."[25] We also sought to show the inadequacy of two poststructuralist theoretical ideas: that culture is best understood as contestation and that holding contradictions *endlessly* in tension so that we expose gaps in ideology should be our goal. This situation, which required consequential judgments and choices, had arrested our own *jouissance* in the free play of the signifier and, as we painfully disagreed, disrupted our easy celebration of multiplicity and difference in collaborative writing. The paper was a complex effort to include irreconcilable perspectives in a framework that would make reconciliation possible.

Looking back after several years and public debate over Clarence Thomas and Anita Hill, it is easier to acknowledge other aims as well: we sought to disrupt the official version of this incident given by the president of the college, Leon Botstein, in *Lingua Franca* and *Harper's*, which was grounded in a humanism that disavows the power differentials within the academy, and to articulate the feminist challenge to his humanism while disentangling it from some of the particulars of this case.[26] While we problematized outsiders' initial judgments of the students or of faculty members and sought to elicit complex sympathies, we were more intent on making the case for those faculty members we felt were unjustly accused and on articulating the principles driving the feminist students than we could acknowledge at the time. We were nervous about how others involved would receive our account and our characterizations of them. Would they agree that we had written what they wanted and needed, or would they, like some contemporary subjects of ethnographic study, "write back" from the margins, decentering our account in its turn?

In Borders, Fran has been known to surreptitiously and strategically replace our *Tattoo* book on the women's studies shelf, where its ethnographic focus on the West, its emphasis on the female body, its analysis of perfume, rape and recantation, horror films and Hawthorne is evident. But recently she discovered Pat had already been placed there in disguised form, under the alias Patricia Sharp (*sic*) of Barrington (*sic*), Massachusetts, a character in Christina Hoff Sommers's academic "mystery" *Who Stole Feminism?* The Simon's Rock Defense Guard case is featured in a chapter on "the feminist classroom," apparently designed to show how students are misled into a misguided "gender feminism." In Sommers's characterization, Pat appears as an embarrassed women's studies professor, dazed and uncomprehending in the wake of Defense Guard action, "disclaim[ing] all responsibility for the behavior of the defense guards ... insist[ing] their attitude ha[d] nothing to do with feminism."[27] What are we to make of Sommers's misnaming and mis-placing? And how exactly are they related to her desire to dis-place academic feminists like us? Sommers's own metaphors expose her as border guard intent on arresting feminist thieves before they go too far. The crime? Usurping the agenda of more "mainstream thinkers" like herself to whom feminism should rightfully belong. And what does this use of a language of rightful possession, thievery, and crime suggest? That we should be locked up or at least locked out. So now where do we stand?


## NOTES

1. Frances E. Mascia-Lees and Patricia Sharpe, eds., *Tattoo, Torture, Mutilation, and Adornment: The Denaturalization of the Body in Culture and Text* (New York: SUNY Press, 1992).

2. George E. Marcus and Michael M. J. Fischer, *Anthropology as Cultural Critique: An Experimental Moment in the Human Sciences* (Chicago: University of Chicago Press, 1986).

3. James Clifford and George E. Marcus, eds., *Writing Culture: The Poetics and Politics of Ethnography* (Berkeley: University of California Press, 1986); Marcus and Fischer, *Anthropology as Cultural Critique.*

4. James Clifford, *The Predicament of Culture: Twentieth-Century Ethnography, Literature, and Art* (Cambridge, Mass.: Harvard University Press, 1988), 186.

5. Frances E. Mascia-Lees and Patricia Sharpe, "Soft-Tissue Modification and the Horror Within," in *Tattoo, Torture, Mutilation, and Adornment,* 1–9.

6. Joseph Conrad, *Heart of Darkness* (1902; reprint edition, New York: Dover Thrift Editions, 1990).

7. Mascia-Lees and Sharpe, "Soft-Tissue Modification," 3.

8. Marilyn Strathern, "Between a Melanesianist and a Deconstructive Feminist," *Australian Feminist Studies* 10 (1989): 49–69.

9. See, for example, Frances E. Mascia-Lees, Patricia Sharpe, and Colleen Cohen, "The Post-modernist Turn in Anthropology: Cautions from a Feminist Perspective," *Signs* 15 (Fall 1989): 7–33; Mascia-Lees and Sharpe, "Culture, Power, and Text: Anthropology and Literature Confront Each 'Other,' " *American Literary History* 4 (1992): 678–96; Mascia-Lees and Sharpe, "The Anthropological Unconscious," *American Anthropologist* 96 (September 1994): 649–61.

10. Naomi Schor, "Female Fetishism: The Case of George Sand," in *The Female Body in Western Culture,* ed. Susan Rubin Suleiman (Cambridge, Mass.: Harvard University Press, 1986): 363–72.

11. Susan Sontag, *Illness as Metaphor* (New York: Farrar, Straus & Giroux, 1978).

12. Frances E. Mascia-Lees and Patricia Sharpe, "The Marked and the Un(re)-marked: Tattoo and Gender in Theory and Narrative," in *Tattoo, Torture, Mutilation, and Adornment,* 145–69.

13. Ibid., 162, 163.

14. Donna Haraway, "Situated Knowledges: The Science Question in Feminism and the Privilege of Partial Perspective," *Feminist Studies* 14 (1988): 575–99.

15. Janet Wolff, *Feminine Sentences: Essays on Women and Culture* (Berkeley and Los Angeles: University of California Press, 1990); Anne Friedberg, *Window Shopping: Cinema and the Postmodern* (Berkeley: University of California Press, 1993).

16. Laura Mulvey, "Visual Pleasure and Narrative Cinema," *Screen* 16, 3 (1975): 6–18; Mary Ann Doane, "Film and the Masquerade: Theorizing the Female Spectator," *Screen* 23 (1982): 74–87; Teresa de Lauretis, *Alice Doesn't: Feminism, Semiotics, Cinema* (Bloomington: Indiana University Press, 1984).

17. Haraway, "Situated Knowledges," 588, 580.

18. Rachel Bowlby, "Walking, Women, and Writing: Virginia Woolf as *Flaneuse,*" in *New Feminist Discourses: Critical Essays on Theories and Texts,* ed. Isobel Armstrong (London and New York: Routledge, 1992): 26–47.

19. Virginia Woolf, *A Room of One's Own* (New York: Harcourt Brace & World, 1929), 24.

20. Frances E. Mascia-Lees, Patricia Sharpe, and Colleen Cohen, "The Female Body in Post-modern Consumer Culture: A Study of Subjection and Agency," *Phoebe* 2 (1990): 29–50.

21. Fredric Jameson, "Postmodernism, or the Cultural Logic of Late Capitalism," *New Left Review* 146 (July-August 1984): 72.

22. Vicki Kirby, "Comment on Mascia-Lees, Sharpe, and Cohen's 'The Post-modernist Turn in Anthropology: Cautions from a Feminist Perspective,'" *Signs* 16 (1991): 394–400; Mascia-Lees, Sharpe, and Cohen, "The Post-modernist Turn in Anthropology."

23. Kirby, "Comment"; Frances E. Mascia-Lees, Patricia Sharpe, and Colleen Cohen, "Reply to Kirby's Comment on 'The Post-modernist Turn in Anthropology: Cautions from a Feminist Perspective,'" *Signs* 16 (1991): 401–8.

24. Bronislaw Malinowski, *The Dynamics of Cultural Change: An Inquiry Into Race Relations in Africa,* ed. P. M. Kaherny (New Haven, Conn.: Yale University Press, 1945), 3–4.

25. Patricia Sharpe and Frances E. Mascia-Lees, "Always Believe the Victim/Innocent Until Proven Guilty/There Is No Truth: The Competing Claims of Feminism, Humanism, and Post-modernism in Interpreting Charges of Harassment in the Academy," *Anthropological Quarterly* 66 (April 1993): 97.

26. "Professors, Students, and Sex: Interview with Leon Botstein," *Harper's* (October 28, 1990): 26–32. Adapted from "J'accuse," *Lingua Franca* 1, no. 1 (June 1990): 21–24.

27. Christina Hoff Sommers, *Who Stole Feminism? How Women Have Betrayed Women* (New York: Simon and Shuster, 1994), 110.

16

# silence and subjectivity
## *(a position paper)*

This essay began as an attempt to discuss, rather than compare or contrast, two diverse sets of women's narratives of the extraordinary—American women's accounts of abduction by UFOs, in which they are experimented on and often impregnated, and East African women's accounts of lethal and near-lethal bloodsucking by some agency of the colonial state and postcolonial state, in which women are captured, penetrated, and their blood extracted, their bodies and minds permanently damaged. Although both sets of material are exceptionally rich and require analyses both as embodied and spatial narratives, for the moment I want to discuss what is contained and expressed—and unspoken—in memories of the extraordinary. This essay is concerned with some gut feminist issues—those of speech, of silence, of how the women talked about these abductions, and of how they spoke about speaking during the abduction and about the abduction. In the pages that follow I will present material that not only conveys the women's beliefs that they'd been experimented upon but illustrates how they talked about talking about such experiences.

Indeed, nothing I could write would explain these issues better than Kayaya Thababu, a woman from eastern Kenya who came to Nairobi in the mid-1920s and became a prostitute there. In Nairobi and in much of East Africa, bloodsucking was performed by the generic *wazimamoto* (firemen, literally the men who put out the fire), who "used to come in the night."

A. They would come into your room very softly, and before you knew it they put something in your arm to draw out the blood, and then they would leave you and they would take your blood to the hospital and leave you for dead.

Q. Couldn't you scream for help?

A. They put bandages over your mouth, and also, these people who worked for the wazimamoto, they were skilled, so if they found you asleep they could take your blood so quietly that you would not wake up, in fact you would never wake up.

Q. Did this ever happen to you or one of your neighbors?

A. No, but I heard about it a lot. . . .

Q. How did you make sure they didn't come into your room at night?

A. I was very frightened and there was no way to be sure they would not come, but . . . if you had a boyfriend staying with you at night you were safe, because they were afraid of waking two people.[1]

However fantastic you might find this account, it raises questions about silencing and consciousness in profound ways. The skillful application of Western biomedicine did not cure, it killed, and the problem with drugs was that they silenced women: Western biomedicine and hospitals were so invasive that they were lethal. Indeed, years later, when women in Uganda described somewhat different experiences of being captured by the bazimamoto—the term for firemen with the local language's prefix—they described silencing as a fate more fearsome than death.

A. They had some rooms and some special equipment like masks that they used to cover your mouth.

Q. Did they put medicine on those masks?

A. Yes, the masks were smeared with drugs.

Q. What happened when you were given that type of medicine? Did the victims live or did they die?

A. They became dull or impotent. And you could not shout. . . . You could not talk again. . . . It is a true story, the bazimamoto and their business were here, when somebody was captured he could not shout.[2]

Although I interviewed many more men in Uganda than women and thus have inconclusive data, men invariably said that "caliform" (chloroform) made them dull and stupid and unable to walk, whereas women all talked about how the drug both covered their mouths and kept them from talking. Mary Poovey's work on anesthesia in Victorian England shows how chloroform in particular not only silenced women, making them passive patients on the operating table and thus open to the medical gaze, but medicalized and pathologized processes as natural as childbirth to put them under the control of male-dominated professions.[3] The comments above show how anesthesia was feared, talked about, and imagined in a colonial context in which African bodies were already pathologized.[4]

In the UFO material, by comparison, speech is more fragmented but never conscious. Aboard alien spacecraft inter-genus conversation is often telepathic and vague; abductees simply "know" what the aliens are doing or what they want. But the women impregnated by aliens or taken to the shipboard nurseries where hybrid fetuses were kept reported long, telepathic conversations about who should mother and why and for how long. Such rarefied speech, if it can be called speech at all, never exists as consciousness: these memories are retrieved under hypnosis and without exception published as "as-told-to" books by the hypnotist.

What do such publications do to feminist and Africanist notions of speech and silence? Silence and consciousness occupy significant places in both feminist and colonial studies: silence is deplorable; it suggests a marginalization of the words and lives of women or Africans. The search for African voices with which to write more authentic African studies has been an academic obsession for almost thirty years; feminists have sought women's words as the proper source for women's history for almost as long.[5] But speech and consciousness are not wholly unambiguous. Speaking is one of the ways subjects participate in modern states and regimes of knowledge that count, classify, and document their experiences; to talk is not only to express oneself but to provide the knowledge and accounting of experiences through which control can be exerted on individuals' private lives. In Foucauldian terms, speech and silence are not opposites but strategies that can be seen to have parallel functions.[6] This is a point Foucault changed his mind on somewhat, but it may be useful for feminist scholars to think that while silence may not actively resist a state's agenda, it does not help it in any way. More recently Susan Gal has argued that the equation of silence with powerlessness and passivity obscures all the cultural and historical meanings silence can have. Women's words, according to Gal, have very precise historical and local connotations, but they are not always the same as women's consciousness.[7]

But since Gayatri Spivak wrote "Can the Subaltern Speak?" in 1988, speech, silence, and the politics of representation have become as bundled as the software in a new computer.[8] For most feminist and Africanist scholars, the impulse to stamp out any silence and replace it with meanings and memories, if not actual voices, has been dampened by the complexities of who speaks for whom and the extent to which speaking about is the same as speaking for. Scholarship and advocacy have been torn apart and conflated.[9] But ideas and anxieties about appropriation assume that speaking in Western texts is as important to colonized women as it is to postcolonial intellectuals. I want to lay down a challenge to all of us, and to Gayatri Spivak, and request that we historicize subjectivity and that we try to understand—however messily—how the subjects of colonial or patriarchal regimes perceived their ability to speak, and the changing circumstances under which they were silenced. That ordinary Africans and ordinary African women were silenced in colonial times seems to be a given. The question is, should we reverse this fact—give voice to the voiceless—or try to understand how the voiceless understood their condition and if they perceived their powers of speech in the same terms we might use?[10] I want to suggest that the very question of whether or not African subjects were silenced was a topic of intense and embodied debate among themselves, about which there was no single or simple answer. As the quotes above show, Africans described the life-or-death advantages of consciousness, as well as the consequences of new technologies to prohibit speech. My argument is that we cannot say whether or not a subaltern can speak until we have looked at all the sites of speech a woman or an African or an Indian has at her disposal. This means examining oral material that was beyond the official gaze, outside official texts, and sources not deemed respectable enough for the task of rescuing subalterns from the condescension of the past—sources that arouse academics' condescension. We must look at the debates that were conducted in unauthorized vocabularies, that were often about things that never happened.

Still, how should feminists approach the implicit question of "Can the subaltern speak?"—how can a white girl cope with the yawning gaps of race and class? Spivak's essay ends with the interpretation of an Indian woman's suicide in the 1920s, an interpretation made possible by the author's connections to the woman's family; other Indian women scholars missed the point, just as Western scholars did. An example from Uganda might suggest other ways to disclose the complexities of representation and how various forms of speech might be incorporated into colonial historiography. Much of the source material for the history of missionary medicine in Uganda from 1895–1935 are the writings of a feisty British nurse, Kate Timpson, in the Church Missionary Society monthly magazine, *Mercy and Truth*. Her early writings in particular are filled with her arguments with African men about the efficacy of various European curative methods, tablets and syrups, in which she was very willing to show the frequency with which African men got the last word. She reported no such dialogues with African women. From the vantage point of the 1990s, we would say that Timpson silenced African women. But that's not true. After Timpson reported her discussions with African men, she described the hospital waiting room: "There are several babies who have never seen a white woman before, or have been told by their mothers on previous occasions, as a means of keeping them quiet, that white people eat black babies. So it is not to be wondered that the little mites let up a piteous howl."[11]

Women are speaking here. This vignette is as much a part of the colonial encounter as are male debates over pharmaceuticals. What has made it less like the kind of speaking we are used to may not be its location at the end of Timpson's article but its location as speech—in the home, out of the ordinary, fantastic, and false.

It is this notion of sites of speech that moves us beyond the either/or dichotomy between speech and silence, between "in their own words" and speaking about. Like all sites, sites of speech are contested, struggled over, camouflaged, and sometimes ignored. Whether or not the subaltern can speak, to coin a phrase, depends on how broadly we are willing to expand our definition of speech to include these fantastic words and worlds, to listen to the vocabularies and rhetorics of blood and ingestion just as we listen to the words of technology and power. Speech and silence are not opposites in scholarly analysis. What is said openly and what is said covertly, what are conscious proclamations and what historian Lyndal Roper has called "psychic imaginings"—these are the distinctions that must be collapsed to truly recover subaltern speech.[12] And equally important, how do feminist scholars respond when the subaltern wants to remain silent, when that particular strategy is most advantageous?[13] To return to the end of Spivak's essay, the young Indian woman commits suicide because she was unable to carry out the assassination that the nationalist movement to which she belonged had asked of her; knowing full well her suicide would be interpreted as a response to pregnancy, she waited until she was menstruating to hang herself in her family's Bombay home. A literate woman, she left no note. Perhaps this was a conscious choice. At the time the act looked deliberately ambiguous; it is possible that any clearer statement would have implicated others, although we have no way of knowing for sure. But from the vantage point of postcolonial India, identifying actions that are nationalist, interpreting "speech," is one of the ways scholars recover nationalist history. From the vantage point of Bombay in 1926, speaking about nationalism may have been dangerous to one's surviving friends and family.

If nationalism is a serious agenda for postcolonial intellectuals, what follows might be considered frivolous: accounts by Americans who claim that they have been taken aboard UFOs and examined and, more often than not, impregnated and then mysteriously but painlessly aborted. Indeed, these are abduction stories beyond the wildest dreams of East African women. These stories contain episodes that the hypnotists who retrieve (and then publish) them call "flights of fancy," which are, as I've said, never conscious speech. But my incredulity raises another question—if these aren't accounts of real abductions by real aliens, what are they accounts of? I submit that they traffic in the very issues that grip and define American women in this decade. Let me give one example from a recent book that uses the testimonies of a number of abductees to weave a coherent narrative collage that "proves" the reality of UFO abduction: if a number of people tell the same story, in other words, it's got to be true. What follows is the hypnotic recollection of an abductee's encounter with an alien, whom she calls "she," aboard a shipboard nursery where the hybrid fetuses of humans and aliens are incubated. The alien "says,"

> "They need mothers. They need something. They need their mothers, they need their mothers. They have to have their mothers." I say, "You should have thought of that before you started them, because I'm not going to get involved." She says, "Don't you care about them. Don't you care?" And I say, "Don't *you* care? Don't *you* care?" And now it seems there's almost something approaching anger in her.... And she says either "They're yours," or "It's yours," or "Some of them are yours," but there's some of those babies in that room are mine. Probably just one, because they're all the same age. And I say, "So what. I don't care, I don't care." And now it's like she shrugs and says, "It doesn't matter if you care or not. They need their mothers, they have to have their mothers."[14] (Emphasis in original)

Here is a debate about mothering, about reproductive rights, of the ethics of neo-natal care, about child custody and maternal responsibility. It is by no means the only position on these issues that is contained in UFO abduction literature—sometimes women are outraged that the children are taken from them and hope one day to help raise them. My point, however, is not merely that various positions are contained in these debates but that debates about reproductive issues are located in UFO abduction narratives. There are many sites of speech with which to debate who parents with which biological imperative. Even fantastic stories about women being impregnated by men from outer space form a debate about hybridity and ambivalence far more animated, and far more mundane, than anyone might read in a mid-1990s literary journal.[15]

In fact, anyone who doubts that UFOs really abducted these women and impregnated them is left with a passionate and varied discourse about sexuality and reproductive rights. It is not the one that most feminists are accustomed to, and it's not the one that has been enshrined in activism; rather, it's one that is found in the words and ideologies published in mass-market paperbacks. Chilling as it may be, it is important for feminists to read what aliens told Betty Andreasson Luca, remembered words she retrieved under hypnosis administered by her husband:

> [The aliens] are standing in front of a glass case. And there's another baby there. A *fetus*. . . . And one of them is saying, "We have to because as time goes by, mankind will become *sterile*. They will not be able to produce" . . . they're telling me that mankind gets so upset when they take the *seed*. And really, the very first part that man and woman, when they came together was to *bring forth*—was not for their pleasure, but to bring forth. And mankind keeps on spilling the seed of life over and over again. And they cannot understand why man gets so upset when *they take the seed*.[16] (Emphasis in original)

By now it's pretty old hat that scholars should read the oral testimony generated in dialogue—whether witchcraft confessions or oral history—as a joint endeavor, whether or not scholars agree that the resulting words are negotiated or totally shaped by the inquisitor's categories and concerns.[17] Obviously, this is pretty subversive to current practices in oral history, and as a result oral historians have tended to ignore it, but I want to suggest that if we look closely at how our evidence is produced, we end up with more evidence—indications of the relations and conflict between interrogator and answerer. Most of the hypnotists who retrieve UFO memories are male; most ask leading questions by Africanist standards, but their desire is to create an exact picture that will serve as "proof." If alien intervention makes mothering a biological imperative, in dozens of hypnosis sessions women resist that vision of themselves. Instead of reading Betty Andreasson Luca's account as having to do with conflict between humans and aliens—in fact, she is strikingly uncritical of aliens' ideologies about "seed"—it might be read as expressing conflicts between human men and human women about the very meaning of sexual relations.

I want to suggest that if we can imagine a feminist reading of oral evidence as negotiating and talking about conflicts, scholars can learn about the extent to which categories are shared and how differently they might be historicized. Just as UFO research discloses the fissures and fault lines in the complicated terrain of gender relations in the United States, we learn from the Nairobi prostitute quoted earlier that speech is a crucial category for me but that for my informant speech is easily controlled by new medical technologies. Opening up the interview itself to analysis gives us another site of speech, one in which the very process of talking and articulation can be explored.

## NOTES

1. Kayaya Thababu, interview with author, Pumwani, Nairobi, January 7, 1977.

2. Julia Nakibuuka Nalongo, interview with author and Remigius Kigongo, Lubya, Uganda, August 21, 1990.

3. Mary Poovey, *Uneven Developments: The Ideological Work of Gender in Mid-Victorian England* (Chicago: University of Chicago Press, 1988), 26–51.

4. See, for example, Megan Vaughan, *Curing Their Ills: Colonial Power and African Illness* (Stanford, Cal.: Stanford University Press, 1991), 77–99; John and Jean Comaroff, *Ethnography and the Historical Imagination* (Boulder, Colo.: Westview Press, 1992), 215–33.

5. This point is developed at greater length in Luise White, *The Comforts of Home: Prostitution in Colonial Nairobi* (Chicago: University of Chicago Press, 1990), 21–28, and "Cars Out of Place: Vampires, Technology, and Labor in East and Central Africa," *Representations* 43 (1993): 27–31.

6. Michel Foucault, *The History of Sexuality,* vol. 1, trans. Robert Hurley (New York: Pantheon Books, 1978), 17–35; for a no-nonsense summary of debates about speech and difference, see also Vaughan, *Curing Their Ills,* 1–28.

7. Susan Gal, "Between Speech and Silence: The Problematics of Research on Language and Gender," in *Gender at the Crossroads of Knowledge: Feminist Anthropology in the Postmodern Era,* ed. Micaela di Leonardo (Berkeley: University of California, 1991), 175–97.

8. Gayatri C. Spivak, "Can the Subaltern Speak?" in *Marxism and the Interpretation of Culture,* ed. Cary Nelson and Lawrence Grossberg (Urbana: University of Illinois Press, 1988), 271–313.

9. See, for example, Daphne Patai, "Ethical Problems of Personal Narratives, or, Who Should Eat the Last Piece of Cake?" *International Journal of Oral History* 8 (1987): 5–27; Marjorie Mbilinyi, "'I'd Have Been a Man': Politics and the Labor Process in Producing Personal Narratives," in *Interpreting Women's Lives: Feminist Theory and Personal Narratives,* ed. Personal Narratives Group (Bloomington: University of Indiana Press, 1989): 204–27; and Susan Geiger, review of *Women's Words; The Hour of the Poor, the Hour of Women;* and *I Could Speak Until Tomorrow, Signs* 19 (1994): 499–503.

10. See Anne Hardgrove, "Witnessing and the Problem of South Asian Women in Communal Identities," Paper presented at the Comparative Studies of Social Transformation Conference on Representation/s, Ann Arbor, Michigan, April 1–2, 1994.

11. Kate Timpson, "Patients and Nurse at Mengo," *Mercy and Truth* 3 (December, 1899): 289–90.

12. Lyndal Roper, "Witchcraft and Fantasy in Early Modern Germany," *History Workshop* 32 (1991): 19–43.

13. See Ann Laura Stoler, "In Cold Blood: Hierarchies of Credibility and the Politics of Colonial Narrative," *Representations* 37 (1992): 151–89.

14. "Karen Morgan," quoted in David M. Jacobs, Ph. D., *Secret Life: Firsthand Documented Accounts of UFO Abductions* (New York, Simon and Schuster, 1993), 164.

15. See Luise White, "Alien Nation," *Transition* 63 (1994): 24–33.

16. Raymond E. Fowler, *The Watchers: The Secret Design Behind UFO Abduction* (New York: Bantam Books, 1991): 24–28.

17. A good historical overview of these debates can be seen in Renato Rosaldo, "From the Door of His Tent: The Fieldworker and the Inquisitor," in *Writing Culture: The Poetics and Politics of Ethnography*, ed. James Clifford and George E. Marcus (Berkeley: University of California Press, 1986): 77–97; and Charles van Onselen, "The Reconstruction of a Rural Life from Oral Testimony: Critical Notes on the Methodology Employed in the Study of a Black South African Sharecropper," *Journal of Peasant Studies* 20 (1993): 494–515.

# PART 5

## sites and spectacles

Building on the notion of the constitutive relationship between metaphor and materiality that concerns previous sections, the writers here, in various ways, focus on the issue of labor—the relationship between economics and the materiality of bodies and places, the gendered division of labor, and the work accomplished by certain narratives' imbrications of space and gender. These pieces take up specific situational contexts—the Sonoran Desert, birthing rooms, Mexican-American women's gardens, strip joints, airplane shows, a ticking clock—in order to expose the kinds of labor that generate the complex production of bodies and spaces as categorical, representative sites of both the mundane and the spectacular.

Ofelia Zepeda's poems express the intricate relations between women's work and constructions of the world. Her mixed use of Tohono O'odham and English suggests that in these constructions identities and place are grounded in language, while place acts as the symbolic and material barometer of seasonal and generational cycles. Helena Michie scrutinizes another version of women's labor in her discussion of the contemporary home birth movement among upper-middle-class women, played out in both the rhetoric of pregnancy advice books and the evolution of the "homey" (and *unheimlich*) birthing room. In her interrogation of the image of home as a site of female autonomy, she elucidates the ambiguous divide between "public" and "private" and considers the simultaneous cultural impulses to separate and collapse the two. Raquel Rubio-Goldsmith's essay on *norteña* women's gardens explores the home in the context of a different binary, that of "civilization" versus "wilderness." Tracing the historical changes in these *corrales*, Rubio-Goldsmith shows how the gardens expressed shifts in moral codes and cultural locations of norteña women brought about by economic and geographic changes. While Rubio-Goldsmith demonstrates how these gardens illustrated Mexican-American women's development of self-representations, Lori Scheer's excerpt from a play by the feminist theater company Bloodhut shows (in several senses) how "Dancing for Dollars" enables a woman literally to re-present herself. Her performative evocation of sex work, in script form here, constructs it as a double game that turns sexual spectacle into a site of female resistance. In her essay on "Upward Mobility," Mary Russo uses the Bloodhut's performance art to launch her own reflections on the liberating possibilities of female bodies in space. Through the exemplary figure of Amelia Earhart, Russo elaborates a theory of female performativity as a kind of stunt, a strategy for eluding confinement within a hegemonic symbolic order. Contemplating the risky flights that made Earhart a quintessential figure of freedom and transgressiveness, Russo sees her deviations and "disappearing act" as potential models for contemporary feminist practice. Finally, Judith Roof explores explicitly a notion implicit in Russo's piece: the ways that the performative invokes and implicates the temporal. Transcribed here from her conference performance, Roof's essay demonstrates how the idea of time proves metaphor and materiality to be inseparable. Roof argues that the "work" of narrative, its production and productivity, is inextricable from a spatial-temporal schema that is material to Western values of both capitalism and heterosexuality.

17

poems from
*ocean power: poems from the desert*

PULLING DOWN THE CLOUDS

Ñ-ku'ibaḍkaj 'ant 'an ols g cewagĭ.
With my harvesting stick I will hook the clouds.
'Ant o 'i-wañ̃'io k o 'i-hudiñ g cewagĭ.
With my harvesting stick I will pull down the clouds.
Ñ-ku'ibaḍkaj 'ant o 'i-siho g cewagĭ.
With my harvesting stick I will stir the clouds.

With dreams of distant noise disturbing his sleep,
the smell of dirt, wet, for the first time in what seems like months.
The change in the molecules is sudden,
they enter the nasal cavity.

He contemplates that smell.
What is that smell?
It is rain.

Rain somewhere out in the desert.
Comforted in this knowledge he turns over
and continues his sleep,
dreams of women with harvesting sticks
raised toward the sky.

## BA:BAN GANHU GE CI:PIA

Ba:ban ganhu ge ci:pia
Ba:ban ganhu ge ci:pia
Kut 'am hema meḍk 'am ha-kakk'e
Kut 'am hema meḍk 'am ha-kakk'e
Ba: mt o ci:pia?
Kut 'am hema meḍk 'am ha-kakk'e
Wa ṣa 'an wo:po ṣon 'oidag

Coyotes moving along over there
Coyotes moving along over there
Someone go over there and ask them
Someone go over there and ask them
Where are you guys moving to?
Running along the foothills
Running along the foothills
Someone go over there and ask them
Someone go over there and ask them
Where are you guys moving to?
With baby's new tenny shoes
And her Merle Haggard and Hank Williams tapes
in the Bashas' grocery bag
And his cowboy boots in another
All worldly goods
Packed up
Moving
Kut 'am hema meḍk 'am ha-kakk'e
Kut 'am hema meḍk 'am ha-kakk'e
Ba: mt o ci:pia?
Someone go over there and ask them
Where are you guys moving to?

## KITCHEN SINK

The light from the kitchen-door window comes through in a special way.
I can see the seasons change in my kitchen sink.
The movement of the sun is shadowed in that sink.
During the afternoon the sink is full with sunlight.
Not necessarily a good time to be washing dishes.
Later in the summer there is a sense of urgency as the shadow gets longer
    and begins to slant
as the sunlight starts to edge out of the sink.
I pretend the sunlight is going down the drain.
The light cannot be stopped by the plug in the drain.
It seeps down around the inner seal where water cannot go,
becoming a part of the darkness that is always a part of drains and pipes.
Winter is coming.
The air is probably cooler already.
I know this because of my sink.

18

# confinements
## *the domestic in the discourses*
## *of upper-middle-class pregnancy*

About two years ago, in my seventh month of pregnancy and halfway through my semester-long course on Jane Austen and Charlotte Brontë—these serve as my calendars and my aids to memory—I found myself teaching a Foucauldian reading of *Northanger Abbey,* trying and failing to explain Paul Morrison's concept of the "domestic carceral" to my students.[1] The class, largely made up of women deeply invested in the euphoric marriage plot and a sense of the ever-expanding domestic spaces it created for women's sexual and social triumph, resisted for the full ninety minutes Morrison's interrogation of the politics of home.

In *Northanger Abbey* the heroine, Catherine Moreland, an avid reader of gothic novels, finds herself in the bedroom of a dark castle owned by the father of the man she loves. Like the gothic heroines upon whom she models herself, she cautiously explores her surroundings, finding, as it happens, a large cabinet, which, according to gothic convention, should contain something crucial to the gothic plot: a mysterious document, probably a will or a confession, or perhaps even a body. Catherine opens the cabinet with some difficulty; it is, to all appearances, empty. As she fumbles for a secret drawer, however, her hand closes on a rolled-up manuscript. Just as she is about to read the document, her candle is snuffed by a gust of wind. Terrified, Catherine retreats to bed. The next morning she reads the manuscript by the light of day: "Her greedy eye glanced rapidly over a page. She started at its import. Could it be possible, or did not her senses play her false?—An inventory of linen, in coarse and modern characters, seemed all that was before her! If the evidence of sight might be trusted, she held a washing-bill in her hand."[2]

The deflation from the gothic to the domestic brings not only comfort but shame. Catherine feels "humbled to the dust" that she could have imagined that a room so "modern, so habitable" could have contained anything like the horrors she had imagined for herself the previous night. The room, then, with its modern furniture, its domestic comforts, acts as a visual guarantee against the incursion of the past and of the gothic. Drained of its gothic possibilities, the room simply signifies benignly the concept of home.

The humor and the moral of the scene both depend on the contrast between the gothic and the domestic, between the horror of the trunk that holds the dead body and the mundanity of the trunk that holds laundry. Feminist critics have argued in fact that, for women at least, this is no simple opposition and that the laundry list and the laundry, which represent both locus and the method of female oppression, are as dangerous to the well-being of a heroine as the ghost or the dead body.[3] The laundry list, as a sign not only of domestic duty but of surveillance, of the listing and categorization of "dirty linen," threatens the female body from a number of directions. The fact that the laundry list belongs to the future husband of our heroine's future sister-in-law also suggests a double or triple entanglement in the marriage plot, which itself becomes sign and method of surveillance.

The phrase "domestic carceral" points to women's imprisonment in the home and in the marriage plot and away from a teleology that sees home and marriage as benign alternatives to a gothic world of ghosts, robbers, and rapists who come in from outside. The phrase begins to explain a series of cultural truths that bear the uneasy and contradictory status of proverbs and surprises: most accidents happen at home; a woman is more likely to be physically attacked by her husband than by a stranger.

It was these truths I took with me in my brief walk across the street to Methodist Hospital, where I, like so many other women of my social class and stage of pregnancy, was attending a series of "birthing classes" preparatory to my delivery. This was to be an especially interesting day; our class was to take a tour of Methodist Hospital's famous and heavily advertised homelike "birthing suites," complete with Jacuzzis, cherry furniture, and pull-out couches for the expectant father.

Trailing behind our childbirth educator, we paused at the threshold of one particular room to admire its many and resplendent domestic accouterments: the armoire, the rocking chair, the chintz-covered sofa, the private bath. If the room looked a little like a motel, it was the kind of motel that looks most like home. If it didn't look exactly like my home, or any home that one might visit, it looked—except, of course, for the IV stand and the fetal monitor snuggled against the wall and in between the pieces of matching furniture—like the home one might have if one were, say, a cleaner and neater person.

One brave man broke the hush of desire provoked in us by the room and by the specter of the perfect birth by which it was inhabited. "What," he asked, "actually happens during delivery?" Our leader paused dramatically before pushing a button on the cherry bedstead, and the room began to move. First, the bed, creaking like the door of a medieval castle, began slowly to fold up until its head was perpendicular to the floor and the foot had moved back to form the seat of a high and narrow chair. Next, a panel in the ceiling opened and metal equipment began to unfold and then to descend. As the equipment locked noiselessly into place, part of it was revealed to be a huge surgical lamp that lowered itself to within about a foot of the now-rumpled surface of the bed. Finally, the nurse opened the door of the armoire to produce a pair of huge black metal stirrups, which she proceeded to attach to slits at the foot of the bed. The living room was now an operating room oddly crowded with remnants from the showroom of Ethan Allen or its perhaps more appropriately named Houston counterpart, Finger's.

As the gothic apparatus descended, my first thought was to flee the scene. I looked around at the other expectant parents for confirmation of a sudden, almost overwhelming fear. They seemed to me impressed, cheerful, absolutely at home with it all. I was edging toward the door when the nurse announced the next stop on the tour: "Next we'll have a look at where you'll be taken if, God forbid, something should go wrong," she said, knocking on what I can now swear was the imitation cherry. "Let's go look at where you'll go if you have a cesarean." She ushered us down a narrow hallway whose plum wallpaper gave way suddenly to greenish tile. "The rooms on that side look like normal hospital rooms, nothing special about them," the nurse explained. "Do you have any questions or comments except 'Please, God, don't let it be me'?"

Was I the only one praying for the green tile and the "normal operating room"? Was I the only one who never wanted to snuggle down in that nightmare of a trick bed or to give birth in a room where everything folded out, up, or down in the process of turning into something else? I think I was the only one who muttered "Foucault" to my husband as the two of us slunk back past the peaches, plums, and cherries of the birthing suite and back to Rice, where two days later I was able, with the help of the folding bed, for the first time to explain the domestic carceral to my students.

The point of this anecdote as I tell it here is to outline a methodological problem involving the place of the reproductive female body in our culture. The birthing suite and the liberal culture of pregnancy management in which it is embedded offer the promise of safety, domesticity, and control. The birthing suite itself, with its overt visual references to home and to the nexus of comforts which that word, however problematically, suggests, serves as the topographical centerpiece to the happy story of female autonomy. By replicating home in the hospital, the birthing suite keeps terror at bay. The irony of the hospital-as-home is, of course, twofold. The closets of the birthing suites, unlike the cabinet in Northanger Abbey, are, in fact, filled with the gothic apparatus of medicine; the birthing suite only looks like home. More importantly, however, the hospital-as-home depends, as does the parody in *Northanger Abbey*, on an uneasy vision of the home as safe place; in this respect the gestures of homeliness, whether they succeed or fail in their referentiality, point to the dangers that lurk in and indeed define so many American homes: poverty, abuse, malnutrition, patriarchy. One cannot escape the discipline of the body by invoking the site of that discipline: it is at home, after all, that women embark on diets, shave their legs and tease their hair, do or do not have sex, and painfully negotiate the conflicting demands of femininity.

Despite increasing feminist awareness of the dangers associated with home, much feminist and proto-feminist discussion of pregnancy and childbirth derives its power and its idiom from a deeply middle-class and heterosexual ideal of domesticity. The remainder of this chapter will look at two exemplary sites of that idiom: the discourse of the home birth movement and the rhetoric of the contemporary pregnancy advice book. In the first section I will look at how and at what cost home gets constructed as a place of safety and autonomy for women, while in the second, through a close reading of one bestselling advice book, I will look at how home becomes both site and instrument of the policing of pregnant women.

In much of the literature of the home birth movement, as well as in feminist and proto-feminist accounts of home birth in more general contexts, home functions in much of the literature as a synecdoche for female autonomy; it becomes the place not only of comfort but of power and freedom. As Sheila Kitzinger puts it: "An overwhelming advantage of home birth is that you control the territory in which birth takes place, and those helping you are guests in your home. You can move around just as you want, eat and drink, take a bath, or go out for a walk—do whatever you feel like doing."[4] Home functions in this enabling fantasy as a place of free choice over one's body, a context safe for the exercise of will, body, and desire. The power of the fantasy lies in its sometimes explicit, always implicit contrast to the scene of the hospital, where, as numerous feminist writers on childbirth point out, a woman routinely hands over power to the institution. The romanticization of home as a place of security may well be as premature as it is—more on this later—nostalgic; according to Pamela S. Eakin's study of women who chose home birth, most "women selecting to give birth outside the hospital were not as interested in maintaining the comforts of home as they were in avoiding the 'stark and regimented' hospital environment."[5] In other words, home itself is a relative value.

Despite the instability of home as signifier, many feminist books on childbirth are structured by a now familiar history, a narrative of devolution from the halcyon days of home births attended by midwives to the medicalized and doctor-controlled present. The shift in this first narrative typically takes place somewhere at the beginning of the nineteenth century when the professionalization of medicine allowed doctors to ban midwives from the bedsides of birthing women.[6] This framing and defining historical narrative can also be condensed to fit the span of one woman's lifetime; Jessica Mitford's *The American Way of Birth* begins with the story of her four increasingly medicalized experiences of childbirth, the first and most fondly remembered of which took place at home.[7] Whatever the chronological scope of the framing narrative, the move from home to hospital is a crucial structural element in the devolution of Western obstetrics. Mirror narratives of recuperation and evolution begin with unsatisfactory hospital births and move toward a home or more homelike birth; this kind of narrative, which we see, for example, in Nancy Wainer Cohen and Lois J. Estner's study of cesarean deliveries, *Silent Knife,* seeks literally to undo the dubious progress of obstetrics and to recapture some ordinary or natural state.[8]

Central to this devolutionary narrative is an embedded history of the revalencing of home and hospital with respect to safety and danger. While at different historical moments for different populations[9] the hospital has signified safety for the birthing woman, in feminist analyses the hospital figures as a place of physical and psychological danger, a place where unnecessary interventions threaten a woman's health, life, and sense of well-being. Home and hospital, then, become, in the debates between feminists and the medical profession, sites not only of contested notions of safety but of referential exchange, where the term "danger" shifts from one location to the other. The marshaling of statistics in support of either position is a murky business, partly because proponents of home birth want, for obvious reasons, to count only planned home births, while official statistics include all births taking place in a noninstitutional setting.[10] Ann Oakley, in her rich and informative feminist history of pregnancy,

*The Captured Womb,* does not even try to untangle the numbers produced by different claims; in an otherwise exhaustively detailed analysis, she remarks only that "the argument about the relative safety of domiciliary and institutional confinement still flourishes in the 1980s. Just as important as the statistics of mortality themselves is the matter of what people make of them."[11] Analysis of the safety of home birth, then, becomes quickly embedded in an analysis of the rhetoric of both sides of the debate and ultimately, I would argue, in the rhetorical status of home.

Kitzinger and others are quick to point out the degree to which medical culture has, for the affluent at least, co-opted the rhetoric of home and autonomy in its advertisements and particularly in its birthing suites. As Kitzinger notes: "Decor and furnishings are an insufficient guide to attitudes. There are hospitals where women are offered flowery curtains, patchwork quilts, a special birthing bed or chair, and soft music, where all this is merely a facade for interventionist obstetric practice. In a commercial system, where medical care is another commodity competing in the open market, some hospitals provide these pleasant rooms to persuade women not to have their babies at home, in out-of-hospital birthing centers, or in rival hospitals" (YB, 169).

Barbara Katz Rothman, in her analysis of various elements of what she calls "natural birth," sees birthing suites with their "flowered linen, photomurals on the walls, and candle-lit postpartum dinners," as competing with home birth through appropriation of the signs of domesticity.[12] While Kitzinger, Rothman, and others are rightly suspicious of hospitals' imitation of "home," they do not take their suspicion a step further into the rhetoric of home itself. They do not mention, for example, that most people's homes are in fact themselves inadequate approximations of the domestic ideal made visible by hospital birthing suites. The problematic nature of the domestic ideal is revealed through a paradox in the statistics about the social class of women who give birth at home. Home births are by far the most common in three groups with very different relations to medical culture: upper-middle-class college-educated women who plan a home birth because of a feminist or proto-feminist critique of medical ideology; conservative and/or religious women who come from patriarchal family structures that emphasize the privacy of the family and the supervision of the father; and poor and/or extremely young women who have had little prenatal care.[13] The teleologies of these women's births meet at home, or rather, in a series of very different homes with different relations, among other things, to privacy, safety, and power. While I am, of course, not arguing that home is, for middle-class women, exempt from the forces of institutional power—as I hope I make clear in the concluding section of this chapter—

"home" might be an especially fraught term for a teenage unwed mother trying to hide her pregnancy from her family by delivering in the bathroom.

While only a small percentage of middle-class women choose home birth, home is nonetheless an important site in much of the contemporary literature about childbirth. Advice literature about pregnancy and childbirth constructs, by definition, a domestic site of information as an alternative to the doctor's or midwife's office. Framed sometimes as resistant and sometimes as a supplement to visits to the doctor's office and to the medical management of pregnancy, these books emphasize a woman's access to information within the confines of her own domestic space. They also, of course, have things to say *about* home and its role in pregnancy and birth; these books routinely make suggestions about diet, furnishings, sex, and clothing, helping and/or coercing women to reconfigure their relations to domestic spaces and activities.

While much recent work on advice literature has focused on the construction of normative femininity through the body, there has so far been very little emphasis on the relation of these books to notions of home and domestic space. Nancy Armstrong, in her introduction to the collection *The Ideology of Conduct*, points to but does not explore the double valence of home in the phrase "domestic surveillance," which she uses to describe the historical function of conduct books.[14] The term simultaneously suggests a surveillance *of* and *from* the home, a literal internalization of disciplinary norms.

The policing of and from the home by advice books directed at middle-class women works as a more subtle alternative to the more literal policing of the working-class home and the working-class pregnant mother within the home. That tradition, as we shall see, becomes most visible in, although it does not begin with, the implementation of home visitation for pregnant women in England at the beginning of the twentieth century. Ann Oakley sees the spread of home visitation as an indication of a paradigm shift in which the state was newly envisioned as having a stake in the health of pregnant women and in antenatal care. The advice book, aimed at a more affluent audience than home visitation, similarly uses the home as a place for education into cultural ideologies of pregnancy, with this difference: it does its work in the name of autonomy and choice.

As my reading of the bestselling advice book *What to Expect When You're Expecting* will suggest, this manual is deeply invested in constructing a middle-class heterosexual domestic space for the education of women into pregnancy.[15] The woman sitting on the cover in a rocking chair is not, interestingly enough, taking care of a baby or preparing either the baby's room or the healthy food upon which the book is so insistent; instead, she sits in the rocker, an open book in her hand, reflecting, perhaps, on something she has just read. The message of the cover is clear; the book in the mother's lap literally precedes the baby; its presence signifies a prepared pregnancy as surely as a plump baby would signify a successful birth. The book represents the baby in two senses: first iconically, as it renders what is inside the mother's body both visible and visual, and second, in a more traditionally political sense, in which the book represents the baby by becoming its advocate. To be pregnant here is to read, to be pregnant with knowledge about pregnancy. The book has entered and constructed the home, has come to rest upon and has all but entered the mother's body as it announces its necessary role in the project of bodily reconstruction.

Sometimes called the yuppie bible of pregnancy, *What to Expect When You're Expecting* by Arlene Eisenberg, Heidi Eisenberg Murkoff, and Sandee Eisenberg Hathaway is a resolutely upbeat book organized simultaneously by two competing structures: a developmental narrative that takes the reader from the first through the last weeks of pregnancy, and a question-and-answer format. Every sign of its intended audience—from the blonde woman rocking on the cover, to its continual invocation of the husband of the expectant mother, to its assumption about restaurants—indicates that it is targeting a white, upper-middle-class, heterosexual audience. The book routinely imagines and invokes a white married woman with money to spend on baby-sitters, vacations, and eating out.

*What to Expect* does exhibit certain crucial markers of the specifically feminist self-help book with roots in the women's health movement of the 1960s and 1970s. Its many diagrams of the female body in various stages of pregnancy, its familiar and experiential tone, and its rhetorical insistence on choice and variation suggest ancestral ties to books like *Our Bodies, Ourselves,* which derive from an explicitly feminist project. The latter text's use of the concept of autonomy is, however, deeply imbricated in a literally developmental narrative that climaxes at the time of labor and delivery. Like much feminist, proto-feminist, and just plain yuppie material on pregnancy, *What to Expect* largely confines the idea of choice to the last few weeks of pregnancy, to the "choice" of various kinds of labor and delivery.

My reading of *What to Expect* focuses on those months before labor and delivery, where the concept of the mother's autonomy is entirely absent as the book both enacts and prescribes a constant surveillance of her behaviors. The mother's every move, whether it be taking a bite of dessert or choosing underpants, is carefully inspected, calibrated, and quantified with respect to the baby inside her.[16]

Nowhere is this inspection more evident than in the book's repeated and sometimes repetitive discussions of food and eating. Although the book is reassuring on the subject of X rays, alcohol, and even drugs in the first chapter, food is fraught with danger to the baby. Indeed, the rhetoric of the book positions the baby as the person eating, the mother as a conduit. The introduction to the section on the "Best-Odds Diet," subtitled "Make Every Bite Count," explains:

> You've got only nine months of meals and snacks with which to give your baby the best possible start in life. Make every one of them count. Before you close your mouth on a forkful of food, consider, "Is this the best bite I can give my baby?" If it will benefit your baby, chew away. If it'll only benefit your sweet tooth or appease your appetite, put your fork down. (*WTE*, 81)

This passage sets up two patterns that recur throughout the book. The first has to do with a particular reproductive calendar that emphasizes the temporal limitation and places the onus of producing a healthy child on the nine months of pregnancy. The warning that the expectant mother has "only nine months" to give the baby a "healthy start" privileges pregnancy over parenting and the fetus over the child. Moreover, it replicates in its rhetorical idiom the "biological clock" that ticks anxiously below the surface of most advice books to professional women and links the discourse of pregnancy to the discourse on infertility. Even in pregnancy, which the book admits in other sections may seem interminable, the mother becomes translated into the idiom of time pressure. In fact, *What to Expect* is not extreme with respect to this collapsed calendar; several pregnancy manuals, most notably Janice Graham's *Your Pregnancy Companion,* begin before pregnancy or with the period of two weeks or so when women are actually pregnant but do not yet know it. This period is, according to Graham, especially fraught with danger to the developing fetus. As she explains in her introduction, where she collapses the two periods mentioned above:

> The idea of "preconception health" is still very new, but the concept is rooted in the belief that many problems occur before most women even realize they are pregnant. ... In these weeks, the embryo is in its most rapid state of development: all the fetal organs are forming and virtually millions of cells are dividing and differentiating. And during this critical stage of fetal growth and development, it is believed that the healthier a mother's body, life-style, and environment are, the lower the risk that something will go wrong.[17]

As the calendar gets pushed back, the onus on the mother becomes greater. Characteristically, this burden is invoked in the name of reassurance: "You can't imagine how planning ahead can make for an easier pregnancy psychologically; there is so much less to worry about or brood over when you know you've provided a pristine environment for your unborn baby from day one" (YPC, 4).

The second emerging pattern in the passage from *What to Expect* has to do with an opposition between the baby and the expectant mother. Like other tensions in the book, this one surfaces most acutely in the discourse around food. The passage positions the baby's health against the mother's "appetites." While for economically disadvantaged women this battle will take place over illegal drugs, particularly over crack, the yuppie mother is represented as working through this problem over food.

While there is some mention of a possibility of problems associated with alcohol in an introductory section on fetal alcohol syndrome, alcoholics and "heavy drinkers" are excised from the text early on by being referred to counseling or to Alcoholics Anonymous. Although alcohol does reappear on several occasions in the month-by-month accounts that make up the body of the book, it is usually relegated to a dependent clause in discussions of *What to Expect*'s more vexing consumable—food. The long and detailed section on eating out begins, "For most pregnant women it isn't substituting mineral water for martinis that poses a challenge at business lunches (or when dining out after hours); it's trying to put together a meal that's nutritionally sound from a menu of cream sauces, elegant but empty starches, and tempting sweets" (WTE, 183). That "most pregnant women" do not go out to expensive business lunches seems too obvious to mention here; "most pregnant women," even those with good jobs, are not regularly confronted with the agonizing choice between "elegant but empty starches" and nutritionally sound meals. By placing the problem of alcohol during pregnancy in the context of the two-martini lunch, the authors manage oddly enough both to trivialize the issue of alcohol abuse and to police effectively all drinking of alcoholic beverages. By speaking only parenthetically about the problem, they suggest that the prohibition on alcohol has been so efficiently internalized that it needs no more discussion. Again, this has a disorientingly double effect, demonizing women who cannot dismiss alcohol from their lives in one dependent clause by suggesting that it is not a problem for "most women," and stressing the impossibility of any discussion of how much alcohol is too much.

The opposition between mother and fetus actually places the latter in the position of monitor. Although agency is not ascribed to the fetus in this process, its very helplessness turns it into a branch of the police; its agency, in fact, derives from its inability to act. This conflict is rhetorically resolved by the disappearance of the mother's body; every forkful of food is imagined as going directly to the fetus. When confronted with the problem of resisting Grandma's special brownies, for example, the expectant mother is advised to say something like "You know I love your brownies, Grandma, but my baby's too young for them" (WTE, 63). The very identification of mother as grandmother places the fetus in the role of fully imagined and resisting personhood. The disappearance of the mother also oddly suggests that the pregnancy is in fact over; the phrase "Is this the best bite I can give my baby?" evokes a child already outside the womb, a child who is "fed" in a more literal sense. The reproductive calendar, then, contracts even further as the baby is represented as being in some sense *already born*.

If the baby polices implicitly, the father is imagined as doing so explicitly. In the section entitled "Fathers Are Expectant Too," the authors discuss the husband's role in the wife's diet. Although a subtitle warns the father, "Don't Be Too Preachy," the husband/father is clearly expected to enforce good eating habits: "If she slips, nagging will only help her to fall faster and farther. Remind, don't remonstrate. Prod her conscience, don't try to become it. Signal her quietly when in public, rather than making a pointed announcement to all within earshot about her ordering her chicken breaded and fried. Most important, do it with a sense of humor and a lot of love" (WTE, 419).

The threat of falling with which this paragraph begins brings us back to what seems clearly to be a sexualized image of "appetite" in the paragraph I quoted earlier. While it would be too simple to see eating simply as a code for sex here or elsewhere, the fall into desire of all sorts is a terrible specter and an efficient way of enforcing control. It is especially interesting to contrast the hysteria of the opening sentence with the reassuring passage on literal falling, in which the authors reassure women who stumble in the street how well protected the fetus is and how little chance there is of actual harm from even the most spectacular accident.

The images of privacy and publicity that structure this paragraph are especially open to a rereading through the domestic carceral. While the fear expressed toward the end of the passage is humiliation in public, it seems clear that in private the husband can feel freer to correct his wife's food choices. Home becomes, in effect, a house of correction, a place where a husband can, by implication, be "pointed" in his criticism of his wife's tastes in chicken.

The emphasis on the dangers of leaving one's house is apparent in the emphasis on guidelines for "eating out." The reader is repeatedly warned about the issue of control in restaurants. Desserts, for example, should probably not even be attempted outside the home. Although the best-odds diet permits fruit and unsweetened whipped cream on the side, women are told to wait and to "indulge in juice-sweetened treats when you get home" (*WTE,* 186). Home, it seems, also has a national dimension. A boxed inset in the 1988 edition helpfully lists national cuisines in order of healthiness: American and Continental, not surprisingly, top the list. In a truly startling moment of xenophobia, the reader is instructed to avoid Chinese, Japanese, German, and Mexican food. No mention is made of the fact that millions of healthy babies are born each year to mothers who eat only the cuisine of these particular countries and that in several of these countries the infant mortality rate, to use only one measure of postnatal health, is considerably better than it is in the United States.

*What to Expect*'s concern with food is, of course, inextricably linked to issues of weight gain and body image in pregnancy. While again, the overt message is reassuring and indeed celebratory of the pregnant body, the underlying message is more anxious. Although there are significant changes in the 1991 edition, in the 1988 edition the authors first tackle the issue of appropriate weight gain in response to the following "question":"I only gained one pound in my first trimester. My friend, who's also pregnant, gained six. What's enough, and what's too much?" The structure of the answer is absolutely typical of the anxious doublespeak that pervades *What to Expect*:

> Weight gain that is just enough for one woman may be too much or too little for another. The extremely underweight woman is probably doing her baby a favor by gaining 6 pounds (as long as they're gained by eating highly nutritious food) in the first trimester, or doing him or her an injustice by gaining only 1. The obese mother-to-be, on the other hand, is doing no one a favor by gaining weight rapidly, and can probably afford to gain only 1 pound (or even none) in the first trimester (as long as she eats adequate amounts of nutritious foods) without jeopardizing her baby's health. For the woman who is average, however, six pounds is probably too much and 1 is not enough. Two to four would be just right. (*WTE* 1988, 122)

The passage begins, like so many others in this text, with a cheery relativism and the implication that one should not compare oneself to other women. Pregnancy, according to this narrative, is an individual matter; no one can set the standards for anyone else—except, of course, the expert answerer of questions. The tone of the paragraph follows a downward spiral through a series of parentheses, qualifications, warnings, and aberrations, until the average woman is admonished in the final sentence. Since the questions are in fact made up by the authors, it is interesting that they choose a negative example—negative at least for the "average woman." As the tone becomes darker, the scale of what is appropriate narrows, and the difference between one and two pounds, one bleary morning misreading, one forbidden cupcake, swells to become, as it were, pregnant with meaning. Since the hypothetical woman asking the question does not tell us whether she is "seriously underweight" or "obese," she and the reader are admonished with the "average"; since if she were underweight or obese she would be aberrant in any case, this hypothetical woman is rendered abnormal in some sense through any of the passages' calculations: she is either, it seems, obese, in which case her original weight was a problem, or "average," in which case she has gained too little. I stress the arithmetic of this answer only because these are no-win equations whose application can only have an anxiety-producing effect. Even wading through the inverted syntax and the parentheses—not to mention the arithmetic—is difficult. The inevitable result ratifies the anxiety of calculation.

Also remarkable in this passage are the allusions to doing someone—first the baby and then, in the case of the obese woman, anyone at all—"a favor." This, of course, gets us back to the language of body image and sexuality. The woman herself is never named as one of the people receiving or not receiving the "favor"; in the case of the obese woman, the "no one" seems to point to a third person, to the husband or father. The authors do reply specifically to a question about the relation of the wife's weight gain to her sexual attractiveness. Interestingly, this occurs in the section on expectant fathers, and the question is posed in the voice of the husband: "As petty as this might seem, I'm afraid my wife's going to get fat and flabby during pregnancy, and stay that way afterward" (*WTE*, 418). The answer is in many ways a canny one that opens with a statement about the primacy of the baby over both husband and wife: "If it were in your wife's obstetrical interest to gain 50 pounds with a pregnancy, you . . . would have no option, of course, but to accept fat and flab as the price of a healthy baby" (*WTE*, 418). Having set up this possibility, this straw man of a flabby woman, the authors proceed to knock it down to size. "A moderate, steady, carefully monitored weight increase of between 25 and 35 pounds, gained on a diet of highly nutritious foods," they explain, will not produce flab and will ensure the wife's "speediest return to slenderness after childbirth" (*WTE*, 418). The section goes on to exhort husbands to help keep their wives from temptation. By giving the husbands a role in the process of fighting flab—a gesture typical of liberal feminism's desire to integrate men into all aspects of the pregnancy process—they also apportion responsibility and blame.

The question of responsibility is articulated through a collapsing of boundaries, not only between mother and fetus but between mother and father. Fathers are expected by the authors to share in some of the physical sacrifices of pregnancy; they should learn to eat steamed vegetables and should themselves abstain from drinking alcohol. When offered a drink at a party, an expectant father should reply, "No thanks, we're pregnant." The "we," figured here as a sign of support, is, of course, also a symptom of a systematic appropriation of the reproductive body. The pregnant body, so resistant to forces from outside the family, knows no boundaries within it. Father collapses into mother, who in turn collapses into fetus. The subjectivity of the mother is eroded from both the inside and the outside.

The disappearance of the mother's body is a key moment in Rosalind Petchesky's productive analysis of the rhetoric of right-to-life movements. In her reading of their most effective piece of propaganda, the film *The Silent Scream,* she notes the repeated presentation of the fetus without the visual context of the mother's body.[18] *The Silent Scream* returns again and again to the image of the free-floating fetus, unconnected to the outside world and to the body that sustains it. The rhetoric of liberal advice culture, with its benign gestures toward working women and its repeated invocations of female autonomy during the process of birth and labor, produces a fetus and a pregnancy eerily reminiscent of the one at the visual and emotional center of right-to-life propaganda. Ironically, that advice culture, with its multiple investments in home, produces a homeless fetus, a baby without walls, as the surveillance of the female body erases that body in the very act of inspection, rendering it not so much invisible as transparent. As we look at the diagrams of fetal development that begin every new chapter, every new monthly installment of *What to Expect,* as we are told to eat, sleep, and exercise for the fetus, we are implicitly being told to look through the body of the pregnant woman.

The transparent pregnant body, spectacularly permeable to the gaze, must itself be fixed within the boundaries of home. Although it may be held up for publicity, its place is essentially private; its confinement within the domestic makes it legible according to a series of culturally sanctioned codes. While the word "confinement" has slipped out of the discourse of contemporary pregnancy and childbirth, it leaves its traces in the domestic carceral and in the elaborate culture of advice, surveillance, and admonition that mark off the "private" sphere.

## NOTES

1. Paul Morrison, "Enclosed in Openness, *Northanger Abbey* and the Domestic Carceral," *Texas Studies in Language and Literature* 23 (Spring 1991): 1–23.

2. Jane Austen, *Northanger Abbey* (1919; reprint, New York: Oxford University Press, 1971), 137.

3. Sandra M. Gilbert and Susan Gubar, *The Madwoman in the Attic* (New Haven: Yale University Press, 1980).

4. Sheila Kitzinger, *Your Baby, Your Way: Making Pregnancy Decisions and Birth Plans* (New York: Pantheon, 1987), 165. Quotes in text will hereafter be identified with *YB* and page number.

5. Pamela S. Eakins, "Out-of-Hospital Birth," in *The American Way of Birth,* ed. Eakins (Philadelphia: Temple University Press, 1986), 223.

6. For various narratives along this line, see Barbara Ehrenreich and Dierdre English, *For Their Own Good: 150 Years of the Experts' Advice to Women* (New York: Anchor, 1979); Ann Dally, *Women Under the Knife: A History of Surgery* (London: Hutchinson Radius, 1991); and Karen Michaelson and contributors, *Childbirth in America: An Anthropological Perspective* (New York: Bergin and Garvey, 1987).

7. Jessica Mitford, *The American Way of Birth* (New York: Dutton, 1992), chapter 1.

8. Nancy Wainer Cohen and Lois J. Estner, *Silent Knife: Cesarian Prevention and Vaginal Birth after Cesarian (VBAC)* (New York: Bergin and Garvey, 1983), xv–xx.

9. For example, Carolyn Fishel Sargent, *Maternity, Medicine, and Power: Reproductive Decisions in Urban Benin* (Berkeley: University of California Press, 1989), 51, notes that many urban women in her study see the hospital as a safer alternative to home birth, and hospitals as more helpful in relieving suffering.

10. See Michaelson, *Childbirth in America,* 28; and Barbara Katz Rothman, "Awake and Aware, or False Consciousness," in *Childbirth: Alternatives to Medical Control,* ed. Shelly Romalis (Austin: University of Texas Press, 1981).

11. Ann Oakley, *The Captured Womb: A History of the Medical Care of Pregnant Women* (Oxford: Basil Blackwell, 1984), 33.

12. Rothman, "Awake and Aware," 172.

13. For a discussion of populations giving or planning to give birth at home, see Michaelson, *Childbirth in America,* 28; Rothman, "Awake and Aware," 171–72.

14. Nancy Armstrong, "Introduction," in *The Ideology of Conduct: Essays on Literature and the History of Sexuality,* ed. Nancy Armstrong and Leonard Tennenhouse (New York: Methuen, 1987).

15. Arlene Eisenberg, Heidi Eisenberg Murkoff, and Sandee Eisenberg Hathaway, *What to Expect When You're Expecting* (New York: Workman, 1984, 1988, 1991). Quotes in text will hereafter be identified with *WTE* and page number. Unless otherwise noted, citations are from the 1991 edition.

16. The decision to use the term "baby" or "fetus" is, of course, laden with and productive of a series of assumptions. We have, when applicable, to echo the choice of

the author we are discussing. When we are not discussing a particular author or point of view, we have chosen to use "fetus" until the moment of birth. We plan, in our introduction, to talk more specifically about rhetorical choices of this kind, and also to provide as a test case a discussion of authorial choices to use "baby," "fetus," "neonate," and "embryo." See Helena Michie and Naomi Cahn, *Confinements: Fertility and Infertility in Contemporary Culture* (Brunswick, N.J.: Rutgers University Press, 1997).

17. Janice Graham, *Your Pregnancy Companion* (New York: Pocket Books, 1991), 3. Quotes in text will hereafter be identified with *YPC* and page number.

18. Rosalind Pollack Petchesky, "Foetal Images: The Power of Visual Culture in the Politics of Reproduction," in *Reproductive Technologies: Gender, Motherhood, and Medicine,* ed. Michelle Stanworth (Oxford: Basil Blackwell, 1987), 36–57.

19

# civilization, barbarism, and norteña gardens

By a happy coincidence, this essay was sched-
uled to be read on the feast day of St. Teresa de Avila, an occasion, like
other religious holidays, always celebrated with flowers. Thus I brought
to the conference a bouquet of the flowers traditionally used on such
occasions: roses, margaritas, and snapdragons, all derived from Euro-
pean-Spanish stock. Although of a pagan origin, for centuries they
have been a metaphor for civilization and Christianity. These cultivated
flowers provided a sharp contrast to the cactus and wildflowers that
bloomed so profusely outside the conference room we occupied in
Tucson, Arizona, a contrast that symbolically prefigured the issues
I would address. This essay suggests that these flowers and the garden spaces that were home for *norteñas*—Mexican women from the
north of Mexico—offer important insights into their construction of
their worlds from the late nineteenth century to the present.[1]

## THE PHYSICAL AND CULTURAL SETTING

From atop the lone tower of the eighteenth-century Franciscan
mission San Xavier del Bac, located twelve miles south of Tucson, Arizona, one's eye can follow the circle of the broad Tucson Basin. To the
north are the Santa Catalina Mountains with peaks above nine thousand feet; east are the rounded Rincon Mountains; far off in the
southern corner are the Santa Ritas, topped with observatories; to
the west are the young, ragged, low Tucson Mountains, known for
their rocky desert growth. Such dry basins and river valleys bordered

by distant desert mountain ranges are typical formations in the extensive geographic space that some know as Aridamerica—the southwestern United States and northern Mexico. In pre-Columbian times these lands were the home of the Chichimec, while Spanish colonial settlers and imperial officials thought of them as Nueva Viscaya or Pimeria Alta; later independent Mexico divided the northern deserts into Nuevo Mexico, Texas, Sonora, and Chihuahua. Today, following the 1853 territorial divisions after the Anglo-American invasion, the area is divided from east to west by an international border separating two nation states—to the north the United States (with Arizona to the west of New Mexico) and to the south, Mexico (with Sonora to the west of Chihuahua). The place names in this region bring to life past histories. Some, like Tucson, come from indigenous roots with Spanish colonial adaptations, and a multitude of Spanish names either venerate merciful saints—for example, the Santa Catalina Mountains or the Santa Cruz River—or pragmatically describe natural features, as in Cañada del Oro or Tanque Verde. This history shared by indigenous peoples, Spanish invaders and their descendants, and the more recent Anglo-American invaders and settlers challenges the historical divisions themselves. Certainly since 1853, the rigid boundaries of maps and treaties that form the national border, so unmovable at crossing points, not only dissolve in desert sands outside the immediate physical barriers but are continuously challenged by cultural scripts written long before nations drew such divisions.

But to understand the world of the norteñas, we must look even further back and beyond the shores of North America. By 1848 Mexican women populating the villages and mountains of these desert lands were heirs to a rich cultural life rooted in Spanish beliefs and Renaissance Christianity. They drew on this cultural heritage to confront the material hardships of this harsh desert frontier, accentuated by violence and hostility. This essay examines how norteñas held in tension their contradictory beliefs and realities, in part by constructing walled gardens where they could both symbolically and actually nurture their visions of a Spanish paradise. It concludes by demonstrating how these accommodations to existence in the desert landscape were turned upside down as norteñas crossed the border into U.S. mining towns during the second decade of this century.

The primary source for this essay is a series of oral history interviews I conducted over a four-year period with ten Mexicanas living in southeastern Arizona and southwestern New Mexico. All of the women had fled from the northern states of Sonora or Chihuahua during the 1910 Mexican Revolution, and all have since died. I have not yet published their stories as oral history because, frankly, I am very perturbed about several issues regarding the publication of oral histories. For a community like mine, the Mexican American/Chicana, the publication of any "good" history is still an event. Our invisibility—so long-standing and profound in the annals of mainstream publications—makes almost any published work on Chicanas a hit regardless of whether or not it represents thoughtful, analytical, and reflective writing. Voices devoid of content soar to become monuments and sole expressions of a heavily woven tapestry of historical complexities. Isolated voices speak for the experience of all others of the same gender and nationality.[2]

Even today for Mexicanas in the United States, our histories, our visions, and our dreams remain prisoners of simplistic stereotypical representations. Our historical experience is reduced to the lowest common denominator, leaving erroneous shadows on the soul of self-identity. To publish one-dimensional "stories" may be profitable at a particular time and place, but such endeavors may not be the best way to provide our communities the opportunity for thoughtful knowledge and dialogue. For Chicanas/Mexican Americans the challenge is great: to communicate at various levels and to do so responsibly.[3]

I use the flower gardens of the norteñas to understand the ways these women merged their symbolic (psychological and spiritual) worlds and the material conditions of their everyday lives. I am trying to figure out how to let theory inform the stories they (and I) tell while allowing their words to inform the possibility of theory. I recognize the importance of theory (my original training was in jurisprudence), and yet my experience convinces me that theory changes lives, very particular lives. As I teach and write, I am conscious of the role of theory and work to incorporate it into narratives that are meaningful for my community. I find it a very difficult endeavor.

Whose voices will we hear? What helped make those voices? Although the norteñas I interviewed represent the general nineteenth-century Mexicana in many aspects, their history is marked by regional distinctiveness that precludes drawing broad generalizations from studies of other Mexican women.[4] These ten norteñas were part of a tumultuous stream of Mexican refugees who had to rebuild their lives in the United States. I am interested in reflecting upon how these women saw themselves in relation to their desert landscape and to other inhabitants of that space. Historical influences are many and sometimes contradictory, but I will examine three that I believe inform how norteñas saw themselves, the desert they inhabited, and those who lived there with them: (1) the visions taught through Spanish Catholicism and inherited by norteñas from their European and Spanish colonial past; (2) the influence of the ideas of positivism, so prevalent in the second half of the nineteenth century throughout Mexico; and (3) the ideas and realities Mexicanas faced in the desert lands across the northern border of Mexico in Arizona mining communities.

Listen to one of the women I interviewed: "Ignacio, my husband, was from Arivechi. His family had lived there for many years before Mexico became Mexico, you know, under Spain. His great-grandfather had come to Chihuahua with the Spanish army to fight the Apaches. Ignacio was born in the same house his father had been born in, and that house had a garden with plants that the great-grandmother had planted. Some real roses from Castillo, you know, plants from Spain." This brief narrative rehearses three themes that shaped the norteña experience: (1) the self-identification as Mexican, descending from the Spanish and therefore civilized; (2) the belligerent relationship between these Mexicans and native tribes; and (3) the image of the garden as both a female domain and a symbol of civilization.

Now, I am sure that she was faithfully repeating the family story, but it tells us something not quite accurate about most people who came to the northern presidios to settle. In fact, very few of them had any direct connections with Spain: most of them were mestizo; some were indigenous, from the central part of Mexico. But even when mestizos or indigenous people from Mexico came to the north, they identified as Spanish.[5] They all came as Spanish settlers, and they all were encroaching on the lands of Apaches, Pimas, Pueblos, Opatas, Mayos, Yaquis, and others. All of the women I interviewed who came from the *sierras* of Chihuahua and Sonora, calling themselves Mexicanas, grew up proud that they were of Spanish heritage—not mixed. As I say, oral history has its problems. But it also has potential for allowing us to better understand cultural meanings for specific individuals and groups. The story above points to the historical context—both factual and metaphorical—that we must explore in order to understand these norteñas' experiences. In these experiences, flowers from Spain became symbols of the women's own identity as civilized Christians, and walled gardens became sanctuaries against the barbarous desert and its inhabitants.[6]

## SPANISH VISIONS

As David Lowenthal writes, "[The] geography of the world is unified only by human logic and optics, by the light and color of artifice, by decorative arrangement and by ideas of the good, the true, and the beautiful."[7] For norteñas a long trail of beliefs regarding the good, the true, and the beautiful helped them create a geography of the world that included an often hostile desert. Historically we can begin with the medieval/Renaissance Christianity that was brought from Spain during the seventeenth and eighteenth centuries.[8]

Later these ideas were augmented by the influence of nineteenth-century positivism, which in Mexico emphasized the classification of races. Perhaps equally important in developing a norteña world view was the actual impact of conquest and the composition of colonial mentalities. Guillermo Bonfil Batalla, a contemporary Mexican anthropologist, has convincingly described the Mexican population as divided into "Imaginary Mexico"—Mexican society that emulates European ways and norms—and "Primitive Mexico"—that portion of the indigenous, marginalized population that is seen as being of an earlier time and in need of civilizing.[9] Norteñas at the turn of the century lived and died in "Imaginary Mexico," submerged in Iberian visions of the landscape.

Spain grew up with ancient cultural ideas about the division between *natura* and *cultura*, reiterated by Christianity: human beings as the center of creation and above nature. While nature may be God's creation, the earth is the primordial creation of God for man. Man has a soul, as animals and inanimate elements do not; therefore man is the pinnacle of God's creation—made in his image. But the height for man is to be a baptized and true Christian. Christians brought to the northern deserts not only the "true faith" but its expression on this earth: "civilization."

Their Spanish heritage also influenced their understanding of the desert. The predominant Spanish view of the desert that made its way to North America with the *conquistadores* was a Christian one—the desert as a place where one goes to do penance, where one goes for forty days to fast, where one goes to seek God, and where, with strong enough faith, one might actually find God. In this sense, then, the desert of Spain already had been Christianized; although the walled garden was still a better, more civilized place, Spanish people had found Christian meanings that allowed them to see the desert as less harsh and evil. The settlers in the north of Mexico brought these beliefs with them, but there they found that the desert really was, in their words, "uncivilized" and "barbarous." As the settlers encroached on the lands of others, bringing what they regarded as "decency," the true word of God, and "civilization," they defended themselves from those whom they saw as deaf to God's calling, and engaged in battles with these "barbarous" people who fought to maintain their place in desert lands.

This was a very different situation from that which existed in the central part of Mexico. This northern area was a frontier where the incursion of Spanish settlers, soldiers, and missionaries into the lands of indigenous people made cross-cultural relationships very problematic. Often the only interactions many norteñas had with the indigenous population were violent ones. Whereas the Spanish conquest of central Mexico had long since concluded the period of military violence, settlers in the northern provinces found themselves on the outskirts of civilized Mexico. It was they who faced the harsh isolation and violence of the desert frontiers. In their view, Christianity and civilization were one, and so it was that the desert reemerged in norteña women's visions of the landscape.

In this world of Christianity, the landscape included all—the heavens, the earth, and below, hell—but all parts were not equal. Yi-Fu Tuan explains such premodern visions of the world as a vertical universe with a hierarchy of good and evil—gods in the heavens, humankind on earth, and demons in the darkness below.[10] The efforts of Catholic missionaries in New Spain from the seventeenth century onward transported these Christian interpretations of civilization to the landscape of Sonora, Chihuahua, and what is now Arizona. Alongside the holy documents in the satchels of Jesuit and Franciscan missionaries came more material seeds of European life—wheat, grapes, olives, oranges, and even flowers. These provided not only the characteristic fields and gardens around the missions but also the *patios* or *corrales* of norteñas.[11] These were the spaces that women dominated—where they carried on domestic labor, took care of a few animals, did much of their cooking, washed the family's clothes, and often raised food crops and flowers.

These spaces were refigured by norteñas living in northern Mexico and the southern United States as they confronted a strange, frightening environment where civilization became more desired and more elusive. As the newly arrived Mexicans snatched bits of land from what they saw as the unchristian "savages," they built walls—walls of the presidios, walls around the missions, walls for their houses. All were ways to close out the desert's barbarism. Safely inside the walls, norteñas tried to reproduce their image of a Spanish, civilized world—a place for peaceful prayer, a paradise of domesticated nature. These patios or corrales—safe spaces of civilization—were quite clearly positioned within the domain of women.

In the land of the Apaches, the Christian view of the desert as the home of the uncivilized—and even of the devil—seemed to many norteñas to be grounded in reality. Apaches sometimes greeted the newcomers with curious interest and help. Other times they felt they had to defend themselves from the encroaching settlers by fighting them off. Apaches raided. The desert became a place of fear for women, an asylum for their enemies. Among Mexican norteño families, terrifying stories abounded. One had lost a father, a brother, or a sister to the Apaches. The protection of God was needed from the "demons" of the desert. Norteñas, like other women from societies of conquest and domination, readily accepted official (both religious and political) rationalizations of superiority. In these accounts they represented those sent by God to civilize the peoples living in ignorance and barbarism. Danger was all around, the devil defending ignorance. To settle in these lands was filled with challenge. But settlers were not alone; God is everywhere and one must invoke His favor and protection. For example, when Patricia Preciado Martin interviewed María Soto Audelo, she described how her mother, María Carillo de Soto, born in Tucson in 1868, saw the Virgin descend onto the Soto lands, appearing on a rocky hillside on this desert land:

> My mother claimed that the Blessed Virgin appeared to her at the ranch many years ago. It was in the summertime. She was young and newly married and somewhat lonesome. She had just given lunch to the cowboys and she was resting—reading a novela, a love story. Then, all of a sudden, she turned to one side and she saw the Virgin appear at the window. My father was in another room reading the newspapers. "Ramon, Ramon!" she called. "Come here! I have just seen the Virgin! Her mantle moved!" My father tried to calm my mother. He tried to comfort her. But my mother believed the Virgin was trying to tell her something—that she was about to die. She used to go out to the arroyo and pray to the Virgin and ask the Virgin if she had a message. So she came to town and confessed and the priest told her that even if it was a dream, nevertheless, it was a beautiful one....
>
> We always knew the story of my mother and the Virgin, and so, after many, many years had passed, we bought her a statue of La Virgen Milagrosa and built the grotto. And the grotto is still there, and the statue of the Virgin is still there. Many people have come and gone, but the Virgin remains. She is looking after the ranch; she is protecting it. It is as if the Virgin were saying, "I belong here. And you must let me stay."[12]

For norteñas words like these bring to life long-held visions of the landscape that came to New Spain from Europe. Tuan explains that "to the man in the Middle Ages, absolute up and down made sense. The earth occupies the lowest place in the heavenly hierarchy."[13] The Christian God created the entire universe, and although he is to be found in all places in nature, his official throne is in the heavenly skies. Earth, the place where God put man, was the center of the universe. "The world was conceived as lodged on the earth and nowhere else, because, that being man's element, the earth was the 'natural place' for his world."[14] But even in this world that God created for his people there are places where evil dwells. The universe includes Satan as well as God.[15] The Virgin protected the ranch. From what? From Satan, from the desert wilderness beyond. The carefully cultivated ranch created a Christianized, civilized space where God and the Virgin might roam, while the untended, harsh desert provided a haven for the evil ones. The Virgin appeared because the ranch was the home of Christians: an island of civilization in a sea of wilderness. The story also points to the center of that Christian civilization in this land. The Virgin appeared to a mother, and when her children wanted to honor her and recall the miracle of the visitation, they placed a statue of the Virgin in a grotto.

## POSITIVIST THOUGHT

Although Christianity provided ample explanation for the dangers of life in these northern deserts, it was not the only ideology at the end of the nineteenth century to rationalize demonization of the colonized. The spreading of positivist teachings throughout the more educated classes reinforced the view that Indians were inferior. Numerous examples of public speeches, legislative justifications, and journalistic essays document widespread acceptance of the belief that Indians were lower on the scale of human evolution than "white" populations with a European biological and cultural heritage. This official discourse was accompanied by concurrent policies that allowed Indians to be exploited and marginalized. During Mexico's march along the road of "civilization," it was even considered good economic policy to rid Mexico of Indians who refused to join the new capitalist regime of Don Porfirio Diaz.[16] No self-respecting norteña living at the turn of the nineteenth century wanted to be "Indian." Norteñas often referred to Indians, perhaps with kindly patronizing interest, as *inditos* or expressed clear superiority with such phrases as "*como indio patudo* [or *india patuda*]," big-footed Indian. In contrast, norteñas saw themselves as the most civilized people of the desert mountains and valleys. It was they who preserved the good forms—*bien criadas*—who in turn brought up their children properly and maintained civilized standards of behavior for the entire family.

The relationship between the walled gardens norteñas created and the uncivilized desert beyond became an important symbol of their status as civilized Mexicanas. Norteñas' walled gardens were figured as vestiges of sacred Christian civilization. In the garden bloomed flowers grown from the seeds from Spain: not the desert flowers of central Mexico—those were weeds—but the roses of Castile. In their corrales norteña women ruled, in a sense. They could create their own worlds, produce the food they wanted, and be close to God in their own way.

These walled gardens also became important places for expressions of spirituality in an area where there were very few priests or churches. In the north we find women within Catholicism and Christianity taking on strong, principal roles not seen in the central parts of Mexico. For example, *rezadoras*—prayer women—would say the official prayers at funerals and at the birth of a child. In most cases they would wait for the arrival of the traveling priest for sacred rites, but in extraordinary situations, such as when a child was born ill, the rezadora would be the one to baptize the child. These Christian rituals used flowers from the walled gardens, as did private devotions and worship of the saints.

## SHIFTING IDENTITIES

However, for the norteñas the landscape was changing. By the 1890s norteñas found themselves pondering their place in the so-called civilized world. The transformation of the Mexican economy during the Porfiriato opened the desert mountains to numerous foreign (especially U.S.) investors and miners. While some pueblos found themselves defending their land rights or losing resources so suddenly they didn't know what had happened, norteño families found themselves living in newly founded mining camps and mining towns, very often owned and managed by Americanos, who, either with or without their families, usually lived apart in compounds with separate facilities.

Norteñas began to understand a new definition of "civilization." In their own country they lived separately, believing that, after all, the real barbarians were the Indians—not them, the Catholic, well-bred norteñas. Now, even in the sierra of Chihuahua, of Sonora, Mexicanas learned that there were those who were more "civilized" than they. Dozens of mining companies brought in foreign people whose degree of civilization was underscored by their whiteness. Thus any trace of uncivilized "Indianness" in the Mexican mestizo had to be educated and whitened away. The belief grew that for Mexico to become a truly civilized nation, Indianness must be eliminated. While this statement may appear extreme, consider the following words of Teodora Brun.

Tuvo hijos muy guapos. Güeros, güeros. Ni parecían mexicanos.
[She had very handsome children. Blond, blond. They didn't even look Mexican.]

El tío José se casó con una India. Era muy buena pero no sabes, los hijos le sacaron e ella—muy salvajes. [Uncle José married an Indian. She was very good, but you know, the sons came out like her—savages.]

La Carmen, una india, trabajó con mi mama. Era la sirvienta y pues era muy lista, y no como las otras de su pueblo. Mi mama le enseñó todo y aprendía muy bien. Como la quise. Pero cuando nos fuímos de los Otates ella se quedó con su familia. Su familia era toda la rancheria; no iba a conformarse en otro lugar. [Carmen worked for my mother. She was the maid and was very smart; not like the others of her village. My mother taught her everything and she learned quickly. I really loved her, but when we left Los Otates she wanted to stay with her family. Her family was the whole village; she wouldn't be happy any place else.][17]

By 1915 thousands of norteñas from ranches, pueblos, mining communities, and cities had poured into El Paso and Nogales to escape the chaos and violence of the Mexican Revolution of 1910. Arizona mining towns, often owned and managed by the same companies that owned and managed mines in Mexico, greeted these Mexicans with open arms. The First World War increased the demand for copper and other minerals, so labor, especially cheap labor, was in high demand. Norteño families streamed into Arizona mining towns. Here civilization had a different face. Clear lines of demarcation—one space for Mexicans and another for Anglos—emerged. The entire community, in its political, social, and religious spaces, reflected this new view of "civilized" and "noncivilized." Separate housing, separate schools for children, lower wages for husbands, inhospitable churches—all exemplified this new civilization. These norteños, who had been part of the conquering population and had held places of privilege, now were treated as part of the conquered.[18] Norteñas responded with age-old mechanisms. They built their walls and within re-created their own version of "civilization." In their homes they maintained their worship of God, the proper food, and the proper care of family.

Norteñas didn't leave behind their favorite Spanish plants. Like their great-grandmothers before them, they carried seeds across mountains and valleys to their new homes. Douglas, Bisbee, Clifton, Superior, and all the other Arizona mining towns soon boasted blooming patches of color. The Mexican barrios were dotted with newly planted corn, chiles, and squash. But food was usually not sufficient. Norteñas also brought the "civilizing" flowers, some for the

Virgin and others to show the desert that beauty was in green, lush, blooming plants that thrived on water. In the mining towns where they lived, to have a *corral* meant to rent a tiny house on a tiny lot that had a tiny square in back. In their small gardens, bordered by fences or even cactus, they walled in paradise and resisted the barbarity of discrimination. Sometimes these spaces were filled with literally hundreds of plants in tin cans, stacked in all kinds of chaotic ways, a collage of colors. There were margaritas, honeysuckle vines, and roses, of course; roses were the most important of all.

They also transported their spiritual roots to these ramshackle corrales in the north. The tiny gardens became sanctuaries because the Catholic churches down the street practiced a kind of Catholicism they were not accustomed to, and in an alien language. As one woman said, "I went to confession for forty years. Of course, I never had a priest who spoke Spanish." But she continued to go to confession every Saturday for four decades.

In these new American Catholic parishes, priests didn't have processions that went down the street with flowers to the Virgin. They didn't allow people to take food to the cemeteries on the Day of the Dead. In fact, in Tucson one of the bishops in the 1930s forbade it, although it had been going on there for more than a hundred years, because he considered it a pagan practice.[19] In this context norteña garden spaces began to have a new function as a site for shrines. Interestingly, in central Mexico up until the 1950s, no houses had outside shrines. Shrines in Mexico had been in public places. Private shrines emerged when Mexican women came to this country and could not find Santa Rita, El Niño de Praga, El Niño de Atocha, and most important, la Virgen de Guadalupe in the Catholic churches. Those figures, so important in the everyday spiritual life of Mexican women, simply were not there. And so they established shrines for them within their domestic spaces, re-creating in their own gardens the Catholicism they were seeking. Today the function of rezadora continues. As a matter of fact, in Tucson there are still several rezadoras. In spite of all the changes that have come about, prayers and devotions have been handed down from mother to daughter. So, too, the gardens have survived.

In addition to these persistent cultural traditions, norteña gardens had special, highly personalized meaning. For example, one woman was asked, "Why did you never leave this house?" It was a tiny little place and she could afford something better. And she replied, "Well, you know, when I first arrived, a few months later my first child was born here, and it died, it was stillborn. And we buried the child in the garden, so I can never leave. I must stay." Another woman had a very big tree there in the garden—a tree planted by her son who had been shot down over the Mediterranean in the Second World War. She, too, would never leave. Yet another woman had a mulberry tree in her yard and said, "I cannot [leave], I love my garden." She saw it quite literally as a paradise in the desert. It was also the place where she remembered her daughter, whose wedding had been there and who had died after she married without ever coming back home. Every year this woman planted poppies in her daughter's memory. For all these women their gardens became monuments, in a sense, to their own families and to their own relationships with nature.

These gardens do not exist anymore in the way they existed before 1940. Since then there have been tremendous changes, changes that reflect an acceptance of much of the consumer Anglo culture. The gardens now have little wells and all kinds of decorations that before had no place. Yet even as they change they remain material manifestations of spaces that women have created and continue to be an expression of their moral code and of how they see themselves and the world around them. Gardens, for norteña refugees, have persistently represented a sanctuary against hostile worlds, be they Apache or Anglo-American. As Rebeca Gaitan so eloquently said, "*Mi jardín es acto de fe. Como todo jardín.*" My garden is an act of faith. Like all gardens.

## NOTES

1. I would like to thank SIROW for the opportunity to move some of these thoughts from oral presentation to written form and very particularly Penny Waterstone for her patience and invaluable editorial help.

2. See Antonia Castañeda, "Women of Color and the Rewriting of Western History: The Discourse, Politics, and Decolonization of History," *Pacific Historical Review* 61 (1992): 501–43; Michael H. Frisch, "The Memory of History," in *Presenting the Past: Essays on History and the Public,* ed. Susan Porter Benson, Stephen Brier, and Roy Rosenzweig (Philadelphia: Temple University Press, 1986), 5–17; and Raquel Rubio-Goldsmith, "Oral History, Considerations and Problems for Its Use in the History of Mexicanas in the United States," in *Between Borders: Essays on Mexicana/Chicana History,* ed. Adelaida R. del Castillo (Encino, Cal.: Floricanto Press, 1990), 161–73.

3. Therefore, to the oral histories I bring archival documentation, numerous secondary works, and in this case, field study of the material base, the gardens.

4. In recent years historiography of the different regions of Mexico has produced extraordinary work. For the Chihuahua region the research and writings of Ana Maria Alonso and of Daniel Nugent provide an excellent portrait of the distinctness of norteña life. Ana Maria Alonso, "Rationalizing Patriarchy: Gender, Domestic Violence, and Law in Mexico," *Identities* (1995): 1–19. Daniel Nugent, *Spent Cartridges of Revolution: An Anthropological History of Namiquipa, Chihuahua* (Chicago: University of Chicago Press, 1993). Also see Maria Teresa Koreck, "History at Work: Peasants and Masked 'Others' in Northern Mexico," unpublished manuscript, 1990.

5. Daniel Nugent, *Spent Cartridges*.

6. The dichotomy of "civilization" vs. "barbarism" is one that has been used in various ways. Daniel Nugent, for example, uses it to signify the civilization of the agriculture of Namiquipa as countered by the barbarous Apaches first and by capitalist development later. For Ana Maria Alonso, "Rationalizing Patriarchy," the terms are also used to examine gender roles among the agricultural communities.

7. David Lowenthal, attributed without citation, in Yi-Fu Tuan, *Topophilia: A Study of Environmental Perception, Attitudes, and Values* (Englewood Cliffs, N.J.: Prentice-Hall, 1974), iii.

8. See my essay "Seasons, Seeds, Souls: Mexican Women Gardening in the American Mesilla, 1900–1940," in *Women of the Mexican Countryside, 1850–1990*, ed. Heather Fowler-Salamini and Mary Kay Vaughn (Tucson: University of Arizona Press, 1994), 140–56.

9. Cited by Elea Aguirre, "Between Here and There: A Nationalistic Widening of Distances," unpublished manuscript, May 1994. Guillermo Bonfil Batalla, *Mexico Profundo, Una Civilazación Negada* (México, D.F.: Grijalbo, 1990), 9, 10, 30.

10. Yi-Fu Tuan, *Topophilia*, 59–74, 75–91.

11. The terms *corral* ("yard" or "corral" in English use) and *patio* are used interchangeably in the oral histories to describe spaces covered with flowers. In central Mexico a patio is an enclosed space surrounded by walls on at least three sides, usually four; a corral is a space enclosed by a fence. The mining towns of southeastern Arizona follow midwestern American urban plans, in which house lots are set back from the streets, leaving a front yard between the house and the street and a backyard in back of the house. Calling the latter *corral* denotes an experience of space akin to the rural Mexican corral, not the patio.

12. Patricia Preciado Martin, *Images and Conversations: Mexican Americans Recall a Southwestern Past* (Tucson: University of Arizona Press, 1983), 41, 43.

13. Yi-Fu Tuan, *Topophilia*, 133.

14. Edmundo O'Gorman, cited in Bernard McGrane, *Beyond Anthropology: Society and the Other* (New York: Columbia University Press, 1989), 33.

15. Bernard McGrane, *Beyond Anthropology*, 33.

16. The Archivo General de la Nación, as well as local archives in Chihuahua, are replete with official documents that contrast Spanish/Mexican civilization with Apache barbarism. I will quote only one such example, which covers all of these points.

> How many scenes of mourning, of desolation, and of blood? Anyone who has
> not seen it, are they capable of understanding the smile of the barbarian as he
> sinks his steel lance in the heart of an already downed victim, and spy with a
> solicitous eye the dying convulsions or the aspect of a ranch that has just
> been the center of love, of happiness, and abundance and now is the victim of
> misfortune and covered with destruction, in ruin and with its members barely
> living; or the luck of a poor settler that, fleeing with an old one, with son and

wife, falls anew in the sights of the astute enemy and has to share the anguish of his loved ones as they all see the horrendous sight of the Apache, with his ferocious screams, his mortal blows. But let's cover ourselves with the dense veil of such an atrocious scene and recognize that Mexican blood circulates in the veins of the victim, as the glory of civilization is interested in her, and it is important to maintain the altars of the true God, erected with such high costs by our forbears amid the wilderness [*barbarie*] and the desert.

"Observaciones sobre el estado actual del Departamento de Chihuahua y los medios de ponerlo a cubierto de las incursiones de los barbaros" (México: Printed by Juan Ojeda, 1939), 9. Translations by author.

17. Interview of Teodora Br٠ . by Raquel Rubio-Goldsmith in 1978 in Douglas, Arizona.

18. Antonio Rios-Bustamante, "Copper Towns, Mexican Miners and Community, 1920–1950: Some Social and Spatial Consequences of the Mining Industry in Arizona," unpublished manuscript, 1993, presented at Seminario de Historia Laboral Mexicana, Centro de Estudios Historicos, Instituto Nacional de Antropologia e Historia.

19. See Jack Goody, *The Culture of Flowers* (Cambridge and New York: Cambridge University Press, 1993), 301–4, for a discussion of the age-old use of flowers and how Puritan societies have debated if flowers are proper for religious uses.

## 20

## dancing for dollars

Economics! Economics! Economics!
That's it—that's why I put it on the line—
I tried it all before—every job that comes to mind!
In just two weeks the rent would be due
—And what about necessities, utilities, food?
With fifteen dollars to my name, I felt I had to play the game.
I put my fear upon the shelf and went to see for myself.

Money, money, money, money . . . MONEY!

Here's the rules of the game if you want to play:
Two-inch heels, at the least, and some lingerie.
Dancing two songs at a time when you're on the stage—
And you better do it right 'cause it's your only wage—
Unless you strike it rich with a solo show
—That's more private, in a booth—
But you're always safe, in truth!
Because there's always glass between him and you
with a slot for him to pass the money through.
Now this is how it works when you're dancing for the jerks.
(I mean the customers, ya know—
the guys who come to see the show)
They go into a stall, drop a token in the slot:
They see onto the stage—they check out what you've got!
For song one: take off your top.
For song two: your bottoms drop.
And make sure you always smile—
Cash makes it worthwhile!

It's a peek show
    freak show
You're dealin' with some creeps so
    let 'em take a peek!
        You'll get the cash you seek.

My dancin' name is Krystl. I would prefer not to see anyone I know here at my new job. It is strange; I don't know how I'm able to do this.

But the CD system sets the pulse, and the dancing is what I come here to do.—And I do it because

I NEED MONEY

and I've been unable to land any other jobs. No one else has ever hired me the very day I applied.—The lady who hired me has a bachelor's degree in music and psychology. I have a degree in theater.

First night on the job, I wear a black camisole and black panties. Gigi says to me, "Honey, you're too covered up, you won't make any money." But she's wrong! I make $15 that night. The next night I wear a T-bar and a lace bustier: I make $80 that night—that's because I score my first solo show.

These are weird. Men actually pay money to masturbate while looking through a glass at a naked woman. They pay $10 for every 5 minutes, and of course the more they pay, the better the show.

There are rules. (And I am glad of that.)

In Arizona it is illegal for a dancer to touch her nipples or pubic area. Also, she may NOT insert anything into any orifice of her body.

That means no chewing gum, either.

You have to be creative to fill the time.

On my side of the glass is an oversized mattress on a platform. And a timer. The walls are mirrored.

On the customer's side is an ashtray, a wastebasket, and a box of Kleenex. We can talk through a small panel of holes in the glass, just below the tip slot.

After the show's over, the dancer changes the sheets on the mattress and cleans the customer's side of the booth. So often you see a lady in spike heels and lingerie donning a pair of plastic gloves, thrusting a roll of paper towels under her arm, marching bravely—ammonia bottle in hand:

going to clean the customer's semen from the glass.

We lovingly call it SPOOGE ...

Figure 20.1 Lori Scheer performing "Dancing for Dollars." Photo by Olive Mondello.

Money, money, money, money ...

The rest of my earnings comes from the enclosed stage. Gigi says to me, "Honey, if you're sweatin' you're workin' too hard ..." But I don't mind sweating because I've always loved dancing! I like getting paid for it. Of course, a lot of the customers are just here to look at pussy.

That is a word that previously referred to a cat, and NOT my vagina. ... But I'm learning to adapt to the jargon.

The customers are all different. There are regulars who come in several times a week, know all the girls' names, have their particular favorites ... like Penlight-Man: he always chooses the fourth stall facing the stage, drops a few tokens, drops his trousers, and holds a penlight over his penis. ... We are not aroused.

I like the little red-haired man. Very courteous. He bought a $30 solo show from me—after making sure I was unmarried (he didn't want to feel disloyal, he said), then halfway through the show, he started a conversation and we talked about self-discovery books until the time went off. Why is such a man paying women to talk to him?

Some of the men are just lonely. I try to remember that.—To me, a man looks vulnerable with his trousers at his ankles.

But some of the customers are just pigs, let's face it.

I came off the stage one night to find D.J. kicking a guy out for pissing in the booth.

Once I had a $40 solo show, and the guy asked me to talk dirty to him. . . . I couldn't do it—but I worked my way out of it—I said, "It would really turn me on to hear *you* talk dirty!"

Well, what would you do? You wouldn't work there in the first place? Well, I don't know a better way to raise this much cash in a day.

One customer said to me, "Ever seen one this big?"

I hated to break it to him.

I've learned that a man's eyes can be a lot scarier than his dick.

The bald man in the tan jacket—smoking his cigarette while stroking his shaft—watches me, then lets the lights go on so I can see his face as he narrows his eyes and flicks his tongue and makes kissing and moaning sounds. . . . This man is paying my rent.

What is erotic?

Sounds like "neurotic" . . .

Let me tell you about my co-workers . . .

I've met some wonderful, bold, colorful women. Several have been dancing for years. But there is only one answer when you ask any of them (and I've asked all of them): Why are you here?

Money, money, money money . . .

Once a dancer ran off the stage and threw the tokens at the man who'd put them through the slot instead of money, screaming, "HOW'M I SUPPOSED TO FEED MY KIDS WITH THIS?!"

The job gets stressful. The place can crawl with frustration. For one thing, your naked body is on display for strangers. You feel like you're under a microscope. It's no wonder several of these women have eating disorders . . . and other problems. . . . A lot of these women have been abused—one girl came in here with cigarette burns on her breasts. . . . So drugs and alcohol medicate the pain and fuel the bravado . . . which you need for this job. Then you find yourself in competition with the other women for the daily dollars.

Incidentally, menstrual periods can be a nuisance, but we strippers have a way of dealing: use tampons, but cut the string first. It becomes a very private joke. The customers never suspect.

You know, when you spend time with a group of women—all in your underwear—an interesting camaraderie can develop. I once conducted a survey: I asked each woman how she felt about men.

Only one woman said she hates men.

Inevitably, she makes the most money every night. I'm talking $300 a night! She wears a blond wig, has a Barbie-doll figure.

One night this lady had a solo show and the customer purposely ejaculated through the holes in the glass. It got on her back and in her hair. She told me, "Krystl, these men would just as soon piss on you as come on you."

I wonder who's really in control here. Most of the women say they're in control—it's their show, their body. But I see the dollar in control, and that comes from the men.

Gigi says, "I'll sell 'em a peek . . . ya gotta sell it: ice to the Eskimos or titties in their face for a minute . . ." I know what she means . . . you have to play the game . . . feed the fantasy—and you have to play a game with yourself to play the game with them.

But I wonder: Why do these men prefer this transaction to a relationship?

I've been unable to sleep at night since I started this job. When I close my eyes, I see the strange images from work. I'm not comfortable with this job, but I've done so many other different jobs—till I burned out on each one—and none of them paid this kind of—

At least the rent's paid, bills are paid; there's gas in the car and food in the fridge . . . and I've seen every dollar of it pass through the slot.

But at this point I'm in constant physical pain. My lower back, my rotators are badly strained.

The art of dancing is getting lost because of the required grinding and pretending to fit the most superficial image of femininity! My anger does not enhance my earnings: nobody likes an angry stripper.

So Gigi says to me, "You're an actress . . . when you come in here, Krystl takes over. The only time Lori and Krystl meet is to handle finances."

That's a fine plan. But it's Lori's face beneath the drag-queen make-up, and Lori's body within the flimsy lingerie. Lori's sensitive skin endures the daily razor to keep Lori's pubic hair within the boundary of the T-bar which is stretched against the crack of Lori's ass.

And I see Lori's eyes in the mirrors that surround me.

Lori looks tired. Lori thinks: "Men are looking at my vagina for a buck."

A very old man buys a solo show from me. I'm quite sure it's an uninspired performance; the minutes seem like hours to me. Afterward he says, "Thanks for reminding me what it's all about."

I say, "Mister, it is not about this."

He slides an extra $20 through the glass.

One night I'm home, not sleeping, and a vision comes to me. I see a little girl in a little dress, dancing in a grassy field.

Suddenly the scene changes and she's dancing on the stage at work—the little girl is bending over, about to assume the most degrading position—where your face isn't visible, only your pussy—

and I am shocked.

I know the little girl is me, and I know I belong in the grassy field. I quit that night.

You know, I had never seen my own body or my own genitalia so clearly as I did in those mirrors—I really saw it—an actual reflection of my vagina as I danced and moved.

And you know, it does resemble a flower.

21

# reflections on upward mobility
## *performance spaces, critical practice, and the spectacle of flight*

Performance art groups, like the Tucson collective called the Bloodhut, whose work is excerpted in the previous contribution, enact the production of abstract space as a series of improvisational possibilities. As performance activists, they ground their work implicitly in the sexual politics of the body. Unlike other performance artists whose work is more *explicit* in the presentation of the sexualized female body, the Bloodhut group relies on life stories that embody specific social and cultural spaces. The narrating performer's body is pointedly not identical with the textually produced body of the narrative. This seems an important and interesting distinction, given the sentimentalization of body and materiality in some feminist writing and performance.

The body, particularly the female body, is typically identified with materiality as opposed to spatial or mathematical abstraction, but as Michel Foucault and more recently Mary Poovey have argued, the rise of discourses of measurement and normalization in the human sciences in the eighteenth and nineteenth centuries effectively abstracted the body and minimized its potential as a site of resistance to regulation and discipline. Furthermore, one might insist that "ground" in the visual field is itself a powerful abstraction, the product of the same processes of rationalization and normalization that have produced the modern body.

If such historical argument concerning the rationalization of the body holds, how can the body (any body) be understood as the

"ground" of a modern politics? The answer lies in the contradictory and sometimes inadvertent reception of texts. In spite of, and in many cases because of,
these dark, cautionary (sometimes antibody, sometimes antiessentialist) tales,
twentieth-century feminisms in the West have continued to look to the body
as a privileged site of contestation. Notions of performance and performativity
have taken on almost hegemonic importance in current theoretical discussions
of the body and sexuality in relation to the limits of necessity and freedom.
Judith Butler's work, for instance, which has challenged us to think of gender as
an act or performance, has generated a facile sense of the possibilities of itera-
tion and acting out as political acts, despite its insistence on the compulsory
nature of such performances. That a text might produce such contradictory effects should not be surprising, since the power of performance (textual or theatrical) to some extent resides in the excesses or gaps between meaning and
utterance in linguistic and corporeal acts or display.

In the Bloodhut text and performance, Lori Scheer tells the story of performing in sex shows. In telling the story, she evokes certain spatial and social
relations involving female nudity. Male-female relations are only one dimension
of the lines of vision mapped out in the storytelling. Relations between the
female performers and between the narrator-performer and the audience
emerge as crucial. Interestingly, in a story about being exposed, a semi-visible
detail complicates the "public" aspect of this display. The bloody tampon, with
its string removed to fool the client, marks a crucial difference between the female body in the commercial sex show as it is seen by the client and the corporeal act that is invisible to the client and effectively interferes with the viewing of female sexuality. That the "matter" is invisible to the theater audience, as
well as to the woman herself, underscores the figural nature of the body and
the scene evoked. Significantly, it becomes a political joke to be shared and repeated between women. In conventional terms, such references might be considered tasteless, unmentionable, or even trivial. But here the commentary on
the concealed tampon locates a place within and without the body where the
female performer can make something happen or change. Menstruation would
presumably take place in any case, but it is here performed with a difference, a
slight difference perhaps, but the devil is in the details. This redesignated in-
ner/outer space as the space of performance confounds traditional notions of
the female anatomical destiny as passive, open, and receptive. Here the body is
figured to the contrary as active, closed to certain standardized meanings, and
acquisitive.

In what may seem at first a turn in a very different direction, I want to
move to another space of female performativity by reflecting briefly on what

seems to me a very compelling historical and ideological link between "women's liberation" and the flight from the immanence of the "material body" directed outward and upward toward spatial abstraction as the place of individual freedom.[1] This link between liberation and "upward mobility" is contemporaneous with the development of the technologies most closely associated with modernity: flight, aerial surveying and mapping, photography, bombing, and consumerism, including especially advertising and travel. Upward mobility suggests the trajectory of class reflected in the corporate language of "glass ceilings" for executive women and low minimum wages for others. Women's liberation of the "you've come a long way, baby" cigarette advertising variety has gone hand in hand with the myths of modernity and has, arguably, a silent partner in First World imperialism and its spatial opportunisms. A healthy ambivalence toward the trope of upwardness takes into account those bodies who are always left behind because of class, age, culture, shape, color, or subalternities of other kinds.

In the modernist conflation of a certain female iconography with bourgeois ideology, freedom is often uncritically conceived as limitless space, transcendence, newness, individualism, and upward mobility of various kinds. Contemporary theories of spatiality and power have suggested, on the contrary, that space is socially and materially saturated, whatever its dimensionality. In a new symbolic geography, the female body in space signifies different desires and ambitions. The yearning for transcendent space has propelled collective as well as individual ambition toward change and resistance, and its attraction for feminism might be read away from the bourgeois model of progress as a model of possibility in times of enormous constraint.

With this goal in mind, I want to remark briefly on a type of performance that, for lack of better terms, could be called stunts. Stunts and stunting bear a theoretical affinity with Michel de Certeau's idea of a *tactic* as opposed to a *strategy,* the possibility of walking through and occupying space differently and subversively.[2] But in place of Certeau, I've chosen another guide to stunting: Amelia Earhart. The Earhart I have in mind is not the heroine of the Virginia Slims advertisement or the icon of modernity figured by her sleek female body unencumbered in limitless space, but the practitioner of a certain kind of literal "upward mobility" who ended her career with a "disappearing act." Since discourses of liberation are so often described as a coming into visibility and a claiming or reclaiming of bodily space, this counter tendency to perform in *invisible* ways in acts of disappearance, stepping or falling down or aside to make way for others, or in the acknowledgment of what is not there or is not yet there, holds promise for a nonidentitarian politics and for critical practice.[3]

Amelia Earhart, in her role as everyday theorist of flying practice (as opposed to modernist, feminist icon), describes her initiation into flying as a convergence of many apparently unrelated and often commonplace experiences.[4] Her belief in the power of everyday randomness and felicitous conjunction is confidently expressed in her choice of chapter headings for her memoirs, like "Growing Up Here and There," "Aviation and I Get Together," "Joy Hopping and Other Things"; preparation for life or for flying (and the two were inseparable in her case) involved a drift from one site of knowledge to another, sometimes literally a transfer from university to university or from one course of study to another. More often she simply traveled and took up whatever seemed promising. Flying lessons, like everything else in her life, were a question of mastering lateral movement. Everyday considerations of what to wear, how to move, and how to wear her hair ("But you don't look like an aviatrix. You have long hair.") all contribute to her approach to flying and to flying lessons (26).

Yet her approach was not entirely idiosyncratic. In general, the content and arrangement of flying lessons were much less hierarchized in the early days of aviation than was the case later, once the protocols of aeronautical professionalism were regulated. In Earhart's day the distinction between serious pilot training and learning stunts was only gradually put in place until eventually the stunt was defined by the Department of Commerce as "any manoeuver not necessary for normal flight" (35). Though constitutive of early flying practice (what one did to become a pilot), stunting became the abnormal and increasingly liminal activity with regard to official flying. Its liminality is underlined in Earhart's account by the association of stunt flying with tightrope walking. This association is by no means original, since many popular histories of women and aeronautics begin similarly with an account of early aerial entertainers from the eighteenth and nineteenth centuries—aerialists, balloonists, and parachutists.

The stunt bears a special relationship to groups who are exceptional or abnormal in relation to the "normal activity." As Earhart notes, a woman in aviation was (and to some extent still is) considered a novelty. Nonetheless, female stunt pilots were quite common. The element of spectacle that Earhart alludes to is what distinguishes the stunt from "normal flying" or practice figures. In discussing women pilots, Earhart mentions Laura Ingalls, who was initially discouraged by her instructors but through her perseverance became an "aerial acrobat" of some note. She held a "feminine record" for 980 consecutive loops (at a dollar a loop, a good wage for a woman in those days) and eventually held the record for both sexes in barrel rolls (179). Of course, such feats were disparaged despite their popularity, because although they contributed to the growing definitions of professionalism within aviation, they were increasingly the sign of the counterfeit, exhibitionistic, unprofessional pilot. Women in this category were doubly suspect, even as they were doubly intriguing to audiences.

Earhart, however, defends stunting and women as stunt pilots:

> Some critics protest against such exhibitions. I myself cannot see what harm they do. Certainly their execution requires sturdy equipment and skill and determination on the part of the pilot. They may not point the way to progress in aviation but they demonstrate its possibilities. As for a woman's doing them, that probably will be necessary for some time—for contrary to legal precedent, *they (women) are considered guilty of incompetence until proved otherwise.* (179) (Emphasis mine)

Earhart is cognizant of the dangers and difficulties of those women who were "already guilty" and marked as novelties within stunt flying: stunts within stunts. Their status as "already guilty" consigned them to the very activities that furthered their marginalization and eventual abjection from "normal" flying. In fact, normal flying came to be defined in relation to "abnormal" moves and vice versa. Significantly, the relationship between the two does not depend upon the prior status of one or the other; rather, they are mutually involved and constitutive.

My interest here is with the status of the stunt and of the stunters or stunted poised in relation to risk and blame. Stunt flying and similar activities, which I characterize as "grotesque performances," are risky activities. On the one hand, they perpetuate the blaming, stigmatizing, and marginalizing of groups and persons who occupy this self-perpetuating loop and are seen as "high-risk" groups; on the other hand, they elicit "risk-control" tactics that, by characterizing risk as almost entirely negative, seek to out-regulate (or make invisible) those performances and groups that enact or embody such double riskiness. In our day this is perhaps most vividly present in the moralizing of the risk of AIDS; indeed, the term "high-risk" is by now laminated to the designations "gay men" and "intravenous drug users," as if these categories and activities were naturally bonded.[5]

A stunt may be thought of more theoretically, then, as a tactic for groups or individuals in a certain risky situation in which a strategy is not possible. Strategies depend upon a proper place, a place of one's own, from which a certain "calculus of force" can be organized and projected outward. By contrast, in

*The Practice of Everyday Life,* Michel de Certeau defines the "tactic" as a "logic of action" for the displaced. In spatial terms, "the place of the tactic belongs to the other. A tactic insinuates itself into the other's place, fragmentarily, without taking it over ... without being able to keep it at a distance. Because it does not have a place, a tactic depends on time, it is always on the watch for opportunities, that must be seized on the wing."[6] As a temporal category, the tactic, or in Earhart's terms, the practice of stunting, belongs to the improvisational, to the realm of what is possible in the moment.

The image of Amelia Earhart—tall, slim, and aerodynamic like the planes beside which she modeled—came to stand for all the liberatory aspirations for individual women in the United States in the 1920s and 1930s.[7] The image has survived into the 1990s as the emblem conflating liberal feminism and consumer progress. Earhart's image, while representing the advancement of women in the postsuffrage era, simultaneously came to represent an unloading of the female body as identified with weightiness—the "unbearable weight" that Susan Bordo has identified as part of "the gendered nature of mind/body dualism."[8] Earhart's body as produced by the media seemed unencumbered. Out in commercial hyperspace, it left behind the marks of the old models of womanhood and, of course, all signs of non-Anglo-Saxon ethnicity. She and her look-alike, Charles Lindbergh, were said to be attractively "boyish" in a distinctively "American" way.

Earhart's "boyishness" and the symbolic virility of flight as active and dangerous opened the way for interpretations of her activities as transgressive, making her a somewhat more ambivalent figure than might first appear. Furthermore, this vastly overproduced modernist image of women's liberation is deliberately compromised in positing a link between freedom and the construction of femaleness as a stunt. As her own writings indicate, Earhart was acutely aware of the need to negotiate this association carefully, and by the end of her short career she was increasingly accused of commercializing aeronautical culture—as if this had ever been absent from its history. Had she survived into the second phase of aeronautical history, with the normalization of flight and aeriality in the military/industrial sphere, her reputation might have merged with that of the many women pilots who contributed quietly to the war effort. Like the liberal feminism she came to represent, she might have "settled down." But then in a final and much-criticized attempt at "long-distance stunt flying," she disappeared.

To conclude, I have tried to suggest that there may be affirmative models of risk and deviance in the high registers of modernism, and ways in which the image of freedom as limitless space, transcendence, individualism, and upward mobility of various kinds may be embodied and diverted, giving way to a model of feminist practice. Earhart's model of stunt flying as pointing to inherent possibility rather than future progress goes in this direction. Furthermore, the compulsory demand to "produce the body" as the sine qua non of identity—to prove that a person or a group is "represented" in the political and technological sense—is answered uncannily with images that are in and out of sight simultaneously. One set of possibilities, therefore, involves acknowledgment of somatic lack so that missing body parts and missing bodies virtual, unrepresentable, disappearing, or dead would be understood as generative. The obsession with Earhart's last flight, understood as a performative stunt, and her repeated sightings years afterward may stand for this invisible potential.

## NOTES

1. For an extended discussion of this theme, see my *The Female Grotesque: Risk, Excess, and Modernity* (New York and London: Routledge, 1995). Some of the following text is excerpted from chapter 1.

2. See Michel de Certeau, *The Practice of Everyday Life*, trans. Steven Randall (Berkeley: University of California Press, 1982).

3. For examples, see Teresa de Lauretis's notion of the "space-off" in *Technologies of Gender: Essays on Theory, Film, and Fiction* (Bloomington: University of Indiana Press, 1987); Peggy Phelan, *Unmarked: The Politics of Performance* (London and New York: Routledge, 1993); and Eve Kosofsky Sedgwick, "Socratic Raptures, Socratic Ruptures: Notes Toward Queer Performativity," in *English Inside and Out: The Places of Literary Criticism*, ed. Susan Gubar and Jonathan Kamholz (London and New York: Routledge, 1993).

4. Amelia Earhart, *The Fun of It: Random Notes of My Own Flying and of Woman in Aviation* (New York: Brewer, Warren, and Putnam, 1932). Hereafter cited in text with page numbers in parentheses. As Earhart tells it, almost everything came in handy eventually: cooking lessons, the influenza epidemic, riding horseback, automobile repair, medicine, French literature, social work at Denison House in Boston, photography, a knowledge of the underground passageways of Columbia University, and the stairwells to the top of the library dome (a knowledge she used to witness the eclipse of the sun in 1925).

5. On social stigmas, see Mary Douglas, *Risk and Blame: Essays in Cultural Theory* (London and New York: Routledge, 1992), 36. For another view, see Sander Gilman, *Difference and Pathology: Stereotypes of Sexuality, Race, and Madness* (Ithaca, N.Y.: Cornell University Press, 1985).

6. De Certeau, *Practice of Everyday Life*, xiv. "A strategy assumes a place that can be circumscribed as proper [*propre*] and thus serve as the basis for generating relations with an exterior distinct from it" (xix). For another example of "tactical" stunts, see

Meaghan Morris, "Great Moments in Social Climbing: King Kong and The Human Fly," in *Sexuality and Space* (New York: Princeton Architectural Press, 1992), 1–51.

7. For an excellent account of Earhart in relation to liberal feminism in this era, see Susan Ware, *Still Missing: Amelia Earhart and the Search for Modern Feminism* (New York: Norton, 1993).

8. Susan Bordo, *Unbearable Weight: Feminism, Western Culture, and the Body* (Berkeley: University of California Press, 1993), 14.

22

# telling time
## *time, metaphor, feminism*

The following essay is a performance piece and can never be anything else to the extent that discussions of time can never escape time. Instead of trying to translate the essay's performative consciousness of time's passage into some kind of print equivalent, I am leaving the traces of its speech as another instance of the imbrication of metaphor, time, narrative, and ideology that the essay addresses. The only equivalent to this consciousness I might suggest would be for readers to place an analog clock face on the page as they read; even with this, the metric quality of speech and presence are much more brashly evident than the subtle and often indiscernible actions of the reading eye.

On the page and years later, this essay is out of time, displaced from the single instance of its presentation in October 1993 in a crowded room on the edge of a desert with a large analog clock in hand. Because I was speaking about time, I was particularly conscious of the time of the paper's delivery, which I thought, not to be self-contradictory, should conform to the letter of conference law and the limits of human attention that papers should not exceed fifteen minutes. Of course, as we all know, fifteen minutes of conference paper time seems more like half an hour, if not a glorious forty minutes, so this paper is remarkably short, being, as it was, really only fifteen minutes long.

Because this was a feminist conference on space, the time of the paper's presence was preeminently spatial, a context that amplified its discussions of the relations between time and space. It was the single presentation about time, following many presentations on space and preceding many others. The essay's warning about the ideologies inherent in our conceptions of space and time also had a particularly contextual (and entirely unintended) application, as the imposed schedule of the conference created too much of a consciousness of linear time and much too much of a consciousness of a demarcated space from which some could not exit and into which others could not enter. In other words, the very structure of a conference with its inherent limitations made this more of a trenchant and pointed critique than it is now, sitting still and fairly innocently on its pages.

## THE TEXT OF THE TALK

(The next paragraph is delivered as if spoken by a cheap used-car salesperson.)

In the next fifteen minutes, ladies and gentlemen, I will attempt to define time without recourse to metaphor; that is to say, I will attempt (if you will excuse my metaphorizing for one moment) to get to the heart, the crux, the essence, the bottom or the bottom line, the very soul of the matter, which is that time and metaphor are reciprocally bound to each other, that neither can be expressed without the other, that both depend upon a particular idea of time, that this idea of time is quite material to Western thought, and therefore that metaphor is material in a very timely way. The real thesis of this paper is that metaphor itself is an ideological construct, materially so, depending as it does upon time, which cannot be conceived without metaphor—and more important, whose metaphors cannot exist outside a specific ideology of narrative.

Time to slow down, however (excuse another metaphor), or do you think that the phrase "time to slow down" is literal, referring, as your most recent experience might suggest, to the speed of my delivery? Or does slowing down refer more to the apparent "speed" of the logic as it unfolds perhaps too swiftly? But applied to logic, the phrase "time to slow down" is clearly metaphorical, and anything having to do with speed, the perception of which is always relative and metaphorically spatial, is always also a metaphor of time. In this instance, however, time doesn't really refer to speed but rather to what might be perceived as timing, as a "when" linked not to simple rhythm but to a sense of progress through time shaped a specific way. This metaphor of when suggests a locus within a pattern that conforms to something like a narrative— it is a narrative—with a beginning, a middle, and an end and certain points in the middle when we expect things.[1] Like (to use a simile) our expectations about how arguments and papers should proceed through time in a development that conforms to a cultural understanding of a sensical cause-and-effect relation in time, ending in synthesis and knowledge, in this case the cause/effect development proper to the scholarly paper. And as in all narrative in this culture at this time (sorry to evoke the time-is-history metaphor), this narrative imports a particular sense of timing linked (metaphorically, of course) to a particular ideology of narrative as conjunctive and productive or reproductive.[2] To be quite literal, time and narrative are wed.

This marriage of time and narrative does not refer to the time of narrative but rather to the idea of what might constitute a narrative in the first place. In the case of a scholarly paper, this ideology of narrative dictates the expectation of some knowledge to come at the end of the paper after the introduction of sets of propositions that may be anything from pure logic to personal experience. These propositions represent the elements necessary to frame a question, or what we might call, after Tsvetan Todorov, a "disequilibrium"—for example, how can metaphor be anything but material? According to its narrative, the paper would then, by arranging its propositions or introducing additional material, establish some synthesis and/or equilibrium, arriving at wisdom, insight, a good end (if we are lucky) or the reproduction of the obvious (as happens so often to the covert delight of the intellectually insecure), or both, but in any case, coming to something that represents a product: knowledge, equilibrium, a paper, or fifteen minutes of occupied time.

Now, clearly in the narrative that shapes this discussion of time and metaphor, time is already defined as fifteen minutes (unless I go over time), and that fifteen minutes could seem like an hour or pass in a flash. Relative to what? To the passage of time as measured by a clock? To some intrinsic sense of fifteen minutes? Or perhaps our perception of duration is relative to the paper's narrative that must, here, shape itself in relation to a specific time limit. Each of these relations through which we perceive temporal duration is a metaphor based on metaphors: duration is not experience but the comparison of one measure of time to another. As when telling time, we can tell narrative and we can judge time from narrative. For example, we know when certain narrative shifts should occur, not from any internal narrative logic but from duration. We all know from watching television sitcoms that the crux of the conflict occurs at seventeen minutes after and synthesis occurs at twenty-three minutes after the narrative has begun. And since at this point I've taken only seven minutes, you know that the argument of this paper is not yet completely developed.

The point is that we understand narrative as a temporal entity, no matter what the ordering of its narration; narrative's temporality functions proportionally; that is, parts occupy certain blocks of time in relation to the length of the narrative, and events occur at certain points, not in an order but in relation to the whole time of a narrative, i.e., halfway through, three-quarters, etc. What this means is both that the timing of narrative is entirely dependent upon its duration and that our understanding of time is dependent upon a specific ideology of narrative as a process that is always going somewhere in linear time, combining elements (sort of like a marriage or the merger of capital and labor) to produce something (sort of like children or a product). And our conception of time is bound to this sense of production; hence, time is not neutral, objective, or literal, but bears in its conception the very material cultural values of both capitalism and heterosexuality.

But if narrative and time are metaphorically bound in this materially ideological way, what does this say about metaphor itself? You knew it was time for the turnabout. Isn't metaphor a primary process, if we believe structural linguists or Freud and Lacan, defining language, thought, shaping our very unconscious in processes analogous to the necessary substitutions of language? Can such a primary process be ideologically inflected, especially with ideologies that might change through history and from culture to culture? Is metaphor in fact universal or do we only think it is? Is it possible that the conception of metaphor as employed in thinking about subjectivity and the very choice of that conception of metaphor as one of the two basic processes of language and thought is already a product of a particular ideology of narrative and time? Which comes first?

Both metaphor and metonymy as used in structural understandings of language and the psyche are combinatory processes, ways of linking and organizing elements perceived as different from one another and from oneself in such a way as to provide the subject an illusory mastery over this difference.[3] The processes evolve in a developmental history around events of metaphorical differentiation: from the mother, from the self, in a trajectory of healthy survival deemed productive. In this, metaphor, or what Freud calls condensation, seems to be both linear and simultaneous, bearing within it, by definition, multiple, instant comparisons that in their apparent simultaneity appear to defy linear time, eclipsing duration in the productive superimposition of similarity and difference. For metaphors work only if both similarity and difference are present at once.

But does metaphor really suggest a temporal simultaneity that contradicts a linear productive time, or does it merely mask its own linear history with a spectacular synthesis that is really the end product of a productive narrative? Aristotelian conceptions of metaphor explain it as the result of a substitution of one term for another, in which the substituting term is both similar and different from the term it replaces.[4] This substitutive process—this apparently simultaneous movement to same through different in what is really a productive joinder of difference—requires a sequence in linear time. If this is the case, is it possible to have metaphor without either linear time or its metaphor of the productive narrative? To test this, let us try to conceive of metaphor within a different conception of time, one that is not linear, unidirectional, or productive. We could, for example, try to take one of Julia Kristeva's renderings of Nietzsche's temporal categories from her essay "Woman's Time."[5] Perhaps either of the two times she associates specifically with female subjectivity would provide us with a different take on metaphor. If, for example, we understand time as both repetition and eternity existing in a kind of cosmic rhythm, do we escape either linearity or the productive narrative? Kristeva says, "There are cycles, gestation, the eternal recurrence of a biological rhythm which conforms to that of nature and imposes a temporality whose stereotyping may shock, but whose regularity and unison with . . . cosmic time occasion vertiginous visions and unnameable jouissance."[6] As she describes it, this time is the prototypical productive narrative, the cosmic version of reproduction, a stereotype of the joyful harmonies of universal reverberation. And in Kristeva's account, this time does not occur by itself, but in narrative tandem with a category she calls "monumental time," a time so "all-encompassing and infinite" that it cannot be perceived as passing yet its narrative is still the narrative of production as it defines the shape of the history of the world from beginning to end. Both tied to the productive narrative and creating a productive narrative of time in Kristeva's account, neither conception of time will give us anything other than metaphor as we know it.

We could perhaps look at two other sources, one outdated in the annals of anthropology, the other current in the paperback tomes of popularized theories of relativity. Anthropologist Edmund Leach describes a time he calls "sacred," a time out of time experienced at the same exact time as the moment of origin, or Eden.[7] In its repetition or what Mircea Eliade might term its "eternal return," this time paradoxically belongs to a scheme of linear time in which sacred and profane time alternate, producing the same narrative of linear productivity as Kristeva's examples.[8] By itself, if it can exist independently, sacred time suggests both that time does not pass in a regular fashion and that time does not pass at all. This is not unlike the uneven passage of time deduced by theories of relativity that, in making the speed of light the constant element in a space-time equation, render time changeable, uneven, relative, not passing reliably or productively but perhaps fitfully.[9] If this is the case—if neither time nor space is continuous—then how can we have metaphor?

Could we have metaphor as we recognize it within the barely conceivable idea of a nonproductive, irregularly passing time? If metaphor requires a sequence in linear time to make its comparison, then in a nonlinear or irregularly passing time, the sequence of comparing would disalign and what appears to be the felicitous simultaneous revelation of meaning would be a disjunctive misfire we wouldn't recognize. Time, both order and a regularly passing money time, must be present for metaphor to make sense. And even if we can reconstruct a misfired metaphor, as in the gross example I just gave you, its function is disrupted; it is not a metaphor except in retrospect—except through the narrative of metaphor in which timing and contiguity are material. If we did not conceive of time as linear and reproductive, even our thought processes, which depend upon comparison and differentiation, would be unreliable, since we could not rely on the next moment coming in time. As I put this, I suggest that our very processes of thought depend upon a conception of time and it may be that time is the most basic conception we have, the one we most confound with an experience we know to be completely unreliable, the one we fervently believe to be real.

Of course, as we round the final turn, my logical processes and vision of metaphor as necessarily linear may be an effect of the ideology working in my very thought processes. Without a linear notion of time experienced as "real," I would probably be unable to speak. And if language is always metaphor, then my task of defining time is doomed, but not the project of revealing, even momentarily, the materiality of both time and metaphor. To give this a *Star Trek* finish (meaning I tie up all of the loose ends in one-tenth of the time of the entire paper), what does this issue of metaphor and time say about the production of feminist texts? It suggests that feminist texts, pinned to language and metaphor, are also somehow pinned to ideologies of productive narrative that import of necessity metaphorically heterosexual and reproductive scenarios. Since it is unlikely that we can alter significantly the time in which we operate or the operations of metaphor that dominate perhaps even our unconscious, the only recourse left is a consciousness of the idea of narrative itself as ideological. If we do that, if like Nicole Brossard or such feminist poets as Olga Broumas we play against the very founding ideology of narrative, we might make small inroads on the easy equation between time and truth, and metaphor might become a more material, conscious, conscionable practice.[10] If Kristeva is correct in her productive narrative of time in predicting that the third generation of feminists would "demassify the problematic of difference," then the problematic of metaphor as the unwitting supporter of our ideological stake in difference and as the defining structure of culture and epistemology might also be displaced. The moment metaphor can no longer be taken for granted, the moment when it becomes awkwardly visible as an arbiter of difference—when it appears to become spectacularly material—is the moment its materiality disappears.

## NOTES

1. This concept of narrative shape is essentially Aristotelian but is assumed as basic by more contemporary narrative theorists. See, for example, Roland Barthes, "Introduction to the Structural Analysis of Narratives," in *Image—Music—Text*, trans. Stephen Heath (New York: Hill and Wang, 1977), 79–124; and Tsvetan Todorov, *The Poetics of Prose*, trans. Richard Howard (Ithaca, N.Y.: Cornell University Press, 1977).

2. Jean-François Lyotard hints at narrative's (re)productive trajectory in *The Postmodern Condition: A Report on Knowledge*, trans. Geoff Benningon and Brian Massumi (Minneapolis: University of Minnesota Press, 1984).

3. Jacques Lacan's mirror stage is an example of one such metaphor, in which the infant seeing an image in a mirror figures the infant's recognition of a potentially wholly separate body. The moment is simultaneously jubilant and premature, since the infant cannot yet do that which it can anticipate. See Lacan, "The Mirror Stage As Formative of the Function of the I As Revealed in Psychoanalytic Experience," in *Écrits: A Selection*, trans. Alan Sheridan (New York: Norton, 1977), 1–7.

4. Aristotle discusses metaphor in the *Poetics*, but for a more thorough discussion, see Paul Ricoeur, "The Metaphorical Process as Cognition, Imagination, and Feeling," in *On Metaphor*, ed. Sheldon Sacks (Chicago: University of Chicago Press, 1979), 141–57.

5. Julia Kristeva, "Woman's Time," trans. Alice Jardine and Harry Blake, in *The Kristeva Reader*, ed. Toril Moi (Oxford: Blackwell, 1986), 187–213.

6. Ibid., 191.

7. Edmund Leach, "Two Essays Concerning the Symbolic Representations of Time," in *Readers in Comparative Religion: An Anthropological Approach*, 2d ed., ed. William Lessa and Evon Vogt (New York: Harper & Row, 1965), 241–49.

8. Mircea Eliade, *The Myth of Eternal Return*, trans. Willard Trask (New York: Pantheon, 1954).

9. For an account of this phenomenon, see Stephen Hawking, *A Brief History of Time: From the Big Bang to Black Holes* (New York: Bantam Books, 1988).

10. See, for example, Brossard's assault on narrative and time in *Picture History*, trans. Barbara Godard (New York: Rook Books, 1990).

# source acknowledgments

Passages from the empirical vignettes in Geraldine Pratt's "Geographic Meta-phors in Feminist Theory" are reprinted with permission from G. Pratt, "Grids of Difference: Place and Identity Formation," *Cities of Difference,* edited by Ruth Fincher and Jane Jacob (Guilford, 1997).

Mary Poovey, "The Production of Abstract Space" is reprinted from *Making a Social Body* by Mary Poovey (University of Chicago Press, 1995) by permission of the publisher.

Joan Dayan, "Codes of Law and Bodies of Color" is reprinted in abbreviated form from *New Literary History* 26 (1995): 283–308 by permission of Johns Hopkins University Press.

In part 3, the lines from Poem 29 of "Contradictions: Tracking Poems" are from *Your Native Land, Your Life: Poems* by Adrienne Rich. © 1986 by Adrienne Rich. Reprinted by permission of the author and W. W. Norton & Company, Inc.

Helena Michie, "Confinements: The Domestic in the Discourses of Upper-Middle-Class Pregnancy," is reprinted from Helena Michie and Naomi R. Cahn, *Confinements: Fertility and Infertility in Contemporary Culture.* © 1997 by Helena Michie and Naomi R. Cahn. Reprinted by permission of Rutgers University Press.

# contributors

**Angelika Bammer** is Associate Professor of Comparative Literature and Humanities in the Graduate Institute of Liberal Arts at Emory University. She is the author of *Partial Visions: Feminism and Utopianism in the 1970s* (Routledge) and the editor of *Displacements: Cultural Identities in Question* (Indiana University Press). Her current project, "Being German: Difference and Identity in Contest," is a book of constructions of German-ness and the exclusions the term implies.

**Mary Pat Brady** is a University of California President's Postdoctoral Fellow in the Department of Ethnic Studies, University of California at Berkeley, and Assistant Professor of English at Indiana University. She is currently revising her manuscript, "Extinct Lands, Scarred Bodies: Chicana Literature and the Reinvention of Space."

**Joan Dayan** is Professor of English at the University of Arizona. She has written extensively on Caribbean women, culture and politics, and the American Gothic and is the author of *Haiti, History and the Gods* (University of California). Her current project is "Held in the Body of the State: Chain, Classification, and the Death Penalty in an Arizona Prison."

**Susan Geiger** is Associate Professor in Women's Studies at the University of Minnesota. She has written on the use of women's life histories as feminist research methodology and on women in the construction of nationalism in Tanzania. She is the author of *TANU Women: Gender and Culture in the Making of Tanganyikan Nationalism* (Heinemann).

**Minrose Gwin,** Professor of English at the University of New Mexico, is author of *Black and White Women of the Old South: The Peculiar Sisterhood in American Literature* and *The Feminine and Faulkner: Reading (beyond) Sexual Difference,* both published by the University of Tennessee Press. She is working on a book that proposes a spatial strategy of reading women's fiction.

**Janet R. Jakobsen** is Assistant Professor of Women's Studies and Religious Studies at the University of Arizona. Her research interests focus on ethics and politics; her book, *Working Alliances: Diversity and the Politics of Difference in Feminist Ethics,* is forthcoming from Indiana University Press.

**Caren Kaplan** is Associate Professor of Women's Studies at the University of California at Berkeley, where she teaches courses on feminist cultural studies, colonial and post-colonial cultural production, and transnational feminist politics. Her books include *Scattered Hegemonies: Postmodernity and Transnational Feminist Practices* (University of Minnesota Press), edited with Inderpal Grewal, and *Questions of Travel: Postmodern Discourses of Displacement* (Duke University Press).

**Cindi Katz,** a geographer, is Associate Professor and Chair of Environmental Psychology and a member of the Women's Studies faculty at the Graduate School of the City University of New York. She is the editor (with Janice Monk) of *Full Circles: Geographies of Women Over the Life Course* (Routledge). Her research is concerned with everyday life and the production of space, place, and nature, and with the intersections of political economy and cultural practice.

**Melanie Kaye/Kantrowitz** is a writer, activist, scholar, teacher, and the former director of Jews for Racial and Economic Justice in New York City. She is the Jane Watson Irwin Professor of Women's Studies at Hamilton College. Her publications include *The Issue Is Power: Essays on Women, Jews, Violence, and Resistance* (Aunt Lute Books).

**Joan B. Landes** is Professor of Women's Studies and History at Pennsylvania State University. She has published widely in contemporary and historical feminist theory, and eighteenth-century French cultural history. She is the author of *Women and the Public Sphere in the Age of the French Revolution* (Cornell University Press) and editor of *Feminism, The Public and the Private* (forthcoming from Oxford University Press).

**Tessie Liu** is Associate Professor of History at Northwestern University. Her current research project is entitled "Genealogies of Race" and is on theories of race in republican thought in nineteenth-century France. She is the author of

*The Weaver's Knot: The Contradictions of Class Struggle and Family Solidarity in West-*
*ern France, 1750–1914* (Cornell University Press).

**María Lugones** works at the Escuela Popular Norteña, a center for popular education in New Mexico, and at SUNY–Binghamton, where she directs the Latin American and Caribbean Area Studies Program and is a member of the Philosophy, Interpretation, and Culture Program. Her publications include "Playfulness, World-Travelling, and Loving Perception" in *Making Face, Making Soul* = *Haciendo Caras: Creative and Critical Perspectives by Women of Color,* ed. Gloria Anzaldúa (Aunt Lute Books); "Purity, Impurity, and Separation" in *Signs* (winter 1994); "The Discontinuous Passing of the Cachapera/Tortillera from the Barrio to the Bar to the Movement," in *Daring To Be Good: Feminist Essays in Ethico-Politics,* ed. Ami Bar-On and Ann Ferguson (forthcoming); and "Enticements and Dangers of Community for a Radical Politics," in *Blackwell Companions to Feminist Philosophy,* ed. Iris Young and Alison Jaggar (forthcoming).

**Nancy Mairs** received an M.F.A. and a Ph.D. in English from the University of Arizona. Her books include *Plaintext* (University of Arizona Press); *Remembering the Bone House: An Erotics of Place and Space* (Harper & Row); *Ordinary Time: Cycles in Marriage, Faith, and Renewal* (Beacon); *Voice Lessons, On Becoming a (Woman) Writer* (Beacon); and *Waist High in the World: A Life among the Nondisabled* (Beacon).

**Frances E. Mascia-Lees** and **Patricia Sharpe** co-directed the Women's Studies Program at Simon's Rock College of Bard from 1986–95, where Mascia-Lees teaches anthropology and cultural studies and Sharpe teaches literature and is Dean of Academic Affairs. They are co-editors of *Tattoo, Torture, Mutilation and Adornment: The Denaturalization of the Body in Culture and Text* (SUNY Press) and of two special issues of *Anthropological Quarterly,* and have co-authored numerous articles for academic journals.

**Elizabeth Meese** is Professor of English and Adjunct Professor of Women's Studies at the University of Alabama. She is the author of *(Ex)Tensions: Re-Figuring Feminist Criticism* (University of Illinois Press), *(Sem)Erotics—Theorizing Lesbian: Writing* (New York University Press), and *Crossing the Double-Cross: The Practice of Feminist Criticism* (University of North Carolina Press). She co-edited with Alice Parker *The Difference Within: Feminism and Critical Theory* and *Feminist Critical Negotiations* (J. Benjamins Publishing Co.).

**Helena Michie** is Associate Professor of English at Rice University. She has written extensively on the representation of the female body in *Sororophobia: Difference Among Women in Literature and Culture* and *The Flesh Made Word: Female Figures, Women's Bodies* (both from Oxford University Press).

**Mary Poovey** is Professor of English at New York University. She is the author of *Making a Social Body: British Cultural Formation, 1830–1864* and *Uneven Developments: The Ideological Work of Gender in Mid-Victorian England*, both published by the University of Chicago Press. She has just completed a book entitled *From Rhetoric to Fact: A History from Double-Entry Bookkeeping to Statistics* (forthcoming from the University of Chicago Press).

**Geraldine Pratt** is Professor of Geography at the University of British Columbia. With Susan Hanson, she is the author of *Gender, Work, and Space* (Routledge). Her current research is on international labor migration and domestic workers in Vancouver.

**Judith Roof** is Professor of English at Indiana University, Bloomington, and author of *A Lure of Knowledge: Lesbian Sexuality and Theory* and *Come As You Are: Narrative and Sexuality* (both published by Columbia University Press) and *Reproductions of Reproduction: Imaging Symbolic Change* (Routledge). She is co-editor with Robyn Wiegman of *Who Can Speak? Authority and Critical Identity* (University of Illinois Press).

**Raquel Rubio-Goldsmith** is Adjunct Professor in the Mexican American Studies Program at the University of Arizona and Instructor in the History Department at Pima Community College. She is the author of "Seasons, Seeds, and Souls: Mexican Women Gardening in the American Mesilla, 1900–1940" in *Women of the Mexican Countryside, 1850–1990: Creating Spaces, Sharing Transitions*, ed. Heather Fowler-Salamini and Mary Kay Vaughan (University of Arizona Press).

**Mary Russo** is Professor of Literature and Critical Theory at Hampshire College. She is the author of *The Female Grotesque: Risk, Excess, and Modernity* (Routledge) and co-editor of *Nationalisms and Sexualities* (Routledge) and *Revisioning Italy: National Identity and Global Culture* (forthcoming from University of Minnesota Press). Her research interests include representations of the body in the visual arts and literature and cultural theory.

**Lori Scheer** is a graduate of the American Musical and Dramatic Academy, New York. As a member of the feminist theater group, The Bloodhut, she has co-authored and performed in several productions, including "Our Own Bodies: Stories from the Bloodhut," "Void of Course," and "I Know an Old Woman." Scheer is a certified Interpreter for the Deaf.

**Rina Swentzell,** an independent scholar, received a Ph.D. in American Studies at the University of New Mexico. Her research focuses on Pueblo social relations and community forms. Her publications include *Ancient Land, Ancestral Places: Paul Logsdon in the Pueblo Southwest* (with Stephen Lexson and Catherine Cameron, Museum of New Mexico).

**Luise White** received her Ph.D. from Cambridge University and is currently a fellow at the Woodrow Wilson International Center in Washington, D.C. Her first book, *The Comforts of Home: Prostitution in Colonial Nairobi* (University of Chicago Press), won the Herskovits Prize for the best book of the African Studies Association. She has just completed "Blood and Fire: Rumor and History in East and Central Africa" and has written several articles on oral history.

**Holly Youngbear-Tibbetts** is Dean of Outreach and Director of the Sustainable Development Institute of the College of the Menominee Nation at Keshena, Wisconsin. Her research interests include native land issues in North America and the Antipodes, the role of indigenous women in community leadership, and the impacts of environmental degradation on the well-being of women and children.

**Ofelia Zepeda** is Associate Professor of Linguistics at the University of Arizona, where she teaches courses on O'odham language and American Indian linguistics, in addition to serving as series editor of Sun Tracks. Her latest publications are *Ocean Power: Poems From the Desert* (University of Arizona Press) and *Earth Movements* (Kore Press).

# index

Cannon, Katie: *Black Womanist Ethics,* 203, 209–10

capitalism, 7, 45–46, 55, 193, 254, 281, 305; and commodification, 110–12; and ethics, 209; and imperialism, 111–12; and social relations, 191; and space, 69–85, 110–14; and technology, 112; and travel, 60–61; in the U.S., 209

cartography, 70–71, 195, 237, 275, 296; cognitive, 176; and imperialism, 4, 11–12, 114–15; as metaphor, 4, 49–51; and nationality, 4, 275

Catholicism, 276, 279; and colonialism, 275, 277–81; and community, 218; and morality, 218; and slavery, 94

Certeau, Michel de, 296, 298–99

Chadwick, Edwin, 74–75

Chicanas, 122–23, 275–86; and borders, 167; in literature, 127

childbirth, 245, 284; home, 253; ideologies of, 258–72

children, 167, 284; custody of, 248; and environs, 190; and everyday life, 192; and identity, 190; Latino, 190; neonatal care of, 248; and political struggle, 192; and remembrance, 184; and social status, 218–19

Christianity, 274, 275, 277, 278, 280–81; and "civilization," 278–79; and homophobia, 212. See also Catholicism

Cisneros, Sandra: *The House on Mango Street,* 166

city, 21–26, 53–59, 70, 72, 176, 196; and home-making, 176; planning, 124n.5; spatiality of, 21–26, 169, 141–59

civil rights, 120, 121–22; movement, 54

class, 16, 18, 22–26, 56, 112, 143, 259, 261, 263, 265, 296; oppression, 79; and spatial distribution, 78; and visuality, 114

Clifford, James, 183, 228–30

clothing, 237: as symbol, 95, 97–98, 100, 141, 145, 151–52, 153, 170

Cobbe, Frances Power, 83

Code Noir, 67; racial classification and, 91–107

Colamina, Beatriz, 8n.1

colonialism, 4, 6, 14, 192, 243, 275; discourses of, 60–64; in New Zealand, 44; Spanish, 276–85; in Tanzania, 141–59; and women, 163, 274–85. See also imperialism

community, 11, 34–35, 40, 42–43, 169; and anti-colonialism, 141–59; and collective memory, 154, 277–81; and lesbianism, 211–12; meanings of, 51; and race, 53–59, 209–10; and travel, 178

Conrad, Joseph: *Heart of Darkness,* 231–32

consumerism, 110–11, 296; and culture, 237, 285

Corday, Charlotte, 135, 136–37; and feminism, 164–65

Crenshaw, Kimberlé, 112, 121–22

crime, 55, 57–58; and race, 55, 114–124

cultural criticism, 62, 234; fictionality of, 194; German, 172; and interpretation, 172; theory and, 19

cyberspace, 164, 175–76, 180, 198; as frontier, 187; and materiality, 187

D'Auberteuil, René-Michel Hilliard, 92

dance, 254; and female body, 288–93

Daniel, Jamie, 20

democracy: and gender, 128–140, and public space, 129–40

Descartes, René, 93

desert, 255–57, 274–75, 276–78: Sonoran, 5; as symbol, 278–80

difference, 16, 239, 307–8; and class, 24–26; and disability, 215–20; metaphors of, 215–16; and morality, 216–20; and social space 216–19; and symbolic geographies, 21; and voice, 165; and women, 15–16; and world making, 216–20

disability, 215–20; and metaphor, 215–16

disease, 75, 84, 196, 215–20, 233–34: abstraction of, 75–76; AIDS, 298; and the body, 203, 215–20; in cities, 74–76; and cultural identity, 170–72

displacement, 67, 190–91; discourses of, 64; and geography, 174; and home, 170–72; as metaphor, 177

domesticity, 79; discourses of, 258–73; and women, 79, 128, 129, 282–85; and writing, 165–66. See also home

drugs, 292, 298; discourses of, 68, 114–19; and gender, 114–115; wars, 115–19

dualism, 5, 15–18, 20, 22, 17, 51; and race, 56; and spatiality, 14–21, 60–64, 115–19; mind/body, 232; public/private, 23, 128–40, 253

Earhart, Amelia, 254, 296–300: as feminist icon, 297, 299

economics, 253; and drug trade, 119; and hegemony, 64; and slavery, 91–107

Eliade, Mircea, 306

Elliott, Ebenezer, 78–79

England: history, 67–89; spatiality and, 67–89

essentialism, 203, 236

ethics, 7, 18, 254; and feminism, 205–14; and gender, 205–14; and labor, 209; and motherhood, 248–49; of place, 20; and race, 206

ethnicity, 7, 16, 171; and fetishization, 123; and nationalism, 171; and specular morality, 112–24

ethnocentrism, 61–62

ethnography, 23, 63, 190, 239–40; postmodern, 233; and representation, 228–31; and symbolic geographies, 21–23

exile, 14–15, 19, 171, 178–79; and home, 171; and identity, 170–72; and language, 171; as metaphor, 14–16; in postmodern discourse, 63

exoticism, 231–32, 235

family, 46–47; and revolution, 129; and subjectivity, 184–88

fatherhood, 129; and authority, 268, 270–71; in Pueblo cosmology, 221–22

feminism, 3, 4, 15, 19, 63–64, 112, 113, 124, 166, 182, 236, 237–38, 243, 245, 259, 261, 294, 295–96; academic, 11, 32, 39, 47–48, 183, 240; and African American nationalism, 141–43, 155; Anglo-American, 7, 11; and art, 4; and class, 47, 163; and communities, 164–65; and consciousness, 17–18; and cultural criticism, 64; and deconstruction, 62; and drug wars, 114–15; and East/West difference, 188; and ethics, 205–14; and film theory, 235; and home, 167; and humanism, 239–40; and indigenous women, 42; and interdisciplinarity, 113–14; and interpretation, 171–73; liberal, 299; and marginality, 39–43; and materialism, 187; and metaphor, 227–42; narratives of, 19, 24–25; and postcolonialism, 14; and postmodernism, 128, 233, 235; practice, 254; psychoanalytic, 183; and spatial politics, 124, 174–76; theory, 1, 13, 26–27, 62, 67–68, 129, 174, 177, 183, 190; and time, 302–08; U.S., 39; and world making, 171–73; writing, 14

Ferguson, Kathy, 15, 18, 20

field work, 232–33: geographic, 190–92; as rite of passage, 233 food, discourse on, 267–69; and slavery, 94–95, 96–97

Foucault, Michel, 4, 76, 234, 245, 258, 260, 294

French Revolution, 68, 77, 91; and gender politics, 128–40

Freud, Sigmund, 178, 305

Friedman, Marilyn, 51

frontier, 275: Mexican, 279. See also borders

Fuss, Diana, 17

Gal, Susan, 245

gardens, 253, 274–85: and Catholicism, 274–85: and colonialism, 274–85; symbolism of, 277, 279–82, 284–85

gaze, 288–93; constitutive power of, 146; regulation and, 72–74, 76–77. See also vision

gender, 18: and class, 46–47; and democracy, 128–40; and ethics, 205–14; gap, 25–26; and history, 172; and ideology, 46–47; in Kenya, 250; and nation, 276, 141–56; and public policy, 131–32; and space, 253; and theory, 7; in the U.S., 250; and visuality, 114. See also feminism, sexuality

gentrification, 20, 21, 123, 176; and home, 176; and television, 22

geography, 13, 19, 21, 173–74, 232, 277; and feminism 20; metaphors of 3–4, 13–30, 31–34, 45, 47–48, 49, 176, 203, 206–08; profession of, 35–36; and subjectivity, 21

Germany, 20, 171; and Nazism, 170

Gilligan, Carol, 206–07, 213n.9

global/local dichotomy, 11; breakdown of, 193; ideology of, 62

Gorelick, Sherry, 57

Grewal, Inderpal, 61, 62

Habermas, Jurgen, 130–31, 134

Haraway, Donna, 164–65; "Situated Knowledges," 235, 236

Hart, M. Cordell, 116–17

Harvey, David, 29n.33

Hatch, John: and Tanzania, 145–50

heterosexuality, 254, 261, 264–65, 305; ideologies of, 112, 192, 210, 307. See also sexuality

Hill, Anita, 239–40

historiography, 246–47, 262; and bodies, 172; and gender, 172; and Mexicanas, 276–77

Hoagland, Sarah, 210; Lesbian Ethics, 203

Hoch, Hannah, 170–71

Hodge, Merle: Crick Crack Monkey, 121, 123

home, 11, 19, 20, 49, 51, 60, 61, 178–79, 183, 190, 193–94, 253; birth movement, 261–63; as category, 36; and drug wars, 116; as fantasy, 261–62; and homelessness, 64; ideologies of, 258–73; meanings of 36–37; and women, 38, 167; and writing, 193–94. See also domesticity

homosexuality, 17, 58, 298; African Americans and, 53–54; closeting, 211; coming out, 211; gay rights movement, 53–54, 120; Latinos and, 53–54. See also lesbians, queer theory, sexuality

hooks, bell, 14, 15–18, 19, 39–40

Hooper, Barbara, 16

hospitals, 262; and childbirth, 258–64; and domesticity, 258–63; and women, 258–64

Hunt, Lynn, 129

hybridity, 62, 96–107, 248–49

identity, 31, 49, 54, 178; authorial, 235; and constructions of 170, 179–80, 192;

cultural memory, 58; and environment, 190; formation of, 17, 19; politics, 14, 15, 51–52, 71, 165, 177, 182; and power dynamics, 60; and race, 96–107. See also subjectivity

immigration, 41, 57, 63, 64, 187; and ethnic stereotypes, 56

imperialism, 4, 7, 111–12, 113–14, 276–78: and Christianity, 278; cultural, 42; Western, 64. See also colonialism

improvisation, 288–93, 299

industrialism, 45–46, 70; and urbanization, 70–84

Ingalls, Laura: and aviation, 297

Jameson, Frederic, 176, 237

Jews, 12, 16–17, 53–59; and African Americans, 53–59; and anti-Semitism, 54–55; and nationalism, 171; and Nazism, 170–72, 179

Kambona, Oscar, 148–49

Kay, James Phillips, 74, 77–78, 80

Kirby, Vicki, 237–39

Kitzinger, Sheila, 261–62, 263

Kristeva, Julia, 183, 306, 307; "Woman's Time," 306

Lacan, Jacques, 187, 305; and "the Real," 187

land, 110; and development, 110–11; and Pueblo cosmology, 221–26; rights, 282

landscape, 11, 110, 274–75, 280; built, 5–6, 41, 223–26, 276–85; Christian view of, 279; and cultural heritage, 36–38, 276–85; and development, 110–11; and geography, 35; and identity, 32, 34–35, 276; and maternal body, 32; and memory, 186–87, 276–81; as metaphor, 32; natural, 5, 39, 41,

221–23, 174–75, 280; and Pueblo cosmology, 222–23; social constructions of, 39

language, 164, 238, 243–51, 305; English, 253; as praxis, 175; and representation, 177; and spatiality, 169; Tohono O'odham, 253; and writing, 194

Lasker-Schuler, Else, 170–71

Latinos/Latinas, 22–23, 50, 53–59; and African Americans, 22–23; children, 190; and drug wars, 117–118; and gay rights, 53–59; and Jews, 53–59; and police, 117–118; use of space, 22–23

Lauretis, Teresa de, 14, 41, 28n.26, 235

law: enforcement, 116–17; and gender, 58, 116–17; and oppression, 64; and race, 18, 116–17

Leach, Edmund, 306

Lefebvre, Henri, 69–70, 71

Lefort, Claude, 130

lesbians, 14, 17, 53–54, 58, 170, 183, 205–14; Chicana, 122–23; and community, 211–12; and ethics, 206, 208–13; and race, 120. See also homosexuality, queer theory

letter writing, 5; as theory, 7, 161–99

literature, 68; and power structures, 121–22

location, 6, 19; and class, 24–26; and gender, 14–26; and geography, 14–26, 174; as trope, 16, 19–21, 60–63

Locke, John, 70

Lorde, Audre, 123, 166, 200n.8

Lugones, María, 7, 12, 168, 179–80, 207

Making Worlds symposium, 3–8, 59, 81, 83, 161, 170, 173, 175, 197–98, 199, 303

Malinowski, Bronislaw, 238

Malthus, Thomas, 70, 73

mapping. See cartography

marginality, 11, 13–18, 19, 23, 39, 45–48, 49, 298; and feminism, 227–40; metaphors of, 14–16, 39, 61

Martin, Patricia Preciado, 280

Marxism, 57, 228

Mascia-Lees, Fran, and Patricia Sharpe: *Tattoo, Torture, Mutilation, and Adornment*, 229, 232

masculinity, constructions of, 16; and rationality 131–37; and subjectivity, 132; and whiteness, 16. See also men

mass media, 54, 191; and gentrification, 22; political influence of, 55; and representation, 55

Massey, Doreen, 61

materiality, 4, 5, 6–7, 8, 12, 43, 70–71; and abstraction, 69–85; and language, 171; and metaphor, 163–65, 173–75, 177–78, 180, 182; and pleasure, 198; and voice, 203

Matterlart, Armand, 60

medicine, 300; in Africa, 243–47; culture of, 263–64; and environment, 225; herbal, 225; and power, 80; and regulation, 80

memory, 58, 61, 184–88, 197–98; and environment, 275–77, 278–85; and law, 95; and the polis, 134; and storytelling, 134–35

men: and the body, 132–33; and capitalism, 73; and ethics, 206; and rationality, 132–133; and sexuality, 288–93. See also masculinity, fatherhood

mentascape, 38, 39, 43

metaphor, 3, 4, 11, 14–15, 17, 26, 31–34, 38–40, 42, 45, 47–48, 59, 166, 305–6; and the body, 228; of cartography, 49–51, 114; confusion of, 227–42; and disability, 215–16; and history, 189; and ideology, 80–81, 234,

302–08; and materiality, 163–64, 173–75, 177–78, 180, 182; and representation, 143, 227–40; and spatiality, 174–75, 189–90; and subjectivity, 174, 177; and time, 177, 302–8; of vision, 114

Mexico, 274–85: Nuevo, 275; revolution and, 275, 283; women of, 274–85

mobility, 6, 15, 17, 19; as metaphor, 18, 49–51; as political strategy, 51–52; as resistance, 167; and subjectivity, 15, 18; as trope, 295–301; and writing, 199

modernism, 60–64, 230, 296, 299

Mohammed, Bibi Titi, 146–50

Moreau de Saint-Méry, Médéric-Louis-Elie, 97, 99–105, 108

mother, 196–97, 268, 281; and drug wars, 117–18; ideology of, 84; "Mother and Child," 225; single, 117; in Pueblo cosmology 221–22; and surveillance, 117–118

mothering, 245, 248

museums: and cultural representation, 231

narrative, 254; as ideology, 307; master, 68, 155; and resistance, 164–65; and temporality, 302–8; and violence, 172; and visuality, 121–22; and women, 164, 183

nationalism, 68, 113, 118, 141–159, 248; and "ethnic cleansing," 142; and gender, 171; and Jewishness, 171; and patriarchy, 64; and race, 171

Native Americans, 6–7, 11; Apaches, 277, 286n.16, 279–80; and capitalism, 281; and colonization, 281; communities of, 34–35, 41; demonization of, 279–80, 28–82; and landscape, 34–35; Pimas, 277; Pueblos, 203–4, 221–26; studies, 7; Yaquis, 277

143–44; women and, 165, 166. *See also* narrative

Strathern, Marilyn, 232

stunts, 254: and gender, 296–98; and tactics, 269, 299

subjectivity, 12, 15, 19, 25–26, 52, 61, 165, 233, 234, 244–46, 271, 276–86, 305–06; and cultural memory, 58; and disciplinarity, 113; and dreams, 181–88; and epistemology, 174

Sudan, 192; and development, 190

Suleri, Sara, 15–16

surveillance, 123, 259, 265, 271; and drug wars, 116–17; spatial implications of, 119–20; and the state, 113; women and, 134

TANU (Tanganyika African National Union), 144–59

Tanzania (Tanganyika), 141–59

Taylor, Jenny Bourne, 19

technology, 112, 246, 296; and capitalism, 112; effects of, 45–46

television, 22, 191; and gentrification, 22

temporality, 5, 33, 162, 254, 299; and capitalism, 69; politics of, 5–6; theories of, 5–6. *See also* time

Thiong'o, Ngugi wa, 188

Thomas, Clarence, 239–40

time, 302; as commodity, 305; ideologies of, 302–8; materiality of, 303–8; and metaphor, 177, 302–8; and pregnancy, 266; representations of, 302–8; and space, 302–8. *See also* temporality

Timpson, Kate, 246–47

Todorov, Tsvetan, 304

Tohono O'Odham, 255–57

travel, 60–61, 63, 296, 297; as category, 36; and class, 178; and community, 178–79; and dreaming, 184–88; meanings of, 36–37; as metaphor, 18, 37, 60–

64, 168, 177–78; and Native American culture, 35; reading as, 168; and women, 178, 183, 207; and women's narratives, 165

travesty, as political strategy, 233–34

Trinh T. Minh-ha, 15

Tuan, Yi-Fu, 279, 280; topophilia, 35

UFOs, 245, 247–49; and women, 243

unconscious, the, 163, 187; and territoriality, 163

urbanization. *See* city

violence, 58; and anti-Semitism, 172; and gender, 58, 136–37, 142, 172; and matter, 193; and narrative, 172; racism and, 58; and sexuality, 193; and slavery, 92, 95– 96; against women, 172, 174–75

vision, 110–27, 265, 280, 296; and cartographic tropes, 114–15; and epistemology, 114–15; and ideology, 119–24; as metaphor, 236; optics, 277; and public policy, 119–24; and spatiality, 114–15. *See also* specularity

Viswanathan, Gauri, 121

*Weaver's Knot, The* (Tessie Liu), 45–46

Western culture, 230, 240, 295, 303; and anti-Semitism, 179; and Nazism, 179

White, Leslie, 37, 204

whiteness, 16; and Creolité, 91–107; epistemology of, 101; ideology of, 281; and masculinity, 16; as property, 126; as racial category, 14, 16–18, 20, 57–58; and slavery, 91–107

wilderness, 5, 253

Williams, B.: ethnography of, 21–23

Wimpffen, Francis Alexander Stanislaus, Baron de, 91

Wolff, Janet, 18, 168, 235

women, 7, 14, 43–46, 67, 255; African, 242–50; and aging, 219; American, 248; Asian, 58; and aviation, 296–300; and the body, 132, 231–32, 235, 240, 258–73, 288–93; and capitalism, 45–46, 70; and class, 45–46; and colonialism, 242–50; of color, 49, 91–109, 168, 207–8; and commerce, 288–93; as consumers, 237; and difference, 16, 24–26; and discursive space, 80; and domesticity, 79, 257, 259; and economy, 46; and ethics, 206; in French Revolution, 129–40; and gardens, 274–85; and gender, 171–72; Indian, 246; indigenous, 39–41, 246; and Islam, 141; and Hinduism, 142–43; Korean, 25; and metaphor, 14; Mexican, 274–85; middle-class, 83; mobility and, 24, 49–52; and nationalism, 141–59; as political symbols, 129; and power, 24; and pregnancy, 258–73; and prisons, 118–19; representations, 142, 143; and resistance, 46; and slavery, 97–98; and spatial relations, 49–52; and technology, 46; and work, 7, 24–26, 45–46; and writing, 32, 38, 120–23, 161–99

Woolf, Virginia, 182; *A Room of One's Own,* 188, 236

work, 16–17, 69, 78, 198, 237–38; and class, 24; migrant, 113, 179; and technology, 45–46; and women, 24, 45–46, 253; and workhouses, 78

worldmaking, 31–32; and disability, 216–20; and morality, 212–13; praxis of, 174

world-system theory, 61–62

writing, 239; epistolary, 161–202; as performance, 169; and politics, 163; and race, 120–23; and repression, 169; and women, 32, 38, 161–99

xenophobia, 269

Young, Iris Marion, 169

# about the editors

**Susan Hardy Aiken** is Professor of English at the University of Arizona. The author of *Isak Dinesen and the Engendering Narrative* (University of Chicago Press), she has published widely on nineteenth- and twentieth-century literature and feminist theory. Her most recent book is *Dialogues/Dialogi: Literary and Cultural Exchanges Between (Ex)Soviet and American Women* (Duke University Press), co-authored with Adele Barker, Maya Koreneva, and Ekaterina Stetsenko.

**Ann Brigham** is a doctoral student in the English department at the University of Arizona. She is currently writing a dissertation entitled "Attractions of a Popular Kind: Tourism and Heterosexuality in American Literature and Film, 1875–1995."

**Sallie A. Marston** is Associate Professor of Geography and Regional Development at the University of Arizona. Her current research focuses on urban social movements among women and minority groups in both the nineteenth and twentieth centuries. The co-author of *Places and Regions in Global Context* (Prentice-Hall), she is completing a book on neighborhood politics entitled "Good Fences, Good Neighbors: The Political Geography of Participatory Democracy in Tucson."

**Penny Waterstone** recently received a Ph.D. in History from the University of Arizona. She is completing a book about gender relationships in an experimental utopian colony in California at the turn of the century.